HOWARD BAKER

HOWARD BAKER
Conciliator in an Age of Crisis

Second Edition

J. Lee Annis Jr.

Howard H. Baker Jr. Center for Public Policy
The University of Tennessee / Knoxville

Second Edition.

First edition published by Madison Books in 1995.

All photographs courtesy of Howard H. Baker Jr. unless otherwise indicated.

This book is printed on acid-free paper.

Library of Congress Cataloging-in-Publication Data

Annis, J. Lee (James Lee), 1957–
Howard Baker : conciliator in an age of crisis / J. Lee Annis Jr. – 2nd ed.
p. cm.
Includes bibliographical references and index.
ISBN-13: 978-1-57233-591-2 (pbk. : alk. paper)
ISBN-10: 1-57233-591-2

1. Baker, Howard H. (Howard Henry), 1925–
2. Statesmen–United States–Biography.
3. Legislators–United States–Biography.
4. United States. Congress. Senate–Biography.
5. United States–Politics and government–1945–1989.
I. Title.

E840.8.B28A56 2007
328.73'092–dc22
[B]

2007002624

Dedicated in memory of five women without whom my first two books would never have been completed:

Elizabeth P. Annis 1932–2000
Elizabeth Pound 1907–2003
Ruthie Edmondson Leyen 19??–2000
Dean Marge Edwards 1919–2002
Beverly Wilson 1953–2000

CONTENTS

ILLUSTRATIONS

PREFACE TO THE SECOND EDITION

In this era of hyperpartisan politics, Senator Baker's story is even more relevant than it was when the hardback edition first appeared in 1994. Inevitably, when scandal has threatened to engulf an administration or party at any point during the last three decades, the first queries reporters or investigators raise are what have become known as the Howard Baker questions: What did the president (or other principal) know and when did he know it?[1]

Especially insightful are comments by journalist Margaret Carlson during the impeachment trial of former President Bill Clinton. "Where was common sense?" she wrote. "Where was Howard Baker?"[2] Why, she could have been asking about so many instances over the last fifteen years, weren't officials of administrations of both parties advising their leaders, as Baker had during the Watergate and Iran-Contra scandals, that cover-ups never work and that the way to limit the harmful effects of congressional or grand jury investigations is by cooperating with them? Why weren't members of Congress seeking the truth about allegations of misconduct by members of their own parties, as Baker had during the Watergate probe, rather than stonewalling those inquiries that might lead to unpleasant conclusions about their colleagues? Why were leaders of all parties spending less time finding bipartisan solutions to problems that affect all Americans and instead casting barbs at or launching investigations of colleagues on the basis of the flimsiest of allegations if it seemed as if it might secure them even the slightest partisan advantage for even the shortest moment? By the early 1980s, the late John T. "Terry" Dolan, the chairman of the National Conservative Political Action Committee (NCPAC) was pronouncing that "the shriller you are, the easier it is to raise funds." By the twenty-first century, the coarsening of American political discussion in both parties and among special interests of all ideological stripes had decayed to such a low level that the veteran Democratic strategist Bob

Beckel was heard bemoaning that politics had become more "about 'shoring up your base,'" than "resolving any issues for the benefit of the country."[3]

Such circumstances distress Baker. Still, as an astute observer of our nation's past, he remembers that political discourse in the early republic as well as in the Vietnam era often reached levels of venom and vitriol far surpassing much of that heard during the twenty-first century. "Where we are," he says, "is the product of a grand compromise that was also the product of this intuition and judgment, the collective wisdom of the people. It has very little logic. Its symmetry is awkward." Even though he finds that "the truth of the matter is that it works," he remains convinced that our system would function with greater efficacy and considerably more public approval were it less necessary for politicos to raise megamillions from self-interested, sycophancy-demanding, often shrill, and always myopic special interests. The adversary system he deems necessary mandates that all interested parties be heard, as well as that all participants afford "a decent respect for different points of view." The "centrist technique" he employed allowed him or others "at least to produce a consensus view on what's possible to do and what's best for the country." It mattered to him not that a president of a different party scored a political victory. "Sometimes," he argued after the Panama Canal Treaties were ratified, "what's best for the country, always what's best for the country, must take precedence."[4] It was his duty, he believed, to see that problems were solved, and he scoffed at the all-too-common sense among today's political operatives that their task was to create or develop issues to divide the public. He expressed his ideals most pointedly in an emeritus address to the Senate of 1998 called "On Herding Cats," which can be found in the appendix. Indeed, the title proved compelling enough that Senator Trent Lott later cribbed it for his own memoir.

The implicit collegiality thus delineated firmly departs from the counsel of so many currently practicing political strategists of all parties to stick to message. Tellingly, Lamar Alexander, as a young legislative aide to Baker, found that many of the speeches he wrote sounded far different when his boss delivered them. "I write these speeches and then I send them into you like I've written them," he lamented to Baker. "What am I doing wrong?" "Lamar," Baker replied, "there is no problem. I see this as an ideal arrangement. You write what you want. I say what I want."[5]

Alexander's subsequent career in the governorship, the cabinet, and the Senate illustrates another Baker hallmark, that of giving several talented and clean-campaigning young politicos their start in government. When Alexander declined Baker's offer to become minority counsel of the Senate Watergate Committee, Baker opted to hire former U.S. attorney Fred Thompson, who later went on to serve in the U.S. Senate as well as argue landmark cases in Tennessee and colorful fictitious ones on NBC's *Law and Order*. Don Sundquist, Baker's original campaign manager during his unsuccessful bid for the presidency in 1980, went on to serve in the House of Representatives and as governor of Tennessee. Baker press secretary Tom Griscom, as communications director for Ronald Reagan, was one of the architects of the "Tear Down This Wall" address and now presides as executive editor of the *Chattanooga Times–Free Press.* Ron McMahan, Griscom's predecessor as Baker's press secretary, won several awards from the Tennessee Press Association while managing editor of the now-defunct *Knoxville Journal.* Baker speechwriter Patrick Butler went on to write presidential speeches for Ronald Reagan and George H. W. Bush and now serves as vice-president of the Washington Post Corporation. Baker counsel A. B. Culvahouse crafted the White House legal strategy during the Iran-Contra hearings. Dan Crippen served as head of the Congressional Budget Office. Campaign staffer Victor "Bulldog" Ashe completed four terms as mayor of Knoxville, then became ambassador to Poland. The late Howard Liebengood, Baker's in-house expert on the intelligence community, went on to serve as sergeant-at-arms of the Senate. Onetime political aide Robert Mosbacher III, who Baker hired at the request of outgoing Congressman George H. W. Bush in 1970, now directs the Overseas Private Investment Corporation. Foreign policy aide Cran Montgomery went on to become ambassador to Oman. Legislative assistant Michael Adams is at this writing president of the University of Georgia. Secretary of the Senate Emily Reynolds got her start as an intern in Baker's Senate office. And former Senate Majority Leader Bill Frist dates his original option to seek a Senate seat rather than a different office to Baker's private counsel in mid-1992 that he and his wife, Karyn, had what it took to make a successful couple in Washington.[6]

In this edition, I have added a chapter covering Senator Baker's life and times since leaving the White House in 1988. While I have had occasion to explore the contents of the Baker papers that have been opened since the publication of the hardback, I have not significantly amended the original text save to add time context or a particularly telling detail or correct a few minor errors. Frankly, I want to preserve as much of the original manuscript as possible, as I believe my conclusions remain sound. With Bill Brock, Winfield Dunn, Dan Kuykendall, Lewis Donelson and a bevy of other talented young urban professionals of the 1960s, Howard Baker built a viable second party and thereby a two-party system in the Volunteer State. With Edmund Muskie and Thomas Eagleton, Baker fashioned the monumental clean air and water acts of the 1970s and pushed them to enactment with little dissent. It was he who focused all Watergate investigations with questions as to the motives of the conspirators and what President Nixon knew and when he knew it. It was Baker who bailed out the Carter administration from near certain failure on the controversial Panama Canal Treaties. Yet it was also this Tennessean who coordinated Republican alternatives to Carter proposals on foreign, defense, and economic policy, all the while cooperating with this Democratic president where the visions of the two coalesced. It was Howard Baker, after losing to Ronald Reagan in the 1980 GOP presidential primaries, who went on to push

Reagan's economic program to enactment and suggest the mechanism that effectively salvaged the Social Security system in the very next year. And, as Stephen Bell, a top aide to New Mexico Republican Pete Domenici, put it bluntly, it was Howard Baker who "saved Reagan's ass" in the aftermath of the Iran-Contra scandal.[7] Future scholars will have plenty more to contemplate, and I'm confident most serious students will craft portraits of the achievements and legacy of Howard Baker fairly akin to mine.

ACKNOWLEDGMENTS

It seems that historians incur more debts than the politicians they analyze. This historian is certainly obliged. Foremost, I owe Tony Edmonds, the chairman of my dissertation committee, for it was he who read many of these pages at their rawest and indeed wordiest. From his labors has emerged a narrative far more cogent than otherwise would have been possible. For their constructive criticism to relatively refined drafts, I am extremely grateful to Dick Baker (no relation to the senator), Bill Connelly, Gary Reichard and David Welborn, as well as to James L. Annis, the late Joseph Backor, Ralph Baker (again, no relation to the senator), Kurt Borkman, Tom Kalucynski, Fred Marcum, and Ray White for a multitude of suggestions about earlier drafts.

I am just as obligated to many members of the Baker staff, past and present. Especially helpful were Ruthie Edmondson Leyen and Teresa Gentry, who graced Senator Baker's Knoxville office, for their generous grants of access to quite thorough files of newspaper clippings. I am also thankful to Doris Lovett at Baker's Huntsville office for the use of her 1966 campaign scrapbook; Katy Barksdale and Tom Griscom, who staffed his press office, for access to speeches, press releases, and other documents; recent aides Susan Ballard, Fred Marcum, and Lura Nell Mitchell, for a variety of assistance; and Bill Hamby, who managed the senator's main Tennessee office in Nashville, for letting me inspect his collection of newspaper clippings. Moreover, I'm grateful to the many people who have consented to interviews. So as not to stigmatize them with responsibility for my errors of fact or stress, I've listed them in the bibliography.

Particularly helpful otherwise were the kind folks at *Human Events*, the *Knoxville Journal*, and the Senate Historical Office for allowing me to scan their files; many librarians at Ball State University, East Tennessee State University, the University of Tennessee at Knoxville, and Vanderbilt University for many kindnesses; Dan Parro of Bailey, Deardourff and Associates, for screening for me the 1980 Baker commercials; Senator Baker and Vince Vawter of the *Knoxville News Sentinel* for allowing me to use some of their photographs; Elizabeth Bruno, Julie Kirsch, Tana McDonald, Melissa McNitt, Meredith Morris-Babb, Jennifer Ruark, Kim Scarborough, and Jennifer Siler for a variety of services; and Hussein El-Fadl and David Horgan, who've done their best, in this case anyway, to eradicate word processor illiteracy.

Thanks also to a number of friends and family members. For help with the original paperwork, I thank Betty Ann Annis, Gayle Annis, and Cindy Gilpin Davis. For hospitality, I thank a number of friends, but particularly Mike Prince and Bob Shearer, and for some inexpensive xeroxing, I thank Tim and Christie Busching. For encouragement at key stages, I thank Teresa Seifert, Ralph Haskins, and a number of my students at Ball State University and Montgomery College. For a great deal of financial aid in the dissertation stage of this project, I thank my parents Jim and Betty Ann Annis, and my grandmother Elizabeth H. Pound. And for keeping me properly focused these past few years, I thank Diane Wynocker, a fountain of support and understanding.

For their help with this edition, I'm first and foremost grateful to Alan Lowe, Nissa Dahlin-Brown, and Bobby Holt of the absolutely superb staff at the Baker Center for Public Policy at the University of Tennessee and Barbara Dewey of the University of Tennessee Libraries for catalyzing interest in a paperback edition. They are resources any scholar of the last third of the twentieth century in America will be happy they tapped for assistance. I need to thank as well Senator Bill Frist for hiring me to be his collaborator and Jed Lyons of the University Press of America for recruiting me for that pleasurable task on *Tennessee Senators, 1911–2001: Portraits of Leadership in a Century of Change*, a work that gave me additional insight on the work of Howard Baker, his colleagues, predecessors, and successors. And I'm equally grateful to thoughtful scholars like Bill Connelly, Ron Foresta, Aram Hessami, Gary Reichard, David Welborn, Carroll Van West, and an anonymous University of Tennessee Press reviewer for their charitable reviews and suggestions; Stan Ivester and Monica Phillips for thoughtfully editing the second edition; Dennis Wile, a superb photographer, for graciously permitting me to use the cover picture; Debbie Durkin and Kiki Kienstra, former assistants to the late Howard Liebengood, for their aid in resolving many bureaucratic problems at the Library of Congress associated with the Liebengood papers; Dave Andrew, Anne Dunn, the late Leonidas Emerson, Harrison Fox, Jack Germond, Claud Gingrich, Tom Goldwasser, the late Ruthie Edmondson Leyen, Steve Marcum, Marnie Ryder, Elkin Taylor, John Tuck, and Bob Worthington for some helpful information in off-the-record conversations; the Montgomery College Foundation, for providing some funding for research; Senators Lamar Alexander, Bill Brock, Bill Frist, William Cohen, and Warren Rudman and Professor Gary Reichard for their kind endorsements of this work, and, as always, Hussein El-Fadl, Fred Marcum, Mike Prince, and Jennifer Siler for so many services and kindnesses.

INTRODUCTION

Washington, February 26, 1987. A dull midwinter haze hung over the nation's capital on a damp, cold Thursday morning. A president recuperating from prostate surgery was now plagued by a pyrotechnic public outrage at some in his administration who had diverted funds from arms sales to Iran to the Contra resistance in Nicaragua. Following the release of the report of the commission examining the scandal, Chairman John Tower declared that Ronald Reagan had been "poorly advised and poorly served" and "not . . . aware of a lot of things that were going on." While placing blame in many directions, members noted the "personal control" of chief of staff Donald Regan over White House aides and his failure to insist upon an "orderly process" of review.[1]

It had long concerned Reagan intimates that Regan's brusque, haughty manner antagonized those who would have to pass on his programs. "Half of Washington wanted him out," Nancy Reagan wrote, and Regan's repeated discourtesies to the First Lady further hastened his demise. But who would replace him? Reagan's first choice was former Transportation Secretary Drew Lewis, who would not leave his position as head of Union Pacific, but recommended former Nevada Senator Paul Laxalt.[2]

A thousand miles southward, Howard H. Baker Jr. was shepherding his four-year-old grandson Daniel on what figured to be their last excursion before he embarked on a second campaign for America's highest office. In the meantime, Laxalt was at the White House professing his disinterest and recommending alternatives. "Whoever was selected," Laxalt said, had to be "someone who . . . knew the Hill, knew the agencies, had . . . credibility with the press and . . . the kind of person to come into a turbulent White House and restore some peace." The name of his affable, patient former Majority Leader "rang out." When he made his view known to Ronald and Nancy Reagan, their eyes lit up, but they reminded Laxalt that Baker was planning a bid for the presidency. "Well," Laxalt replied, "there's one way to find out." Minutes later, Joy Baker answered the phone at her family's condominium in Bal Harbour, Florida, and heard a familiar reassuring voice asking about her husband's whereabouts. "Howard is at the zoo," she said. "Well," Reagan replied chuckling, "wait till he sees the zoo I have in mind for him."[3]

Six weeks earlier, Baker had turned down Donald Regan's offer to replace William Casey as director of Central Intelligence. But now a man Baker once saw as "a movie star who'd fall flat on his face," but whom he had come not only to admire but to like, had asked him to rescue him at the low point in his political career. With the administration in what Labor Secretary Bill Brock termed a blue funk, Baker took the offer as an obligation, and accepted it with little hesitation, knowing it extinguished any chance he had of becoming president.[4] How did he fare at a post he often calls the worst job in Washington? "Sometimes people say one man can't make a difference," said Hawaii Democrat Daniel Inouye, the chairman of the Senate panel investigating the Iran-Contra scandal. "That one man made a difference." Baker, added former Tennessee Governor Don Sundquist, was "able to keep the White House functioning, as opposed to what happened during the Nixon Administration, when there was a siege mentality and all they could think about was . . . protection." While historical considerations factored little in Reagan's choice of a replacement for Regan, Sundquist's analogy demonstrates the appropriateness and wisdom of the Baker choice. Baker's prior service as vice-chairman of the Senate Watergate Committee had given him a perspective ideally suited to the task at hand in early 1987, that of limiting damage to a government whose very existence was threatened by public outrage over the crimes of a small band of overzealous aides. It had been Baker's advice to Richard Nixon in 1973 to come clean quick and thereby liquidate rather than merely contain the damage that might accrue to his party, and he would extend the same advice to another beleaguered president in 1987. Although Baker and Reagan had been close working partners since 1981, they had never been intimate associates. Nearly a generation apart and hailing from dissimilar backgrounds and political bases, their ambitions had collided in the late 1970s. Implicit within the friendly, innately decent, and incurably optimistic characters of both were somewhat calculated aloofnesses that led neither man to reveal themselves or the fullness of their thought patterns to even their closest associates. But Reagan, unlike Nixon, had the capacity and inner security to seek out good advice in times of trouble and to take heed. That he would reach out to someone outside of his bases in California or the conservative movement and ask him to abort a presidential campaign said much about his determination to not allow a budding scandal to linger in the public consciousness, in no small degree because the public gained a perception that there was, as Utah Reaganaut Orrin Hatch put it, "bona fide presidential timber" in both the presidency and the chief of staff's position. That Reagan, leaning on Baker, succeeded in diverting attention from a scandal that threatened to incapacitate his presidency and focusing it upon the timeless concerns of war and peace and bread and butter can be seen in both the landslide victory of George Bush in 1988 and in the rise in Reagan's approval rating from a low of 36 percent prior to Baker's arrival to a more typical 61 percent level at the time of his departure.[5]

It was Baker's role in uncovering the misdeeds of the Nixon administration that won him universal recognition as a Leader of the Senate. More formally, Senate Republicans elected him their Leader in 1977, and his effectiveness in Reagan's first term was such that many agreed with Colorado conservative William Armstrong that "the success . . . Reagan had was 60 percent Ronald Reagan and 40 percent Howard Baker." "There's Howard Baker," Dan Quayle liked to say in his senatorial days, "then there's the rest of us as far as senators are concerned." Such sentiment might be mistaken for boosterism from two Republicans for their Leader, but it reflected a clear consensus. Every time senators, Senate staffers, and congressional reporters were polled between 1980 and 1984 as to who they found the best senator, the most influential, the most effective, or the most persuasive, Baker finished first. Privately, many of Baker's strongest boosters were Democrats, one of whom asked, not completely in jest, "If the Republicans lose control [after the 1982 election], could Howard Baker stay on as Majority Leader?" Another guessed that Baker would get 80 or 90 votes if there were a secret ballot in the Senate for president, a not uncommon estimate. After *Newsweek* in 1978 asked a sample of Democratic senators off the record who they would like to see elected president in 1980, a reporter told a senior Democrat that the responses indicated that a plurality of his colleagues privately backed Baker. "You're wrong," the member responded. "He'd win a majority."[6]

The esteem most Senate Democrats held for Baker resulted because he, as Abraham Ribicoff put it, "played it straight" with them in his friendly but quietly authoritative way in moving toward shared ends in often nonexpedient circumstances. Even when he was about to blast the ideas of one of their Leaders, he, having made an agreement with Democratic counterpart Robert Byrd not to surprise each other, made it a point to let them know beforehand. His word was his bond, and many deemed him a statesman, or as Abba Eban put it, one who could build a "bridge between his experience and his vision, between ancient fidelities and new hopes, between echoes of the past and calls of the future."[7] In times when his view of the national interest differed from sizable and vocal sectors of his own party, it was clear that he had the courage and the capacity to make decisions he believed in the national interest that he knew might not only thwart his lifelong ambition to be president but also his reelection to the Senate.

As indicated in his role in securing ratification of the Panama Canal Treaties, his most striking break from a position seen as the Republican one, Baker believed that leadership could be not just the "slave of the spectacular," but also "the care with which its groundwork is laid, the persistence of its follow through and the consistence of its proposals in the face of challenge." His definition is especially appropriate in its recent congressional context, as the patience and planning of floor leaders has come to be as crucial to the life and death of legislation as their parliamentary and substantive knowledge. James Squires wrote during the Ervin Committee hearings that Baker was not a brawler but a "chess player, the kind of gritty, patient little guy who could win a smiling contest, holding the perfect grin until his own insides are screaming with pain." Baker accepts such a designation, finding two tracks in his personality. "One of them tries hard to do the job here. The other runs along more or less parallel, sort of watching what's going on." In his early years in the Senate, his aloofness caused him problems. "He is either the nicest, most honest man in the . . . Senate, or . . . the most deceptive," a GOP colleague told Squires. "I haven't decided which." Such doubts wore off. Abraham Ribicoff reflects a common view when he says that Baker is "one of the fortunate few in politics who is very, very secure in himself." If his closest associates had a worry, it was that Baker was too trusting of his own instincts. But this hampered him little in the Senate, for he clung passionately to the idea that his colleagues were as dedicated to serving the public interest as he. "There is no higher secular calling," he often said, and he, perhaps to his detriment and unlike many in the same business, looked upon his brother and sister politicians as potential allies. A novel he began writing in 1973 and shunted aside when he and the publisher could not agree on the story line embodied the same values. Leaving it devoid of melodramatic scenes, he used his protagonist, a young East Tennessee lawyer elected to the Senate, to explore the "ideals, motives and principles" which "make men act." He carried the same lessons into the real legislative arena. "It is a very rare thing when Howard Baker attacks the ideology of other people," said John Seigenthaler, the former publisher of the *Nashville Tennessean*. "He has respect for them. It is his way to take . . . something from everybody and . . . use it as clay . . . to mold policy."[8]

Such words suggest that the oft-used nickname, "the Great Conciliator," should supplement Squires's designation of Baker as a chess player. Indeed, Baker found merit in Walter Lippmann's view that the "only feasible goal which statesmen can set . . . is to reconcile the conflicts which spring from . . . diversity." In part, Baker saw himself as a scoutmaster, doing whatever was needed "to take care of your troops." Taking pride in what colleagues revere as his gift of listening attentively, Baker, said Barry Goldwater, "took the time to find out what every Republican wanted." "What does it mean?" he frequently asked senators and close aides. While rarely substituting someone else's judgment for his own, he used his talks with colleagues to sharpen his perceptions of the issues involved.[9] His pragmatic, often eclectic approach allowed him to sift through rhetoric to the heart of highly complex issues before virtually any of his colleagues, a knack seen by the public when he framed "What did the president know and when did he know it" as the focal point of all Watergate investigations. But senators quickly discerned Baker's conciliatory hand in compromises covering such realms as fair housing, mass transit, the Panama Canal, revenue sharing, the environment, and budget and tax policy. Although many can claim as broad a range of interests, only Everett Dirksen, Russell Long, Henry Jackson, Hubert Humphrey, and Edmund Muskie among those he served with could point to as wide a scope of achievement.

While Baker captured the hearts of few ideologues, Republicans and Democrats alike saw him as eminently electable, if he could only win his party's nomination. Some say his problem was a moderate posture in a conservative party, even though his voting record was demonstrably conservative. He developed his philosophy in *No Margin for Error: America in the Eighties,* the work he wrote in conjunction with his 1980 presidential campaign that highlighted calls for fiscal restraint and reinvigorated defenses. Its premises confirmed Albert Gore Sr.'s assessment that Baker was "called a moderate because he's got a bland attitude; he's a purebred conservative with a bland attitude . . . sometimes mistaken for moderation." Another senator found it remarkable that he could take the same stand . . . as Barry Goldwater and Goldwater will come out looking . . . reactionary and Baker . . . moderate." Such claims are borne out by a voting record that never rated higher than a 25 on a scale of 100 graded by the liberal Americans for Democratic Action (ADA). But conservative groups rarely reciprocated. Baker found particularly amusing the 1969 ratings of the ADA and the Americans for Constitutional Action (ACA). "I didn't get thirty percent with either," he joked, "which was a great comfort . . . because I publish my own rating, and . . . always make a hundred percent."[10]

Baker explains the divergence in attitudinal terms. In a 1970 commencement address, he endorsed morality, or "the effort of one person to behave in such a way as to respect the rights and freedoms of other people," but rejected moralism, or "the effort of one person to insist on how another should live and think and behave." More bluntly, Hugh Scott, his predecessor as Senate GOP Leader, termed the far right's disgruntlement with Baker as stemming from a demand for "total . . . subservience to an ideal." Those who allied themselves to a cause, he said, "reserved their right to dispute not only the approach . . . but facets of the cause. Subservience to an ideal means . . . you have given up your powers of ratiocination and substituted those of someone else. If you vote for fluoridation of water for fear . . . you're going to get licked, that's subservience to an ideal, or against fluoridation, whichever that silly issue was."[11]

A. James Reichley, in *Conservatives in an Age of Change: The Nixon and Ford Administrations,* uses nonpartisan indices to classify Baker as a stalwart in the tradition of Howard Baker Sr. and Everett Dirksen, as opposed to a fundamentalist, who he found not "content with moderating the rate of change" but intent upon a "counterreformation." While the fundamentalist form of conservatism developed after World War II "in response to a number of economic, social . . . and even spiritual concerns," stalwarts had a century-long identity as the voice of small town, middle-class Protestants and Main Street businessmen. Seeing the marketplace as the proper arbiter of economic decisions, their pragmatism led them to accept federal intervention if it might protect the interests of their constituents. Proud of their heritage as the party of Lincoln, they remained committed to the enactment of laws guaranteeing civil equality long after most blacks had abandoned the GOP ticket.

The last great hero of the stalwarts was Robert A. Taft, to whom the elder Baker and Dirksen pledged allegiance in the late 1940s and early 1950s and the younger Baker adopted as a hero. More than any other politician of his generation, Baker can claim legitimate philosophical descent from Taft. Their similarities in what Gary Hart calls a "thoughtful and humane brand of conservatism" are as evident from their general adherence to the stalwart model of decentralized, fiscally responsible government as from their occasional deviations. Just as Taft justified his support of housing and education programs by holding that the government must maintain a floor beneath which no American should fall, Baker cited a commitment to expanding opportunity as his basis to support welfare reform and a Department of Education. Even his support for the Panama Canal Treaties, which led some who proclaim their descent from Taft louder than he to term him a traitor, is entirely compatible with the anti-imperial view of the national interest Taft expounded several decades earlier. "Panama," Baker wrote, "got what was necessary to her dignity and we got what was essential to our security."[12]

Even more striking than the ideological parallels are the circumstantial ones. After waging unsuccessful bids for the GOP nomination, both returned to the Senate to manage the fights for the programs of the men who defeated them. Just as historian James T. Patterson found Taft indispensable to the legislative prowess of Dwight D. Eisenhower in 1953, Warren Rudman wonders if Ronald Reagan "really understands how much he owes Howard Baker." Like Taft, Baker began preparing his caucus to assume a governing role long before a Republican reentered the White House, believing that a party out of power could not merely oppose presidential initiatives but had a duty to present alternatives. While scholars labeled this concept as "responsible parties" in Taft's day, the lone congressional leader to honor its dictates between 1952 and 1976 was Gerald Ford, and the only support for it elsewhere seemed to come from scholars interested in making the system more accountable. Thus, it was Baker who revived the idea of "responsible parties" on a broad scale. Largely because of his efforts at conciliation, his caucus adopted GOP alternatives to the foreign, defense, economic, and energy policies of Jimmy Carter. Once his party became the majority in 1981, Baker worked to see that his GOP colleagues united behind Reagan's tax and budget programs in some form, knowing such a course would allow his party to take credit or blame for any fallout from the outcome, minimize any need to cut deals with Senate Democrats, and strengthen his hand in conference committees with representatives of the House. His success led predecessor Hugh Scott to call him "the best Republican leader in my time. He has shown courage, as in the Panama

Canal issue. He not only shepherds his flock with care and tact and humor, but he knows how to hold off the no-win issues until such time that they can't destroy the forward movement of legislation."[13]

Like anyone who attains a leadership position in Congress, Baker was a partisan, but his partisanship was not the blind, somewhat glandular zealotry that often characterizes recent converts. Rather, it was rooted in the heritage of his Appalachian homeland. Growing up among descendants of victims of rebel rather than Yankee aggression during the Civil War, it came quite naturally for him to identify with the party of Lincoln, just as it came naturally for antebellum East Tennesseans to link with the Whig Party of Henry Clay, which, unlike the Jacksonian Democrats, promised their region equitable proportions of state and federal benefits and internal improvements that would facilitate the transport of their products to northern markets. Never terribly prosperous, East Tennessee has always accepted some federal programs, even those like TVA, the most locally far-reaching of them, that were initiated by Democrats. But East Tennessee Republicans were also socialized to accept the free-market economic system embraced by the small businessmen among them and identified with their stalwart GOP compatriots of the Midwest. Baker was doubly so, having ties to both the mountain Republicans and professional classes of his homeland. His instincts were those of a problem solver and a conciliator. "Problems are solved," E. J. Dionne wrote in *Why Americans Hate Politics*. "Issues are . . . what politicians use to divide the citizenry and advance themselves." "It is the resolution of conflict," Baker told students in 1990, rather than its perpetuation, "that makes the difference between successful self-government and civil warfare." While Baker always found time to hail GOP compatriots and take issue with the programs of the Democratic Party or the claims of its candidates, it was rare that rancor entered his approach or his rhetoric. Unknown to him, says liberal journalist John Seigenthaler, were cheap shots. When asked at the end of his tenure as Majority Leader as to his greatest legacy in that position, it was, simply, "that this place works."[14]

Within the Senate, Baker followed a bifurcated approach in formulating strategy. He would devise plans, informing only trusted associates, and them only in increments. He drew his big picture at regular Tuesday caucus luncheons and then allowed his chairmen to sketch in the details, thus in Pete Domenici's words, "letting you think you're doing it, not that it's being done to you." Rarely if ever did he attempt to preempt prerogatives of his chairmen or involve himself in petty jurisdictional struggles. When asked in the midst of one such squabble why he wasn't involved, he responded, "Ain't got no dog in that fight."[15]

In part, Baker's success stemmed from his manner. To Richard Lugar, Baker was "sufficiently self-effacing so there's plenty of room for others to feel they play an important role. But he's never so obsequious that you doubt he's the leader." Using a mixture of persuasion, flattery, and cajolery, he, in the words of Warren

Rudman, tried to make "everybody feel . . . important, whether we've been here for one day or twenty years." Rare was it when important debates concluded without him congratulating both managers for maintaining "the finest traditions of the Senate." His attention to his colleagues' concerns and his magnanimity led members to think twice when they entered the chambers of the Senate and saw him sitting on a table in the well in the midst of a difficult vote. "Howard, geez, I can't vote for that. Do you really need me?" When the response was an "I really need you" followed by an earnest smile, Republicans generally and even a few Democrats would contemplate their ballots in anguish for a few moments before casting them with their Leader.[16]

Baker's reputation for finding solutions to complex issues approached that of Henry Clay, "the Great Compromiser" of the nineteenth century. "To hear them talk," Lisa Myers once wrote, "Howard Henry Baker . . . could bring together a boll weevil and a cotton planter." He would keep his options open as long as possible, often advising colleagues that "of a dozen disasters that are coming down the track at you, eleven . . . are going off the track before they ever get to you" and the twelfth "is going right over you and you can't do anything about it." If such a steamroller missed, Baker had a knack for building coalitions through a disarming and conciliatory brand of bargaining. As a lawyer, he had a knack for bringing civil suits to settlement by treating all parties with courtesy and respect, using his briefs in a somewhat novel way to outline the points on which all sides agreed and then crafting rational, practical solutions that satisfied all parties that justice was being served. In executive sessions of the Senate Watergate Committee, he would often annoy single-minded liberal staffers while delighting their more pragmatic bosses by countering Sam Ervin's proposals, commending those parts he deemed acceptable, adding, "We may have to do just that, but I wonder if it might be better if first we . . . ," and then presenting an alternative. Almost always, the Baker proposal became the focus of discussion and an amended version dissimilar to Ervin's initial instinct became committee policy. Indeed, Baker often got much of what he wanted when a less conciliatory course would have left him with nothing. At times during his stint as Leader when shouting seemed likely to become the tone of operation, Baker would say, "Let me turn up my hearing aid," then tell those present, "I want you and you and you to get together and talk this thing over and give me a brief memo on the options." Ensuing delays generally served to calm tensions. Even if the two sides could not find common ground, the myriad options they outlined generally left sufficient room for Baker to forge a compromise both sides could accept. The frequency of Baker's success led Bill Armstrong to feel better when he saw him coming and William Roth to dub him a "political neutron bomb" who "destroys his opponents and leaves their egos standing." Presidents and senators alike knew that many controversial initiatives would not have become law without some Baker-induced modification, and saw just as well that the final product was likely to resemble Baker's desires more than their own. And Baker's flexibility had limits. "You . . . can't change that man's mind once it's made up," said Neil Sexton, who watches and maintains Baker's home when he is away.[17]

Implicit in Baker's manner is a historical consciousness Allen Tate found common among educated southerners. Intuitively recognizing predicaments facing each member, his sense of time and place extended to what Dan Quayle called a "sixth sense of when to push and when not to." In the process, he maintained his dignity and insisted that others be accorded the same treatment. "By 1972," says John Seigenthaler, "it was . . . clear that he would never use race for a vote and his instincts would follow the tradition of the party of Lincoln." It was rare when he adopted the buzzwords of any interest group, nor would he don funny hats to win the support of groups of regional or ethnic boosters. But his aloofness never reached the point of pomposity. None of the awards he received, not even the Medal of Freedom Ronald Reagan presented him in 1984, succeeded in eliminating an uncommon democratic air. He was one of the few members to be seen in line at the basement cafeterias of Senate office buildings and perhaps the only senator to express a fondness for Goo-Goo Clusters or Krystal burgers. When pulled over for speeding in 1983, he refused an offer of a warning citation and insisted upon being "treated like everyone else." He reacted in much the same way a few months earlier when he learned that he had been ranked as the second-best-dressed man in America. A bit flabbergasted, he told friends he was a slob and spoke of how often tailors had called him and how often Joy had not let him leave the house without changing because his clothes were mismatched or too rumpled.[18]

Such a democratic spirit extended to Baker's idea of the desirable nature of legislative service. Although born, bred, and wed into families with long histories of public service, he never aimed to spend his entire career in the Senate. Nor did he deem it wise for most of his colleagues to spend most of their time in Washington. Afraid members had become "elected bureaucrats" and "tourists in their own constituencies," he regularly trumpeted his father's view of his proper role as a "Tennessean, temporarily in Washington to speak for his neighbors" who "never thought about giving up his profession or his . . . enterprises and personal interests." Indeed, the citizen-legislature that Baker wished he could re-create would meet no more than six months of any year, thus allowing members to "think big thoughts," commune with their constituents, and pursue other interests.[19]

An outsider at heart, Baker derived as much satisfaction from his photography as from his work in politics. "Those photographs that generally appeal to me," he wrote in *Howard Baker's Washington,* a collection of his pictures of the nation's capital adorned by his impressions of its architecture, "are straightforward and simple and direct." Much the same could be said of his fondness for the residents of his hometown. A scenic isolated community nestled high on the Cumberland Plateau twelve miles south of the Kentucky border, Huntsville, the seat of Scott

County, retains a rugged frontier character. The independence and candor of the natives, memorialized in Scott County's secession from Tennessee and creation of the Independent State of Scott when the Volunteer State left the Union, led Baker to solicit their ideas on national issues. He remains a deacon at Huntsville's First Presbyterian Church and even had its pastor, Martha Fairchild, join former colleague John Danforth in conducting his remarriage to second wife Nancy Kassebaum, then the senior senator from Kansas. "This church means a lot to the senator," previous pastor Charles Boonstra declared before Baker brought Ronald Reagan to worship in 1982. "Every Sunday he's in town, he's in church." Such weekends became fewer, a circumstance that disturbed him deeply. Determined as a senator not to let Washington become his home, Baker has always maintained that Huntsville remains his mooring. In his early days in Congress, his wife, Joy, would take their children to Huntsville for the summer so they would never lose sight of where they came from. Knowing Baker consciously missed his mountain perch if he stayed away too long, staff members took care to schedule visits as often as time permitted. A trip there, said his daughter Cissy, left him feeling like he could conquer the world.[20]

Chapter 1

POLITICIAN'S SON
1925–1964

Baker's roots extend deep into Appalachian history. His ancestors formed a small ripple in the stream of hearty settlers who migrated via Virginia and North Carolina in the late eighteenth century. Some more adventurous Bakers moved to Campbell County, the domain due east of Scott County, in 1811. Their influence spread quickly, as the hamlet of Baker's Forge was named after his great-grandfather. Both of Baker's paternal great-grandfathers, George Washington Baker and Alderson T. Keen, shared the fervent Unionism of their East Tennessee neighbors, enlisted in the Union army, and rose to the rank of major. Local historians credit Keen with convincing General Ambrose Burnside to move his troops through Scott and Morgan counties en route to Knoxville in 1863.[1]

Baker and Keen linked with the Union Party during the war and its parent body, the Republican Party, afterward. Over the next four generations, their descendants followed their example devotedly. Many actively participated in the affairs of the party of Lincoln. Those disinclined toward political pursuits voted Republican as a matter of course.

James Francis Baker, George's son, was the first Baker to gain political prominence. A native of Cedar Creek in Campbell County, Jim Baker began studying law early in life and opened a practice that extended to encompass Campbell's adjoining counties. One early case was tried in Huntsville, where he, overeager to prepare a defense, arrived a week early without sufficient funds. To pay for lodging, he accepted money and other necessities from another customer who went by the alias of "Frank Howard" and roomed with his brother Jesse. Legend has it that the Howards were known as Frank and Jesse James in other parts of the country.[2]

While the Howard boys left, Jim Baker grew fond of Huntsville and decided to stay. He established a law firm, published the *Cumberland Chronicle* newspaper, and opened the Huntsville Supply Company, a general store. His business interests extended by the 1890s as far north as Hustonville, Kentucky, where he met and married Helen Keen. After the wedding, they lived in her hometown of Somerset, Kentucky, until Baker moved his family back to Huntsville in 1909. A congenial gentleman known for his candor and common sense, Scott County's first Baker was elected district attorney general, the Tennessee equivalent of district attorney, and elevated to a judgeship late in his life. Successful at business and law, Jim Baker belonged to the upper stratum of Scott County society. While his fortune paled by Gilded Age standards, it far exceeded those of the hill farmers and lumber-yard workers who comprised most of Huntsville's population. He stayed in close contact with his neighbors through his businesses and civic activities and shared their mountain heritage and individuality. They admired him for the breadth of his knowledge and the diligence of his work habits. Jim Baker never forgot those who helped him out in times of need, for he named his first son in honor of Frank Howard, who had staked his rent years before.[3]

Howard Henry Baker was born on 12 January 1902 in Somerset, where he lived until he reached age seven. A first grade classmate was distant cousin John Sherman Cooper, the future Kentucky senator. While Jim Baker moved his family back to Huntsville in 1909, his work placed him in Knoxville much of the time and he moved his family there during school years when Howard entered his teens. Howard Baker's academic record was distinguished at every level. He entered the University of Tennessee in fall 1918, helped found UT's Sigma Nu chapter, coanchored the debate team with Ray H. Jenkins, who later served as chief counsel to the committee investigating Senator Joseph McCarthy's allegations of Communist infiltration of the U.S. Army, and was elected president of the class of 1922. Upon graduating, Baker entered the University of Tennessee Law School, where he served as the first editor-in-chief of the *University of Tennessee Law Review*. But his tenure was short-lived, as he completed the three year course of study in two years.[4]

Not long thereafter, Howard Baker married Dora Ladd, the daughter of two future sheriffs of Roane County, returned to Huntsville, and became a partner in his father's firm. Lawyers have always prospered in Scott County, where murder, bootlegging, and moonshining rates are high and many manage properties for absentee owners. But Howard Baker, in the mind of Wilbur Mills, had as broad a knowledge of general principles of law as anyone he had ever met. Impeccably honest, Baker was instrumental in building Huntsville and Scott County high schools and the Scott County courthouse and in forming the Plateau Electric Cooperative. He inherited much of his father's law practice after his death in 1924 and expanded the clientele to include the Plateau Electric Cooperative and the First National Bank of Oneida. He also became involved in the land business, representing Frank Payne, a Pennsylvania manufacturer, in the purchase of forty thousand acres in Scott and Morgan counties and gaining a one-ninth interest for his work.[5]

While it might seem that a maldistribution of wealth separated Howard and Dora Baker from the rest of the mountain folks of Scott County, neither Howard nor Dora Baker saw their neighbors condescendingly. While friends remembered Dora Baker as "a friend of the poorest hillbillies" as well as the upper crust of Scott County, Howard Baker also mixed comfortably among rich and poor alike. Scott County Republicans relished in contrasting Howard Baker's brand of benevolence with the paternalistic Crumpian variety rendered in Memphis. He and Dora Baker belonged to all of Huntsville. So would their children.

Howard Henry

Howard Henry Baker Jr., their eldest, was born on November 15, 1925. Young Howard Henry, said his eighth-grade teacher, was a "quiet young man with a good vocabulary" who was very "easy to get along with." Howard Henry displayed an ability to turn a phrase at an early age, winning a speaking contest at eleven. But forensic skills did not come easily. A shy young man, he was cast as a singing cowboy in an early school play. Stage fright set in and young Baker did not appear. Teachers searched for minutes and finally pushed the blushing tyke on stage. "I'm supposed to be an old cowhand," he blurted, "but I can't remember the words." His audience chuckled at his confession, but smiles turned to grimaces when he admitted to not wanting "to sing the damn thing anyway."

Ordinarily, however, the studious young Baker fared well in Scott County schools with little effort and read much more than his classmates outside of school, particularly from the *National Geographic*. Easily bored with the monotony of classroom busywork, the mechanically adept Howard Henry dreamed of becoming an engineer or a pilot. Like many southerners, he familiarized himself with the history of his homeland. Equally significantly, he met many of the pivotal figures in Tennessee while a child. Ray Jenkins was a frequent visitor to the Baker home and Estes Kefauver, another of his father's classmates, stopped in when legal business took him near Huntsville.[6]

Some of young Baker's political talent must have been inherited. Three of his grandparents served in county offices, while Howard Baker was elected to the Tennessee General Assembly in 1928. The elder Baker served one two-year term before retiring to devote more time to his law practice. He did not leave politics entirely, being elected in 1932 as Scott County GOP chairman, a post he held for sixteen years, and by voters in seven counties in 1934 as attorney general in the nineteenth judicial district.[7]

Dora Ladd Baker died the April before her husband became attorney general, a traumatic event in the life of young Howard Henry. "I remember vividly seeing her the last time in the hospital, where she had been taken for a gall bladder operation," Baker says today, and "being gotten up in the middle of the night to take me with my grandmother and my uncle to Knoxville. I don't recall anybody ever told me she died. We just sorta knew. . . . Even to this day, I don't like the sound of organ music, which is a direct result of that." Otherwise, while remembering a vivacious and outgoing woman, his recollections of his mother are sketchy, of the sorts of "things kids remember." "I remember she brought me a cat," Baker says, chuckling and flashing his familiar wide toothy grin. Characterizing his memories of his mother as not "well-rounded," he notes his sister, Mary, has no recollection of her, as she was two when Dora Baker died. What eight-year-old Howard Henry understood was that he would have to assume more responsibilities. From what Mary characterized as their father's "stern talking-to that put things into perspective," he also knew what the consequences would be of not performing them. Howard Henry would have to look after Mary when his father was away. His paternal instincts came readily enough that his half sister Beverly, twelve years younger than he, once declared him "as much a father . . . as a brother," because he, among other things, prodded her to learn a new polysyllabic word each day.[8]

To fill the void in the maternal role, Howard Baker Sr. persuaded Lillie Ladd, his recently widowed mother-in-law, to move in and guide the lives of young Howard Henry and Mary. A strong woman, Lillie Ladd had become the first female sheriff in Tennessee two years earlier when she filled the unexpired term of her husband, John Christopher Ladd, who had to resign because of the debilitating effects of a fatal illness. Her character is seen in a tale of her capture of five prisoners who escaped from the Roane County jail while she was attending to John in an Illinois hospital. She caught the next train to Kingston, found a friend, and drove to Walden's Ridge, where two ringleaders were hiding out. Spotting them immediately, she began honking her horn and shouting. Two of her deputies had guns, the unarmed sheriff cried, and were prepared to shoot to kill. The two alarmed escapees quickly surrendered. Three others turned themselves in after learning that their leaders had been captured.[9]

Not surprisingly, Howard Henry became attached to his firm but colorful grandmother, and it was another trauma for him when his father remarried slightly more than two years after his mother's death. Baker's bride was Irene Bailey, a widow who abstracted legal titles for the Great Smoky Mountains Park Commission. Many times she traveled to Claiborne and Campbell counties, both of which fell under Howard Baker's jurisdiction. The two fell in love and were married in 1936. Howard Henry resented his stepmother at first, a short-termed sentiment stemming from her replacement of his mother and grandmother. Irene Baker was a more forceful disciplinarian than either Dora Baker or Lillie Ladd had been, challenging him to achieve his potential, in part by curbing a tendency to procrastinate.[10]

Young Baker acquired two passions during his teens that stayed with him for the rest of his life. He took up photography no later than 1937. While the results of his early efforts were occasionally ominous, as he once melted the paint off the kitchen cabinets with photographic chemicals, Howard Henry soon became an accomplished photographer. Joking today that he learned in the Boy Scouts that he was better at taking pictures than tying knots, he often earned small sums of money by taking pictures of cadavers the days before funerals. Photography was an especially appropriate hobby for the friendly but introspective youngster, allowing him to recapture poignant memories and serving as an outlet for whatever creative energy he had. Later his pictures served as a form of diary, but to him they were imminently more useful, as each snapshot elicited thousands of images from which he could recapture memories and gain additional insights. Photography also served as an escape from the day's business. In reflective moods, he found his pictures a personal vehicle to establish fresh perspectives on the affairs of the moment.[11]

Howard Henry experienced his first taste of politics about the time he developed his interest in photography. Aspiring young politico Howard Baker took his ten-year-old son on a tour of Tennessee in 1936 for the Landon-Knox ticket. But while the excursion was an exercise in political futility, Howard Baker took it as a duty, and Tennessee Republicans rewarded him with their nominations for governor and senator in 1938 and 1940, respectively. Standing no chance of winning either race, as the already strong Democratic majority had been further solidified by the popularity of New Deal programs, especially the TVA, Baker faced strong Democrats both times. State Senator Prentice Cooper, an honest, soft-spoken conservative graduate of Princeton and Harvard Law School who was closely allied to Shelby County boss Ed Crump, received their nod for governor in 1938. Baker's 1940 opponent was the thoroughly entrenched Memphian Kenneth McKellar. It is not surprising that Baker failed to capture 30 percent either time.[12]

Nominations for statewide office in the 1930s and 1940s were what one Tennessee GOP leader saw as rewards politicians were very happy to honor someone else with. As all knew their chances were slim at best, the offices Tennessee Republicans most coveted were the First and Second District seats in the House of Representatives, both of which seemed to be held by entrenched incumbents. Avenues for the advancement of the young attorney general were thus blocked. While realizing that he was a sacrificial lamb, Baker worked as if the races were tight, traversing Tennessee again and again, as one early chronicler wrote, to acquaint "voters with Republicanism and the name Baker in much the same way medieval villagers worked on a magnificent cathedral that would never be completed in their own lifetime." From 1936 on, young Baker was active in his father's campaigns, seeming to know even then how to handle crowds.[13]

Howard and Irene Baker were much more concerned about Howard Henry's scholastic progress than any of his extracurricular activities. Young Baker had always performed well in Huntsville schools, but there, as in most southern communities, education suffered from insufficient funding. Howard and Irene Baker ardently desired a better education for the naturally inquisitive Howard Henry than

Huntsville schools could offer, and sent him to McCallie School, a military prep school four hours away in Chattanooga. While a bit cocky at first, Howard Henry found McCallie's program much more rigorous than the one to which he was accustomed. Classmates found him to be a pleasant enough guy who played junior varsity soccer and served as photography editor of both the student newspaper and yearbook. Not terribly fond of the military parts of McCallie's program, senior private Howard Henry wound up working his pants off before graduating in 1943.[14]

HB

Under normal circumstances, Howard Henry would have embarked upon a four-year course in engineering, but America was at war. Seeing a duty to contribute to the effort, the fully grown, five-foot-seven, baby-faced adolescent enlisted in the Navy's V-12 program, which required him to spend the academic year in college. The Navy ordered young Baker to begin his pursuit of a B.S. in electrical engineering at the University of the South in the fall of 1943. He spent a year at the Sewanee, Tennessee, institution before transferring at the Navy's instruction to Tulane University, accumulating three years of academic credit in two years. Summers and holidays he spent on training maneuvers on bases from Rhode Island to Florida. Just before the war ended, he was commissioned a lieutenant, junior grade in the Naval Reserve, given command of a PT boat, and responsibility for decommissioning other PT boats. After his discharge in 1946, Baker aimed to resume studying engineering at the University of Tennessee, but worked as an underground mining engineer, setting place markers to help survey the areas where miners would dig for coal at the Payne-Baker tract. There, he apparently began to consider other lines of work. When he went to register for classes, he stood in line for a day, then left for home frustrated. Passing the law school, he noticed "the door . . . open, the light . . . on and . . . no line," then parked his car, went inside, and filled out an application.[15]

Baker was not terribly fond of law school, either, but did quite well, earning a sufficiently high grade point average to enter Phi Beta Phi, the legal honorary, and the even more prestigious Scarabbean Honor Society. His passion even then was politics, and he would offer his opinions on current events to anyone who would listen. HB, as his Pi Kappa Phi brothers called him, became active in the student government, attaching himself to Tom Vaughan, the charismatic president of the student body during the 1947–48 school year. Many saw HB as Tom Vaughan's protégé, but James Toomey Baker, his free-spirited cousin who also belonged to Pi Kappa Phi, found it "a case of the tail wagging the dog." When Vaughan graduated, his quiet but not particularly well-known advisor ran for election in his own right. He had done his work without fanfare and belonged to a small fraternity, hardly an advantage in the realm of Greek politics but a real detriment when fraternity and sorority members were outnumbered, ten to one. In a manner instructive of how he would woo Democrats in his Democratic majority state, HB courted independents arduously, promising them the use of a college-bought jukebox in the gym, an improved system of campus transportation, and a lowering of social barriers separating independents and Greeks. To all students, he vowed to establish a small radio station on campus, a pledge he kept by seeing to the opening of WUOT in early 1949.[16]

"Ol' Two to Ten"

Howard Henry returned to Huntsville after graduating and became the junior partner in the firm of Baker and Baker. He tried his first case against Haywood Pemberton, a local legal legend then in his seventies. So soon out of law school, the cocky twenty-three-year-old was anxious to make a name for himself. He prepared his case along the lines recommended at the University of Tennessee Law School, peppering his case with what circuit court clerk Ted Q. Wilson called seventy-five-dollar words. But Howard Henry received a rude awakening when he entered the courtroom. Haywood Pemberton was a master courtroom psychologist and constantly referred to Baker as "son." "He sonned me to death," Baker said later. "Mr. Pemberton . . . knew what the squire wanted and he gave it to him. When the squire ruled in his favor, Mr. Pemberton winked at me and said, 'I thought he would see it our way.'"[17]

A few months later, Baker and Baker tried a case together. Howard Henry delivered what he was sure was a poignant summation with florid rhetoric and lofty exhortations and inquired how he had done. His father looked him in the eye. "You were all right," he said. "But the clarity of your words sometimes exceeds the wisdom of your thoughts." Baker accepted the advice and soon shed a bit of his vocabulary from his courtroom repertoire and took to addressing East Tennessee juries in twangy vernacular and in commonsense terms they could understand. His legal reputation grew enough that Haywood Pemberton and other veteran barristers were soon sending him their leftover business.[18]

Baker Jr. also became active in the civic life of Scott County. He had joined the American Legion shortly after returning from the war, and his involvement increased after he graduated from law school. He, like his father, taught an adult Sunday school class at the First Presbyterian Church of Huntsville and also became active in the Scott County Bar Association, the Scott County Chamber of Commerce, and the Oneida Kiwanis Club, the latter of which elected him its president in 1952.[19]

Howard Henry came as well to handle a steadily increasing share of legal business, as his father became more involved in politics, chairing the Tennessee delegation to the 1948 Republican National Convention. Like most Tennessee delegates, the best known of whom were Republican National Committee Chairman B. Carroll Reece, a former twelve-term congressman from Upper East Tennessee and the GOP nominee for the Senate, and Guy Lincoln Smith, the publisher of the *Knoxville Journal*, Baker supported the candidacy of Senator Robert A. Taft, the scholarly conservative from Ohio. The leading advocate of the fortunes of eventual nominee Thomas E. Dewey was Second District Congressman John Jennings Jr. When Dewey chose Jennings to direct his fall effort in Tennessee, he created enmity by bypassing the party leadership. Had Dewey won, Jennings might have kept his seat. But Dewey's loss left him with virtually no patronage to bestow at a time when he had rankled many by proclaiming that a Dewey win would end "the . . . corrupt alliance between certain Republican leaders in Tennessee and Crump-ism."[20] Here was a reiteration of allegations long made by Reece's enemies that a working arrangement linked the organization of Memphis boss Ed Crump and East Tennessee Republicans, whereby Crump's East Tennessee Democratic allies conceded the First and Second Districts in the House in return for GOP support for Crump allies in Democratic gubernatorial primaries, thus allowing East Tennessee Republicans to control federal patronage and Democrats to manage that accruing at the state and local levels.[21]

Years ago, Baker looked into such allegations and found them a myth that took on a life of its own. Regardless of their veracity, the steady reiteration of such tales gave them credibility and rendered negligible public belief in the viability of the Tennessee GOP. It bothered many Republicans that such charges were made in 1948, for Reece, the alleged beneficiary of such deals, was waging a vigorous campaign for an open Senate seat. Angered, Reece opted to run for the seat he had held and concluded that Jennings's replacement was every bit as much in the interest of the people of Tennessee. Guy Smith arrived at the same conclusion, withdrew from Jennings the support of his newspaper, the only metropolitan GOP daily in the South, and found a ready opponent in the elder Baker, an ambitious attorney who wanted to follow in the path of the late J. Will Taylor, Jennings's predecessor and one of his heroes.[22]

It was his young law partner to whom the elder Baker entrusted to run his campaign, and the Bakers believed their chances were fairly good. Baker Sr. had a strong base in the counties he had served as attorney general, and his outlook seemed ideal for his constituency. He favored the Taft-Hartley Act, an increase in the defense budget, the expansion of veterans' benefits, and the enactment of anti-Communist legislation while opposing deficit spending and "socialized medicine." While a conservative, Baker attended assiduously to the interests of his would-be constituents, arguing for expanding TVA, new safety laws for mines and businesses, and increased funding for projects at Oak Ridge, and against restrictions on workers in that scientific center that limited their rights to own homes and manage businesses.[23]

Even though Jennings's record was hardly impressive, as he had answered but 89 of the 236 roll calls in 1949, he was not without resources and was widely known, having served the Second District since 1939. While all signs pointed to a neck-and-neck finale, Baker unseated the incumbent by a better than two-to-one margin, a rare occurrence in any state.[24]

Baker's primary margin was somewhat illusory. Some Jennings backers resolved to stay home or cross over to Democratic nominee Frank Wilson, an able Oak Ridge attorney hardly typical of the sacrificial lambs Second District Democrats generally nominate to go through the motions of running for Congress. While predominantly Democratic Oak Ridgers appreciated Baker's sympathy, they maintained their allegiance to hometown boy Frank Wilson. Intraparty bickering detracted enough from GOP strength in the rest of the district that a tired, frustrated candidate looked at his campaign manager one night and asked him to promise never to run for office, a request Howard Henry flatly refused. Small boosts near the end of the campaign allowed the Bakers to regain their enthusiasm. An overwhelming majority of his constituents in this, the only district in America not to have elected a Democrat since the Civil War, identified with the GOP. Fences mended sufficiently by election day to give Baker 52.4 percent of the vote.[25]

Howard Baker and his family left for Washington two months later. Howard Henry helped his father organize his new office, then returned home once a staff was chosen and trained. Mary Baker remained in Washington and was chosen as Tennessee's princess in the Cherry Blossom Festival, where she befriended Joy Dirksen, a fellow congressional brat who represented Illinois. Both were bridesmaids in the September wedding of Louise Reece, the daughter of B. Carroll Reece. Early on the day of the wedding, Joy and Mary lit up a cigar on a dare. Spying them in a car near the Reece home, Howard Henry pulled Mary from the car. When Joy emerged defending her friend, an ever-protective Howard Henry rebuked her for her "very corruptive influence" on his sister and pushed her into a rose bush. That night, Joy covered the scars of her first meeting with Howard Henry Baker with band-aids and mercurochrome.

Baker reflected and concluded that he had overreacted and phoned Joy from Huntsville less than a week later. He was going to be in Washington and wondered if he could drop by to deliver a more formal apology. She agreed to hear him out. Upon arriving at the Dirksen apartment, he very apologetically regretted his abruptness. Within a few minutes, he became enthralled with her charm, the grace of her acceptance of his apology, and her mischievous wit. Apparently, the sincerity of his gesture moved her, for she accepted his proposal twenty-five minutes after he arrived.[26]

Joy and her mother Louella began making plans for the wedding soon thereafter. They scheduled the ceremony for December 22, 1951, at the First Presbyterian Church of Pekin, Illinois, without informing the father of the bride. Everett

McKinley Dirksen had been preoccupied during the summer of 1951 with his duties as chairman of the Republican Senatorial Campaign Committee. A crafty congressional veteran gifted with rare eloquence, Dirksen had figured in GOP presidential speculation since the early 1940s and was the most formidable character Baker had ever met. When Joy brought him to the Dirksen cottage near Chesapeake Bay in late September, Baker invited the senator, a friend of his father's, to take a walk on the beach. There, Dirksen listened as Baker informed him of his feelings for Joy and of the planned nuptials. Touched, Dirksen gave the union his blessing.[27]

Howard and Joy Baker were wed in December by the same minister who had married Everett and Louella Dirksen. After returning from their honeymoon in Puerto Rico and the Virgin Islands, they settled in Huntsville. Joy Baker assumed she had married a country lawyer. Her feelings toward her father's profession were somewhat ambivalent. She had majored in political science at Mount Vernon Junior College and Bradley University and her interest came naturally. Her father had served in Congress for seventeen of her twenty-two years. In his initial Senate campaign, she and her mother drove, attended meetings, collected messages, and wrote and typed press releases. After his election, she acted as an unpaid receptionist in Dirksen's office. While a politically astute woman of the traditional school who begged away from speaking engagements until 1978 on the theory that "your husband never has to account for anything if you don't say anything," her interest and enthusiasm were tempered by a realistic streak developed from her childhood separations from her father. The 1950 campaign had only added to her discomfort. After one exhausting day, she looked at her mother and vowed with a sigh to marry a ditchdigger.[28]

Respectful of his wife's feelings, Baker remained an interested but generally passive observer of politics during the first twelve years of their marriage. He filled in for his father on speaking engagements when the congressman's schedule prevented him from appearing and was always on the periphery of his father's campaigns. With both he and Joy the offspring of members of Congress, they were invited to fill in for absent guests at White House state dinners often enough that Dwight D. Eisenhower eventually asked him, "Why are you here?" When his visits to Illinois coincided with Dirksen's campaign tours, Baker generally helped in some way. Occasionally, he was the butt of Dirksen's jokes. "I've got a son-in-law who . . . served on a PT boat," the "Wizard of Ooze" quipped in 1960, "but nobody . . . suggested we elect him to anything."[29] Had Baker been inclined to pursue a political career, his options would have been limited. Tennesseans were not yet prepared to abandon their Democratic heritage, and the most prestigious plum available to Republicans, the Second District seat, was held by his father.

Baker thus opted to work at establishing his law practice, and today says he enjoyed this part of his career more than any other. He was especially adept at murder cases, the variety he found the most pressure filled, trying sixty-three over seventeen years. As no Baker client was ever sentenced to the electric chair, observers took to calling him "Ole Two to Ten," in view of the light sentences his clients customarily received. People from all over Scott County flocked to their courthouse to watch Howard Henry Baker, in part because he defended some of East Tennessee's most colorful criminals but also because they appreciated his forensic talents. Indeed, Baker had a folksy manner and an ability to frame questions that drew out more information than witnesses wanted to reveal and endeared himself to jurors, courtroom audiences, and opposing attorneys alike. He, too, had a knack for getting to the heart of his cases and making his points succinctly enough to convey his message. Especially revealing was a workers' compensation case where a man was injured by a fallen electrical wire. Representing the employer, Baker asked the victim how high he could reach. After the man responded that he could move his arm just barely above his head, Baker queried as to how high he could reach before the accident. The man grasped high in the air, whereupon Baker rested for the defense.[30]

One who took notice was Ray Jenkins, East Tennessee's most noted trial attorney of the middle third of the century. A master of courtroom theatrics, the tall, crew-cut Jenkins became counsel to the Senate committee investigating Senator Joseph McCarthy's charges that Communists had infiltrated the U.S. Army, and hired Baker as an unpaid assistant to undertake chores Baker remembers as pure drudgery. But taking the opportunity to observe the cross-examinations of Jenkins and minority counsel Robert F. Kennedy, Baker gained a unique education about congressional investigating committees and a wariness of their potential for abuse. More significantly in the short run, he gained insight into the techniques of a man he found could hold his own with the best and met several times on the opposite side of the courtroom. These lessons evidently proved helpful, as Jenkins by 1961 was hailing Baker as the "outstanding young lawyer in East Tennessee."[31]

Baker's clients were a diverse group, with many coming from the Scott County civic community. He was instrumental in the 1950s in forming the Highland Telephone Cooperative, the Huntsville Utility District, and the new Scott County Hospital, chairing the Scott County Airport Authority and serving on the boards of the Tibbals Flooring Company, the Stearns Coal and Lumber Company, the Colonial Gas Company, and the Brimstone Railroad Company. Most profitable of his legal ventures was his representation of Stearns, which with three other coal companies won a $1 million judgment from the United Mine Workers in 1959 after the UMW tried to win recognition through violence and sabotage when the firms contracted with a rival union. Baker's most profitable business interest was his partnership with Bill Swain, his best friend and the head of Swain Lumber Mills, and Dr. Milford Thompson in buying in 1959 the controlling interest in the First National Bank of Oneida, which the former owners had been preparing to close. Stockholders elected Baker chairman of the board soon thereafter and

Baker appointed Swain as president. The two lowered credit requirements and the bank emerged from its lethargy.[32]

Howard Henry was developing into one of Scott County's leading citizens and his family was growing. Darek Dirksen Baker, the firstborn of Howard and Joy Baker, was born in 1953. His sister Cynthia, who from an early age answered to "Cissy," the nickname her "Gramps" Dirksen gave her, followed three years later. Baker associates have often noted that for him, unlike many of their colleagues, his family comes first. Indeed, Cissy Baker, a former managing editor of Cable News Network who now serves as vice-president of the Tribune Broadcasting Company, recalls many times her father catching "a plane from Chicago at three in the morning just to be home when I got up."[33]

Baker made time as well to pursue three hobbies. While photography remained his principal diversion, he also fulfilled a dream of earning his pilot's license and built Scott County's first tennis court next to his home. Upon completing the facility, he found himself the only soul in town who knew how to play. After banging the balls against the wall for days, Baker invited neighbors over. "Folks," he commanded with a grin, "we're going to learn a new game."[34]

Baker wound up playing less tennis than he would have liked when his firm opened a Knoxville office. Accounts piled up quickly from insurance companies and other businesses, and Baker was away from Huntsville often enough in the early 1960s that he bought a house in Knoxville for his family to live in during the school year. While deeming himself a journeyman lawyer, he traveled the East Tennessee circuit extensively and appeared less frequently before the Tennessee Supreme Court, the Sixth Circuit Court of Appeals in Cincinnati or courts and regulatory agencies in Washington.[35]

Baker was arguing a case before the Federal Power Commission on January 7, 1964, when Everett Dirksen arrived in shock. Howard Baker Sr. had suffered a fatal heart attack while shaving that morning. Like much of East Tennessee, Howard Henry was stunned by the passing of his father, a robust, soft-spoken counselor who remained his law partner while in Congress as well as a constant source of wisdom.[36]

Dubbed "the outstanding Republican leader in this state" by Governor Frank G. Clement, the shoes of the elder Baker would be difficult to fill. With several ambitious Republicans anxious to assume his mantle, GOP leaders feared a struggle might give Democrats a fighting chance and asked Irene Baker, who had worked in each of her husband's campaigns since 1938 and served as Republican National Committeewoman, to run. A reluctant Irene pointed to her stepson and said, "Here's your candidate." "Oh, no, Mother," Howard Henry responded, "you run." Succumbing, Irene Baker campaigned on her husband's record. A warm conversationalist, she met with small groups, while Howard Henry and others rallied the faithful at larger gatherings. While Democrats banded behind Willard

Yarbrough, an editor at the *Knoxville News Sentinel* who tried to link Mrs. Baker with Barry Goldwater's anti-TVA stance, their efforts were in vain, as Irene Baker won with 58 percent of the vote, a small margin by her husband's standards, but still a compelling one.[37]

Irene Baker took her seat in the House in mid-March and gained a reputation for doing her job quietly but well. She completed her husband's term and then returned to Knoxville, where she became welfare commissioner.[38] But Washington had not heard the last of the Bakers, for another would announce his candidacy for the United States Senate on May 26, 1964.

CHAPTER 2

TRAILBLAZER 1964–1966

Prior to 1964, Baker resisted all suggestions that he run for office, believing "one man in the family at a time . . . enough in politics." But he had spoken with his father at length about the possibility of his running for the United States Senate.[1] No longer were the barriers in place that made the elder Baker's 1940 bid an exercise in futility. As the healthy statewide victories of Dwight D. Eisenhower and Richard Nixon in 1956 and 1960 indicated, conditions were ripe for a re-creation of the antebellum Whig coalition under the auspices of the party of Abraham Lincoln.

Pre-1964 Tennessee GOP Growth

A suitable recipe for victory for a Tennessee Whig mixed healthy majorities from East and West Tennessee with the votes of enough middle-class Middle Tennesseans to carry the state. The East Tennessee sectionalism long fueled by disproportionately low appropriations from the rural Middle and West Tennessee–dominated General Assembly still flourished. Similar discontent emerged from middle-class migrants to Democratic areas who were appalled by the low quality of services they got for their tax dollar. Just as important, many professional groups, such as Memphis cotton merchants who blamed federal and state planting restrictions for pricing southern cotton out of the world market, had come to doubt the efficacy of various New Deal and Fair Deal programs.[2]

No longer would Tennesseans shop around until they found a Democrat who held their viewpoint. Many of the more educated found the ideology of the GOP more closely attuned to their thinking than the party of their fathers and grandfathers. The Cumberland Mountains no longer served as a barrier to the expansion of Republicanism to those Tennesseans better acquainted with neighbors in Alabama and Mississippi than those of fellow Tennesseans in towns like

Bristol, Sevierville, and Huntsville. Good roads traversing the mountains created closer ties among East, Middle, and West Tennessee, and Tennesseans, like other Americans who shared in the cult of the automobile, took advantage of a seemingly inexhaustible supply of gasoline to travel in other parts of the state and renew contacts they had made in Tennessee's expanded system of higher education. Ideas were flowing and suspicions receding, a process hastened by the advent of radio and newsreels, which diminished the influence of hopelessly provincial party organs whose influence ended at the county lines of their subscription areas. From the new, less polemical media, changes would come in the way voters perceived the parties. Republicans and Democrats alike came to see the scapegoating that had served as political dialogue since Reconstruction as a bit harsh. After World War II, a number of competitive GOP organizations arose outside of the historic GOP strongholds of Upper and Middle East Tennessee. The first strike came in McMinn County in Lower East Tennessee in 1946, where a bipartisan group of returning GIs ousted an entrenched machine at gunpoint after incumbents beat up detractors and locked themselves in the county jail to "count" the ballots of an electorate that had ousted them. Similar disturbances in Polk County two years later resulted in three deaths. GOP growth emerged in Chattanooga after 1956 when "Bald Bill" Carter and Bill Brock founded a school for poll watchers aimed merely at "some sort of clean . . . election." The two began attending training schools and a sufficiently strong organization was in place in Hamilton County by 1962 to capitalize upon Democratic discontent and make Brock the first Tennessee Republican elected to Congress from outside the First and Second Districts since 1920.[3]

Similar developments were proceeding in Memphis, which the paternalistic segregationist Edward H. Crump had controlled for much of the first half of the century. In 1954, the year Crump died, the Shelby County GOP primary attracted 750 voters, so few that a participant joked that it could have been held in somebody's backyard. That vote emanated largely from blacks who aligned with the GOP in days when they could not participate as Democrats. Led by George W. Lee, an extraordinarily eloquent orator who seconded Robert Taft's nomination at the 1952 GOP convention, blacks congregated in the Lincoln Leagues and gathered the bounty of patronage when Republicans won the presidency. But there was no patronage between 1932 and 1952, and many blacks drifted into the Democratic Party. Lee's standing, even after his efforts in 1956 helped lead to a 54–46 margin for Eisenhower in Memphis's black precincts, ultimately depended upon the support of East Tennesseans B. Carroll Reece and Guy Smith.[4]

Becoming more influential in the Shelby County GOP was an able group of young white professionals who had met in the Eisenhower campaign, many of whom had been Democrats who had seen their path to power blocked by remnants of the Crump machine. Two generations younger than Crump, most were fairly tolerant on racial questions and quite conservative on fiscal ones. Finding their outlooks akin to those of the East Tennessee Old Guard, they were surprised to find themselves not welcomed by Guy Smith and B. Carroll Reece. Grievances accumulated over the next few years. Black Republicans found it "all right to them for us to be here as long as we were at the back of the boat and they were on the front." But their numbers were declining, and their leaders were aging, factors prompting the young to align with Democrats who had started to admit them into their deliberations. In the meantime, GOP affiliations grew sufficiently by 1962 among white professionals to allow the GOP to attract candidates for every legislative seat. Malapportioned districts meant that none expected to win and none did, but the races catalyzed the enthusiastic involvement of hundreds of volunteers for years to come. GOP growth in the white community portended conflict with blacks who had been active far longer. When racially moderate attorneys Lewis Donelson and Harry Wellford tried to assure George Lee in the early 1960s that there was "plenty of room . . . for both of us," Lee replied, "there isn't." "Well, move over," said Donelson, "because we're going to run you off." And run Lee off the New Guard did, defeating the World War I lieutenant for reelection to the state GOP executive committee in 1962 and then denying him a seat on Tennessee's 1964 delegation to the Republican National Convention. While some termed them racists, Benjamin Hooks, a Lee protégé then moving away from his GOP affiliation, better describes his rivals as "conservatives . . . who sought power . . . because they were dissatisfied in the way the Democratic administration was going in programs for people" and had sufficient backing to take control of the Shelby County GOP.[5]

Television was transforming the Tennessee political landscape even further. Voters still expected candidates to stump at rural courthouses, a skill Lamar Alexander jokes involved "raving and ranting about everything from tax sharing to the Communists" to "spittin' and whittlin'" old-timers who were likely to notice only "if you ended too soon." But stumping had become more of a means to call attention to a candidate's empathy for his audience than a way to convey his knowledge. That talent voters now expected candidates to exhibit in radio or TV ads of thirty seconds to five minutes that would reach them and five million others. Here was a medium readymade for Baker's cool, conversational style. It ironically was his stump speeches for his stepmother that prompted senior GOP officials to notice him coming on like gangbusters. Tennessee Republicans were optimistic in 1964, a rare year when both Senate seats were available. By late 1963, Dan H. Kuykendall, a shrewd Memphis businessman who had been active in the Eisenhower and Nixon campaigns, had wrapped up the nod for the seat of Albert Gore Sr., an incumbent long seen as too liberal for Tennessee. Three perennial candidates vied for the nod to fill the remaining two years of the term of the late Estes Kefauver. Fearing the presence of any of the three would limit the credibility of the entire ticket, Kuykendall, state GOP chairman Ernest Koella, and attorney John B. Waters Jr. called on Baker at his law office in spring and asked him to make the race to spare embarrassment to the party. Baker agreed to mull over the possibility. His father's death had removed the sharpest obstacle, and he and Joy concluded that Darek and Cissy were old enough to move to Washington if he were to win in a healthy way. A week later, Baker phoned Waters, an old college friend, and told him that he would run if Waters would manage his campaign.[6]

The Initial Campaign

Citing unparalleled growth, Baker declared on May 26 in announcing his candidacy that it was the GOP's duty to "rise to full maturity and offer to the people . . . the choice of candidate, principles and issues to which they are entitled in the concept of the two-party system." His would be a conservative campaign in the classical sense. Paraphrasing Lincoln, he forwarded his conviction that the obligation of government was "to do for the people those things which they cannot better do for themselves within the limits of financial and moral responsibility." "We're witnessing a unique phenomenon . . . this year," he later elaborated, "caused by fear of a giant federal government about to devour us." America, he said, faced a "drift toward centralized government which obsesses the notion that the people can be governed only by Washington," and he professed fear that "galloping federalism" might reach the point where the "federal government can tell you where you must go to school, who you must employ, where you must work and the wage you must accept." Intent upon reversing the flow of power from Washington to states and local communities, he proposed a tax sharing program, whereby federal revenues would be transferred to states and localities to allow those more aware of a community's priorities to determine where tax dollars were spent without constraint from anonymous bureaucratic directives.[7]

Recognizing revenue sharing would only partially restore the prerogatives of state and local governments, Baker pledged to oppose further encroachments on their authority. Matter-of-factly, he announced his opposition to Titles II and VII of the pending civil rights bill, saying that only state government could know all its problems and cope with them effectively. He was more forceful in his condemnations of federal intrusion into the private sector, blasting the Hill-Burton hospital construction program because it gave the federal government too much control over the operations of hospitals once they were completed, and the Medicare proposal being considered, as its cost might destroy the solvency of the Social Security system.[8]

Baker's outlook meshed well with the predominantly conservative mindset of Tennessee GOP primary voters, and his name became well known throughout Tennessee over the summer of 1964. While not a spellbinding orator like his father-in-law, Baker had a knack for choosing the appropriate word or down-home analogy to get his point across. Acquainting voters with his rational, folksy demeanor and youthfully exuberant conservatism by campaigning in every Tennessee county, including some no GOP candidate had ever worked before, he won 85 percent of the votes cast in the GOP primary.[9]

Democrats waged a more spirited contest for the seat occupied by Herbert S. "Mr. Hub" Walters, an elderly conservative who was a stand-in for Governor Frank G. Clement until 1964, when Clement might gain the seat without repercussions for leaving the governorship so soon after his 1962 election. Kefauver partisans were inclined to fight Clement's accession. Tensions had flared between the camps for years, but were rarely more acute than in 1964. For Clement to bid "to fill the seat of Senator . . . Kefauver," said one Kefauverite, "is almost an insult to his memory. His many friends are well aware of the efforts of Clement to defeat him in every attempt he made." Kefauverites banded largely behind Ross Bass, a World War II veteran who had been a florist, a nursery owner, a soft drink bottler, and a postmaster in Pulaski before being elected to five terms in the House. But Clement was the favorite, as he controlled the state Democratic organization and retained the unwavering loyalty of thousands of rural Tennesseans who clung to traditional values and were attracted by his Bible-quoting, fist-pounding eloquence. "Hysteria turns into history," he liked to say, and he won national acclaim for sending the state national guard to Clinton in 1956 to disperse a mob that gathered to block a court order to desegregate public schools. But his popularity declined after he raised the state sales tax in 1963, with discontent especially salient among unions and blacks. While Clement had long sympathized with union aims, he could not persuade the legislature to follow his lead. And while he was the first Tennessee governor to appoint blacks to major state offices, many believed that he had not moved fast enough and cited his defense of his 1964 refusal to sign a fair employment practices code because some portions violated state purchasing law. Distrust mounted after he tried to mollify conservatives by blasting Bass for voting to deny jury trial in criminal contempt procedures against those accused of violating civil rights laws. "You aren't going to convince your enemies," Benjamin Hooks told Clement, "and you're sure going to lose some of your friends." And so it was, as Bass, a signer of the Southern Manifesto of 1956, who Hooks said "had to have his arm twisted up to his head" to get him to back the Civil Rights Act, won the endorsement of the Tennessee Voters' Council, the state's most influential black organization. Labor, too, backed Bass, whose voting record reflected a commitment to its aims.[10]

Factional differences were exacerbated by whispering about the occasional irascibility of both Bass and Clement. Congressman "Fats" Everett had to pull Bass off Howard Baker Sr. at a party after the elder Baker gave a less than adulatory response to a Bass query about his performance on the Ways and Means

Committee. Clement's irritability was exacerbated by his alcoholism, a condition that was a source of whispers. While occasionally good natured, tales of the governor's battle with the bottle proved damaging for the rest of his career.[11]

Bass identified himself with Kefauver and painted Clement's administration as a dictatorship. Lambasting Clement for ignoring education, notwithstanding unprecedented increases in pupil performance, teachers' salaries, and school funding during Clement's tenure, Bass aligned himself with Lyndon Johnson, proclaiming his support for the Texan's housing, antipoverty, and tax-cut programs. Clement countered by declaring Bass a stooge of liberal *Nashville Tennessean* publisher Amon Carter Evans as well as an ineffective and often absent congressman. But he could not overcome the ire of those angry about his tax increase, and only Bass's 97,000 vote margin surprised local pundits. While Bass's win made him the favorite, it had come at the cost of Democratic unity. Clement, while backing Bass, let backers follow their consciences and many of the more conservative of them, especially in the business community, drifted toward an increasingly optimistic Baker camp.[12]

Unfortunately for Baker, 1964 was not the best year to make headway among disaffected Democrats. The militancy of some of Barry Goldwater's supporters led many to deem all in his party extreme. Particularly offensive to many was the rhetoric of Ninth District congressional nominee Robert James, who declared it his "object . . . to make people realize there is more to life than bread," and complained that federal employees could not teach Sunday school in segregated churches. Just as distasteful to moderate Democrats and black Republicans was the presence at the head of the ticket of Goldwater, the one GOP presidential hopeful who opposed the Civil Rights Act of 1964. While no segregationist, Goldwater saw efforts to regain a sizable chunk of the black vote as futile and urged their abandonment. Instead, he opted to try to merge the traditional Appalachian GOP base with West Tennesseans in the cotton industry, white supremacists, ideological conservatives, suburbanites discontented with poor services and high taxes, and leaders of finance, industry, and insurance. Traditional Democrats, said John Grenier, the Alabama attorney who handled Goldwater's southern operations prior to the convention, "could not be jarred loose without somebody they thought was a segregationist." While this assessment may have been appropriate for the Deep South, it was one that disrupted a coalition that had carried Tennessee in three previous elections and angered many Republicans. George Lee vowed to do everything he could to defeat Goldwater and James. While friendly to Baker, he withheld his support, one reason being Baker's enthusiastic support for Goldwater.[13]

Equally problematical for Baker was Goldwater's view that TVA "would be better operated and . . . more of a benefit for more people if it were part of private industry," a statement Howard Baker Sr. described as a serious mistake upon learning of it in November 1963. Baker echoed his father's dedication to TVA, often trying to reassure audiences that Goldwater was not for its dissolution and destruction. While his pleas were seconded by Richard Nixon, who tried to distract attention from Goldwater's position by assuring crowds that Goldwater would change his position once he learned all of the facts, and Everett Dirksen, who declared that the Arizonan aimed only to sell TVA's steam power plants, Goldwater disregarded their warnings. Even so, GOP leaders hoped that his general outlook would elicit a favorable response and invited him to speak in Knoxville on September 16. Baker was tapped to introduce Goldwater, whose standard speech exalting the principles of a strong national defense, free enterprise, and decentralized government was well received until he spoke of TVA. "What I have said with respect to TVA," he said, "is within the . . . framework of that philosophy and I stand by it." Here was a godsend for Bass, who began concentrating his attacks on Goldwater and brought in Lyndon Johnson to Tennessee to vow that there would be no sale of TVA while he was president.[14]

Baker developed "an intense desire to sink into the dust" the moment Goldwater reiterated his stand, recognizing that his chances had slipped gravely. He still fought gamely, reviving Clement's recitation of Bass's poor attendance record and declaring that Bass "flew the coop" on Tennessee farmers. With the farmer's share of the food dollar at its lowest point since the 1930s, price supports dropping from 89 percent to 74 percent of parity, farming costs increasing and prices decreasing, Baker declared that Bass had proven himself a friend of the Australian farmer, while American farmers were suffering by decisions not to cut imports of Australian beef. While his assignment of full responsibility to Bass was hardly fair, the issue stuck, as Bass had answered only ten of the House's eighty-five roll calls in 1964, with three of those on motions to adjourn. Baker claimed not to be overly upset, labeling the absences the greatest service he rendered, as Bass had not voted against a single position of the Americans for Democratic Action (ADA), the highly liberal lobby, that year.[15]

In his one head-to-head debate with Bass, Baker declared the chief domestic priority of government as the preservation of essential freedoms. Arguing that overcentralization set governors further apart from the governed, he, as Goldwater might have, claimed that Bass "lacked confidence in himself and in the people . . . to do things for themselves." While his support for Goldwater never flagged, he distanced himself from the Arizonan's proposed cuts from the Rural Electrification Administration and made voters aware of his disagreement with Goldwater on TVA. When Bass tried to paint him as a closet sycophant of these discredited positions, Baker responded by charging Bass with harping on TVA as a smokescreen to cover up the ties of Lyndon Johnson with accused influence-peddlers Bobby Baker and Billie Sol Estes.[16]

Baker was making headway. While most expected a Bass victory, they noticed a steady decline, and Bass won by a narrow margin of 568,905 (52.1 percent) to 513,330 (47.4 percent). Baker congratulated Bass, then pledged his support to the furtherance of an effective two-party system. Privately, he maintained his good cheer, boasting to Guy Smith of good news. "I'm running ahead of Goldwater," he said. "You dumb son of a bitch," the crusty editor shot back. "You don't run ahead of the top of the ticket and win."[17]

Baker had run fully 3 percent ahead of Goldwater, who won just 44 percent of the vote, lost Hamilton and Shelby counties, both of which went for Nixon in 1960, and carried the historically Republican Second District with but 50.5 percent of the vote. It is hard to disagree with the contention of Dan Kuykendall, who ran just behind Baker and well ahead of Goldwater, that he and Baker easily would have won if someone else had headed the ticket. Indeed, those Tennessee Republicans who had established records before the campaign generally fared well. Jimmy Quillen and Bill Brock won reelection to their House seats, while John J. Duncan captured the Second District seat that Irene Baker was vacating. And the GOP gained five seats in the Tennessee General Assembly, largely because of court-ordered reapportionment. But those with close ties to Goldwater or without previous records of elective service suffered. Thousands of mountain Republicans were alienated by Goldwater's proposed cuts in aid to Appalachia, and thousands more in other parts of the state were angered by his suggestions to make Social Security voluntary and sell TVA.[18]

The one jurisdiction where Goldwater outpolled the two GOP Senate nominees was Shelby County. The fact that Robert James also ran ahead of the two suggests that Goldwater swayed many segregationists. But, as James concluded after the election, "the respectable people have been outvoted." If, as James suggested, only Republicans were respectable, then one must wonder why Memphis was so much less respectable than in 1960, when Richard Nixon carried Shelby County handily. Indeed, Goldwater and James, in courting segregationists, had written off the black vote for the entire GOP ticket. Kuykendall later guessed that he and Baker won but 1 percent of the black vote statewide. George Lee agreed, saying the party of Lincoln had been kidnapped by extremists who ignored the examples of Dwight D. Eisenhower and Richard Nixon of honoring the principles of a party rooted in freedom and individual rights. In Nixon's view, Goldwater had lost because voters rejected the reactionary caricature pinned on him by opponents and, ironically, some supporters. This perception had also rubbed off on Baker and Kuykendall, both of whom Nixon believed would have won had they garnered a normal quota of black votes.

Even in defeat, however, Baker had put himself into a strong position to advance. He had won more votes than any GOP candidate in Tennessee history and more than twice as many as any predecessor. Having waged an effective campaign only to lose because he had been linked to the extremism attributed to Goldwater, it was no surprise that the *Knoxville Journal* touted him as the new titular head of the Tennessee GOP. Biding his time, he resisted overtures to become state GOP chairman and maintained a light speaking schedule. Privately, he and associates concluded that a bare-boned race they deemed at first little more than fun and games had been lost solely because Baker had been victimized by the reactionary tag pinned on many Republicans in 1964.[19]

The Breakthrough

No one could be certain that 1966 would offer a better opportunity, but several delegations descended upon Knoxville to ask Baker to run for Bass's seat when a full six years would be available. Many, including his law partners, Joy, Everett Dirksen, and Bill Swain, counseled him against running. Uncertain of the impact a race would have upon his family, his firm, and his fortune, or that Tennessee's two-party system had progressed to sufficient maturity to allow the election of a Republican, they advised Baker to let someone else take the defeat they foresaw. Of a different mind was John Waters, who found a wide range of contacts all across the state urging Baker to run again. Baker mulled over his options for months and guessed that his chances of winning were better than even. He had run the strongest race of any GOP Senate candidate in Tennessee history in a most un-Republican year and created very little anti-Baker sentiment. As his name was becoming more widely known, Lyndon Johnson's and Ross Bass's popularity were plummeting. Polls of fall 1965 indicated that 65 percent of the state's voters would consider voting for a Republican under the right circumstances. More optimistic than his most intimate associates, Baker, feeling duty bound, did his best to dispel their carefully and lengthily stated concerns and opted to make a second race.[20]

The only problem was that there was no longer a clear field. One of those who had encouraged Baker to run in 1965 was Kenneth L. Roberts, a genial Vanderbilt law professor who had coordinated statewide volunteer activities for Goldwater and been named Tennessee's outstanding Young Republican. When Baker suggested to some that he might not run, financier David K. "Pat" Wilson asked Roberts to make the race. Roberts was agreeable but found that Baker had changed his mind. Who should withdraw? The two met privately, concluded that a civil primary would involve more people and generate more interest, made a gentleman's agreement not to attack each other, and went about organizing across the state. Here was a tedious process, as only forty-one of the state's ninety-five counties had held GOP primaries in 1964. Even after Bill Brock and state GOP executive director Bill Carter began executing a blueprint to strengthen the GOP in the Democratic strongholds of Tennessee, some local organizations were so primitive that Baker said that he would "rather have people vote for my opponent than . . . vote in the Democratic primary." In no small part because of the efforts of Baker and Roberts, seventy-five counties had GOP committees by 1966 and seventy-eight held primaries.[21]

Baker announced his candidacy in Nashville on February 16, hoping to signal with his choice of the capital city that this campaign would be better financed and more successful than his initial foray. He designed his platform to appeal to a broader constituency, too, having learned the hard way that successful minority party candidates must develop attractive alternatives to proposals of the majority. "We can't simply react to the Democrats' proposals . . . , but we must offer . . . positive proposals," he said. "We must see that the Republican Party is so broadly based that it can support widely divergent viewpoints and express the majority view."[22]

Just as antebellum Whigs of the stripe of Henry Clay focused on promoting measures designed to spur economic growth while limiting social disharmony, Baker settled upon revenue sharing as his platform's centerpiece. Revenue sharing had the conservative virtues of rechanneling authority back to state and local officials and thus giving those most familiar with the needs of their communities more latitude in funding projects of pressing local concern, and the liberal ones of providing Tennessee, one of the few states without an individual income tax, with added funds for an improved system of education, better roads, and other services traditionally funded by state and local governments. Always pragmatic, Baker did not see decentralization as a panacea for all domestic ailments. He believed the federal government had a number of legitimate duties, including the initiation and expansion of opportunity that it was not fulfilling. Aiming to unite business-oriented Republicans of Tennessee's cities and suburbs with traditional mountain Republicans of East Tennessee, some of whose ardor had been lost in 1964, he advocated an Economic Opportunity Corporation that federal and private donations would finance to catalyze job training, housing, slum clearance, and small business loans in America's poorest corners, and said opportunity could be stimulated further through a series of tax credits for businesses seeking to hire the hard-core unemployed. His concept of opportunity extended to higher education, and he advocated a federal tax credit to anyone paying for their tuition or their children's in a university or college. While revenue sharing would add funding to long-strapped southern educational systems and render them more able to compete with those in the North, Baker also called for the creation of a southern regional university center to provide top-notch scientific and technological training for the region's best young scholars.[23]

Fiscal restraint, Baker argued, must supplement opportunity to ensure prosperity, as the growth in federal spending had caused a surge in inflation that wage and price guidelines could not stop. "The planners of the so-called Great Society . . . provided lots of fat salaries for Democratic politicians," he declared. "But they failed to provide for millions . . . who have to pay 21.5 percent more per pound . . . for meats than in 1965. The fuzzy-headed planners overlooked those . . . Americans who . . . turned to substitutes" and "found that these foods were up . . . 15.5

percent over a year ago." Baker also cited a need for cuts in foreign aid. He did not reject the concept of foreign assistance but called for the donation of goods and services, rather than cash, a process he believed would benefit taxpayers, investors, and recipients. Baker demanded reforms in other federal agencies, too, urging the addition of the Cumberland River to the jurisdiction of TVA and the extension of Social Security benefits to many not covered.[24]

Baker waged the bulk of his primary campaign in East Tennessee and in Memphis, having learned from aide Hugh Branson that Hamblen County, an East Tennessee county of 49,000, played a larger role in GOP primaries than the city of Nashville. He campaigned his heart out, traveling in a rented Greyhound bus every day except Sundays to what he remembers as every village, hamlet, city, and crossroads in Tennessee. At the same time, campaign manager John Waters was traversing the state, telling local pols how well things were proceeding at the other end. While it was assumed that the more conservative image of Kenneth Roberts rested nearer to the center of GOP thought, Baker and Roberts generally agreed on issues that conservatives used as litmus tests. Baker, too, was better known. While the two remained friendly competitors, Roberts could bemoan only Baker's late entry and his refusal to debate.[25]

Baker indeed had captured the loyalties of many Tennessee conservatives in 1964. While his fiscal conservatism won him considerable acceptance among the professional classes, more appealing to less well-off socially conservative Tennesseans was his support of Everett Dirksen's constitutional amendment to reinstate voluntary prayer in public schools. "The United States Senate opens every session with a prayer," he argued. "The least we could do would be to allow the children in the public schools . . . the same privilege." Baker took a generally conservative position on most foreign and defense issues as well. While declaring it the patriotic duty of all Americans to support President Johnson's handling of the war in Vietnam and that all other issues were secondary to bringing that conflict to a swift and honorable end, he acknowledged that Tennesseans were getting tired of this war, a shift he attributed to confusion over American objectives. Viewing the administration's credibility gap as the result of a misguided bid to build a consensus through chaos, Baker urged Johnson to justify American war aims more candidly and demanded an increase in the bombing of prime military targets. Vacillation, he said, had convinced Vietnamese Communists that there need be no rush to commence peace negotiations. Believing Johnson's failure to restrict the flow of trade through Haiphong had encouraged North Vietnam, Baker left the details for the State Department to work out but called for drastic cuts in aid to North Vietnam's trading partners.[26]

Roberts fully agreed with Baker on school prayer and Vietnam, but he knew he needed the near-unanimous support of the Goldwater faithful to win the nomination. Recognizing that Goldwater's identification with the extreme right had damaged his campaign irreparably, Roberts did not encourage extremist support, but his silence was taken as assent. Baker had no such qualms. "We must turn back all efforts of . . . ultraconservatives or ultraliberals to take over the Republican Party," he told several gatherings, making his point especially forcefully after learning that John Birch Society members were circulating vicious anti-Baker leaflets. "Organizations which place their own objectives above loyalty to the Republican Party or to the country," Baker warned, "do a disservice to both party and country." When asked if he was referring in part to the John Birch Society, he answered, "Yes," a stance that won him the endorsements of the *Chattanooga Times* and the *Memphis Press Scimitar*.[27]

Equally strong support for Baker emanated from traditionally Republican organs like the *Knoxville Journal*, the *Maryville-Alcoa Times* and the *Oak Ridger* and from key GOP politicos. Among recognizable names, only Harry Carbaugh and former Congresswoman Louise Reece, Tennessee's Republican National Committeeman and Committeewoman, and two-time House nominee Robert James lent their backing to Roberts. Baker, in contrast, retained the virtually unanimous support of the mountain Republican hierarchy of East Tennessee, centered in the subscription area of the *Knoxville Journal* and symbolized by the backing of Congressmen John Duncan and Jimmy Quillen. His support in Memphis was sufficiently strong that Lewis Donelson could playfully taunt Roberts a few weeks before the primary, saying, "Howard's going to beat on you like a drum." And Baker regained some black votes the GOP had lost in 1964, as the Reverend C. M. Lee had formed a largely black Free Republican organization in Memphis primarily to back him.[28]

Baker was hardly concerned about the identity of the Democratic nominee; he was displaying polls in mid-July showing him beating either Bass or Clement. Bass's standing had dropped appreciably from a quick-tempered response to a nickname he had worn for much of his career. While he served in the House with Perkins Bass of New Hampshire, reporters labeled him as "Big Mouth" and Perkins as "Small Mouth" Bass, based on the sizes of their oral features. Baker and Clement both adopted the "Big Mouth" theme in 1964 and threw in a "Large Mouth" or a "Loud Mouth" for good measure. Bass ignored the taunts until April 1966, when he was introduced at a Democratic fundraiser with the ditty "He's known in the Senate as "Big Mouth Bass, what's more he has a pretty lass, The Senator from Tennessee, Ross Bass, Avenell's husband." Angrily throwing down his napkin, Bass announced, "I'm no big mouth—I didn't want to come—I think I'm going to leave—I'm leaving."

With furor over taxes subsiding and some blacks returning, Clement had regained much of his strength. But while Clement had appointed Benjamin Hooks to a judgeship in Shelby County, making him the first black judge in Tennessee since Reconstruction, and established precedents like hiring black secretaries in his office and black officers in the state highway patrol that the new breed of southern governors of the 1970s would follow religiously, he could not command the support of the Tennessee Voters' Council. Impressed by Bass's loyalty, the TVC endorsed him without giving Clement a hearing. Organized labor also stuck with Bass, who had voted to repeal Section 14-B of the Taft-Hartley Act. Little separated the two on other issues. Both favored increases in Social Security benefits, a higher minimum wage, and tax exemptions for lower-income families. Both, too, supported new federal agencies: Bass's pet project was a Department of Education, while Clement championed a Department of Consumer Affairs. But Bass wore the image of a big-spending liberal, and Clement effectively painted him as a Johnson administration rubber stamp.[29]

Such perceptions allowed Clement to win votes from many Republicans who switched to have a voice in the gubernatorial contest. While Baker told Republicans they had "no dog in that fight," thousands switched to vote against liberal businessman John J. Hooker, who lost to Buford Ellington by more than 53,000 votes, indicating that GOP crossovers were not determinative. What crossovers did affect was the senatorial primary that Clement carried by 18,243 votes, as Ellington backers generally opted for Clement.[30]

The Republican primary was a relatively quiet affair, as Baker and Roberts kept their agreement not to attack the other. But Baker, having wrapped up the support of the rank-and-file in 1964, exuded confidence and promised to finish what we started in 1964. While Roberts sensed defeat, he fought on at a pace equal to Baker's. A gentleman, he conceded forty-two minutes after the polls closed and predicted Baker would win convincingly in November. Baker heaped praise upon Roberts for a fight in the American tradition and made him his campaign chairman for the fall election. He said nothing about size of his victory, which, in a race many figured to be close, he carried with 77 percent.[31]

Most cast Clement as the favorite. Noting Baker's relatively small number of votes (122,617), many expected Tennessee to remain loyal to its Democratic heritage. But while Bass pledged to support Clement, his speeches were perfunctory. Nor would Ellington, who had been less than friendly with Clement for years, tie his campaign to Clement's, fearing his own effort against token opposition might be harmed, as Clement had never approached the vote total Baker had polled in his 1964 loss.[32]

Realizing that many Democrats were caught between their dissatisfaction with Clement and their reverence for the party of their forebearers, Baker tried to ease the transition of Middle and West Tennessee Democrats with the most conciliatory tone possible. He discarded all remnants of 1964 and painted Clement and his organization as complacent guardians of the status quo. "You are about to witness a . . . revolution," he said. "The Democrats of this state are no longer concerned with what their Democratic granddaddies may think if they vote Republican, but with what their grandchildren may think if they don't." His message appealed to young Tennesseans, as shown by the presence of his organizations at four-fifths of the state's colleges and his victories at most college mock elections by wide margins.[33]

Baker likewise made what Stephen Hess and David S. Broder called "the most ardent appeal for Negro votes of any southern candidate save Alabama Attorney General Richmond Flowers." He opened headquarters in the black areas of Tennessee's major cities, hired black aides, encouraged black groups to participate more fully in the democratic processes of government, and counseled against what he saw as a counterproductive strategy of becoming owned by any party. Urging them to "turn out government that is more concerned with enslaving you than about your needs," he promised to "speak your voice and your needs and speak them on the Senate floor without fear." While not yet prepared to support the open housing section of the pending civil rights bill, citing qualms about its wording, he did declare the principle of open housing just, assuring the TVC in October that he did not oppose the equality of man. Clement's position was less certain, and he used his TVC appearance to recite his past accomplishments, leading members to quibble for seven hours before finally settling on him. A spokesman for West Tennessee delegates, the bloc that pressed for the endorsement, said the choice hardly reflected a real preference. "The Republicans crossed the line . . . to kill our candidates," he said. "We've got to have some way to rebel."[34]

Labor support was equally slow to emerge for Clement. While Tennessee Labor Council head Matt Lynch remained loyal, he could not persuade his organization to render its support. Nor did the AFL-CIO back Clement, although state chairman Harry Morgan did issue a personal endorsement the day before the election. But Clement was not without resources, winning the editorial support of the *Memphis Commercial Appeal*, the *Nashville Banner*, and the *Nashville Tennessean* and maintaining thorough control over the Democratic organization, the operations of which often seemed indistinguishable from those of the state government. State employees were expected to give time and money to the Clement campaign, while state policemen delivered campaign literature and chauffeured former governors to Clement campaign events. While warning that Clement would pull every trick in the book, Baker more often noted his failure to take clear stands on issues like Vietnam and open housing, declaring that "the days when a machine politician can get elected through secret deals and empty platitudes have passed."[35]

Even though he had painted the Democratic primary as a contest between a "very junior, do-nothing senator" and a "tired out do-nothing governor," the adversary Baker usually described was not Clement, whom he had known since Clement's tenure as counsel to the Railroad and Public Utilities Commission in the late 1940s, but Lyndon Johnson and his program of "guns and butter and a little fat." Baker warned of a tax hike and termed it the "least imaginative and most painful way to control spending." "Let me say that I feel for the people of Tinnysee, too," he said, aping Clement's pronunciation, as Clement, if elected, would "have an Administration collar around the neck." Standard fare in GOP circles, such barbs assured whites who weren't comfortable with Baker's appeals to blacks that he would resist the more extravagant programs of the Great Society.[36]

Having secured East Tennessee in the spring and summer, Baker spent much of the fall in Middle and West Tennessee, the latter of which appeared ripe for GOP gains. Dan Kuykendall was waging a strong challenge for a Memphis House seat and another Republican had a shot of winning in the Seventh District. Baker generally took a more conciliatory line than his cohorts, a posture allowing him to attract support from blacks, labor, and other Bass supporters. East Tennessee Republicans had rarely been more united and Richard Nixon, John Sherman Cooper, and Gerald Ford all traveled to Tennessee to speak on his behalf. *Human Events*, the ultraconservative weekly, even featured the Baker-Clement contest in its "Race of the Week" section and gave Baker a resounding endorsement.[37]

A late October poll indicated that 65 percent of those surveyed believed Clement would win, but 56 percent of those who had made up their minds preferred Baker. To inspire confidence, Baker took to projecting a 100,000 vote win. Here was a move that Lamar Alexander, a bright young attorney who was calling most of the shots by October, considered "gall gone crazy." But Baker had gained enough confidence from warm receptions in labor halls and on Beale Street to allow him to ban volunteers from handing out his literature at the polls, a practice he had always found annoying anyway.[38]

Still trusting the tradition that the Democratic primary was tantamount to winning the general election, Frank Clement was slow to sense the shift. Bob Clement, who served in the House from 1988 to 2002, thinks his father did not have the same fervor to be a senator as he did to be governor. It always confounded Frank Clement as to how he could get at Baker. "How," he asked his son, "do I attack Howard Baker, who's never been elected anything except student body president at the University of Tennessee?" Neither had an answer, and Bob Clement advised his father he would lose days before the election. In what Bob Clement and Kenneth Roberts today call one of the cleanest elections ever, Baker landed just 580 votes short of his projected margin, with his victory being declared by Tennessee newsmen even before the polls closed in West Tennessee.[39]

Baker had run nearly 9 percentage points ahead of his 1964 showing, carrying more than two-thirds of East Tennessee's votes and making solid inroads into Middle Tennessee. More strikingly, he carried West Tennessee by 6,700 votes, becoming the first Tennessee Republican since Reconstruction to do so. He ran especially strong in the state's urban areas, carrying all save Nashville. Surprising nearly everyone, he also won, by Harry Morgan's estimate, 60 to 70 percent of the votes of Tennessee union members and increased his share of the black vote from virtually none to 15 to 20 percent.[40] Here was the Whig coalition reassembled in an elephant's garb. Even so, many saw Baker's achievement as accidental because of the Democratic Party's tatteredness and wondered if the new GOP coalition would hold if a united group of Democrats mounted a strong challenge. Scarcely concerned, Baker set out to ensure the permanence of a two-party system in Tennessee, a system of which is the trailblazer.

Chapter 3

IN DIRKSEN'S SHADOW 1967–1969

Baker entered the Senate as the first Republican ever elected by the people of Tennessee. Even so, his presence, like that of many freshmen senators, was little noted. Southern reporters harped upon the achievement of Winthrop Rockefeller, a more flamboyant racial moderate who had been elected governor of Arkansas. And the freshman GOP class of the Ninetieth Congress was top-heavy with more experienced leaders like Edward Brooke of Massachusetts, the first black senator since Reconstruction; former Wyoming Governor Clifford Hansen; Governor Mark O. Hatfield of Oregon, a vocal critic of U.S. involvement in Vietnam; and Charles H. Percy of Illinois, the president of Bell & Howell, Co., long seen as the boy wonder of GOP politics. In such company, many dismissed Baker rather casually as a "junior-grade Everett Dirksen."[1]

First Stirrings

Baker adhered to the deferential code of conduct traditionally prescribed for new senators, plunging into the work of the Government Operations and Public Works Committees, familiarizing himself with the issues those panels covered, and reporting on them to a study group composed of newly elected colleagues and Robert Griffin of Michigan, the next most junior Republican. Baker took every opportunity to forward his revenue-sharing program. Beginning with his maiden address in March, he commenced a series of pronouncements for the bill on the floor. Often rising to salute significant converts, he berated Lyndon Johnson for his opposition and hailed liberal economists Walter Heller and Joseph Pechman for their support. Realizing that Vietnam costs had forced Johnson to reduce spending for several Great Society programs dear to his heart, Baker argued for a minimally funded program for the duration of the war in the hope that its establishment would reinvigorate states and cities and provide a framework for further decentralization. As Johnson allies Wilbur Mills and Russell Long would not hold hearings on any of the bills introduced, Baker realized that his bill would not be enacted but continued to forward it, recognizing more positive action was likely in the future.[2]

Baker believed the Founding Fathers had empowered state and local governments to administer and perform most services, a healthy distribution since those closest to the people were more aware of local conditions. With more and more problems transcending state and county lines, Baker called upon communities to cooperate in developing economic development, job training, and environmental control programs. Baker, a product of the TVA region, had called for developing pilot air and water pollution projects under TVA jurisdiction in 1966. Soon after being assigned to the Air and Water Pollution Subcommittee of the Public Works Committee, he asserted that Congress had a duty to place barriers between the public and the causative agents producing stress. He warned that pollutants needed to be dispersed rapidly to protect the public's health from not only conditions posed by excessive concentrations of debris but also equally disruptive social and economic side effects. Were pollution left unchecked, an aroused public might demand unrealistic standards upon polluters, thereby forcing millions out of work.[3]

Thus seeking to balance environmental and economic concerns, Baker, realizing the impossibility of pristine pure air, wanted to legislate a high but flexible standard of air quality. He rejected the concept of national air quality standards, finding it absurd to govern smog-ridden California by the same rules applicable to the Smoky Mountains. But contrary to his generally conservative instincts, he concluded that maintaining any standard would require stringent federal regulations upon polluters. Shippers would have to pay for spillage, coal-generated factories would have to use scrubbers, and automakers would have to reduce emissions levels in their new models. Most of the initial work would have to be done at the federal level, with generous contributions from states and localities.[4]

As the most junior minority member, Baker could hardly match the influence of Edmund S. Muskie, the soft-spoken if fiery-tempered chairman from Maine, or his own cousin John Sherman Cooper, the venerable Kentucky moderate who served as ranking Republican. But Muskie soon was describing Baker's work as indispensable, recognizing like other less mechanically inclined members that Baker had studied engineering, continued to skim scientific journals and understood far better than they the technological complexities of pollution control. Just as important, Baker had what Thomas Eagleton called a rare ability to "argue his point, . . . persuade others, . . . then reduce that point into usable legal language." Baker was even more valuable as a conciliator. To Cooper, he was "one who could find solutions for difficult problems. . . . Muskie would get so nervous and angry. Finally, he . . . would say, 'Well, . . . Baker, see what you can do about it,' and Baker worked out a great number of solutions on all these environmental bills. . . . He had a way of effecting compromises which did not gut . . . the bill, but . . . gave it a chance to get started."[5]

Later, Baker would say that only his father had a greater influence upon him than Cooper, a rock of integrity and champion of civil rights who formed his ideal of Lincoln Republicanism. Baker's closest Senate associate on a personal level, naturally, was Everett Dirksen. Fond of each other, Baker and Dirksen took pains to keep work from disrupting their relationship. "I think he told everyone . . . except me how to vote at one time," Baker said. When they disagreed, they agreed to disagree cordially. In private moments during such periods, they discussed gardening, Dirksen's hobby and a secondary Baker pastime. Professionally, Baker made it a point to inform Dirksen in advance of any forthcoming floor battle that might embarrass the GOP Leader.[6]

"One Man, One Vote"

The first Baker-Dirksen clash loomed four months after Baker entered the Senate. A staunch supporter of the Warren Court's decisions in *Baker v. Carr* and *Reynolds v. Sims,* which ordered states to apportion legislative districts equitably, Baker knew that the results limited the power of rural-dominated southern legislatures to malapportion election districts and thereby deny blacks and Republicans representation in proportion to their numbers in the population. But while Baker opposed any attempt to delay compliance, Dirksen feared such a move might limit the power of midwestern Republicans to preserve their bastions of support. Early in May, Baker called upon Dirksen and informed him of his position. Shocked by Baker's firmness, Dirksen looked his son-in-law in the eye. "Howard," he said, "if you are going to fight, try to win."[7]

Baker allied with Edward M. Kennedy in a bid to preserve the newly mandated doctrine of "one man, one vote." The House had forced the issue earlier in the year with a bill allowing a maximum deviation of 30 percent between the largest and smallest congressional districts in any state, with the permissible variance receding after 1972 to 10 percent. When a bill by Sam Ervin allowing 35 percent discrepancies reached the Judiciary Committee, Kennedy commanded the support of but four Democrats for an amendment reducing the leeway to variations of 10 percent. With the panel more rurally oriented than the full Senate, Kennedy reintroduced his amendment on the floor on May 25. Baker added his name and argued that Congress should not tinker with the reapportionment decisions, as the Court would not tolerate the deviations that remained in twenty-one states five years after *Baker v. Carr.* On a moral level, he declared the Kennedy-Baker amendment even more justified, as inequities denied an equal voice to all by giving rural denizens a disproportionate share of seats in the House of Representatives.

Citing Tennessee's limitation of the variance separating the largest district from the smallest to 1.3 percent, Baker declared that the amendment's adoption would end such discrimination against urban inhabitants.[8]

Baker's duty lay in collecting Republican votes. Privately telling waverers that malapportionment had helped the Democrats for nearly a century in Tennessee and other states, he showed them statistics indicating that GOP House gains in 1966 would have surpassed the actual forty-seven-seat pickup if all districts had been equal in population and convinced eleven Republican colleagues to bolt from Dirksen's position and help carry the vote, 44–39. When, after months of negotiation, a conference committee resolved differences in a way almost identical to the House approach, Baker and Kennedy then led the Senate to reject the report by a 22–55 vote, with but four ayes coming from Republicans.[9]

Baker had accomplished much while managing his first major piece of legislation, having, with Kennedy, persuaded the Senate to affirm a controversial ruling that effectively ended rural dominance of state legislatures and congressional delegations. Change was most visible in the South, where groups concentrated in metropolitan areas, such as inner-city blacks and suburban Republicans, were granted representation proportionate to their fraction of the population and thus guaranteed unprecedented opportunities to win elective office.

Baker, too, benefited, as the debate marked the beginning of his identity as an independent force. While some continued to deride him as a creature of his father-in-law's creation, GOP National Chairman Ray Bliss hailed him as "exhibit A for the Republican Party." His stock was rising in Tennessee as well, as the state GOP executive committee endorsed him as its favorite son for the 1968 presidential nomination. Holding no illusions that he might be chosen for either slot on the ticket, Baker admitted that the ploy was designed to hold Tennessee's delegates in line until an opportune point prior to the convention. The only opposition to Baker among Tennessee Republicans, in fact, emanated from the ranks of the John Birch Society and other small likeminded groups. He had earned the respect of most of his colleagues, and few lobbies, save those with a near-exclusive alignment with the Democratic Party, found major flaws with his voting record. African American organizations applauded Baker's vote to confirm Thurgood Marshall's nomination for a seat on the Supreme Court and his fight to expedite reapportionment.[10] While each vote cast by a member of Congress can become a doubled-edged sword, no vote had yet won Baker much enmity at home.

Open Housing and Gun Control

Henry Horace Williams, the "Hegel of the cotton patch" who taught philosophy to Sam Ervin and Thomas Wolfe at the University of North Carolina, once asserted that the choice between "good and evil was not the thing that tries the souls of men, but choosing between conflicting loyalties is." Such a dilemma faced Baker in the debate over open housing after Minnesota Democrat Walter F. Mondale and Massachusetts Republican Edward Brooke amended the measure to bar anyone from discriminating on the basis of race in selling their home. While Baker, like his father-in-law, believed that the amendment infringed upon the rights of individuals to sell their property to whomever they pleased, he, unlike Dirksen, had been on record for the concept of open housing for two years and was one Mondale found, unlike many southerners, interested in some progress on civil rights. Mindful like Brooke and other junior Republicans that his party's public image might be painted on the basis of their performance in this debate, Baker joined fellow freshmen Griffin, Hatfield, and Percy in urging Dirksen, whose support had been the key to passing any civil rights bill since the 1950s, to find common ground with Mondale and Brooke that might bridge the conflicting principles of open housing and private property. Without Dirksen's backing, the first two bids fell short by 55–37 and 56–36 margins. But after weeks of soul searching, Dirksen let it be known that he would back a plan barring discrimination by realtors or agents but exempting individual homeowners, a course maintaining property rights while covering 90 percent of all real-estate transactions.[11]

Dirksen gave Baker the task of placing their ideas into workable language. As he announced his shift on February 26, negotiations were proceeding amongst Baker, Brooke, Attorney General Ramsey Clark, liberal New York Republican Jacob Javits, conservative Republican Roman Hruska of Nebraska, and liberal Democrat Philip Hart of Michigan. As a result, Baker and some of the participants in a bevy of meetings were unaware of some of the details when Dirksen introduced the substitute. Upon learning that a provision had been deleted exempting individuals who employed agents to sell their homes if they did not instruct the agent to discriminate, he tried to amend the substitute. While his amendment was not a central feature, he felt compelled to raise the point, as he had described the substitute to some conservatives with that provision included. Halfheartedly, he raised his addendum, labeling its deletion an honest misunderstanding. The amendment was defeated, albeit by a narrow 38–43 margin.[12]

Baker's handling of open housing, the least popular civil rights measure, won favor in some corners of Tennessee, but a shrill reaction arose from realtors and some white suburbanites. Baker's detractors remained vocal until April 4, 1968, when an assassin's bullet felled Dr. Martin Luther King Jr. in Memphis. Shocked that such a tragedy had occurred in Tennessee, many conservatives grew reflective. Few objected when Baker was the first southerner to rise on the Senate floor to eulogize King. Struck by the grim irony and poignance by which this champion of nonviolence had been slain, Baker called for "renewed resolve that . . . vigorous national efforts toward full equality of opportunity . . . will be carried on within the flexible but peaceful framework of justice and legal order."[13]

Historians often credit the enactment of the Civil Rights Act of 1968 to a collective congressional desire to atone for King's death. While the assassination explains John Anderson's decision to vote to dislodge the conference report from the House Rules Committee, a check of the dates indicates that the slaying of King had no impact upon the Senate, which had approved the bill more than three weeks before his death. The killing did lead several members to demand new restrictions upon the interstate sale of firearms. Baker, who had long defended the Second Amendment right to keep and bear arms, resisted temptations to yield to the sentiment of the moment. While he supported passage of the Omnibus Crime Act of 1968, a package including bans on the sale of guns to minors and mail-order sales of handguns, he opposed further restrictions not in the final draft save bans on the ownership of hand grenades or bombs by anyone not authorized by the FBI or the Defense Department. Gun control advocates were more vocal after the June 5, 1968, murder of Robert F. Kennedy. While shaken by the slaying of Kennedy, a friend since the Army-McCarthy hearings, Baker remained opposed to most forms of gun control, especially objecting to registration, fearing certificates might be used in the future to confiscate all privately owned firearms. As approval of a second gun control statute was certain, he, like all but four GOP colleagues, supported the relatively mild bill that passed, explaining that "if it were not passed, an even worse bill would have been enacted."[14]

The Nixon Loyalist

Matters of a more partisan nature occupied Baker for much of 1968. As the only Republican elected statewide in Tennessee, he was aware that blacks were still disturbed about the lily-white delegation the Tennessee GOP had sent to the 1964 convention. While he wanted to make amends by reserving for them a number of seats on the 1968 delegation, Tennessee Republicans rebuffed his efforts by including only one black, Sarah Moore Greene, the president of the state NAACP and a future Baker aide, in the fifty-six-member contingent. Delegates followed his lead more closely in opting to support former Vice-President Nixon, who Baker hailed upon withdrawing as favorite son as the man most keenly tuned to the times. Applauding Nixon's commitment to justice and equal opportunity to every man in housing, jobs, and voting and his rejection of centralization and civil disorder, he assured listeners that he had nothing against Governors Nelson Rockefeller of New York, who had announced, or Ronald Reagan of California, who had not. When Rockefeller came to Nashville looking for support, Baker served as a gracious host, said the governor deserved a hearing, and told him he had no support in Tennessee.[15]

Baker reiterated his message in a keynote address to the state GOP convention, declaring that mistakes during the two previous administrations had caused

Democrats to forfeit the confidence of the American people. Aware that a winning coalition for a minority party candidate must combine the near-unanimous backing of his own party with a significant number of independents and defectors, he urged Republicans to adopt his conciliatory tone, warned against ever again letting itself be ruled by a narrow philosophy, and called upon his compatriots to set aside all petty grievances and support the choice of the national convention.[16]

Baker thought that the Republican nomination would be meaningless to Nixon or anyone else if the GOP platform was limited to recitations of the party's past laurels and harsh denunciations of the Democrats. Hoping to win approval for several of his pet programs, he resolved to secure their inclusion in the platform, which a panel chaired by Everett Dirksen would draft. While aware of his father-in-law's inclination to help, Baker knew the specifics would be determined by the contenders for the nomination. Using his position on Nixon's Key Issues Committee to maximum effect, he lobbied the former vice-president to accept some of his most significant initiatives. Quickly endorsing revenue sharing, Nixon also backed Baker's call for the peaceful employment of nuclear energy, remembering the international goodwill that flowed from the "Atoms for Peace" proposal. Nixon studied more closely Baker's aim to end the draft. Only when Baker, who had held since 1964 that conscription ran against a two-century-old tradition of voluntarism, and Mark Hatfield assured Nixon that any proposal they submitted would specify that an end to the draft would await the end of the Vietnam War did Nixon agree to incorporate an antidraft plank.[17]

Recognizing Baker's attractiveness as an issue-oriented representative of the New South, Nixon tapped him to second the nominating address to be delivered by Spiro T. Agnew, the unknown governor of Maryland. Baker lauded in youthful hyperbole "America's greatest son." In a speech composed largely of snippets he had delivered often in Tennessee, he noted trials of "bitterness and frustration" and "peril and promise" and exhorted delegates to nominate a man with "new relevant ideas" who could unify America by recognizing the "brilliance and diversity" of its people.[18]

Baker's homespun manner won generally good reviews. Distributors of the Nixon-Baker buttons that many Tennesseans were sporting found many takers that night. A minor boom, centered in the Tennessee delegation but scattered among many, surfaced for a Nixon-Baker ticket once the convention settled upon Nixon as its nominee. While doing nothing to encourage the movement, its intended beneficiary revealed to friends that he would welcome the nod if Nixon offered it.[19]

Unbeknownst to virtually anyone, Nixon had opted tentatively for Agnew, thinking Agnew would have appeal in the border states and among ethnics, groups he was targeting, and had experience with urban problems that he could not match. Nixon valued even more Agnew's anonymity, as his polls showed that those figuring most prominently in speculation (Hatfield, Percy, Reagan, Mayor John Lindsay of New York, and Governor George Romney of Michigan) would actually detract from his total in November. While Nixon had not finalized his decision, anyone who would supplant Agnew on Nixon's dream ticket had to share qualities Nixon found in Agnew: integrity, personal and political strength, a moderate-to-conservative philosophy, and adherence to Nixonian conceptions of foreign policy.[20]

Only Nixon mentioned Agnew during any of the first three meetings he convened to test his choice. While he remained secretive, intimates knew of his desire to exclude the "glamour boys"—Hatfield, Lindsay, Percy, and Reagan. With predictable objections raised to each, participants arrived at a consensus that only the choice of a centrist would assure unity. Baker fit this category perfectly, and his name was mentioned often before dawn on August 8, most notably by Strom Thurmond, the aging ex-Dixiecrat, who ranked him just behind Reagan. Baker survived the second meeting well, as did two governors Thurmond deemed acceptable, Agnew and John Volpe of Massachusetts. A southern participant found "it . . . clear. For the North, it was Volpe. For the South, it was Baker."[21]

After a nap, Nixon convened a fourth meeting at 9 A.M. Again Agnew's name surfaced only when Nixon mentioned it. But among this contingent, Baker had the advocacy of only Everett Dirksen, whose support for his son-in-law drew guffaws from other participants. Baker soon faded from consideration, a development Nixon explained by characterizing him as too new. Baker took the decision in stride, knowing his chances had been remote, and promised to do everything he could to elect Nixon. Days after the convention, Nixon designated him and nine others as his surrogates at events he could not attend in states too small to justify his own presence, a delegation allowing him to concentrate on winning the states with the largest blocs of electoral votes.[22]

The Breaking of a Chief Justice

Even the most conciliatory of legislators are not immune to the demands of partisan politics as elections draw near, and Baker was no exception. It was his belief that Nixon, if elected, should have the prerogative of nominating a successor to Chief Justice Earl Warren, who announced his intention to retire in June 1968 with his departure contingent upon the Senate's confirmation of a successor. Lyndon Johnson's choice to replace Warren was Associate Justice Abe Fortas, whose seat would be filled by Judge Homer Thornberry. Johnson informed Everett Dirksen of his plans and convinced the Minority Leader to help him secure confirmation. Dirksen phoned Baker that night, told him of Johnson's intentions and asked for his vote. Citing his belief that the new president should fill the post, Baker refused Dirksen but agreed to keep the names confidential.[23]

Baker met the next day with Paul Fannin, Hiram Fong, Robert Griffin, and George Murphy to draft a petition holding "that the next Chief Justice . . . should be designated by the next President . . . and that if such an appointment were made in the waning months of this Administration . . . , we would not vote to confirm it." Fourteen more GOP senators added their names before Johnson made public his choices on June 26. Baker restated his opposition that day, saying he had nothing against Fortas and nothing against Thornberry. Declaring his vote a matter of principle, he coyly denied a partisan motivation, noting that a new Democratic president could resubmit the nominations in January. While predicting swift confirmation if that were the case, Baker professed fear that confidence in the Supreme Court might recede even further if the choices were made by a lame-duck president. Once Griffin organized a filibuster, a course helped by news that Fortas had advised Johnson on foreign policy issues and accepted $15,000 to conduct seminars while on the Supreme Court, the campaign progressed rapidly enough that a mid-September head count revealed forty-one senators, seven more than needed to block cloture, committed against Fortas's elevation.[24]

While Baker and Griffin could not block Fortas's rise in the Judiciary Committee, they did keep Griffin's vow of extended debate. Baker's role lay in refuting administration attacks on the anti-Fortas lobby. In a three-and-one-half-hour floor address on September 23, he restated his opposition and denied Fortas's ideology had been part of any senator's decision. Pointing out that he had never been a Supreme Court baiter, he found the charge especially inapplicable to eighteen other Republicans who had vowed to fight any nominee before the election. He blasted Ramsey Clark and others who tried to impugn the motives of adversaries, many of whom had backed every civil rights bill, with cries of anti-Semitism, noting that Jacob Javits, who backed Fortas and shared his creed, declared such charges invalid. Regretting he could not support a fellow Tennessean, he declared that the Senate had a responsibility to give its advice and consent. With battle lines well in place, Majority Leader Mike Mansfield saw no way out but to file a cloture petition. When but forty-five senators voted aye, Fortas asked Johnson to withdraw his name.[25]

The GOP Returns to Power

Fortas's withdrawal had little impact upon the politics of his home state. Tennessee Democrats again were divided, albeit this time over the choice of a president. Thousands of whites were moving to the camp of independent candidate George C. Wallace, leaving Democratic organizations in disarray. In contrast, Republicans, save for a small group of reactionaries, rallied behind the Nixon-Agnew ticket. Surrogates Baker and Bill Brock spoke often, especially in East Tennessee and in Memphis, where they figured a maximum GOP turnout would offset pluralities for Humphrey and Wallace in Middle and West Tennessee and give Nixon the state's electoral votes. As they guessed, Nixon carried the state with 38 percent. More surprisingly, the GOP gained eight seats in the State House and elected its first Speaker since Reconstruction.[26]

Baker was elated. Not only had Tennessee taken another step toward a mature two-party system, Richard Nixon's victory signified that his initiatives would get a hearing at the White House. Work began on January 31, 1969, on one of his most desired changes when he introduced a constitutional amendment lowering the voting age to eighteen. Praising the present generation of American youth as one of activists and idealists, he condemned as absurd stereotypes of them as an alienated generation and said the extension of the franchise would capture the energy and enthusiasm of the youth of America and channel them into directions of less cynicism. As chairman of the southern division of the Senate GOP campaign committee, he aimed to market a moderately conservative image of the southern GOP that would appeal to youth by comparing Richard Nixon's challenge with that met by Lincoln a century earlier, that of reuniting a divided country while maintaining law and justice to all.[27]

Baker proved one of Nixon's staunchest allies on foreign policy. He resolutely defended the president's course in Vietnam, saying that North Vietnam had refused to consider any initiative America had forwarded at the Paris Peace Talks. Likewise, he backed Nixon's defense policy, voting early in 1969 to ratify the Nuclear Non-Proliferation Treaty and holding with Nixon that America should deploy an antiballistic missile (ABM). Believing it would allow more flexibility in response to an attack, he hoped that the deployment of a Safeguard ABM would serve as a bargaining chip that U.S. negotiators could use to force the Soviets to dismantle their intercontinental ballistic missile systems (ICBMS).[28]

Baker likewise found much to applaud in the Nixon domestic program, particularly the revenue-sharing program that had long been his pet. Early in 1969, he introduced such a bill that twenty GOP colleagues, the National Governors Conference, the National League of Cities, the Tennessee General Assembly, and the United States Conference of Mayors all endorsed. Aware of his work, Nixon asked him to introduce his version. More quietly, he added his name to two of Everett Dirksen's pet projects, a constitutional amendment to allow voluntary prayer in the public schools and a bill to ban the mail-order sale of pornography to minors.[29] The measures proved the last collaborations of the two, as Dirksen passed away on September 7.

The day before, Baker had visited his father-in-law and emerged to tell reporters that Dirksen looked great. Confident Dirksen would recover from the removal of a cancerous lobe of his right lung, he left as planned for a meeting with the president in San Clemente on the seventh, but learned shortly after landing in Los Angeles that Dirksen's heart had ceased to beat. Shocked, he called Nixon, canceled the meeting, secured the president's agreement to deliver the principal eulogy, and caught the next plane back to Washington.[30]

Services for Dirksen were held in the Capitol Rotunda on September 9, with much of official Washington present. Following an eloquent presidential tribute, Baker responded for the Dirksen family by defining his father-in-law as a "man of imposing presence and bearing . . . , eminent wit, humor, and perspective, who kept himself and others constantly on guard against taking themselves too seriously."[31]

A few months earlier, an observer had lamented that oratory may perish with Dirksen. While some younger colleagues complained that his outlook was also a relic of a bygone age, Baker, a student of history and a devotee of Senate tradition, believed that much could be learned from his elders. "I think he loved that old man," a friend said of his relationship with his father-in-law, and today, references to Dirksen are far more frequent from Baker than those to any other associate. Years later, Baker wrote that Dirksen gave a spice to life that he appreciated even more then than he did at the time and he joked about all of the times that he had to endure Dirksen's terrible singing.[32] Professionally, he dedicated himself to emulating the example of Dirksen, a lawmaker of rare talents even critics were wont to deny. While he, like Dirksen, had earned the respect of his more senior colleagues early in his congressional career as a bright, independent-minded young member with a promising future, several believed him too young and too new to the Senate to fill his father-in-law's shoes.

Chapter 4

THE RISE TO SENIOR SENATOR 1969–1972

It had been a privately stated Baker ambition to someday follow in Dirksen's shoes as GOP Leader since he entered the Senate. While preoccupied in the days immediately following Dirksen's passing, he was approached by Bob Packwood, a first-year senator from Oregon who informally led a caucus of the GOP class of 1968 and encouraged to make a bid to succeed his father-in-law. With Baker neither discouraging nor encouraging him, Packwood began preparing with Baker's administrative aide Hugh Branson for what he hoped would be a Baker race and election after Baker, then immersed in planning Dirksen's funeral, returned from Illinois.[1]

With fellow first-year senators Henry Bellmon, Marlow Cook, Bob Dole, Edward Gurney, and Ted Stevens, Packwood aimed to install a younger member as Leader. Caucusing to find a candidate, they considered Robert Griffin and James Pearson but opted for Baker, as he seemed the most interested. The early line favorite was GOP Whip Hugh D. Scott, a cagy Philadelphian and self-styled Aristotelian who had served sixteen years in the House, eleven in the Senate, and a stint as Republican national chairman, who won many quick pledges from moderate and liberal colleagues from the Northeast and Midwest. Also interested were veteran conservatives Roman Hruska and Gordon Allott, who both had support from likeminded senior colleagues from the Midwest and Far West.[2]

Baker's chances appeared good, as several senior conservatives pronounced him acceptable if neither Allott nor Hruska could muster a majority. Allott had angered other westerners in a water rights dispute, and the knowledge that he would not get their votes led him to withdraw. Hruska, having been defeated by Scott for the Whip in January, realized that he would not benefit from a freshman senators' revolt, leading him to pull out and endorse Baker. Organizations as divergent as the liberal Republican Ripon Society, which found Baker's youthful image attractive, and the American Conservative Union, which urged GOP senators to select "a leader from the ranks of such men as . . . Howard Baker . . .

or other qualified conservatives," added their support. Some Scott backers grew anxious enough to suggest electing Scott as Leader and Baker as Whip if Baker conceded. While Baker said he might be interested in the second slot if Scott defeated him, he would not deal for it.[3]

To the surprise of many, several conservatives favored Scott. Norris Cotton backed him because of their long friendship. John J. Williams, a fiscal purist who opposed revenue sharing, claimed that he did not believe in dynasties. More common was a view that Baker's two-and-one-half years in the Senate were not enough to prepare him for the rigors of the Leadership. Packwood tried to alleviate such concerns by pointing out that Lyndon Johnson had risen to a leadership post after but two years, an even shorter period of apprenticeship than Baker's. But many senior Republicans had been victims of the pressure tactics known as the "Johnson treatment" and were more fearful than allayed. Although some conservatives complained that Scott stood to the left of the GOP median on domestic issues, they also noticed his general adherence to the Nixon line on foreign policy and saw his experience as more valuable than anything Baker offered. Nixon agreed but refrained from telling anyone until the day before the vote, leading Harry Dent, his chief political advisor, to tell at least one senator that Nixon backed Baker. Dent's intrusion led moderates and liberals to fear Baker's election was part of a southern strategy favored by the most conservative elements of the GOP. In fact, Dent's stratagems ran counter to the desires of Nixon. While the president had informed Baker and Scott that he would not intervene, he reneged on his vow just prior to the balloting. Believing Scott could occasionally sway some moderate and liberal votes behind his program, while Baker's influence, because of his youth and geographic base, would be limited to the core group of Nixon loyalists, Nixon told chief congressional liaison Bryce Harlow the day before the vote to notify undecideds that he preferred Scott.[4]

As indicated by the 24–19 outcome, those who claimed indecision generally opted for Scott because of his experience. While some were inclined to give Baker the consolation of being Whip, others found a list of Baker supporters and saw that the only four approaching the label of moderate were freshmen Cook, Packwood, Stevens, and Baker, thus leading many to fear that Baker might be overly anxious to please the right wing if elected to a leadership position. Baker, moderates Griffin and James Pearson, and the conservative John Tower vied to become Scott's assistant. Griffin led after the first ballot with fourteen votes. Baker and Pearson garnered thirteen apiece, and Tower but three. Baker picked up Tower's votes on the second ballot and two of Pearson's. But Griffin added nine Pearson ballots on the second and third counts, giving him a 23–20 victory. Although a double loser, Baker hailed Scott and Griffin as men of exceptional ability. Scott returned the favor years later by characterizing Baker as one of his most valued senators. Indeed, Baker's and Scott's voting records were quite similar in the seven remaining years of their joint service, especially on foreign questions, as both, while uneasy about committing 500,000 troops, still staunchly supported Nixon's Indochina policies.[5]

War and Peace

While Baker had a "nagging concern that we were in over our heads," he opposed an immediate unilateral withdrawal of American troops, fearing Southeast Asia might be left "to the cannibalism of another Maoist adventure or another exercise in elimination." Desiring like most a mutual withdrawal from South Vietnam, Baker urged the Vietnamese Communists to negotiate seriously and provide information about American prisoners of war. Noting continued Communist intransigence, he recommended that Nixon accelerate his Vietnamization program, which he hoped might allow expanded troop withdrawals without appreciable effect upon the war effort.[6]

Nixon, unlike Johnson in Baker's view, had a track record for candor and did not deserve the blasts of those who attacked him for expanding the war to Cambodia; responsibility, he argued, belonged to North Vietnam, which had established sanctuaries there for its troops. Baker likewise opposed the Cooper-Church amendment, which banned U.S. aid to Cambodia after July 1, 1970, believing it amounted to the Senate ordering the president around. While never disputing the First Amendment rights of demonstrators, Baker did question their wisdom, believing their conclusions far more emotional than rational, and suggested that they aim their slings and arrows at the real target of their movement, the Vietnamese Communists who had rejected several reasonable peace initiatives. The invasion of Cambodia prompted him to urge dissenters to consider the circumstances of Nixon's decision, a tack he thought would convince them that Nixon had acted in the interest of peace. While believing students had overreacted, he was just as quick to condemn counterreactions that culminated in six students being killed at Kent State and Jackson State Universities.[7]

The protests and reaction, both of which accentuated the shrill and the sopho moric, symbolized to Baker a breakdown in a pattern of civility that had once governed American politics. While this trend manifested most openly in antiwar demonstrations, he suspected the problem might have the more pernicious ramification of poisoning dialogue on every conceivable issue for years to come. Baker was especially disturbed by the violence shown French President Georges Pompidou and his wife in Chicago by a group of pro-Israel demonstrators opposed to his sale of fighter jets to Libya. Upon learning a few had broken through police lines and accosted the couple with obscenities, Baker, who believed the sale a threat to Israel, took the Senate floor to lambaste his ostensible allies for street tactics and hail Nixon, another sale opponent, for flying to New York to apologize to the Pompidous.[8]

Black and White

Of more consequence were Baker's positions on domestic issues, where again, he usually aligned with Nixon. He voted for unsuccessful Nixon nominees Clement Haynsworth and G. Harrold Carswell as well as Harry Blackmun, Nixon's third choice, for seats on the Supreme Court. Today, while conceding Carswell's mediocrity, Baker says that he would again vote with his party if the vote took on a partisan configuration, but he hopes the Senate will advance to where nominees are considered on their merits, character, personality, legal training, and experience, with a minimum of partisan consideration. At the time, he was moved by a desire to avert a second humiliating defeat for Nixon. Even so, his approach to civil rights differed substantially from those of most of his southern elders. Unlike them, he voted to extend the Voting Rights Act and increase funding for the Office of Civil Rights of the Office of Education. More conspicuously, he had never advocated segregation and outlined to black audiences much earlier than most the negative effects upon children by the denial of contact with playmates of a different race.[9] Finding no point separating the injustice of the little-challenged practice of northern de facto segregation from the rapidly dying de jure variety that had long poisoned southern race relations, he differed from many northerners by insisting that federal efforts be conducted the same way in all parts of America.

Baker never deviated from his call for a national transition to unitary school systems. Recognizing the difficulties, he counseled the use of devices involving a minimum of social disruption and voted to add funds for school systems undergoing desegregation. Warning that desegregation needed to win the cooperation from the people involved in a short time, he urged school boards and federal officials to design programs to keep as many children as possible in neighborhood schools. He suggested that rural districts consolidate dual systems into a single unit and that urban areas use with some discretion solutions like rezoning districts and pairing all pupils of a similar age group in a community in a single school. Two methods he objected to were freedom of choice and busing. White southerners too often had allowed whites to choose their children's schools while denying blacks the same choice through intimidation, and he voted to table an amendment establishing freedom of choice as federal policy. He was just as adamantly opposed to busing, believing schools could be desegregated in ways less likely to exacerbate tensions. While voting often to deny funds for busing, he resisted for a time temptations to "circumscribe constitutionally based decisions" of the Supreme Court by statutes depriving the Court of jurisdiction over such cases.[10]

Clean Air and Water

Baker's principal focus in 1969 and 1970, however, was his work on the Muskie subcommittee on air and water pollution. Baker considered the environment his issue,

Muskie aide Leon Billings once declared, and "flat out told the . . . White House to leave him alone." Concerned that uncontrolled emissions were creating hazards in all parts of the country and that Congress had not conferred sufficient enforcement powers upon federal agencies, Baker listened to spokesmen for industry and labor, enforcers and polluters, and environmentalists and developers, and concluded that Congress had to act quickly to prevent the ecological crisis from becoming a catastrophe. Convinced that any action would be better than none, he signed on as a cosponsor of bills drafted by both the White House and the Muskie panel, thus patterning a commitment to action, if not a rigid adherence to the initial solutions of either source.[11] While his work won him little public acclaim, the two most far-reaching environmental laws ever enacted, the Water Pollution Act Amendments and the National Air Quality Standards Act of 1970, bear his imprint.

While a consensus had formed in favor of tough new environmental legislation, questions of approach remained unresolved. Should Congress regulate standards of environmental quality or, rather, the flow of pollutants? Who should pay? Despite his disdain for regulating private industry, Baker determined that Congress must control emissions of harmful substances, as the alternative of regulating air and water quality standards would add exorbitant burdens upon taxpayers, transfer considerable authority from Congress to the bureaucracy, and shift the burden of cleanup from polluters to the government. Convinced of the merits of the emissions standards approach, Baker helped Chairman Muskie incorporate the plan into the working models of both the air and water pollution bills of 1970.[12]

Alarmed by massive oil spills off the California coast, the panel approved a water pollution package establishing an Office of Environmental Quality and, in a Baker amendment, requiring owners of ships that had spilled oil to bear full cleanup responsibility. The full Public Works Committee, with senators as dissimilar as conservative Edward Gurney and liberal Thomas Eagleton, soon added its unanimous endorsement and the Senate returned an 86–0 verdict. Infuriated, oil barons mounted a bid to weaken Baker's addendum by persuading the House to pass a bill allowing them to escape cleanup costs. Conceding minor points in the conference committee, Baker and Muskie insisted upon assessing those responsible for spillage with absolute liability and eventually convinced House counterparts to relent.[13]

Drafting air pollution legislation proved far more complex as emission technology was in development. Members quickly incorporated language requiring the abatement of emissions from the burning of municipal waste but searched for months for a way to reduce automotive pollution. Some initially were intrigued by the possibility that the auto industry might develop a pollution-free steam engine that someday might rival the internal combustion engine. But such zeal subsided once carmakers detailed the structural and environmental deficiencies of steam-powered vehicles. On a more practical note, Edward Cole, the president of General

Motors, told the panel that manufacturers by 1975 could install antipollution devices in every car they made. Noting GM's progress with the catalytic converter, Cole prodded the panel to require the installation of such a device in every new model in the not too distant future. He convinced Baker, whom Muskie found a great believer in the potential of American technology and one who saw a need to write in the law standards that would force industry to expand the potential of technology for dealing with environmental problems. Like Muskie, Baker regretted that car buyers would have to pay more for new models but calculated that atmospheric modes of cleanup would result in even heavier tax burdens and they moved to incorporate the Cole approach.[14]

No senator quarreled with the Cole-Muskie-Baker plan. Conservatives hailed its efficiency, while the environment-minded, although disappointed that it did not regulate air quality, applauded it as an important first step. Dealers and distributors were placated by an addendum by Baker and John Sherman Cooper exempting them from liability for defective converters. Chrysler and Ford, whose research and development programs were not as advanced as GM's, were placated by another Baker-Cooper measure establishing a review procedure if their 1975 models did not meet the bill's standards.[15]

Baker labeled the measure the toughest and most far-reaching piece of environmental legislation ever adopted. But even this bill needed some revision. While Nixon's consolidation of most environmental programs into two superagencies, the Environmental Protection Agency and the National Oceanographic and Atmospheric Administration, resolved many jurisdictional questions, Congress had not required the Atomic Energy Commission to comply with environmental statutes until Baker got such a provision included in the environmental amendments of 1971. Six years later, he devised a compromise revising the Clean Air Act by cutting back delays in compliance schedules for hydrocarbon, carbon monoxide, and nitrous oxide emissions proposed in an industry-backed House bill. While Baker's attention to the environment was widely noted among his colleagues, many ecological groups hesitated to credit him, regretting that his commitment to technological progress sometimes led him to back programs they abhorred, like the Nixon SST and space shuttle programs. Even so, Baker remained proud of his association with Nixon and firmly backed even the most controversial Nixon programs, such as the Family Assistance Plan, which was devised to streamline the welfare bureaucracy and increase benefits.[16]

The First Real Two-Party System in Any Southern State

The 1970 elections were approaching. At his own expense, Baker traveled thousands of miles to campaign for GOP Senate candidates George Bush of Texas, George Murphy of California, and Robert A. Taft Jr. of Ohio. In the fall, he spent more time in Tennessee, where Albert Gore's Senate seat and the governor's chair were available. Gore's seat seemed more enticing, as "the old Gray Fox" had cast unpopular votes against the Vietnam War, the ABM, and the Haynsworth and Carswell nominations, and for gun control. While others contemplated the race, the field narrowed to Congressman Bill Brock and Tex Ritter, the venerable actor and country singer. Ritter, a well-educated man with some legal training, aimed to stand as the candidate of the "dynamic Republican mainstream" against Brock, whom he labeled the choice of the "extreme right wing." But Brock, who before being elected to Congress had led a march through Chattanooga with his father to spur compliance with court-ordered desegregation and had chaired drives for adult and black literacy, mental retardation, and the disabled, had built a firm base over the past decade among Republicans of all stripes and co-opted most of Tennessee's abler GOP organizers. While recognizing the likely outcome, Baker, fearing that the race might become divisive, proclaimed his neutrality and warned his staff that any who involved themselves should first seek other employment.[17] A similar ban extended to the governor's race, where four little-known pols—Dr. Winfield Dunn of Memphis, Nashville industrialist Maxey Jarman, House Speaker Bill Jenkins, and former state GOP chairman Claude Robertson—sought the nod.

With the platforms of the four differing little, the contest was reduced to one of which candidate could attract the most support from his own end of the state. With two East Tennesseans in the race, a surprisingly large seven-point edge went to Dunn, an articulate, fatherly, forty-three-year-old dentist who carried a near-solid vote from Memphis. But this margin paled in comparison with Brock's over Ritter. In a race seen as close, more than three-quarters of the votes went to Brock. Quickly, Baker moved to facilitate the GOP unity portended by the strong endorsements of the ticket from the four losers. While Senate business and prior commitments limited his time, he vowed to help wherever possible. As a start, he persuaded Lamar Alexander to leave his job as assistant to White House congressional liaison Bryce Harlow and return to manage Dunn's campaign.[18]

Democrats were divided. An unknown conservative had held Gore to 51 percent in the primary, and many conservatives were withholding their support in the general election. Frank Clement's death in 1969 had made businessman John J. Hooker the gubernatorial nominee. Thousands with stock in Hooker's industries blamed him for their losses when shares fell from a high of sixty-nine dollars to two dollars. These events Dunn exploited with calls for sound management in state government amid a comprehensive economic development program for Tennessee. While such appeals made some headway, the balance of power belonged to supporters of George Wallace. Dunn, a racial moderate, believed the Wallace core included not just lower-class whites "determined to keep a segregated society" but many alienated souls "who saw . . . something besides the routine" and voted for Wallace to "take a slap at folks in conventional seats of power."

Hooker appealed to their populistic instincts by berating Dunn for joining the GOP because he opposed Medicare. Gore stressed his support for Medicare, tax reform, and increased Social Security and veterans benefits.[19] But they addressed only the economic portion of the paradox of Wallaceism, and many Wallaceites were more worried about an assault they saw upon traditional virtues, values Brock and Dunn appealed to by trumpeting their support for school prayer and stiffer sentences for drug dealers and pornographers and their opposition to gun control and busing.

Aware that some Gore-backed programs were popular, Brock tried to paint him as the third senator from Massachusetts. But Brock's campaign staggered until October 13, the day Baker tried to amend the Equal Rights Amendment (ERA) with a rider allowing voluntary prayer in any public building. Baker had signed on as an ERA cosponsor in July 1969 and continued to recommend its adoption. After the House passed the ERA in October, opponents rushed to amend it, knowing any addition would kill it for the time being. While an amendment allowing states to implement freedom-of-choice plans failed, Sam Ervin found thirty-five votes for an addendum exempting women from the draft, enough to win with many members away. Seeing the addendum as a mere clarifying measure, Baker voted with Ervin. But some ERA supporters believed it dilatory; others rued that it required further action. Such disagreements had killed the ERA for 1970 and its managers prepared to withdraw it. Before they could, Baker brought up his prayer amendment as he and Everett Dirksen had in the past whenever a chance presented itself, arguing that a joint ERA-prayer amendment would present the states a more attractive package. The Senate, after an unusually brief debate, approved Baker's amendment 50–20, but managers then withdrew the resolution, knowing two-thirds of the Senate would never rally around such a package.[20]

While Baker's amendment never won congressional approval, it had an enormous effect in Tennessee as it put Albert Gore on the spot. Once Gore voted no, Brock began to declare prayer the real issue and cited three Gore votes against it. "That amendment put Brock over the top," Jim Sasser said later. Brock's margin, as Sasser inferred, was quite narrow, as he carried less than 52 percent of the two candidate vote against an opponent who had voted often against the wishes of his constituents. Brock, in fact, had run behind Dunn, who garnered more than 53 percent of the two candidate vote.[21] Noting that both Tennessee senators and its governor were Republicans, many touted the Volunteer State as the first GOP majority state in the South. But GOP candidates for lower offices did not fare as well as Dunn and Brock, whose victories, while as attributable to Democratic factionalism as GOP strength, added proof that able GOP candidates could win in Tennessee.

Brock's election gave Baker hope that his colleagues might reconsider his qualifications for GOP Leader if he challenged Hugh Scott again. While Republicans made a net gain of one seat (two, if one includes James Buckley of New York, who was elected as a member of the Conservative Party but voted with the GOP to organize the Senate), the composition of the caucus was virtually unchanged. Baker's chances nevertheless seemed to have improved, as Scott's support of the Family Assistance Plan had offended John Williams, a Scott supporter in 1969 who retired in 1970 but continued to prod George Aiken, John Sherman Cooper, and Milton Young to withdraw their support from Scott, regardless of who ran. While Aiken resisted, Young and Cooper switched. The choice was agonizing for Cooper, a Baker cousin who respected Scott. Near seventy and considering retirement, Cooper declared Baker "the right age—45 years" in a letter to a dozen colleagues. Even so, Baker's second bid proceeded slower than did his first, as Williams was the only senator with a serious objection to Scott. Nixon authorized Bryce Harlow to notify waverers that Scott remained his choice, prompting Barry Goldwater and Ted Stevens to switch, thus countering Cooper's and Young's defections. Still thinking he had enough votes for a tie, Baker signaled Cooper to place his name in nomination. But with no other switches, Scott was reelected, 24–20.[22]

Lying Low

Discouraged, Baker adopted a low profile. Save for his nostalgic resurrection of Everett Dirksen's biennial resolution to make the marigold the national flower, he contented himself with reintroducing legislation Congress had overlooked. He reattached his name to three constitutional amendments—those mandating equal rights for women, voluntary school prayer, and the direct election amendment—that Congress had not completed action upon and cosponsored another—the amendment granting the right to vote at eighteen—which became necessary after the Supreme Court ruled a similar provision of the Voting Rights Act extension of 1970 unconstitutional. But he spent the bulk of his time lobbying for a revenue-sharing plan that Richard Nixon described in his 1971 State of the Union message as the cornerstone of his New Federalism. Again, Nixon tapped Baker to introduce his bill in February, and thirty-seven colleagues, nearly all Republicans, signed on as cosponsors. His action prompted Edmund Muskie, Hubert Humphrey, and Congressman Henry Reuss to introduce similar bills. Unconcerned with specifics, Baker urged the three to help him devise a bill all could accept, as a major obstacle, House Ways and Means Committee Chairman Wilbur Mills, remained in their paths. But upon learning of a poll showing 77 percent of the people backed some form of tax sharing, the man who had held Baker's "pet bill by the throat" opened hearings in June. When called to testify, Baker urged members to approve any proposal they could agree upon.[23]

Baker followed the Nixon line on more divisive questions as well. While never doubting the nobility of defending South Vietnam, he came to believe that

America had overextended its defense perimeters, venting his uneasiness most clearly following the publication of the Pentagon Papers. Unlike Nixon, who was more concerned that the documents were leaked, Baker wanted to force former Defense Secretary Robert McNamara to testify about why he was telling Congress one thing and President Johnson another. But Baker could find common ground with Senate doves on just one meaningless rider, a disagreement stemming from a belief that the final settlement should allow the South Vietnamese people to choose their own destiny, a demand many doves found unnecessary. From a military standpoint, he believed Nixon's Vietnamization plan the best and most rational guarantee of South Vietnam's survival and ending American combat involvement. Deeming a strong deterrent vital to Nixon's ability to negotiate a comprehensive armistice, he hailed the president's May 1972 order to resume the bombing of North Vietnam as a measured, courageous, and necessary response to overt North Vietnamese aggression.[24]

Baker saw Vietnamization as sufficiently in place by June 1971 to allow an end to the draft. After joining just twenty-one senators behind a bill ending the draft immediately while requiring eighteen-year-olds to register, he joined only three Republicans—Goldwater, Hatfield, and Schweiker—in opposing a two-year extension. Undeterred, he vowed to continue his efforts to reinstitute all volunteer services.[25] Time was on his side, as Richard Nixon and many colleagues had pledged long before to lend a hand once the war ended.

Recognizing that he and Baker agreed on most issues while aware of Baker's capacity for independence, Nixon saw Baker as one of his ablest Senate advocates. Soon after Associate Justice John M. Harlan retired in September 1971, Attorney General John Mitchell called Baker to his office. "What would you do," Mitchell asked, if the president "offered you a seat on the Supreme Court?" "I'd say that I'd just as soon he didn't," Baker responded. Mitchell declared the offer legitimate, then asked Baker about his reluctance. Baker replied that he wanted to remain in a lawmaking capacity. Mitchell asked him to mull over the possibility. Baker did, halfheartedly. Out of curiosity, he visited Justice Potter Stewart, an acquaintance since Stewart's days on the Sixth Circuit Court of Appeals and confirmed his suspicion that he would feel removed from the process of governing. "Funeral homes," he later told Orrin Hatch, "are livelier than the Court." After returning from Stewart's office, he phoned Mitchell, reiterated his distaste for the reactive role of a justice, but said he would accept the offer if that was Nixon's wish. Understandingly, Mitchell opined that all would be better off if Nixon nominated William Rehnquist.[26]

Servant of Tennessee

At the same time, Baker proved a conscientious servant of Tennessee interests, although occasionally his proposals angered some of his constituents. Since entering the Senate, he had called for a comprehensive study of America's fossil fuel reserves and an equally elaborate proposal to meet future needs. By 1971, he was advocating the creation of a National Energy Board to coordinate federal energy policy and facilitate research and development programs for alternative fuels. Like every other Tennessean in Congress, Baker emphasized nuclear power, believing diminishing supplies of fossil fuels would result in growing needs for energy, of which breeder-created power seemed the most abundant, clean, and economical. The primitive state of breeder research programs and the AEC decision to concentrate upon the less efficient fast breeder distressed Baker. Finding European programs much more comprehensive, he urged the AEC to emulate their example and expand plans to include the thermal breeder, a safer and more efficient tool than the fast breeder then being tested.[27]

Baker's advocacy of breeders coincided with his view that producers had environmental responsibilities. Land users, he believed, should be subject to the same regulations that applied to those who dumped debris into the air or water. Most abusive of any had been strip miners in his native Appalachia, many of whom had dumped whole sides of mountains into nearby streams and roads. Not only had unregulated mining destroyed much of the region's natural beauty, the failure of many strippers to reclaim their land had rendered much of it unusable for generations. Outraged, Baker and John Sherman Cooper introduced a bill in the fall of 1971 to regulate the most disruptive aspects of strip mining by requiring all strippers to secure permits from the EPA and the Bureau of Mines, which would be authorized to license only those who practiced the most advanced techniques of reclamation. Many operators feared that reclamation costs would drive some of them out of business and force a hefty rise in consumer prices. Some even had employees drive freighted coal trucks outside both Baker's house and office in Huntsville and threaten to unload their coal in his driveway. Lonnie Strunk, who usually flew Baker between Tennessee and Washington in his Senate days, was in Huntsville and called Baker to quip that he had "some of the maddest old friends and some of the strangest new ones." But on the floor, Baker quoted reclamation costs as but two dollars a ton and declared current stripping policy an unfair subsidy by the poorest people in the country for low power rates everywhere. Knowing coal producers in the regulation-ridden West faced different conditions from those faced by his Appalachian neighbors, he assured their senators that he would incorporate provisions more suited to western topography. But neither Baker nor Cooper could convince Richard Nixon, and the bill was relegated to oblivion. Strip miners, who remembered that major tracts of the Payne-Baker lands in Scott and Morgan counties had been stripped, were furious at Baker, who, as the executor of his father's and Payne's estate, had managed the property and honored existing contracts. But once the agreements expired, stripping stopped, and Baker oversaw the reclamation of every acre of strip mined land he had managed, a fact irate competitors ignored.[28]

Even more volatile in Tennessee was anger over busing, which had risen dramatically after the Supreme Court affirmed a ruling directing the Charlotte school board to use busing as its principal means of desegregation. A similar case was pending in Davidson County, where the school board had tried to devise a desegregation program consistent with federal guidelines. None of their proposals won the approval of federal Judge L. Clure Morton, who ordered the school board to implement a program leaving none of the city's 141 schools entirely black, but allowing thirty-six to remain all-white. Forty-nine thousand of the eighty-eight thousand children in the county school system would be bused. Some passed seven schools serving their grade before reaching their destinations. Many schools had to revise their schedules by creating two shifts, one from 7:00 A.M. to 1:00 P.M. and the other from 10:00 A.M. to 4:30 P.M., forcing thousands of children to leave home before sunrise and dictating that thousands more would not get home until after dark. Thousands of parents began sending their children to private schools, with heated rhetoric accompanying white flight. Morton and other federal judges were easy targets, but opposition leaders found other scapegoats. Hoping to become Nashville's mayor, Casey Jenkins lambasted incumbent C. Beverly Briley, a conservative Democrat and staunch critic of the decision, for not leading a campaign of defiance, and chastised Baker for recommending Morton's appointment to Nixon. Baker defended Morton, explaining that the judge had merely ruled in the light of the decisions the Supreme Court had set down.[29]

Baker's statement hardly disguised his disdain for busing. Unlike many northerners, he believed an anti-busing position conveyed a commitment to common sense. "Busing," he said, "visited upon . . . children to satisfy some numerical equality and . . . judicially decreed proportion . . . is also inherently unequal and . . . creates the same lack of opportunity cited in the [Brown] decision." A cosponsor of many anti-busing amendments, he offered one, unsuccessfully, postponing all court orders requiring busing until school districts had exhausted their appeals. Soon after busing commenced in Nashville, he and other Tennesseans met with sympathetic White House officials who, while not committing themselves to action, did continue to monitor events. Over the next few months, violence spread to northern cities, including Boston and Pontiac, and George Wallace carried Democratic primaries in states from Michigan to Florida on the strength of the anti-busing furor. Stung, Nixon met with Baker and others on February 14, 1972, and announced his support for a moratorium on new court orders. While other southerners were angry as a moratorium allowed previous orders to stand, Baker was encouraged by the Justice Department's amicus curiae brief for the appeal of the Nashville school board.[30]

Reelection

Baker vowed to continue his fight as he announced for reelection. "We have already proved . . . here in Nashville," he said, "that busing for . . . some artificial numerical racial balance . . . is unworkable." Busing remained a constant Baker theme throughout 1972. He and John Tower secured Richard Nixon's pledge at a September White House meeting to continue adding his voice to those urging immediate action.[31] Baker counseled Nixon at the same meeting to lobby for revenue sharing. Once passage of a House bill appeared imminent, Baker approached Hubert Humphrey, the sponsor of a similar bill, and suggested that they join together. With forty cosponsors as diverse as George McGovern and Strom Thurmond, Baker and Humphrey introduced the House bill and promised to accept any changes that the Senate might make to render the House bill more palatable to recalcitrants. In fact, the Senate passed a measure strikingly different from the House bill. After Baker urged them to be flexible, conferees agreed in early October to Wilbur Mills's suggestion that states choose between the Senate formula, which was more generous to more rural states, and the House formula, which benefited more populous urban dominions.[32]

Baker appeared with Humphrey as Nixon staged the signing ceremony in October in front of Independence Hall in Philadelphia and used the bill's passage to convey the image of a leader during his reelection bid. It was a natural emphasis, as he in 1966 had described the enactment of such a bill as a primary goal for his first term. Tennesseans of both parties were quick to credit him. "Without . . . Howard Baker," Winfield Dunn said, "we would most likely be a great distance from the passage of a bill." Nashville Mayor Briley called Baker's work magnificent.[33]

Baker's GOP constituents were firmly in his camp, giving him 97 percent of their votes in the primary. His nearly 200,000 votes far surpassed the number any GOP candidate had ever won in a Tennessee primary. His strength was augmented in the general election by Richard Nixon's presence at the head of the ticket. Long popular in Tennessee, the president was a prohibitive favorite in the state once Democrats nominated George McGovern, whose platform included pleas for an immediate withdrawal from Vietnam, a ban upon the private ownership of handguns, and an extension of busing to areas not already covered. Baker, finding these planks radical, sought to identify himself with Nixon and his moderately conservative image, featuring a photograph of himself with the president in his literature and describing himself as "a close friend and trusted advisor of our President, Richard Nixon."[34] But his identity as a Nixon ally did not prevent him from making vigorous appeals to young voters and blacks, who Nixon and most other Republicans had written off.

Voters under thirty had played a significant role in both previous Baker campaigns, and his base among them was stronger than ever. Sixty thousand of his 100,000 volunteers ranged between the ages of eighteen and twenty-four. While his youthful appearance undoubtedly swayed many, more were impressed by his advocacy of an all-volunteer army, increased funding for education, and the eighteen-year-old vote. Support was especially strong on the state's campuses, where McGovern-Baker buttons were common. The junior partner of this unlikely tandem carried most of the mock elections sponsored by Tennessee colleges and universities by near record majorities.[35]

Blacks, in contrast, had provided few votes for Baker in 1964 and 1966, but many had come to view him more favorably. Knowing he held to his father's admonition that "there are Democrats and Republicans in elections, but afterwards . . . just constituents," black leaders found him a strong voice when their viewpoints coincided. On other occasions, they, like John Seigenthaler, discerned that he would never use race for a vote. Even in the midst of heated busing debates, Baker insisted upon the permanence of integrated schools and supplemented his abhorrence of racial demagoguery with his active promotion of the federal hiring of blacks. Most visible was his persuasion of Richard Nixon in 1972 to nominate Judge Benjamin Hooks to a vacant seat on the Federal Communications Commission (FCC). Hooks, the first black FCC commissioner, gratefully endorsed his sponsor before a convention of Black Masons in August.[36]

Baker's opportunity for gains in the black community grew after Democrats nominated three-term congressman Ray Blanton, whose rural West Tennessee House seat had been carved up in the 1970 census. Unlike much of the state's Democratic hierarchy, he identified with George Wallace's base of poor white farmers and laborers and his votes against open housing, the Voting Rights Act extension, the eighteen-year-old vote, revenue sharing, and several pieces of antipollution and education legislation, reflected the reactionary elements of their collective psyche. He aimed his criticisms of Nixon's handling of the Vietnam War at the same constituency, claiming that he knew the Paris Peace Talks were a farce when North Vietnam sent a woman to negotiate. While it was often suggested that Democratic regulars were backing him for the Senate to use his loss to dissuade him from running for governor in 1974, several of Tennessee's best-known Democrats were backing Blanton, leading him to believe that he could prevail if he could unite his party behind him.[37]

It thus became Blanton's aim to engage Baker in a partisan fight, a stratagem his record rendered next to impossible. Blanton needed to strengthen his ties to labor and blacks, but there was little to recommend him to either. To compensate when speaking to Democrats, he attacked Baker for supporting the economic policies of Richard Nixon. "It costs two dollars and fifty cents to buy a rubber stamp," he declared, "so why should you pay one $42,500 a year?" Rhetoric designed to arouse the class-consciousness of lower-income Tennesseans became Blanton's staple. Tennessee's two senators, he said, were "two millionaires from East Tennessee" who had made careers out of ignoring the little guy. Such rhetoric won him many friends in the state's labor community, who hoped that he might be more receptive if he represented a statewide constituency. Blacks were less enthusiastic. While the Tennessee Voters' Council endorsed Blanton lukewarmly, many blacks openly advocated Baker's election. Nashville City Councilman Morris Haddox, citing Blanton's negligence on civil rights, endorsed Baker while Walter Bailey, a Memphis counterpart, went even further, heading an adjunct group known as Democrats for Baker.[38]

A similar split existed among Wallace backers. While Blanton received Wallace's support, he could not match Baker's credentials as a spokesman for constitutional amendments to end busing and reinstitute voluntary school prayer. Viciously and foolishly, he tried anyway. Citing a 1970 vote against a statutory ban upon court-ordered busing, he characterized Baker as "downright deceitful and hypocritical" and laid the blame for busing in Nashville upon Baker, as he had recommended Judge Morton's appointment to Nixon. He was just as critical of revenue sharing, labeling it a "farce" and a "boondoggle." While Blanton aimed to strip the aura of leadership from Baker, his choice of issues perplexed Democrats, most of whom knew that Tennessee, one of the few states without an individual income tax, had long been strapped for funds and stood to benefit as much as any state. Democratic local officials, elated by the $98.4 million Tennessee would get, were especially critical. One of the most influential, Nashville Mayor Beverly Briley, even attended a salute to Baker the day after the bill became law. Baker continued to expound upon the benefits of the program to Tennessee, but his speeches contained only one reference to his opponent's record. "Wilbur Mills changed his mind," he said, "but Ray Blanton never got the word."[39]

Still, Blanton remained within striking distance. Out of the blue, he, while some of his supporters were making anonymous harassing phone calls to the Baker family and plotting to grease the tracks in front of Baker's campaign train with enough vegetable oil to stop it cold, charged Baker with running "the filthiest campaign in history" in 1966, and added that several black leaders would swear they had been offered bribes to endorse Baker and other Republicans. Quickly, leaders of several black groups who had endorsed Blanton refuted his charges and the Shelby County Democratic Club found them distasteful enough to give Baker their tacit support.[40]

The emergence of the character issue coincided with several Baker endorsements from generally Democratic sources. Citing Blanton's "essentially negative" record, chairman David Gray of the Tennessee Sierra Club issued a ringing endorsement of Baker, with whom he had worked often. Baker, too, won the backing of every major urban daily in the state. While much of the East Tennessee press had backed him in the past, it surprised some that the boards of the *Memphis Commercial Appeal* and the *Nashville Banner*, which had backed Frank Clement, had shifted. But the *Nashville Tennessean*, the state's most liberal daily, shocked nearly everyone when it declared "Senator Baker . . . a broader, deeper, heavier man than . . . Ray Blanton,"[41] as it had never before endorsed a Republican in a federal election.

While confident, Baker took nothing for granted. Ten days before the election, he launched a whistle-stop tour beginning in Bristol and ending in Memphis, on a ninety-year-old locomotive once used to rescue victims of the Johnstown flood. Redubbed the *Baker Cannonball* by Roy Acuff, the *Rose Bud* was met by large crowds at every stop. Each audience was treated to a set by Acuff and other country stars before Baker would appear and link his fortunes to those of Richard Nixon, who he said was ending the Vietnam War and keeping inflation to a minimum. Baker exhibited his good nature on many occasions, but most tellingly when he spotted Mrs. Maybelle G. Clement, the late governor's mother, waving from the Dickson hotel, where her son had been born. Baker praised the memory of his 1966 opponent, a man he considered a friend, and recalled that he had never had to set the record straight with Clement as he had had to do many times with Blanton.[42]

When the *Rose Bud* reached Memphis, Baker heralded "the dawn of a new day in Tennessee electoral history." Tennesseans gave him 716,534 votes, more than they had ever before given any candidate for any office, to Blanton's 440,599. As usual, his margin was strongest (71.8 percent) in East Tennessee. While he did not fare as well in West Tennessee, his 60.3 percent represented a higher proportion of the vote in this battleground division than any GOP statewide candidate had ever received. Even more surprising were results from Middle Tennessee, from which he became the first Tennessee Republican since Reconstruction to carry. Richard Nixon carried the state by an even larger majority of 813,147 to 357,293, leading Blanton to write off his loss as the result of the liabilities of McGovern and insufficient funding. But this explanation is unconvincing, as Democrats kept control of the General Assembly and all but one of their congressional seats and elected Bob Clement, the former governor's son, to a seat on the Public Service Commission. The presence of ticket splitting is further demonstrated by a subtle variance in the two coalitions. While Nixon ran 6.2 percentage points ahead of Baker statewide, his total was five points less than Baker's in the congressional district encompassing Memphis. The difference is found in the showings of the two in the city's black wards. While Nixon mustered approximately 15 percent of the vote, Baker carried nearly 40 percent. Statewide, Baker's share of the black vote was five points lower, but it remained one of the highest showings of any GOP Senate candidate in America.[43]

The increasing frequency of ticket splitting indicated that a two-party system was flourishing in Tennessee. To Dan Kuykendall, a major effect of his party's emergence was that "Democrats can't run bums anymore."[44] With Tennesseans deciding fewer elections on the basis of the memories of their forebears and more upon their perceptions of the abilities of candidates to solve the problems of the future, those Democrats who sought to ride the horse of class envy to election would have to prove some concrete and longstanding commitment to the realization of the aspirations and values of lower- and middle-class constituents. Otherwise, they would be swept aside like Blanton by Republicans like Baker, who hailed from the socially conservative sectors of Tennessee but remembered that the Whig heritage of East Tennessee and its emphasis on the harmony of all classes dictated that they promote ideals and policies designed to uplift all within the Volunteer State community, and not just the most fortunate.

Tennesseans, too, expected their officials, once elected, to rise to positions of authority within the inner councils of government. While Baker was rising in seniority and stature within the Senate, it took the size of his landslide to prompt national pundits to speculate about the possible fulfillment of his ambitions. The speculation late in 1972 generally centered around a third bid for the Minority Leadership, but conservative columnist William Rusher went so far as to tout him as a viable contender for president.[45] It was the hope of Baker that his party would become the new majority envisioned by Richard Nixon, whose standing seemed stronger than ever after the January 1973 signing of the Paris Peace Accords that ended U.S. military involvement in Vietnam. But Nixon had reached the apex of his approval. Undercurrents linked to the June 17, 1972, bugging of the Democratic National Committee were charging the political atmosphere with ever-increasing static. While seven former employees of the Committee to Re-elect the President (CRP) were in the process of being convicted for their complicity in the crime, many questions remained unanswered. With the unwillingness of Nixon and his top associates to cooperate with prosecutors, many in both parties suspected a cover-up and demanded an investigation.

Chapter 5

WHAT DID THE PRESIDENT KNOW AND WHEN DID HE KNOW IT? 1973–1974

It was Baker's role as vice-chairman of the committee investigating Watergate that propelled him into national attention. Here was just the kind of assignment that sent tremors into the hearts of many colleagues. Having been asked to make the idea of a third race against Hugh Scott for the GOP Leadership, Baker told Scott that he couldn't afford to run against him again. "Lord knows what you'll make me next time."[1]

Creation and Early Business of the Ervin Committee

Baker's Democratic counterpart was Sam J. Ervin Jr., a constitutional scholar whose thick, occasionally stuttering North Carolina drawl, seventy-six years, and eyes that seemed to dart aimlessly hid an uncanny capacity to pierce witnesses with probing queries that got to the heart of often morally and legally complex matters. His motion to create the committee stipulated that a seven member panel would investigate any unlawful or improper activities during the presidential campaign of 1972. Republicans sought to limit the panel to six senators and broaden the investigation's scope to include the elections of 1960, 1964, and 1968, when allegations of Democratic misconduct were common. The leadership in these fights fell upon Baker, who had considerable experience in debating election reform issues. Believing an evenly divided panel could operate successfully within Senate rules, he suggested guaranteeing victory to the side backed by the chairman if the panel split its votes. Once Ervin countered that the best way to avoid ties was with an odd number of members, Democrats rallied en masse against Baker's amendment and one by Edward Gurney broadening the panel's charter to cover the 1960, 1964, and 1968 elections. But concerns that the probe might turn into a partisan witch hunt were alleviated by Ervin's promise to allocate one-third of the funds authorized for staff to the minority, thus leading Republicans to join Democrats in approving the resolution by a 77–0 count.[2]

Six of the seven seats on the committee remained vacant. Choices of Republican members proved easy, as three senators were interested. Believing slots would improve their political standings at home, Edward Gurney, a Florida conservative, and Lowell Weicker, a vocal Connecticut maverick, notified Hugh Scott of their interest. More discreetly, Baker let Scott know that he would accept a slot under certain conditions.[3] With no other Republicans interested, Scott convened a meeting of the leadership and asked members to list the names of the five best-qualified colleagues to serve on the panel. While suggestions varied, each compiler listed Baker, whom Scott deemed "a good lawyer, a good interrogator, . . . in the middle of the road" and the owner of "the best television personality in the Senate." Scott then informed colleagues of the interest of the three and his aim to pick from among interested members. Gurney and Weicker accepted immediately. When Scott assured him that he and the others could pursue the probe independently, Baker agreed to serve as ranking Republican. Ervin chose his supporting cast from those who could project a nonpartisan patriotic image. Majority Leader Mansfield first got a reluctant agreement from Herman Talmadge, a onetime segregationist and former Georgia governor whose intellect demonstrated while chairman of the Agriculture Committee had garnered him respect across party lines. He next approached an equally hesitant Joseph Montoya, a New Mexican whose fluency in Spanish was assumed of value in interrogating the four Cuban American burglars, then assented to Ervin's request of Daniel K. Inouye, a Hawaiian who had lost his right arm fighting in Europe during World War II and was apprehensive enough to decline the offer several times.[4]

Staff selection proceeded at a slower pace. For his chief counsel, Ervin tapped Georgetown law professor Samuel Dash, an expert on electronic surveillance. Rufus Edmisten, a politically astute Ervin aide, would be Dash's chief deputy. Baker's task was more difficult, as Nixon domestic chief John Ehrlichman authorized aide Wally Johnson to phone Baker and suggest the names of lawyers, such as former Attorney General Herbert Brownell, they deemed friendly. But, to Baker, choosing anyone the White House suggested would negate his intention to convey the appearance that he would conduct a fair and independent investigation. Wanting aides whose first loyalties were to the truth and to him, he first asked and was turned down by his former legislative aide Lamar Alexander, who feared that his past service with Nixon would put him in the awkward position of investigating people with whom he had worked. He then named Fred D. Thompson, a hard-nosed, pipe-smoking onetime assistant U.S. attorney with a reputation for convicting crooked sheriffs, bank robbers, and bootleggers who had been the Middle Tennessee director of his 1972 campaign. Thompson brought with him Howard Liebengood, a shrewd conservative he had known since law school. Thompson's deputy, however, would be Donald G. Sanders, a quiet but tough former FBI agent who had spent four years as chief counsel to the House Internal Security Committee.[5]

Liebengood, Sanders, and each of the others eventually hired were chosen on the basis of their intelligence, willingness to work long hours, and propensity to shun a limelight many young men find irresistible. "We're going to try our best to have a bipartisan investigation," Thompson told his staff, "but if it comes down to 'us' and 'them,' I don't want to worry about who is 'us' and who is 'them.'" Once hired, however, staff members heard one constant and direct order from Baker, to pursue every lead and "let the chips fall where they may."[6]

Without any direct evidence linking Nixon and his allies to either the break-in or the cover-up, it was the initial belief of Baker, a GOP loyalist who took Nixon's assurances of his own innocence at face value, that the probe was the Democrats' "best effort to put a different face on a bad defeat." Late in March, he, like other members, was shocked by a rather forceful assertion by Lowell Weicker at an executive session that "this . . . could go all the way to Bob Haldeman." Even so, he feared that a sizable chunk of the populace might conclude that Nixon had breached faith with them when he forbade anyone on his staff from testifying. Aware that Sam Ervin had come to entertain misgivings because his half century as a lawyer, judge, and senator had taught him "that when a man has . . . evidence which will exonerate him . . . , he cannot run fast enough to present it to any tribunal which may have the power to pass on it," Baker, a well-traveled attorney himself, felt certain that rapid and full disclosure was the only way for Nixon to limit damage to himself and to his party. He was sufficiently concerned to tell Hugh Branson that he wanted to meet privately, a message Branson relayed to White House congressional liaison Bill Timmons. A meeting was arranged for February 22, whereupon Baker informed Nixon upon entering his Executive Office Building office that he would use every resource he had to combat intrusions upon presidential prerogatives. Even so, he expressed frustration with Nixon's refusal to allow his staff to testify. "There's enough lawyer left in me to presume to advise you how to do this," he said, "and what . . . you ought to do is send your witnesses up there, pounding on the door to testify. If they can't tell your story better than a collateral and secondary witness, you're in real trouble." This Nixon rejected nervously but categorically, saying he would invoke executive privilege but allow his aides to answer written interrogatories. "I assume . . . everybody's all right," Baker shot back, "and I worry . . . about my old friend John Mitchell." Nixon shrunk. "Well, John may have some problems," convincing Baker there was more to Watergate than he had thought, although he did not know what, and that he should try to change Nixon's mind. He and Branson thereupon called Bryce Harlow, a seasoned White House counselor, and convinced him that full disclosure might lead to Nixon taking some heat but lead to an early exoneration of a man all three believed innocent.[7]

Swaying a wise, impeccably honest veteran like Harlow was one thing; getting Nixon to budge was another. After talking with Baker, Nixon concluded that Edward Gurney was on the only loyalist on the panel and that Baker was an "impressive . . . smoothy." With Baker having informed Nixon that the proper future channel of communication was Attorney General Richard Kleindienst, Nixon ordered counsel John Dean to inform Kleindienst of Baker's wishes and that he wanted the panel run like a court of law, with hearsay evidence being expunged. Kleindienst's inability to reach Baker infuriated Nixon, who ordered on March 22 to act as "Baker hand-holder" and "babysit him starting in about ten minutes." Baker, in fact, had authorized Branson to ask Nixon aides for guidance and reiterate his disdain for executive privilege. The White House eventually designated Wally Johnson to meet with Branson, but, "To this day," Branson jokes, "I haven't heard from Wally."[8]

Baker's position on executive privilege paralleled that of Ervin, who found Nixon's assertion that the Senate could not subpoena White House aides ridiculous. After Nixon reiterated his claim at a press conference, Ervin vowed to arrest any Nixon aide who refused to answer a committee subpoena. Baker backed Ervin, saying that the testimony of Dean, then the highest-placed individual believed implicated, was essential, but remained hopeful that the White House and the committee could reach an accord. Nixon succumbed and arranged for Ervin and Baker to meet John Ehrlichman on April 9. There, Ehrlichman relayed a Nixon offer to waive executive privilege if the panel closed the hearings, a proposal Ervin and Baker rejected while promising to allow Nixon to invoke executive privilege upon the testimony of any member of Nixon's staff with the committee to determine the validity of any claim.[9]

Squabbling over executive privilege was hardly the only Watergate news. New revelations about the complicity of various White House and CRP employees emerged quite regularly after convicted burglar James McCord alleged in a letter to Judge John Sirica that several CRP and White House employees had perjured themselves before the grand jury and that others had pressed the seven original defendants to plead guilty and remain silent. McCord spoke with the committee staff a few days later and leaked a full account to the *Los Angeles Times*, including charges that John Dean and deputy CRP director Jeb Magruder had advance knowledge of the bugging. Because Samuel Dash had met with reporters, many thought he was the leaker, thus mounting pressure on the panel to grant McCord immunity. Such developments perturbed Baker, who believed that only members should hold press conferences, a concern heightened by the fact that each step in the probe was fraught with complex ramifications. After a lecture from Baker, Dash declared that staffers would not meet the press without Baker's or Ervin's authorization. Baker left the meeting and told reporters of his "full confidence" in Dash, thus letting everyone know that he would make every effort to preserve a united front but would not tolerate any further slipshod maneuvers.[10]

McCord met the committee in executive session on March 28, detailed his charges against Dean and Magruder, and added John Mitchell's name to those he implicated. The panel quickly determined that McCord's allegations came from hearsay derived from discussions with G. Gordon Liddy, who refused to talk to the committee or prosecutors. Abhorring hearsay and skeptical of the eccentric Liddy, each senator voted to deny McCord immunity. But knowing McCord's statement, the strongest yet, would tantalize the public, Baker, presiding in Ervin's absence, reminded all present of committee rules banning the dissemination of any material unauthorized by the full panel. This admonition proved unavailing, as an account of the session, again from McCord, appeared in the next day's *Washington Post*.[11]

While Nixon aides cited the leaks as evidence of the committee's bad faith, their cries fell upon deaf ears. Each day brought new charges and countercharges. Some of Nixon's strongest supporters joined Barry Goldwater in observing that Watergate was "beginning to smell." Publicly, Baker counseled Nixon to "send his men up here . . . to testify in public and under oath." Privately, he advised John Ehrlichman on April 13 that a White House plan to close the hearings but make transcripts available was a mistake to "note away." But while vowing to back such a plan if Ehrlichman could convince Sam Ervin of its efficacy, he would not talk to Ervin or try to persuade him. GOP National Chairman George Bush agreed. When Ehrlichman told him that he'd "rather have you out telling our story" and expressed fear that H. R. Haldeman had "no experience with this kind of thing" and that Dwight Chapin might "choke," Bush guessed that "the more open the thing, the better we'll acquit ourselves." Such advice from loyalists like Bush and Baker led Nixon to contemplate John Dean's warning of a month earlier that a cancer was growing on his presidency and to announce on April 17 that any member of his staff called to testify would do so voluntarily. This Baker greeted quite typically by congratulating Nixon for acting as he had recommended.[12]

The Sam and Howard Show

When hearings opened on May 17, Baker followed Ervin's opening remarks by promising an "objective and evenhanded but thorough, complete, and energetic" probe that would develop the facts before the American people and recommend appropriate statutory changes. Confessing an initial fear that the probe might become a Democratic maneuver to "exploit the temporary vulnerability" of the GOP, he declared that events, especially the panel's customary unity, had convinced him otherwise. Chairman Ervin had gone out of his way to highlight the committee's credibility as a bipartisan body, most strikingly by designating Baker as vice-chairman and empowering him to sign subpoenas, authorize staff travel and expenditures, and preside in his absence, a rare delegation of authority to a minority member that helped legitimize the panel's work in most eyes.[13]

If tensions were present, they involved GOP members and the majority staff, especially Sam Dash. The initial incident drawing Dash's ire was Hugh Branson's refusal to let him use Baker's signing machine to sign subpoenas in April while Baker was in the Soviet Union. After Baker and Thompson produced a list of witnesses Dash objected to on May 8, Dash restricted access to sensitive documents to his staff alone. Discord became evident the first day of the hearings, when Baker rebuked Dash for introducing evidence no member had seen.[14]

While drawing Dash's wrath, the firm but amiable Baker was receiving considerable attention from the media and the general public. "I try to get a picture of who the man is," he said, "how he relates, and what I'd like to inquire about." Baker would generally peruse a package Fred Thompson had prepared, then pose questions unrelated to the material he had just read based upon his overall knowledge of the case. Often, Thompson wrote, "he would wait until seconds before his turn to question, jot down two or three words . . . and open a dialogue . . . that gave the impression that he had been rehearsing . . . all night." Baker tended to shun detail-oriented questions, preferring to examine broader issues of motivation from witnesses as to why they had undertaken clearly illegal and even more pointless actions. From financially secure and capable men like James McCord and Bernard Barker, he sought to determine why they were involved in bugging the DNC headquarters at a time when the identity of their presidential nominee was unknown. Of McCord's first attorney Gerald Alch, he queried why he had not advised his client to plead guilty after being caught redhanded.[15]

As the panel heard the testimony of higher-placed officials, Baker continued asking about motives. He was most stern in his examination of Herbert Porter, a young CRP aide who had perjured himself to the grand jury at the direction of Jeb Magruder. Baker was interested in what led such an apparently conscientious individual to participate in the Nixon campaign's dirty tricks. After Porter cited a fear of being seen as disloyal, Baker admonished him that "the greatest disservice that a man could do to a president of the United States would be to abdicate his conscience." Baker's questions to Magruder, who had joined in the reluctant decision of John Mitchell, Fred LaRue, and Gordon Strachan to approve a $250,000 intelligence-gathering plan of G. Gordon Liddy, were equally pointed. "If you were concerned because the action was known to you to be illegal," he dug in, "because you thought it improper or unethical, you thought the prospects for success were . . . meager and you doubted the reliability of Mr. Liddy, what on earth would it have taken to decide against the plan?" Once Magruder guessed the opposition of anyone present would have prevented the break-in, Baker asked why he had not reported what he knew to Nixon or the FBI. Magruder cited a fear that knowledge of Mitchell's involvement might have imperiled Nixon's reelection and that the cover-up was a decision acquiesced in by all involved from the moment the break-in was foiled.[16]

While Magruder's testimony was important—as he linked Mitchell and H. R. Haldeman, two of Nixon's closest associates, to the break-in and cover-up, respectively—John Dean's figured to be even more damaging. Having warned Nixon and his top aides in early April that he would not let himself be made the scapegoat, Dean and attorney Charles Shaffer commenced negotiations with Dash shortly after Dean was forced to resign as White House counsel on April 30. Two meetings convinced Dash that Dean's story justified a grant of immunity. Weicker, too, met with Dean, his neighbor, and believed his story valuable. Ervin, after hearing a broad outline from Dash, was equally supportive, and his three colleagues added their votes. Baker and Gurney were wary of Dean, as were many on both sides.[17]

Unaware of what Dean would testify to, as Dash had promised to inform only Ervin of the basis of the request, they, as attorneys, had seen many defendants escape sentences by implicating higher-ups and were angry as Dash had previously supplied all members with summaries of the evidence to which witnesses seeking immunity could be expected to testify.[18] Gurney feared Dean was trying to use the committee to escape punishment. Baker, thinking Dean as culpable as anyone for the escapades categorized under the heading of Watergate, likened a grant to buying a pig in a poke. But after convincing no one, Baker said that he would change his ballot and persuaded Gurney to join him, thus preserving the committee's customary unity.[19]

Only three days prior to the scheduled beginning of Dean's public testimony on June 19 did Dash let Baker and Thompson meet with Dean, who aimed to neutralize Baker by revealing his February 22 meeting with Nixon.[20] What Dean did not count on was that the date scheduled for his testimony coincided with the visit of Soviet chief Leonid Brezhnev. At the request of the joint Senate leadership, who did not want Nixon's bargaining position with Brezhnev to be weakened, Baker moved in executive session to delay the hearings for a week and allow Dash and Thompson to continue questioning Dean. After only Weicker dissented, Baker told Shaffer that he expected Dean to give Dash and Thompson the testimony he had withheld. A day later, the *New York Times* reported that Dean had used $4,850 of CRP cash to pay for his honeymoon, thus letting Shaffer imply that Baker and Thompson had leaked the information, say that he would no longer let his client testify before them, and convince Ervin to block any attempt to cite Dean for contempt of Congress. The panel's unwillingness to compel Dean to testify left him as the only witness allowed to testify publicly without having been thoroughly interviewed beforehand by both staffs.[21]

The honeymoon leak merely highlighted a problem that plagued the panel from start to finish. As early as April 2, Ervin told John Ehrlichman that the committee and its vicinity were the "leakinest place in the world." "We didn't invent the leak," Baker quipped, "but we raised it to its highest art form."[22] But this leak intensified the hype prior to Dean's testimony. Hugh Scott, who had hailed the panel for a "fair and unbiased" investigation, blasted Dean, who had lied to him in their one prior meeting, as a turncoat and a liar. Lowell Weicker termed the leaks another bid to block the airing of the truth. The preponderance of such leaks and the assumption that Dean would link Nixon to the cover-up led reporters to dub Dean as the most significant witness the committee would hear.[23]

Dean lived up to his billing, testifying that Nixon seemed to know what had happened as early as September 15, 1972, and had lied about a nonexistent Dean report as early as August 29. He further alleged that Nixon had ordered him on February 27, 1973, to report directly to him on all Watergate matters, knowing Haldeman and Ehrlichman were principals. After being pushed by E. Howard Hunt for $122,000, Dean told Nixon on March 21 that a cancer was growing that might end his presidency if he did not act to remove it. Hush money, he added, had been paid to the original defendants and he had helped Magruder prepare to perjure himself. Later that day, he told Haldeman, Ehrlichman, and Nixon that he believed himself and Nixon's two top aides indictable for obstructing justice.[24]

Baker did not begin questioning Dean until June 28, three and a half days after he took the witness chair. He was more than a bit perturbed by the attempt of Dean, whom aides deemed "that little son of a bitch," to discredit him. Hiding his displeasure, he called Dean's story "fairly mindboggling." Believing the probe unfocused, he had told his press secretary, Ron McMahan, at lunch that the committee had been "chasing rabbits, and we need to find the central animal." To Dean, he declared that his testimony had established that animal as "What did the president know and when did he know it?". After establishing that Dean could not implicate Nixon in the planning of the break-in, Baker moved to the cover-up, seeking to focus attention upon Dean's firsthand information and prod him into a statement that might lead Nixon to respond. Such a refutation was needed, Baker thought, as the charges represented an outline of presidential malfeasance, with his answers to his pet inquiry being (1) substantially more and (2) six months and six days earlier than Nixon had acknowledged.[25]

More volatile if less consequential events following Baker's first round of questions further established his independence. Lowell Weicker followed by describing the course of a smear campaign against him perpetrated by some on the White House staff and read into the record the transcript of a March 28 phone call where Richard Kleindienst is heard telling John Ehrlichman that Baker had told Weicker to "shut up," comments he quickly refuted. Finding it "difficult to overlook the presumptuousness of a man . . . five foot seven telling a six foot sixer to shut up," Baker corroborated Weicker, who then concluded with an impassioned lambasting of some Nixon aides who had tried to discredit witnesses and committee officials with threats, intimidation, and innuendo. Baker backed him completely, informing those who sought to produce a malicious impact on anyone connected with the probe that they were subject to inquiries from the special prosecutor.[26]

Baker grew reflective during the Fourth of July recess. Having told his own aides a year earlier that "we don't want half the power those guys have down there now" if he were ever president, his concern that Nixon's senior staff had exceeded their authority mounted as he learned that Nixon had no knowledge of a number of decisions that had profoundly affected his presidency. Disturbed that John Mitchell had not informed Nixon of G. Gordon Liddy's intentions, Baker asked him to cite "the constitutional basis for arrogating unto yourself or anyone else . . . a Presidential-level decision?" Mitchell conceded the absence of such a basis, but defended a fear that Nixon "would have unloaded . . . on all of the White House horror stories," a course he thought would have impeded Nixon's reelection.[27]

Baker concluded by asking Mitchell to suggest a means the committee might use to obtain testimony from Nixon. While Mitchell had few ideas, Baker, who like his colleagues was interested in gaining access to White House documents, continued to suggest that Nixon meet with the committee, publicly or privately. When the committee debated the issue, Ervin, Montoya, and Weicker argued for an immediate subpoena. Baker counseled restraint, believing abruptness would fuel the arguments of those who deemed the panel unfair to Nixon and urged Ervin to find an accommodation. If this did not work, Baker pledged to declare that no president was immune to a congressional subpoena and vote accordingly. While skeptical, Ervin consented, thereby avoiding an immediate confrontation with the president.[28]

The very next day, the committee learned of other evidence Nixon had withheld. In response to a question from deputy minority counsel Donald Sanders behind closed doors, former Haldeman aide Alexander Butterfield disclosed that Nixon had installed listening devices in the Oval Office, the Cabinet Room, the Lincoln Sitting Room, his office in the Executive Office Building, and his desk at the Aspen Lodge at Camp David. Now having a foolproof method of determining what the president knew and when he knew it, the panel asked Nixon to submit the tapes of five conversations with Dean. Nixon denied their request after listening to the tapes, saying different people might construe them in different ways and that their release would violate the principle of executive privilege. After reviewing Nixon's letter, the committee approved Baker's motion to subpoena the tapes and documents it had been seeking. Even so, Ervin and Baker remained hopeful they could reach an accord that would negate the need to sue. Agreeing that a private auditing of the tapes they would make would satisfy the committee, they joined Dash and Thompson in meeting with Nixon counsels Fred Buzhardt and Leonard Garment on July 27. But the meeting resolved nothing, as Buzhardt and Garment had no room to maneuver.[29]

John Ehrlichman sat at the witness table as the committee considered the motion. As debates over constitutional issues between Ervin and attorney John J. Wilson interrupted his testimony, the crowd began to hiss at some of his remarks. Upset, Baker convinced Ervin to cut off what had become his cheering session and commended him for acting as he had urged, declaring their job "infinitely tougher if we are cast in the role of conducting a circus." H. R. Haldeman followed Ehrlichman, and he had listened to some of the tapes. Baker was angered by the preferential treatment given Haldeman, a target of the investigation. But agreeing with Ervin that Haldeman had waived his Fifth Amendment rights and could be compelled to testify about what he had heard, he asked Haldeman what Nixon had said when Dean informed him that the original defendants would demand a million dollars to remain silent. Nixon replied that he would have no trouble raising the money, Haldeman responded, but then interjected that "it would be wrong." Baker asked Haldeman if he were sure. Haldeman answered that he was "absolutely positive."[30]

By this time, several members had concluded that an early end to the hearings might be desirable. While some believed this could be facilitated if the panel met in August, Baker fought the idea. Although some tensions had long been present among staff members, some of whom, without authorization from any senator, withheld evidence from members of the other party, overt rancor entered the caucus room for the first time when Inouye concluded his questioning of Ehrlichman by uttering "What a liar" and John Wilson responded by describing Inouye as a "little Jap." With such bitterness only making the panel's work more difficult, Baker sought to calm tensions with quips like "Who thought you up," to Anthony Ulasewicz, the jovial bagman for payments to the original defendants, or by promising to "sprawl across the committee table and suck my thumb" if the hearings ran into August.[31]

When Baker returned to Tennessee in August, he found that many Republicans wanted him to conduct a Gurney-like defense of Nixon and his subordinates. "I get the reaction," Chattanooga Congressman LaMar Baker remarked, "that he is not representing . . . Republicans like the Democrats on that committee are representing Democratic interests." Dan Kuykendall, his colleague from Memphis and a close Nixon friend, added, "Howard Baker is doing a service to this country and to the presidency. But . . . some . . . don't understand his tactics. . . . Through the years, his friends have always had to push Howard when the time comes to be political." Winfield Dunn spoke for a larger group who felt Baker had "conducted himself with dignity in a difficult situation." Democrats were hard-pressed to find ground to criticize Baker. Nashville Congressman Richard Fulton, in fact, said he was proud that a Tennessean had played such a role in uncovering the wrongdoings of the administration. State party chairman Jim Sasser was left lamenting that Baker "wasn't as tough on the big boys as he was on the spear carriers," a complaint not echoed by John Mitchell or H. R. Haldeman, the latter of whom was convicted for a dishonest answer to a Baker query.[32]

If Tennesseans weren't sure what to make of Baker's performance, many Americans appreciated his focus on the why of Watergate spiced with a mixture of tension-relieving humor, country wisdom, and deference to Ervin. *Time* characterized him as the "most relaxed and polished" interrogator. Jack Waugh of the *Christian Science Monitor* depicted him as "Watergate's Lancelot." In-depth stories in newspapers across America took note of his marriage and his legal career. Others reported upon the diet (a strict adherence to the principles of Dr. Adkins combined with the resumption of smoking, a habit he had kicked) that had allowed him to lose thirty pounds and forced him to use safety pins to keep his pants up. More dubiously, *Women's Wear Daily* added him to its "fifteen studliest" men list, and the editors of *Playgirl* offered him a hefty sum to pose for their centerfold, an overture he refused, citing a fear of being arrested for "unbecoming exposure." And while Bill Brock was the only figure of national stature to urge him publicly to run for president, 11 percent of the GOP voters the Gallup organization polled in August listed him as their first choice, a ten-point gain since April. Baker fared equally well in match-ups with Democrats. A July poll showed him narrowly defeating Democratic frontrunner Edward Kennedy, a feat only Charles Percy could duplicate.[33]

Upon returning to Washington, Baker used the panel's authority to hear evidence of dirty tricks against the Nixon campaign. In one session, he introduced forty affidavits showing that several local CRP headquarters had been vandalized; shots had been fired through the window of the Springfield, Massachusetts, GOP headquarters during working hours; demonstrators had taken over the Washington office of Democrats for Nixon, and burglars had broken into the office of Nixon's physician and strewn his medical records across the floor. Dissidents had been especially violence prone at the GOP convention. Baker brought Kentucky Congressman Tim Lee "Doc" Carter, one of the earliest congressional critics of U.S. involvement in Vietnam, to testify that he and his wife had been physically attacked by demonstrators who cursed at him and attempted to tear off his suit as they tried to enter their hotel the night before the convention opened. One soul who screamed "murderer" tried to block Carter's path and got a "Sunday punch flush on the jaw." When Carter could not find his wife, he ran to a policeman near the hotel entrance and learned that she had had to crawl on her hands and knees to get through the crowd. Three days later, another mob broke the fuel line of the Kentucky delegation bus, forcing Carter again to seek police aid. Remembering his experiences at the 1968 Democratic convention, Ervin noted that the First Amendment protected only peaceable assembly. Baker was on the Tennessee delegation bus in Miami Beach when its engine was disabled and its tires slashed, forcing he and Winfield Dunn to catch a ride in a Tennessee patrol car. "I admire you," he told Carter, while confessing little could be done by law other than recommend that security be tightened if violence seemed imminent.

Carter, under Baker's questioning, opined that the demonstrators were not genuine war protestors but ignorant troublemakers with no ties to the McGovern campaign or the Democratic Party. While most anti-Nixon demonstrations in

1972 were organized outside of the McGovern campaign, the panel learned that McGovern's southern California coordinator had allowed organizers of a demonstration at a Nixon appearance in Los Angeles to use their phone banks and that a paid employee in McGovern's Los Angeles headquarters had let volunteers xerox three thousand copies of a leaflet calling Nixon "treyf"—the Yiddish word for unkosher—which went on to say, "Thanks to modern technology Nixon brings the ovens to the people rather than the people to the ovens." GOP staffers called Rick Stearns, McGovern's western coordinator, to testify after learning that this tome was distributed in Jewish neighborhoods, as it was Stearns whom aides said had let demonstrators use the phones. Stearns denied the charges, then chided Republicans for making him appear. Baker, having spent five months listening to evidence of GOP wrongdoing, was angered. Noting that the issue was one of propriety and not criminality, Baker admonished Stearns that he "screamed" before he was "stuck" and informed him, as he had Nixon's henchmen, that the committee's mission was one of fact-finding and not casting judgment.[34]

Zonked on Saturday Night

Remaining conflicts could only be resolved with an airing of the tapes, nine of which Judge Sirica had ordered Nixon to produce for him to examine. This ruling and an appeals court reaffirmation irked Nixon, who began searching for a reason to fire Special Prosecutor Archibald Cox. White House Chief of Staff Alexander Haig and Counsel Fred Buzhardt met with Attorney General Elliott Richardson and suggested a plan that they hoped would satisfy everyone but Cox. Richardson would fire Cox, and Nixon would present an authenticated summary of the tapes to Judge Sirica. Richardson threatened to resign, having promised not to fire Cox save for extraordinary improprieties. Haig devised a compromise letting Cox stay if he accepted an authenticated summary prepared by someone both he and Cox trusted. When Richardson suggested the plan, Cox demanded to see it in writing.[35]

Haig and Buzhardt then asked John Stennis, a Mississippi Democrat trusted by all of the principals, to listen to the tapes and transcribe their Watergate-related contents for the Ervin Committee. Stennis was agreeable, if Baker and Ervin approved. Richardson and Charles Alan Wright, Nixon's new attorney, tried without success for the next three days to get Cox to accept the transcripts that Stennis would be preparing for Ervin and Baker. Nixon therein made public his offer to Cox in language crafted to convey the notion that he was generously waiving executive privilege. With time limited, as the deadline for filing an appeal was midnight on October 19, Nixon summoned Ervin and Baker from New Orleans and Chicago. They were met by Haig, Wright, and Buzhardt at the White House, told that Nixon hoped to reach an agreement with Cox by midnight, and ushered into the Oval Office where Nixon informed them of Haig's talks with Stennis. Ervin and Baker indicated their approval if Nixon let experts who could determine the authenticity of the tapes assist Stennis. Advising Nixon they were but two members of a seven-member panel, they assured him that they would call a meeting to consider the proposal at the earliest possible date and agreed to withhold comment until Nixon issued his statement.

That night, the White House Press Office issued a statement saying Nixon would not appeal the ruling but would prepare summaries of the tapes and deliver them and the tapes to Stennis, who would verify and submit them to Sirica and Ervin. Nixon triumphantly announced that Ervin and Baker had agreed to this procedure and ordered Cox not to try again to obtain tapes or documents. Couched in terms making it seem like a compromise, the statement was misleading, as Stennis had agreed to prepare transcripts for only the Ervin Committee and only if members approved and, like Ervin and Baker, had not been told of his intended function, one he saw as improper, as the verifier of Nixon-prepared summaries for the special prosecutor.[36]

In Cox's view, the Stennis proposal did not comply with court rulings, and he declared the next day that the directive ordering him not to issue further subpoenas was inconsistent with Richardson's guarantee of independence. Taking this as insubordination, Nixon ordered Richardson to fire Cox. Richardson refused and resigned, whereby Alexander Haig, under Nixon's orders, directed Deputy Attorney General William Ruckelshaus to dismiss Cox. Ruckelshaus also ignored Nixon's directive and was fired before he could resign. Soon thereafter, Solicitor General Robert Bork, the third-ranking official in the Justice Department, agreed to obey the dictum in a letter to Cox. A few minutes past nine, the FBI sealed off Cox's office and sequestered all files.[37]

The "Saturday Night Massacre" made it doubly important to Baker that the panel have access to the tapes. Trusting like Ervin that their deal was still intact and hoping to expedite resolution of all Watergate questions and thereby limit political damage to the GOP, Baker called Alexander Haig the next Tuesday and Wednesday to suggest that Nixon consider some middle ground, perhaps allowing Judge Sirica to supply the panel with all relevant excerpts. But Nixon was of no mind to keep his word, citing to Haig the committee's many leaks and Sam Dash's announcement to Charles Alan Wright that he would appeal Judge Sirica's decision that the panel had no authority to sue for the tapes. Ervin's and Baker's colleagues were supportive enough to vote in executive session to approve their actions but not until Lowell Weicker noted that they had been "zonked."[38]

Public opinion turned irretrievably against Nixon thereafter. Dozens of House members filed resolutions asking their Judiciary Committee to determine if Nixon had committed impeachable offenses. Baker, with Bill Brock, introduced a bill calling for two special prosecutors—one from each party—to be appointed to investigate campaign violations. Once other senators killed the plan by insisting upon a single prosecutor, Baker and Brock joined Marlow Cook and Charles Percy in sponsoring a measure barring Nixon from removing the special prosecutor without Senate approval.[39]

The firestorm of criticism alarmed Nixon, who embarked in mid-November upon what he called "Operation Candor," part of which involved meetings with Republican members of Congress as well as with friendly Democrats. Baker attended one with other GOP senators with surnames between A and G and found most present strongly behind Nixon. In contrast, Edward Brooke, who had been a surrogate speaker for Nixon in 1972, told Nixon in his respectful but firm manner that he had lost the confidence of the American people and suggested that he consider stepping down. "Ed's right," followed the conservative James Buckley, who said that governing would be next to impossible without the trust of the people. Baker took a middle ground, advising Nixon that he could not regain his credibility through a press conference or a speech and again urged him to appear before the Ervin Committee. Nixon's refusal left Baker frustrated. "I'm going out of this meeting without knowing where we're going," he told Nixon. "I want . . . you to remember that this comes from friends of yours and I hope those friends will share in your decision." "That's what this . . . is all about," Nixon tried to reassure him, "and when I make the decision, I'll meet with the leadership." Baker was still taken aback by Nixon's stonewalling of his closest allies. "Mr. President," he shot back, "I meant as you meet with them, not before you meet with them." Here was advice that so startled Nixon because of its audacity that he had his congressional liaison Bill Timmons ask onetime employer Bill Brock to speak to Baker about his demeanor.[40]

Even though Brock convinced Baker that his tone had been off-base, Baker remained concerned that Nixon was doing nothing to mitigate doubts about his professed noncomplicity. In a speech at Whittier College, Nixon's alma mater, two days later, Baker reiterated his call upon Nixon to make a full disclosure in a public forum. Nixon's failure to come clean at this date, he said, was either "another in an unbroken chain of bad decisions" or meant that evidence existed that they didn't want to disclose.[41] His association with Nixon continued to lead him to give him the benefit of the doubt, but the absence of new evidence prompted him to attend to matters the minority staff had deemphasized.

One of the First Opponents of PACs

It was always Baker's view that one of the Ervin Committee's principal tasks was developing legislation to prevent future Watergates, even though he feared that "the great danger is overreaction." Having warned against an "orgy of reform without direction," Baker saw the public financing provisions of the March 1974 campaign reform bill pushed by Common Cause, organized labor, northern Democrats, and Hugh Scott as an abridgement of the First Amendment rights of the people, as it gave voters no voice in who got their tax dollars. While conceding that large donors had disproportionately influenced past elections, he deemed the private financing of campaigns an irreplaceable means of involving citizens and offered with Ervin an amendment giving individuals a 100 percent tax credit for the first $50 they gave each year. Seeing the bill's $1,000 ceiling on individual donations as too low, he advocated a $3,000 cutoff and expressed fear that the Congress might be "burning down the barn to get to the rats." "Corporations cannot vote," he argued. "Common Cause cannot vote. Chambers of Commerce cannot vote. Why should they contribute?"[42]

Baker also regretted that the bill did little to reform the nonfinancial aspects of campaigning. Having talked with Democrats who had run for president in 1972, he was convinced that the process of electing a president needed change. He remained committed to a constitutional amendment substituting a direct election for the electoral college. As the networks had declared that he had been elected in 1966 before the polls closed in West Tennessee, he also advocated a uniform twenty-four-hour polling period to halt disenfranchisements of workers whose shifts conflicted with the standard twelve-hour period and to prevent eastern returns from prejudicing the decisions in the West. Convinced as well that the primary season was too long, abused the health of candidates, and bored the public, he proposed a time zone system of primaries consisting of but four preliminaries spread in three-week intervals between June and August. Like the regional primary concept, the time zone system would shorten the primary system and end the undue influence granted New Hampshire and other states. But Baker deemed his proposal superior, because the time zone format precluded strictly regional candidates from capturing a nomination through unstoppable momentum from carrying every state in their region if that section held the first primaries.[43]

Disturbed by the Senate's inattention, Baker joined Robert Griffin and James Allen in a filibuster that was relatively successful at first. Proponents fell seven votes short of cloture on the first try and the Senate approved an amendment by Baker and Peter Dominick mandating the simultaneous closing of all polls.[44] But those who depended upon labor money defeated Baker amendments to ban donations by groups, remove public financing provisions, limit public financing to the presidential election, and repeal the law requiring broadcasters to sell time to candidates at the lowest unit rate, and Baker voiced a hearty no to the bill.[45]

Unexplained Surreptitious Activities

At about the same time, Baker concluded his report on CIA involvement in Watergate. Since the onset of the investigation, he had suspected that the CIA played a larger role than its leaders were admitting if only because the agency was less than cooperative with routine inquiries. Much evidence linked the CIA tangentially to Watergate. Five of the original defendants had worked for the CIA. Eugenio Martinez was on a CIA retainer at the time of his arrest. E. Howard Hunt had received disguises and equipment to burglarize the office of Dr. Lewis Fielding, Daniel Ellsberg's psychiatrist. James McCord kept in close contact with his former superiors. These revelations coincided with the testimony of deputy CIA Director Vernon Walters, former Director Richard Helms, and former deputy director Robert Cushman that Haldeman and Ehrlichman had tried to pressure the agency into joining the cover-up.

Journalists Miles Copeland and Andrew St. George were not convinced by CIA protests of innocence. While Copeland, a onetime CIA agent, guessed that McCord had sabotaged the bugging knowing that the CIA hierarchy feared the creation of a separate White House intelligence unit, St. George alleged that Martinez had kept his CIA superiors informed about the break-in planning and that they had forwarded their findings to Helms. Disturbed, Baker prompted new director William Colby to say that Robert Bennett, the president of Robert Mullen & Company, a public relations firm and CIA front, had been debriefed by his CIA case officer shortly after the break-in. Baker interviewed Bennett, who said that he had been an intermediary between Hunt and Liddy for a time and that Hunt protégé Tom Gregory had notified him of his distaste for Hunt's plans hours before the break-in.[46]

Hunt shed light on his relationship with Bennett in a subsequent interview, alleging that Bennett had suggested that *Las Vegas Sun* publisher Hank Greenspun had documents that would interest both the CRP and reclusive billionaire Howard Hughes, a Mullen client. Soon, Hunt and Liddy met with several Hughes associates to discuss burglarizing Greenspun's office. Bennett had also arranged for Hunt to meet Clifton Demotte, who he believed had damaging information about Edward Kennedy's accident at Chappaquiddick. Baker and Thompson determined that Bennett was keeping the CIA informed while withholding evidence from the FBI and the Watergate grand jury, suspicions further aroused when they learned that the CIA had paid Bennett's legal fees. With these revelations coming more than eighteen months after the bugging, Baker said that he could hear "animals crashing around in the forest" that he could not see and created a task force of Thompson, Liebengood, and Michael Madigan to probe the extent of CIA involvement.[47] An early witness was former agent Victor Marchetti, who suspected that the CIA maintained a central taping system. While William Colby confessed that the CIA had used such a system and promised to provide all relevant tapes, the agency had destroyed its tapes before Colby took office but after Mike Mansfield had written every federal agency and asked that they keep all materials that might be used as evidence. A few days later, Helms's secretary told the task force that the tapes destroyed included some of Helms's conversations with Nixon, Haldeman, and Ehrlichman.

The unit further determined that the CIA learned of the Fielding break-in promptly after it occurred and that it maintained separate files on Hunt, Martinez, and Watergate, all of which they refused to produce. Members also found that agent Lee R. Pennington had entered the home of James McCord just after the break-in and burned documents linking McCord with the CIA in a fire causing thousands of dollars in damage. Such findings infuriated Helms and other CIA hands, who sent reports to members of panels with oversight duties denying any agency complicity. Without reading the Baker report, chairman Lucian Nedzi of the House Armed Services oversight subcommittee pronounced the CIA blameless and charged an unnamed sinister force with trying to blow smoke. Senate counterpart Stuart Symington, a close Helms friend, alleged that Alexander Haig had convinced the same senator, obviously Baker, to attack the CIA to divert attention from the House Judiciary Committee's impeachment probe.[48] At the same time, CIA officials were denying critical information about the tape destruction, the fire and other incidents, claiming that oversight panels had all relevant documents.

Disturbed, Baker summoned Helms on March 8, 1974. After thanking Helms for the cooperation he knew he would receive, Baker asked if the tapes contained conversations with Nixon, Haldeman, or Ehrlichman. Helms's noes grew louder as Baker raised each name until he complained that he did not appreciate the tone of the inquiries. Baker responded that he was equally resentful of rumors that he was conducting a hatchet job. When Symington interjected that he had come to see what Mr. Thompson wanted, Baker said that he, not Thompson, had initiated the requests. Citing rumors in a conciliatory manner, Symington asked if Thompson had said Helms was likely to be indicted. A confounded Thompson refuted the charge and told Symington of some of the more curious matters the task force had been looking into. Symington thanked Thompson, but Helms continued to deny any CIA involvement. Ehrlichman later told Thompson that Nixon had ordered him to demand a report on the CIA role in the Bay of Pigs fiasco from Helms, who declined until Nixon himself made the request, and even then submitted an incomplete record, leading Baker to conclude that "Nixon and Helms have so much on each other, neither of them can breathe."[49]

Baker was even more frustrated after aides learned that a young clerk in the Joint Chiefs of Staff liaison office with the National Security Council, Yeoman First Class Charles Radford, had been stealing NSC documents and funneling them to JCS Chairman Thomas Moorer. Could this relate to Watergate, they asked David Young, a youthful Ehrlichman aide who had headed the "Plumbers Unit." "Yes," Young replied, and Baker scheduled a meeting with Young. Impressed with Young's informativeness and demeanor, Baker asked him about the relevance of the Radford-Moorer matter. "That is the one thing I promised the President I would not discuss," Young responded, staring at the ceiling. "I cannot tell you why, but you ought to ask the President, because he is in a position to tell you." Baker backed off and sought out Nixon privately. "If you love your country," Nixon told Baker, "you'll never ask that question again." Baker never did, but he did urge Nixon to make the matter public as he could not see how the presidency or the country could be hurt any more than earlier disclosures had already done.[50]

Equally frustrated because of his inability to gain access to CIA documents, Baker ended his investigation, turned his report over to Armed Services Committee Chairman John Stennis and the CIA, and noted that it raised more questions than it answered. The CIA held the report for three months for "sanitization" before allowing Baker to release it. While few paid attention then, the press began examining Baker's leads when issues surrounding Richard Nixon were relegated to the back pages of America's newspapers.[51]

The Final Days

It was always Baker's and Ervin's intention to see that their staffs agreed upon a single report. When infighting seemed to erode the panel's common sense of purpose, Baker would tell Thompson, "we've come too far to let this happen." He further maintained that the report should omit conclusions about anyone's guilt or innocence, saying those tasks were more appropriately handled by the special prosecutor or the House Judiciary Committee. Ervin agreed, telling Dash, "The best way to draw a horse" is to "just draw the horse and know that any damn fool . . . will see that it is a horse."[52]

While the committee's report reflected Ervin's and Baker's intentions, it was more vivid than expected, as it was not finished until members had time to digest evidence from transcripts Nixon had submitted to the House. While not moralizing about Nixon's salty private language, Baker was offended that Nixon had entertained the idea of paying hush money. He agonized over the course Nixon should take, believing a resignation "would create a precedent . . . that would plague us for years," but reserved comment on the issue of impeachment. While not convinced that the high standard that he believed the Constitution prescribed for proof that a president had committed an impeachable offense had been met, all such questions became academic on August 5, 1974, the day Nixon released transcripts of tapes he had withheld even from his lawyers revealing that he had ordered H. R. Haldeman on June 23, 1972, to direct the CIA to block the FBI probe of the bugging. What the president knew about the cover-up was a great deal, and when he knew it was no later than six days after the break-in was foiled. Baker's first exhibition in the area of his first love—photography—opened at the Washington Gallery of Photography that week. The occasion was not an entirely happy one because of developments in the field he speaks of as his hobby—namely, politics. There had been nothing satisfying about investigating a man with whom he had been closely associated, and he expressed grief for the fate of the Nixons, especially the president's wife, Pat, and daughters, Julie and Tricia.[53] But one question was and still is unanswered, one Baker had put so often to so many witnesses: Why?

If any portion of Howard Baker's career has aroused controversy among scholars, it is his role in the Watergate investigation. In *The Wars of Watergate*, the most recent attempt at a thorough chronicle, the liberal historian Stanley Kutler depicts Baker as a "Byzantine" defender of Nixon who developed "back channel lines to the White House, constantly sending word that Nixon was not to be misled by his public statements." Here was a portrait that first emerged in *Chief Counsel*, the memoir of Samuel Dash. But what Dash really believed is a matter of conjecture. In chance encounters with GOP counterpart Fred Thompson and Howard Liebengood, Thompson's assistant, just prior to *Chief Counsel*'s publication, Dash tried to alleviate fears the two had developed after seeing newspaper snippets describing the book's tone. "I have the highest respect for you and Senator Baker," he told Thompson, "and I . . . want you to tell Senator Baker that." It is unlikely that Kutler was aware of this conversation, as the only two sources he used on the payroll of the Ervin Committee were Scott Armstrong, a man Dash suspended for leaking unfavorable material about nearly everyone associated with the panel, and Dash himself, two dedicated investigators who nevertheless lacked the perspective that ordinarily comes from some experience in the battlefield of electoral conflict or the everyday life of Capitol Hill. With several other members of both the minority and the majority staffs kind enough to make themselves readily available to scholars, one looks further and finds that Kutler has selectively quoted the often inconclusive notes of Haldeman and Ehrlichman and misattributed the transcript of at least one significant conversation between Ehrlichman and Ervin to Baker. Kutler also ignored considerable evidence in the Nixon project of the National Archives as well as in the Watergate-related portions of the writings of Senators Baker, Ervin, and Talmadge of Baker's counsel to Nixon, given once privately and often publicly, to disclose all evidence relating to Watergate as fully and rapidly as possible, not to mention his lack of responsiveness to White House bids to choose the minority counsel, limit the scope of the probe to merely the break-in, or block the testimony of those Nixon aides who were implicated in the planning of either the burglary or the cover-up. These efforts, the liberal journalist J. Anthony Lukas concluded in *Nightmare: The Underside of the Nixon Years*, still the most thorough and accurate account of the events known as Watergate, "never paid off."[54]

Kutler's interpretation rests in part on an overreliance upon both the hearsay evidence of Watergate defendants and sources like Armstrong and Dash who treat differences of opinion as evidence of bad faith or even sinister motives. Here is a criticism few schooled in the ways of Washington or electoral politics would make. One intended victim of the break-in was George McGovern, who, to be sure, hails Sam Ervin as the "driving force" in the probe and "What did the president know and when did he know it?" something of an "indirect way to build a defense" of Nixon, as the answer, if it established that Nixon's knowledge was little and late, would have limited a public consciousness of Nixon's responsibility for creating the atmosphere that led to Watergate. Even so, McGovern found Baker an "honorable" and "effective" inquisitor, recognizing in part a trait of conservatives like Baker to see individuals as legally accountable for their actions, and not those of their aides, a legitimate view, albeit one with which he disagrees. He, too, had to know of assessments from men like Terry Lenzner, an ideologically similar Dash aide, that Baker's role was that of a "statesman," as Baker was constantly supportive of his inquiries and "at no time . . . undercut the investigation or subpoenas even in the most sensitive areas involving the President."[55]

If the assessment of any Democrat of Baker's role in the Watergate probe should matter, it is Sam Ervin's, whose view meshed unabashedly with Lenzner's. "I have the highest opinion of Senator Baker and . . . the deepest appreciation for all the help he furnished to me," he declared in 1981 in a chuckle that turned into a mischievous and infectious wide-mouthed belly laugh with a broad twinkle in his ever-roaming eyes. "I'd be glad to support him for President if he'd only run on the Democratic ticket." Why? From a half century of experience in politics and in the law, Ervin expected any seven lawyers distinguished enough to be elected to the United States Senate to have seven different ideas about how such a probe should be conducted. Astonishing to Ervin and other congressional veterans was the fact that the panel divided along party lines only once, on a January 1974 motion to authorize additional hearings. This the chairman attributed in no small part to his belief that Baker was "a man of remarkable intelligence, . . . devotion to his country and . . . the possessor in an outstanding degree of what can only be called an understanding heart." With Baker as insistent as he was in rejecting executive privilege claims forwarded by John Ehrlichman in private meetings, the chairman believed that his vice-chairman had "put his loyalty to the country to try to ascertain what the truth about Watergate was" above his "devotion to the Republican Party . . . , an institution which he revered." Here was a perception that struck the White House as well, as indicated by Nixon's March 22, 1973, observation that "Baker is not proving much of a reed."[56]

Here rests clear evidence of Baker's independence, albeit it is equally clear that Baker never lost sight of his fear of the fallout that might amass upon the political fortunes of the millions of Republicans who had no connection with the misdeeds of the Nixon administration. As a Republican, he was certain that the way to control damage to his party was to see that all evidence related to Watergate came to the public's attention quickly and forthrightly. Here was advice that he gave Richard Nixon early and often, and revived when Ronald Reagan came under fire for less venal but perhaps more consequential mistakes during the Iran-Contra affair. That Baker held true to his oft-stated commands to follow every lead and let the chips fall where they may is demonstrated in Ervin's eager and frequent salute that he "gave primacy to his country and to his duty to ascertain what the truth was" and perhaps even more so in Stanley Kutler's reluctant acknowledgment that he "emerged from a Democratic-dominated show with his reputation substantially enhanced."[57]

Chapter 6

THREE TIMES A BRIDESMAID 1973–1976

While Baker's legislative talents had long been evident, the Watergate probe gave credibility to his national ambitions. A *Newsweek* poll showed him running behind only John Connally and Barry Goldwater when Republicans were asked in mid-September 1973 who should succeed Spiro Agnew if Agnew left office. But Nixon insiders looked in other directions when Agnew resigned after being convicted of tax evasion, a trend summed up in the one mention of Baker's name among White House memos to the president. "No," advised speechwriter Raymond Price, "because of the Ervin Committee investigation." It thus did not surprise Baker when Nixon opted for Gerald R. Ford, the overwhelming favorite of members of Congress. "It's a darn good choice," said Baker. "He will have no trouble being confirmed."[1]

Energy, Mass Transit, and Big South Fork

While the Ford choice proved popular, GOP hopes were deteriorating from Watergate and an economy was souring from shortages of gasoline and home heating oil that ensued after an Arab oil embargo in October 1973. With a view of energy like many Tennesseans, with one eye toward Oak Ridge, Baker had been proud to announce in 1972 that a liquid metal fast-breeder demonstration project would be built near the Clinch River. With issues of oil supply becoming paramount in 1973, he voted to authorize the Alaska pipeline without mandating environmental impact statements, believing a delay would add $6 million daily to the balance of trade deficit and make America more dependent upon foreign oil. Realizing Alaskan oil would not begin flowing to the Lower 48 in the months to come, he advocated the deregulation of new natural gas and resisted a host of price-fixing schemes. Deeming conservation as important as production, he joined Edmund Muskie in advocating a temporary relaxing of standards to allow the winter burning of low-sulfur coal to keep factories and businesses open.[2]

Baker also worked with Muskie on a measure letting states and cities use Highway Trust Fund revenues for mass transit for the first time. While they could not win in the rural-dominated Public Works Committee, they attracted support from Richard Nixon, Common Cause, the United Auto Workers, and the Teamsters Union. Rejecting more expensive proposals, they tried to reassure small-state senators that the bill would not delay completion of the interstate system or deny rural officials the right to build highways, but merely allow urban executives to use their funds to pay for bus lines or subway systems. While many remained opposed to using the Highway Trust Fund for anything but roads, senators were more cognizant of a need to conserve fuel, and a 49–44 majority appeared for the Muskie-Baker amendment. The divisions separating the House and Senate versions of the highway bill were reflected in the conference committee. While seven of nine senators favored the Muskie-Baker amendment, seven of nine House members opposed it. The panel met twenty-nine times before Baker devised a compromise allocating one-quarter of the funds for mass transit in 1976.[3]

Occasionally, Baker raised more parochial issues. Most controversial was the creation of the Big South Fork National River and Recreation Area due north of Baker's Scott County home. For years, John Sherman Cooper and Howard Baker Sr., hoping to spur development in McCreary County, one of the poorest areas in Kentucky, had pressed Congress to build a dam along the Big South Fork. Upon entering the Senate, the younger Baker joined Cooper in sponsoring the bill, which, while backed by local utilities and the Army Corps of Engineers, was opposed by environmentalists and never brought to the floor. In its place, Baker and Cooper suggested creating a park surrounding the waterway that environmentalists and most locals endorsed, save for coal operators owning mineral rights to the land being partitioned. Their bill was signed into law by Richard Nixon in 1974, two years after he vetoed a bill containing funding for the park, as it, to Nixon, resembled a Christmas tree in that it was loaded with money for projects that he did not deem worthy of federal support.[4]

Revived Ambitions

Baker's general focus, however, was on national politics. In early 1974, he let it be known that he was contemplating a bid for the presidency, a distinct change, as he had previously remained coy, even among close friends. As late as his annual Fourth of July picnic of 1973, he had spotted press secretary Ron McMahan sporting a "Senator Baker for President" T-shirt and grinningly ordered him to take it off. When he was on the stump, audiences generally wanted to hear his view of the latest Watergate developments, and he obliged by hailing his party for "a conscious decision to do that . . . unpleasant, dangerous job of investigating ourselves in full, public view." He continued to expound upon Watergate after Nixon left office. Standing in at a gathering Gerald Ford was scheduled to address on the day after Ford ascended to the presidency, Baker hailed the transfer of power as an affirmation of the "rule of the law." Even so, he feared that Nixon's departure might establish the act of resignation under fire as an unwritten part of the Constitution and saw it as evidence of an erosion of the idea of a strong president held by the Founding Fathers. While anxious to remove the trappings of the imperial presidency, Baker feared that Congress might be overemphasizing the needs of the moment to restore a sense of equilibrium. Enough of a Senate man to cheer the larger role granted Congress in the foreign policy-making process by the War Powers Act, he feared that the Congress might overrestrict the options available to the executive in future crises.[5]

Baker's warnings received little credence in 1974. Humbled by the arrogations of authority and lies of the Johnson and Nixon administrations, members of Congress guarded new prerogatives with zeal. Few constitutional discussions were held outside of academic circles after Nixon resigned. Gerald Ford saw his chief duty as healing the wounds to the national psyche from Vietnam and Watergate, with his secondary goal being the revival of an economy crippled by soaring inflation and unemployment rates and plummeting stock prices. In contrast, the White House press corps focused upon the status of the case that might be initiated against Nixon and whom Ford would choose as his vice-president.[6]

This time, Baker's name surfaced often in vice-presidential speculation. Tennesseans like Winfield Dunn, Bill Brock, John Duncan, and the editorial board of the *Nashville Tennessean* all openly recommended his nomination, while Congressmen Robin Beard, Dan Kuykendall, and Jimmy Quillen privately urged Ford to take the same course. Baker was also backed by Senate colleagues Roman Hruska, Bob Packwood, and Ted Stevens, who joined Brock in naming him as their first choice in their letters to Ford. Several others listed him as their second or third choice. Among senators, only Nelson Rockefeller and Barry Goldwater fared better. Grassroots Republicans found him nearly as acceptable. Eleven percent of the Republicans polled by *Newsweek* in the two days after Nixon's resignation listed him as their first choice, placing him in fourth place behind Goldwater, Rockefeller, and Ronald Reagan. Conservatives saw Baker in an increasingly favorable light after learning that Rockefeller ranked high. LaMar Baker told reporters that conservatives in the House GOP Steering Committee generally favored Goldwater or Reagan but would accept George Bush or Baker. Evans and Novak reported likewise that North Carolinian Jesse Helms would attempt to unite his conservative brethren behind Goldwater, Reagan, or Baker to block Rockefeller.[7]

Baker would have nothing to do with such schemes. While hoping to be chosen, he would say only that it would be his duty to accept the nod if Ford offered it. He considered his chances slim, as Bush and Rockefeller were generally seen as the favorites. Moreover, many Republicans recoiled at his independence on the

Ervin Committee. "Whoever heard of Howard Baker before Watergate," a House Republican asked. "That finishes him." Unbeknownst to anyone, Ford had opted against choosing a sitting member of Congress and concluded that Rockefeller's long experience in government, broad knowledge of foreign affairs, and ability to attract talented men and women to public service made him the best possible vice-president, or if anything should happen to him, the best possible president. Realizing with Pat Buchanan that Rockefeller was the "strong and safe choice," Baker declared after the nomination was announced that the choice guaranteed the GOP's continuity as a broad-based party. If he was disturbed by anything, it was the Democratic refusal to consider the nomination until November and the attempts of right-wing purists to sabotage the nomination with chirps about the governor's remarriage and financial empire. As thoughtful a student of procedure as he would have been a champion of virtually anyone Ford might have chosen, he suggested replacing the Twenty-fifth Amendment with a reconvening of the Electoral College to confirm the president's choice, a process he believed would guarantee that the vice-president would reflect the will of the public expressed in the last election.[8]

With the Rockefeller nomination in hiatus and Washington awaiting the trial of major Watergate defendants, the press continued to focus upon the legal status of Richard Nixon. At Ford's first presidential press conference, nine of the twenty-eight questions dealt with Watergate. While Baker urged him to "cool it," Ford aimed to "get the [Nixon] monkey off" his back. Without even a statement of contrition from Nixon, Ford issued a pardon on September 8. While finding the decision "principled and highly motivated," Baker was troubled by Nixon's lack of an admission of guilt and saw the pardon as a mistake at a time when Nixon had not been indicted. Thankful the GOP had survived Watergate intact, he feared "the whole thing" had been thrown "back in our laps."[9] His concern was well founded. Many Republicans regretted the lack of a confession, while just as many Nixon haters alleged without proof that Ford had issued the pardon as part of a deal with the former president, charges which placed GOP candidates again on the defensive. With Watergate compounded by a deteriorating economy, Republicans lost forty-five House seats, three in the Senate and four governorships, including Tennessee's, where Baker protégé Lamar Alexander was defeated, as were two GOP congressmen and fourteen GOP state legislators.

Continued Reaction to Abuses of Power

Disturbed but not surprised, seeing the GOP showing as an inevitable result of Watergate, the pardon, and a slow economy, Baker was concerned that the size of the Democratic wins, especially those in Tennessee, might be enough to allow Democrats to claim mandates for whatever policies they pleased. Not just concerned about the heavy outlays Democratic Congresses had provided over the previous decade, which he held largely responsible for the state of the economy, he had learned of many unreported abuses of the CIA and FBI in earlier administrations. Disturbed by the CIA's unresponsiveness to requests from congressional committees, Baker introduced a bill creating a Joint Committee on Intelligence Oversight. Assuring defense-minded senators that he was "not engaged in a vendetta" and believed a "strong, vigorous, and viable" intelligence capacity vital, he denounced in no uncertain terms a measure outlawing all CIA covert and clandestine functions. But while opposed to an absolute ban, he did not believe America should meddle in the internal affairs of other countries except those which were clear enemies of the United States or threats to its security.[10]

The Baker-Weicker legislation aroused opposition from many, including John Tower and Barry Goldwater, who believed oversight should be handled by Armed Services subcommittees and whose bargaining position strengthened after Democratic Congressman Michael Harrington declared erroneously in fall 1974 that CIA Director William Colby had said that the agency had conducted a massive destabilization campaign in Chile during the troubled tenure of Communist President Salvador Allende. Liberals blasted the alleged subversion of a democratically elected government. Conservatives focused upon the violation of a pledge to keep material confidential and predicted more harmful leaks if oversight functions were removed from existing committees. While Baker argued that his bill would merely streamline oversight, the allegations allowed Senate elders to block the creation of a separate committee until it was reported late in 1974 that the agency retained files on more than ten thousand U.S. citizens, most of them critics of the Nixon administration. With new stories breaking daily, Gerald Ford, hoping to quell outrage, named a commission headed by Nelson Rockefeller to investigate the reports. Baker applauded the move but believed the Senate should conduct its own inquiry. Once the body voted to create such a panel, Mike Mansfield designated Frank Church as its chair. Hugh Scott selected Tower and Goldwater to represent those Republicans who wanted to maintain unrestricted intelligence, Charles "Mac" Mathias and Richard Schweiker from those critical of American involvement in Vietnam, and Baker.[11]

Baker, less senior than Tower and thus not the GOP's chief spokesman, focused his attention on unanswered Watergate questions. "Why," he still wondered, "were so many people going out of their way to fuzz up the answers to questions we felt were completely harmless?" His task was facilitated by reporters who months earlier had seen the degree of Richard Nixon's culpability as the only story in town. Seymour Hersh, describing Baker's difficulties in gaining access to CIA logs, diaries, and files, revealed that former CIA Director Richard Helms had ordered aides not to provide Watergate-related evidence to prosecutors in the six weeks following the break-in, an especially improper directive that precluded inquisitors from learning of the existence and activities of the Plumbers Unit for months and made certain that John Ehrlichman's unheeded order to the CIA to block the FBI probe of laundered money would go undiscovered. Continued CIA noncompliance added to Baker's suspicion that "elements of our intelligence community had an interest in the Watergate break-in . . . unofficially, that has yet to be . . . explained." His concern mounted after the June 23, 1972, tape was discovered. Why, he wondered, had Nixon tried to use the CIA and not another agency to block the probe? One conclusion was that Nixon had learned of activities that would discredit the CIA if they became known, thus causing him to question whether any president could control the agency. CIA officials grew concerned, knowing a negative conclusion from him, one of the more defense-oriented senators, might damage its ability to function.[12]

Once William Colby agreed to let him examine every available Watergate-related diary, log, or file he had wanted to see at the CIA's headquarters, Baker learned he could not substantiate a belief that the CIA as an institution had been involved in the break-in. What he did regret was that the distancing plan initiated after the burglary and the death of Lee R. Pennington precluded investigators from learning why James McCord had burned his files after his arrest. To Baker, these developments merely added to the need for fulltime CIA oversight, a belief strengthened when senators learned of agency plans to assassinate Marxist dictators Fidel Castro and Patrice Lumumba in the 1960s. They, too, prompted him to cosponsor bills banning any federal agency from participating in assassinations of foreign leaders and reopening investigations into the murders of John F. Kennedy and Martin Luther King Jr. Talks with Ed Redditt, a black former Memphis policeman and Bill Brock's Memphis office head, convinced him that others besides James Earl Ray had been involved in the King assassination. He held fewer doubts about the Warren Commission verdict that Lee Harvey Oswald acted alone, but the proliferation of conspiracy theories led him to believe that such doubts could only be assuaged by an airing of all of the evidence.[13]

Seeing a proposed permanent Senate Intelligence Committee as the proper forum for such a probe, Baker cosponsored the bill creating such a panel. But he objected to a recommendation by a majority of the Church Committee that the CIA be required to notify the permanent panel of all foreign covert actions and allow it to declassify any material it deemed appropriate, believing such steps imposed undue restrictions upon legitimate intelligence functions. While urging Congress to establish a review committee of senior members to decide upon any appeal of a decision not to declassify information, he could not convince the Senate to make it a criminal offense to publish the names of CIA agents working undercover overseas.[14]

Gerald Ford's Ally

On these and most other foreign and defense issues, Baker was a staunch ally of Gerald Ford. Baker agreed with Ford that stronger commercial and diplomatic ties with the Soviet Union would reduce the threat of war and hopefully buttress the positions of the less militaristic elements of the Soviet leadership. His optimism was tempered by beliefs that the Soviets intended to foment revolution throughout the world and that détente would only work to America's advantage if matched by a viable deterrent. While supporting both the SALT-I and Vladivostok Accords, he voted repeatedly against funding cuts for weapons systems Nixon and Ford deemed vital and insisted after twice inspecting NATO nuclear storage facilities that U.S. installations in Europe be secured against terrorists, as several depots were located uncomfortably near the borders of East Germany and Czechoslovakia and guarded only by pistol-toting GIs.[15]

Baker had conducted this investigation with John Pastore for the Joint Committee on Atomic Energy, a body more commonly concerned with domestic uses of atomic power and one Baker used to monitor research operations in Oak Ridge. Largely because of his work, Congress routinely approved appropriations in the mid-1970s for the Clinch River breeder, and Ford agreed to extend the life of the Appalachian Regional Commission, a body Richard Nixon wanted to terminate. But Baker could not convince Ford to sign the strip-mining bill of 1975 nor sway enough House Republicans to override Ford's veto. Blaming this defeat upon operator-induced pressure, he crafted his statement to allow the continuance of a productive working relationship with Ford. His approach proved wise, for revenue sharing, his onetime pet bill, was under attack from budget-conscious White House aides and a long-shot Democratic candidate for president named Jimmy Carter. With a reauthorization due, Baker, more convinced than ever that revenue sharing strengthened state and local governments, urged colleagues to act to recharter the program and thus facilitate long-range planning. As revenue sharing had a strong, resilient appeal, only four senators voted no.[16]

Had Ford not been interested in a full term in 1976, Baker would have sought the nomination. Never a Ford intimate, he discounted suggestions that Ford might run, as Ford, unlike many Democrats and Ronald Reagan, had hardly begun the tedious organizational chores that modern presidential politics requires. Without such preparation, Baker calculated that any campaign would fail, believing the value of incumbency had been diminished by public financing and subsidies for primary candidates. Ford's withdrawal, he guessed, would lead to a bitter struggle for the nomination, leaving Nelson Rockefeller, the standard-bearer of GOP progressives, and Ronald Reagan, the champion of conservatives, the frontrunners. This confrontation Baker thought many would shy away from, fearing such a struggle would divide the GOP as disastrously as in 1964. This vacuum could then be filled by someone acceptable to all wings of the party. He, as a southerner with a moderate image, was perfectly situated. Aside from those not excited by Reagan or Rockefeller, he figured he could cut into his native South and Rockefeller's base in the Northeast, much as Richard Nixon had in 1968.[17]

Whatever the political viability of Baker's philosophical underpinnings, his standing and Ford's were far from equal. Baker still ran behind Ford, Reagan, and Charles Percy, and Ford's approval rating had risen from 31 percent to 40 between April and June. Disagreeing with the incumbent on little other than the strip-mining bill and the Nixon pardon, Baker wrote Ford on July 9, 1975, a day after Ford announced his candidacy, and promised his aid.[18]

Ford faced a serious challenge from a man much more eloquent than he. Ronald Reagan appealed to the core constituency that had nominated Barry Goldwater in 1964 and had hired some of the most talented GOP operatives anywhere. Later, Ford admitted that his backers were "crisscrossing America lining up endorsements." While most GOP officeholders were supporting Ford, a December poll showed 40 percent of Republicans behind the challenger, with only 32 percent for Ford.[19]

Baker became Ford's honorary chairman in Tennessee, promised to support him as long as his candidacy was viable, and undertook a heavy schedule across the country as a Ford surrogate. Small declines in unemployment and food prices and a Reagan suggestion that Social Security funds should have been invested in the "industrial might of the nation's economy" allowed Ford to narrowly win the New Hampshire and Florida primaries, both of which Reagan had hoped to carry. While Ford also won primaries in Illinois, New York, Wisconsin, and Pennsylvania, Reagan's first victory in North Carolina on March 23 revived his candidacy and renewed talk of an alliance with supporters of George Wallace, whose paralysis had eliminated any chance of his ambitions being fulfilled. Such a coalition was possible in states with open primaries and one emerged for Reagan in Texas on May 1 that won for him its 100 delegates and produced momentum that allowed him to carry Alabama, Georgia, and Indiana, three states where Wallace had always been strong. Once a delegate count found Ford behind Reagan, a sense of doom fell over the Ford camp. Some even feared that Ford was in trouble in Michigan, as its laws allowed crossover voting. But the state GOP organization was mobilized down to the township level and separate appeals were made to Democrats and Independents. Home state pride had its effect, and Ford carried Michigan, 2–1, which, coupled with a win in Maryland, allowed him to pull near Reagan. But Ford's troubles were far from over. Six primaries—Arkansas, Idaho, Kentucky, Nevada, Oregon, and Tennessee—were set for the next week, and Ford was considered likely to win only in Oregon.[20]

Baker had been predicting a Ford win in Tennessee since early May, leading one Reaganite to suggest he was "confusing the President's popularity with his own." But he had become the actual chairman, and an active one. While he could not convince Ford to wage a media-intensive swing through the state, he and Tom Beasley, Ford's state campaign director, had been working to convince local GOP leaders to stick with the president, and they and Hugh Branson had forged a delegate slate of prominent Republicans of all stripes. Winfield Dunn, Robin Beard, Jimmy Quillen, Dan Kuykendall, and George W. Lee had all endorsed Ford, and Ford organizations were in place in most parts of Tennessee. Baker crafted his statements to reflect his belief that only a Ford nomination would keep the "torch of Republicanism lit," but that his position did not mean he was against anyone. He would back Reagan if the convention opted for him, a courtesy Ford did not mind. But Ford became irate when he learned that Reagan would spend the night at Baker's guest house, an invitation Baker had earlier made to Ford and defended by noting it was longstanding and that Reagan would be addressing a Scott County gathering where he would speak for Ford. "We are . . . rivals right now," Baker said, "but I have never let politics stand in the way of my friendships."[21]

Ford's ire lasted only the few hours between Reagan's departure from Huntsville and his declaration that TVA, which at the time was noted for inexpensive power, was an example of the "government starting out with . . . a legitimate . . . operation . . . becoming a . . . part of the power-producing combine of this country, competing with private enterprise . . . on a tax-free basis and with its own bonding power, able . . . [to] put the people into debt for . . . millions of dollars." When someone suggested that his position resembled Barry Goldwater's and asked if he agreed that TVA belonged in the private sector, Reagan declared it "something to look at." Ford campaign manager Rogers Morton alerted Baker, who proclaimed a sale "out of the question." While Reagan tried to explain that he had merely urged against further federal intrusions into private prerogatives, his reiteration of the theme caused aides to hedge their bets. "A Reagan defeat," state coordinator Gene Cantrell declared, "would not be a mandate for Gerald Ford, but a tribute to Howard Baker."[22]

Tennessee Republicans gave Ford a 2,170 vote margin out of 240,000 cast, a win stemming from his strength in Upper and Middle East Tennessee, which, matched with a smaller edge in Memphis, let him withstand slim Reagan margins in the other five districts. Even with the votes of many backers of George Wallace, who carried a majority in the 1972 Democratic primary but managed but 11 percent in 1976, Reagan still lost. Ford had "Howard Baker to thank," said Reagan West Tennessee coordinator Jere Griggs, "or he'd never have carried Tennessee—that and TVA."[23]

Believing his victory "attributable directly" to Baker, Ford thanked him at the White House. "You were magnificent," he said in a letter, "in your strong expression of support" and "in the enthusiasm you activated in your workers." Ford's nomination seemed more likely, as 207 Pennsylvania and New York delegates announced for him, and Kentucky and Oregon joined Tennessee on May 25.

Nowhere did Ford win big. Tennessee even gave 22 of its 43 delegates to Reagan, as delegates were apportioned by district. But, psychologically, "Tennessee and Kentucky turned it around," a Ford aide said. "Then all we had to do was play out the string."

Playing out the string was harder than expected. When primaries ended, Ford was 170 votes short of the 1,130 necessary for nomination and Reagan 100 further behind. Two hundred seventy delegates remained to be chosen in conventions. One hundred seventy more were uncommitted, confusion portending trouble for Ford. Nowhere was the superiority of Reagan's preparations more evident than in Missouri, the site of the first postprimary convention. Believing he could sweep the at-large delegates, Ford traveled with Baker, Bob Dole, Robert Griffin, and John Tower to St. Louis to address the convention that morning. He returned to Washington immediately thereafter, leaving the four to oversee his operations. But Reagan, having won one district by a wide margin and holding a ninety-vote edge overall, won all but one at-large delegate. When Ford invited the four to the White House, each warned that Reagan could still be nominated and that Ford needed to create the perception by the first ballot that he held 1,150 rather than 1,130 delegates to offset similar claims from Reagan. Ford's projections became more realistic, letting him better target states for personal visits. When America's ambassador to Lebanon was assassinated on June 16, Ford canceled a trip to Iowa so he could oversee the evacuation of Americans and sent his wife Betty with Baker, Dole, and Griffin. Noting strength for Reagan in a state where he had once been a broadcaster, Ford strategists split the at-large delegates with Reagan. Combined with near-solid blocs from four other states, the outcome helped change a perception that Ford's team was outclassed. With announcements from dozens of delegates, James Baker, Ford's chief delegate hunter, declared on July 23 that fifteen pledges from Hawaii had put Ford over the magic number of 1,130.[24]

The Vice-Presidency Slips Away, Again

While Baker continued to meet with delegates, he had begun preparing to deliver the keynote address at the Republican National Convention, a speech he believed important to both his party's success in November and the fulfillment of his own ambitions. Not terribly interested in being vice-president, he saw the nomination as the surest route to the White House. A spellbinding piece of oratory might propel him into the nomination. A lackluster effort would end any chance of his being picked. He began by reading every keynote delivered at both conventions since 1856 and found most to be pretty awful, a piece of research that gave him hope. With his party devastated by Watergate and torn by the Ford-Reagan fight, he set out to include a realistic assessment of the position of the GOP and an uplifting message to convince the faithful that a victory was still possible. Working with former Nixon wordsmith Raymond Price, Baker completed the first draft in early August and sent copies to the Ford and Reagan staffs. Reagan aides made merely technical suggestions, but fears from the Ford camp that the text had too many Watergate references led Baker to remove a few.[25]

Indeed, Baker had to placate Ford if he wanted to be Ford's running mate. It was clear that Ford was considering him. Once nine Maine delegates vowed to abstain unless Ford promised not to choose John Connally, and Mississippi GOP Chairman Clarke Reed, a Connally supporter, countered that the names of Edward Brooke, Mark Hatfield, Charles Percy, and Lowell Weicker on a list of twenty-three semifinalists "came as a shock," Ford had to assure several groups that the offending names were included as flattery and that he would select someone compatible with his own defense-minded internationalism in foreign affairs, frugality on domestic questions, and tolerance on social ones.[26]

These criteria suggested Baker. Generally aligned with Ford, he had a reputation for integrity that many figured would defuse the Watergate and pardon issues. That many Ford aides shared this view is demonstrated by the unparalleled attention counsel Philip Buchen and deputy counsel Edward Schmults gave to interviewing Baker about his 1972 campaign's acceptance of an illegal $5,000 corporate contribution from Gulf Oil lobbyist Claude Wild and the legal status of the Payne-Baker lands. Explaining that Wild had misrepresented his gift as an individual one and that the check had been returned once Baker had learned that the money had come from corporate funds, Baker gave Buchen a packet of newspaper clippings and the canceled check, and added that his interest in the Payne-Baker lands had been placed in a blind trust with instructions to sell. Not satisfied, Buchen phoned several Baker associates in Tennessee. With all corroborating Baker's accounts, he remained near the top of Ford's list.[27]

Ford also charged Buchen and Schmults with inquiring about the health of his semifinalists. Baker produced a doctor's corroboration that he was in good health for a man of fifty and told Buchen and Schmults that his wife had conquered an eight-to-ten-year bout with alcoholism. This was no secret. Joy had been most severely affected in the two years after her father's death, when her mother noticed that she "fell to pieces." She spent eight months in a Connecticut hospital in rehabilitation in 1971, using her time to knit and make jewelry. She had sufficiently recovered by spring 1973 to work without pay in Baker's office and serve on the boards of Knoxville College, the Knoxville Symphony Society, the Knoxville YMCA, the Dirksen Library, Ford's Theatre, and the Kennedy Center. Still, she occasionally overindulged until she resolved to quit, and did so in early 1976.[28]

Ford's attorneys asked Baker's friends and associates about Mrs. Baker and found his account accurate and his conduct exemplary. Cissy Baker, then in her teens, said that her father "never broke down. . . . At one point I turned on him for not giving up. He told me she'd pull through it someday. He knew what was underneath." Later, Peggy Smeeton Stanton, an Ohio congressman's wife, wrote that friends knew Joy Baker to be a "warm, intelligent, outgoing" friend "with an illness." "Everybody knew," Cissy added, "but nobody except Dad and Darek and me knew to what degree." "One of us was there, day in and day out" to help her mother. Cissy Baker can never recall seeing a "more understanding person" than Baker, who declined scores of engagements to stay with Joy. "Howard would be in the middle of a trip," Joy said later, "and . . . have to come home . . . because I couldn't cope," while her daughter declined a good summer job at Opryland in 1976 to see her "through a lot of crises."[29]

Support mounted in the meantime for a Baker nod for vice-president. A survey published on August 11 showed 11.3 percent of 449 responding delegates favoring him, placing him a close second behind Connally. His support emanated most strongly from Tennessee. Bill Brock asked Ford to withdraw his name and give the nod to Baker. Tennessee Reagan chairman Harold Sterling called upon Tennessee delegates to do everything they could to ensure Baker's nomination. Jimmy Quillen, spurred by bids by Reaganites in other states to allow delegations they had stacked to vote against the will of those who elected them, tried unsuccessfully to allow Tennessee's fourteen at-large delegates, eleven of whom backed Ford, the same authority. Such plugs were echoed by the *Nashville Banner,* which cited his "steadiness and strength," and John Seigenthaler, who saw the one unanswered question as if Ford had had the good sense to pick Baker. Baker support was also growing on the floor, where Congressmen Robert McClory and Clarence Brown, Senator Roman Hruska, Governor Christopher Bond, the Connecticut delegation, and OMB Director James Lynn all declared him their first choice.[30]

While grateful, Baker steadfastly refused to promote himself on talk shows or allow his staff to rally support. Likening the process to "driving a car on a sheet of ice," he publicly urged the choice of a Sunbelt representative to link Jimmy Carter with the virtually undaunted liberal record of his running mate, Walter Mondale. Reagan had earned the right of first refusal, he said, having won nearly enough votes to head the ticket. Aware of Reagan's disinterest, Baker saw his own chances as still good, even if Ford made an offer to Reagan. His position as keynoter gave him one advantage, and he rehearsed his speech assiduously. Thoroughly prepared, he made his way to the Kemper Arena shortly after eight on August 16 to deliver what figured to be the most important speech of his career.[31]

Baker approached the podium hand-in-hand with Joy to the "Tennessee Waltz." A demonstration ensued, centered in the Tennessee delegation but scattered throughout the hall. Baker grinned and pronounced the time one for "common sense . . . about . . . our party" and "straight talk about the needs of our nation." Calling the past few years "painful, . . . embarrassing, . . . and humiliating" for his party, he said the GOP had the "strength to . . . go forward," "because we faced our problems . . . with honor and dignity," unlike Democrats, who had not faced "abuses in prior Democratic administrations and . . . in the present Democratic Congress." "Running around . . . rattling the dusty old skeletons of Watergate," he said, would not work, because the people knew that no one held a monopoly "on . . . bad judgment," and a Republican victory was likely because they were "looking to the future . . . while . . . Democrats are . . . chasing the ghosts of the past." Virtue would not be an issue, or "love or patriotism or compassion." Instead, the primary issues of 1976 would be "How much government is too much government? How many laws are too many laws? How much taxation is too much taxation? How much coercion is too much coercion?"

The answers to these and other questions, Baker lectured, holding the lectern and occasionally clenching his fist, would come whence they had always come, from "the good common sense of the people," which in bygone days had mandated the creation of an egalitarian government, a resolve to defeat "Nazi terrorism" and "Soviet expansion" and "help those in need and right the wrongs" against victims of discrimination. The common sense of 1976, he said, was that "government taxes too much, it meddles too much, and it is up to us to do something about it." Painting his party as "one which had fought for . . . limited government in good years and in bad" and the Democrats as those for "more of the same—more programs, more promises," he noted that the federal budget had grown from less than $4 billion a year to more than $400 billion since 1932. Accepting that Franklin Roosevelt founded "big government," he charged that "based upon the record of that Democratic Congress, Jimmy Carter and his friends make Franklin Roosevelt look like a piker back in Paris," as Democratic promises guaranteed another annual $110 billion in outlays. "Why, a billion here and a billion there," he quoted Everett Dirksen, "and . . . the first thing you know, it adds up to real money." "Somehow," he added, "Democratic words of compassion always . . . translate into programs of coercion, . . . control, . . . and compulsion." He painted the differences more sharply thereafter, arguing,

> The Democrats start with government and we start with people. . . . For decades now, leaders of the Democratic Party have peddled the patronizing notion that only in Washington are officials wise enough . . . to decide for the rest of us what our priorities should be, how we should spend our taxes, . . . how we should organize our communities, even how close to home our children should go to school. And they do this with the best of intentions, because they really believe that they do know better and that the rules and guidelines that they write are for our own good and that some . . . nobler motive entitles them to tell the rest of us how to run our personal lives. But . . . the notion that notion that they know better what is best for Nashville or New York or Kansas City is . . . nonsense. They don't know better; you know better what is best for this country.

Past Democratic platforms Baker likened to "Roman candles that lit the heavens of hope, only to fizzle and disappear." But America had "had its fling with Roman candles" and would not be fooled again. He expressed optimism even in the face of a thirty-three-point Carter lead, confidence rooted in his belief that the government the people demanded resembled the limited model idealized by the GOP. "The people want restraints on the arrogance of power," he said, "because the people . . . want a nation with the strength to defend its vital interests and the wisdom to define them; because the people want leadership that has a heart but uses its head; because what . . . Republicans say . . . is not 'Trust me,' but 'Trust yourselves.'"[32]

Reaction was swift and positive. With shouts of "Baker" and "Ford-Baker" filling the arena, temporary chairman Bob Dole called Baker back for two curtain calls and quipped that "he may have a future in politics." Commentator Eric Sevareid labeled the address "the best effort of the evening," while the *Nashville Tennessean* editorialized that it "should place Baker at the top of Gerald Ford's pecking order." The next day, Nelson Rockefeller hosted a breakfast for Baker and said he "would do a great job at whatever job he undertook." Ford was impressed enough to watch the speech a second time and compliment Baker for a "damn good job," leading one Baker aide to boast that his boss was "the hottest thing in town."[33]

Such optimism was unwarranted. While Ford told Melvin Laird that Baker was the safe choice in a golf game the day before the convention opened, this was no boost for Baker when Ford trailed Carter 62–29. One House stalwart who hailed Baker for "a damn good job" made his statement regretfully, thinking circumstances demanded a bold choice. And muttering was heard from southerners who questioned the southernness of Tennessee's senior senator, even as Strom Thurmond was hosting a reception in his honor. After Bob Dole lobbied him on his own behalf, North Carolina chairman Bob Shaw passed the word that he was not high on Baker because of his pro–civil rights record and his role on the Ervin Committee. Clarke Reed added that many in Mississippi were angry that Baker had joined Bill Brock in blocking William Hooper, the husband of his state's Republican National Committeewoman, for a seat on the TVA Board of Directors, and that Baker had declined many invitations to address Mississippi GOP gatherings.[34]

Such talk disturbed some on the White House staff and encouraged others. After one of the unfavorably disposed leaked Baker's account of Joy's alcoholism, Ron McMahan was asked to comment. Putting his hand over the phone's receiver, he told Baker that the story was out. "Confirm it," Baker ordered, and the political community reacted in an almost uniformly understanding fashion. Many echoed a delegate who called the Bakers "an inspiration to any American who has ever fought the bottle." Winfield Dunn and Jimmy Quillen proclaimed their revulsion at a leak they saw as a shameful exploitation of a good woman's suffering to discredit her husband.[35] With the exception of an error-laden broadcast by Jack Anderson falsely accusing Joy of having been drunk when involved in a fender bender a few days earlier, further discussions of Baker's merits focused on his base of support and his qualities as a campaigner.

Counter to the prevalent view, Baker had but two advocates in Ford's inner circle. One was photographer David Hume Kennerly, whose judgment Ford respected. "If your Vice Presidential selection isn't a fresh face, someone of Howard Baker's caliber," Kennerly wrote Ford, "it will be a mistake." While he had listened to Kennerly on other matters, the president denied him a voice in the choice of the vice-president. Baker's other advocate was Robert Griffin, who characterized Baker's support as widespread as any remaining candidate's. But some Ford intimates took Griffin's advice as suspect, knowing Griffin saw Baker as his chief rival for the Senate GOP Leadership, which would become available in January.[36]

Ford had held three meetings before leaving for Kansas City, and the names of William Ruckelshaus, Dole, and Baker survived well. While some urged the choice of a flamboyant candidate like Ambassador to Great Britain Anne Armstrong, John Connally, Nelson Rockefeller, or Ronald Reagan, Reaganites bristled at Rockefeller's name and many industrial-belt delegates expressed equal shock when they heard Connally's. Reagan sent word that he would only appear with Ford if Ford would not offer him the nod. Minutes after being nominated, Ford went to Reagan's hotel, exchanged a few pleasantries, then stepped into Reagan's suite and inquired about Armstrong, Baker, Connally, Dole, Ruckelshaus, Commerce Secretary Elliott Richardson, and Treasury Secretary William Simon. After declaring Richardson unacceptable and that some of his followers might find drawbacks in Ruckelshaus, Reagan led Ford to believe he would accept Baker, but Dole would be excellent.[37]

Ford returned to his suite to meet with Rockefeller, Senators Griffin and Tower, aides Richard Cheney, Robert Hartmann, John Marsh, Stuart Spencer, and Robert Teeter and trusted friends Bryce Harlow and Melvin Laird. Before asking for ideas, Ford declared that his running mate needed to be qualified to assume the presidency, ideologically akin to him and acceptable to Reagan, thus ruling out Richardson. It was agreed that Connally and Simon could not shake images Ford knew would remain liabilities, leaving Armstrong, Baker, Dole, and Ruckelshaus. Tower and Spencer backed Armstrong, saying that her addition would transform the election. But Teeter's polls indicated that this coupling would lose more GOP votes than any other, even if it gained thousands of Democratic votes. Teeter's candidate and Rockefeller's was William Ruckelshaus, a Catholic they believed would help Ford among ethnics and remove some of the Nixon taint from Ford because of his role in the Saturday Night Massacre. Cheney and Harlow, who pushed for a conservative, held that Reaganites saw Ruckelshaus as the most liberal and might precipitate a floor fight. These arguments made sense to Ford, whose silence led some to think Ruckelshaus would be chosen. But Ford had used the group solely as a sounding board and had, in fact, ruled out Armstrong and Ruckelshaus.[38]

While neither Baker nor Dole had had an advocate, neither had any detractors, either. But Ford saw many supposed Baker strengths as weaknesses, fearing that Baker's selection or Ruckelshaus's might perpetuate Watergate memories rather than remove them. Dole, in contrast, had no connection with the scandal or the probe. Just as important, Ford believed that Baker's reputation as a skillful legislative leader projected the image of a compromiser, while choosing the slashing, sharp-witted Dole would convey the perception of a stronger ticket. Recognizing Dole's acerbic wit might on occasion sting the gums of his own ticket more sharply than the skin of Carter and Mondale, Ford still believed his partisanship would confer upon him a stronger image. And Ford liked Dole, whose persuasion of three colleagues to vote for him for the House GOP Leadership in 1965 he credited for his narrow victory. He and Baker, in contrast, had never been close. Ford's uncertainty grew as he took the Reed and Shaw messages to mean that Baker might not be terribly helpful in the South. Indeed, moderate Illinois Congressman John Anderson and others had advised him that Carter's strength was such that Ford should face up to losing Dixie and concentrate upon the Great Plains states, where many remained angry about his 1975 embargo upon grain shipments to the Soviets. Believing Dole more likely to convince farmers that there would not be another embargo than Baker, Ford phoned a few high-ranking northeastern liberals to test their reaction. A consensus among them that Dole was acceptable led Ford to finalize a close call for Dole and announce it three hours later.[39]

Sam Ervin, John Seigenthaler, and Herman Talmadge, to name three astute southern Democrats, have all argued that Ford beat himself with his choice. Even more tellingly, Walter Mondale believes that he and Jimmy Carter would have been defeated had Baker been his opposite rather than Dole.[40] While "if" theories of history cannot be proven, considerable evidence supports their conclusion, even if it is likely that Iowa would have switched from Ford's to Carter's column. Especially enigmatic is Ford's belief that circumstances demanded a running mate from the historically Republican farm belt. While cases can be made that Reagan or Ruckelshaus might have added more than Dole, a better one exists for Baker, as the ten Confederate states Carter carried supplied more than his victory margin in the popular vote and 118 of his electoral votes. Twenty-one more electoral votes came from Missouri and Kentucky, states bordering Tennessee. Save for Arkansas and Georgia, none of these states returned a large margin for Carter. Ford fell five or fewer points short of victory in Florida, Louisiana, Mississippi, Missouri, and Texas. Democratic Senate nominee Jim Sasser worried openly throughout the week that Baker's coattails would help Bill Brock, knowing Reagan and his followers would fall in line if Ford chose Baker. Reagan always fondly evoked Baker's hospitality in his primary swing as evidence of a considerate opponent, words seldom used in 1976 to describe Dole, whose references to "Democrat Wars" many saw as evidence of an unguided missile or a gutcutter.[41] With the issues Baker raised in his keynote about the powers of the federal government made to order for a moderately conservative southerner to use against Jimmy Carter and Walter Mondale, Ford's option for Dole may have cost him a full term as president.

Sobbing Tennessee delegates perceived this better than anyone. "Maybe we weren't praying just right," said John Duncan. When Baker arrived at their meeting, delegates greeted him with a five-minute standing ovation. Baker defended Dole, whom he commended for a very sharp tongue and a quick wit. Acknowledging the difficulty the ticket would have, he tried to assure delegates that there was time. Duncan and Jimmy Quillen added halfhearted statements for Dole. Robin Beard, a tough ex-Marine, tried to follow but could not. Bill Brock stood up, said a few words for the ticket, then commended his senior colleague and "a lovely, lovely lady who's been very, very courageous." The delegation rose and applauded for two minutes. Baker, stone-faced with tears rushing down his cheeks, joined them and worried that his wife feared that the publicity given to her had led Ford to choose Dole. "I'm sure Joy thinks that," he said, "but she doesn't think it very much and she handled it well today." Believing he had been done in by a few Ford advisors, he said he "got along within the state and country" but had "troubles with small groups." "If I ever again get involved in a Presidential race," he said, "I'll be in the driver's seat."[42]

Chapter 7

THE LEADER, AT LAST 1976–1977

Baker left Kansas City deeply discouraged. Never comfortable in denying that Ford's choice had wounded his pride, he still traversed the country from New York to Hawaii to speak and make television spots extolling the virtues of Ford and GOP Senate candidates. He did the brunt of his work in Tennessee, a state Ford strategists saw as "just plain . . . bad luck," fearing that traditionally Democratic born-again Baptists, whom they saw as the swing vote there, would opt for a southerner of the same mind-set. Baker urged Ford not to write off the South, as polls showed Carter's twenty-point lead had been cut to five. But Ford deemed only Texas and Virginia winnable and ignored Tennessee save for a jaunt down the Mississippi, a decision Baker knew would harm every GOP campaign in the state.[1]

When not at the United Nations, where he was serving a stint on the U.S. delegation to the General Assembly, Baker spent much of his time acting as honorary chairman of the reelection campaign of Bill Brock, whose seat was in jeopardy. "I knew once that [Dole] choice was made," said Shelby County GOP chairman Don Sundquist, "that we had lost Tennessee" and Brock's seat. Democrats put up virtually unknown state chairman Jim Sasser, who had ties to all Democratic constituencies and enemies in none. While Brock tried to link Sasser, a gravelly voiced Nashville attorney, to the "Blanton machine," his efforts were rendered futile by Sasser's attention to his tax records that showed that he, albeit legally, had paid very little in federal taxes in 1975. The result was disastrous for the state GOP. Ford managed but 43 percent of the vote, a showing sealing the fates of Brock and six GOP members of the Tennessee General Assembly. Even in the most Republican areas, Carter's appeal was irresistible. Ford managed only 50.3 percent in the Second District, and Brock carried it with but 56.7 percent, far below his 1970 total.[2]

The Third Time the Charm

The Democratic sweep led Baker to consider running for governor in 1978. Viewing that race as the best way to rekindle enthusiasm among GOP workers, he believed the State House a better platform for a presidential bid as it would allow him to avoid positions on many no-win issues and give him more time for a national race. Defeating Ray Blanton, the first incumbent allowed to run for a second consecutive four-year term, would be even easier than winning the Senate race the two had contested in 1972 in view of Blanton's steadily deteriorating popularity and the growing number of investigations into his affairs. A win would strengthen his image as a conservative reformer and thus enhance his chances of winning the presidency. Never deeming a governor's work as challenging as a senator's, he was sidetracked by the opening in the GOP Leadership left by Hugh Scott's retirement, which offered him visibility as a national party spokesman. As onetime Scott supporters like Charles "Mac" Mathias and Edward Brooke had gone to Bob Packwood, who had managed his earlier campaigns, and said that "we assume Howard's going to run . . . and we want to be with you," Baker saw his chances as better than even and started telling colleagues of his interest the day after the election.[3]

Several other GOP senators were also contemplating bids. The favorite was Minority Whip Robert Griffin, who would have been unopposed had Ford won. But Carter's election caused more articulate Republicans to believe that they might make better spokesmen. Reports appeared that Bob Dole and John Tower were entertaining bids, but neither challenge materialized. Barry Goldwater withdrew after finding he would get fourteen votes at most. These developments led Griffin to feel certain of the support of many with whom he had worked. In truth, it was difficult for Griffin to prepare. Ignoring Hugh Scott's advice to make a complete tour, he found it hard to guess what to expect. Baker, while uncomfortable with pushing anyone, even close friends, had firm pledges of support from liberals Brooke, Mathias, and Richard Schweiker, moderate Packwood, and conservatives Dewey Bartlett and Pete Domenici, all of whom were lobbying diligently for him. On Christmas, he learned from Malcolm Wallop that the eight GOP newcomers would stay uncommitted until January 3, news that buoyed him, as he had heard that Griffin expected the votes of all eight. Having seen a list of Griffin's expected votes that included five of the first six senators who had promised him their support, he grew more confident but declined to declare his availability, fearing a third loss might irreparably foil his presidential bid.[4]

Baker's silence was seen as noninterest. New GOP senators did not invite him to their January 3 breakfast for those seeking leadership positions. But freshman Harrison "Jack" Schmitt phoned fellow New Mexican Pete Domenici that morning and told him the meeting was proceeding. Domenici called Baker at home and told him that he wanted to see him in his office. Domenici was on the phone with Schmitt when Baker arrived. "You just have to go over there," Domenici pleaded, "and you can't just go there and say if I run I want you to know what I'm like if you decide to vote for me." Baker rushed to the Capitol and entered the meeting midway through Griffin's speech. When invited to follow, he gave a talk and answered questions. Many wanted to know if he planned to use the job as a springboard to the presidency. Not denying his ambition, he declared his primary goal as strengthening a badly weakened party, a response prompting three freshmen to pledge their support within an hour. By midnight, he was certain of sixteen votes.[5]

Baker went to work on January 4 uncertain if he would run. With Charles Percy away, he was three shy of a majority. "I don't have the votes," he told Domenici, Packwood, Mathias, and Hugh Branson, and he contemplated withdrawing. "You can't do that," Packwood responded. "Bob probably doesn't have the votes either." With Packwood's tally showing six members undecided, Baker agreed not to make up his mind until he reached the Caucus Room. When he arrived, John Chafee pledged his support. Seconds later, Baker bumped into Griffin. "Bob," he said, "I've got seventeen votes and I don't know what the hell to do." "Well," Griffin replied nervously, "good luck if you win."[6]

Seeing anguish and terror in Griffin's eyes, Baker signaled Mathias to nominate him. He moved to the back and eyed Edward Brooke, who would count the ballots. His mood brightened when uncommitteds Clifford Case and Lowell Weicker entered a half hour late and smiled at Ron McMahan, his press secretary. But experience led him to remain nervous even when he saw Brooke nodding at him with bright eyes. Only upon uttering "Baker, nineteen; Griffin, eighteen" did Brooke flash a telling grin. Tension remained until the characteristically magnanimous Griffin walked over, shook Baker's hand and popped open the case of champagne he had brought to celebrate his own victory.[7]

"It could just as easily gone the other way," Baker conceded. Few had any complaint with Griffin, whose tactical astuteness was invaluable on the floor. Others, from Mark Hatfield on the left to Orrin Hatch on the right, opted for him, guessing correctly that he might be in electoral jeopardy if not elected. But six of eight freshmen, a majority of the progressive Wednesday Group, and a few conservatives like Carl Curtis found Griffin's parliamentary skills a far less necessary quality in their Leader at a time when they held but thirty-eight of one hundred seats than an eloquent voice who could give their party a youthful, dynamic image. What GOP senators had done, wrote Pat Buchanan, was elect a "spokesman more articulate than Jimmy Carter," a view shared by Jack Germond, who commended them for their maturity in opting for the "cheerleader with the dimples" over the "diligent secretary of the Glee Club."[8]

Almost immediately, Baker initiated a series of strategies with Whip Ted Stevens and Policy Committee Chairman John Tower to mold their thirty-eight members into a solid counterforce. Mindful that GOP interests would not be served by either blind negativism or me-tooism, they aimed to present attractive alternatives to Carter programs. While Gerald Ford had followed the same strategy in the House, neither Ford nor any other minority leader ever assembled as cohesive a bloc as the one Baker forged in 1977. Like Ford, Baker created task forces to shape party programs and named to each an amenable group of members from all shades of GOP opinion. Members of the two principal task forces produced bills reflecting the free-market principles of the party at large, which the caucus agreed virtually unanimously to recommend. The economic centerpiece was a permanent tax cut of 4 to 14 percent for families making less than $18,000 per year that members preferred to Carter's one-time $50 rebate, which would be matched by incentives to businesses to catalyze job creation and training, savings, and investment. The energy program accelerated Carter's schedule for deregulating oil and natural gas prices, with the aims of spurring oil production for more fuel and reducing America's dependence on foreign energy. While neither plan received much attention, the presence of alternatives rallied members and served as blueprints for programs that GOP candidates would develop and articulate in 1978 and 1980.[9]

While Senate Republicans had become more united following a 1975 debate over whom to seat in a contested senatorial race in New Hampshire, Baker forged an even more solid bloc. He maintained close contact with each of his colleagues and encouraged all to come to him with their concerns. Knowing where each senator was likely to come down on any issue, the political standing of each and the projects they deemed important, he could determine which members were persuadable and how to negotiate. Unavailable were the arm-twisting tactics of Lyndon Johnson, which had reached the point of diminishing returns by the time Johnson left the Senate. Accustomed to Hugh Scott's low-key style, GOP senators, said Ted Stevens, "wouldn't take too well to being told what to do." But scare tactics ran counter to Baker's preference for a mixture of persuasion, flattery, and appeals to party loyalty anyway. Those up for reelection remembered his vow to campaign for them. Others appreciated his attention to their concerns in discussions with Majority Leader Robert Byrd about the Senate schedule. When members believed that Byrd overstepped the bounds of fair play, they reciprocated by giving Baker their votes on procedural matters even if they agreed with Byrd on substance.[10] As Republicans held two less votes than the sixty needed to block cloture, his influence appeared limited. But with a united front and a few defections, he could tie up any measure Democrats deemed important. While Baker used this option sparingly, the degree of unity within his caucus gave him substantial leverage.

Having pledged to consult often with Gerald Ford, Ronald Reagan, and Nelson Rockefeller and incorporate their ideas for a course of opposition, Baker met with each whenever they traveled to Washington or he ventured into their home states.

He especially urged Ford to remain active, issuing this advice most forcefully after Carter aides blasted the former president in April 1977 for criticizing their boss's airing of Soviet human rights violations before Secretary of State Cyrus Vance presented an arms control package to the Soviets. Baker also encouraged Reagan, whom he saw less often, and took pride in noting that Reagan now agreed that the GOP had to devise new appeals to Democrats and independents. Rockefeller, who had championed that idea for twenty years, met with Baker less frequently, but his legacy remained through a host of protégés. While Henry Kissinger was Baker's most prominent occasional consultant with Rockefeller ties, the most proximate was James Cannon, whom he hired as his administrative assistant.[11]

Baker's efforts were matched by House counterpart John J. Rhodes, a pragmatic conservative from Arizona and new Republican National Committee Chairman Bill Brock, who combined a soft-spoken enthusiasm and genius for organizational innovation with a reverence for the free-market system. Brock supplemented policy-oriented panels with a series of committees having the long-range goal of devising new appeals to groups long regarded as part of the Democratic coalition. When the networks gave the GOP time to respond to Carter's addresses, Brock would discuss the implications and GOP alternatives with a freshman Republican Baker would recommend. Appearances with Baker and Rhodes, all agreed, would be held only when the three wanted to give particular emphasis to their statements, thus limiting descriptions of the GOP as an establishment-dominated party and of such meetings as second-rate reruns of the "Ev [Dirksen] and Charley [Halleck]" shows of the 1960s.[12]

Early Dealings with Jimmy Carter

Carter's relationship with Baker was distant at first. While Baker quips that he got off to a bad start with Carter because Carter remembered their first meeting and he did not, Carter heeded the counsel of Thomas P. "Tip" O'Neill, the robust, white-maned Speaker from Boston, to rely upon the advice and votes of members of his own party. But Carter, determined to be a "peoples' president," rankled congressional Democrats, almost all of whom had been elected by larger margins than he, by relying upon pollster Pat Caddell and public relations guru Gerald Rafshoon, who they feared might blur his image with imprints of gimmicks. Many blamed Carter's "Georgia Mafia," whom they deemed arrogant and unavailable. A rift was apparent when patronage became an issue in 1977, one Baker believed stemmed from Carter's difficulty in getting out of his candidate's role and into the president's role.[13]

A warning signal of problems Carter would have came when he chose Ted Sorenson, a top aide to John F. Kennedy, to head the CIA, instead of sitting director George Bush, whom many in both parties backed, or Lieutenant General James Gavin, the dovish hero of D-Day, whom O'Neill supported. With Sorenson, who had little experience in intelligence, having requested conscientious objector status during World War II, advocated declassifying secret documents, and worked for a law firm that represented several countries with less than ideal human rights practices, Baker joined Republicans Goldwater, Thurmond, and Garn and Democrats Biden, Huddleston, and Morgan on the Intelligence Committee in opposing Sorenson. With Chairman Daniel Inouye, Baker let Carter know that Sorenson could expect at most five of fourteen votes, thus leading Sorenson to withdraw on the first day of hearings.[14]

"Nobody declared war on Carter," Baker said, assuming that the choice was a newcomer's mistake, but the anti-Sorenson sentiment signaled that the Senate would carefully scrutinize each nominee to a key foreign policy-making position. Democrats were divided on foreign affairs. One group, led by Henry "Scoop" Jackson, alarmed by the Soviet buildup and the adventurism of its surrogates, urged a substantial increase in U.S. conventional and nuclear forces. The other school, exemplified by George McGovern, saw attention to the Soviet rearming as irrelevant to the more serious problem of preventing nuclear war. While Carter placated both groups by choosing centrists Cyrus Vance, Harold Brown, and Zbigniew Brzezinski to head the Departments of State and Defense and the National Security Council, his choice of Paul Warnke to serve as both chief negotiator at the Strategic Arms Limitation Talks (SALT) and director of the Arms Control and Disarmament Agency prompted a fear that he had opted for the McGovern line, as Warnke had opposed the B-1 bomber, the Trident submarine, the mobile Inter Continental Ballistic Missile (ICBM), and the XM tank, and called for sharp cutbacks in U.S. tactical nuclear weapons in West Germany.[15]

While some, like Paul Nitze, a hawkish arms control negotiator who had served every president since Truman and was motivated largely by jealousy, believed Warnke should not be part of the administration in any capacity, Baker focused upon his dual role as head negotiator and ACDA head. Prepared to vote for Warnke to head the agency, he believed that the controversy rendered negligible Warnke's effectiveness as a negotiator. While only two Republicans opposed either Warnke nomination in the Foreign Relations Committee, much dissent emerged from the Armed Services Committee. Carter took the votes to label Warnke's detractors as those opposing any new agreement, but his statement flies in the face of the fact that only two senators opposed the original SALT Treaty, but forty voted against Warnke.[16] While Carter's SALT-related meetings with Warnke's most influential critics—Republicans Baker, Griffin, and Tower and Democrats Jackson, Daniel Patrick Moynihan, Sam Nunn, and John Stennis—grew more frequent, seldom did he incorporate their suggestions into his bargaining position.

Even so, Baker found some redeeming features in Carter, quipping that he "had to like" it that Carter "didn't have an accent." More important was their agreement on a strip-mining bill Baker had long sponsored and GOP presidents had heretofore foiled. Baker was less enthusiastic about Carter's aim to consolidate many agencies in a Department of Energy. Happy that the plan eliminated some overlapping, he rued that it removed autonomy from the Federal Power Commission and feared that it, with an initial $10 billion budget, had a potential for great mischief. While backing an unsuccessful measure requiring Congress to approve each of its regulations, he reluctantly voted to establish the department.[17]

In contrast, Baker was incensed to learn that a demonstration plant for gas centrifuge technology would be located at Portsmouth, Ohio, and not Oak Ridge, where the technology was developed, so Carter could keep a vow to the people of Ohio. As estimates indicated that the project would cost hundreds of millions less at Oak Ridge, Baker termed the decision a "reckless use of taxpayers' money" and joined James Sasser and Clifford Hansen in calling for a GAO investigation. Baker and Sasser were more successful in delaying Carter's plan to terminate the Clinch River breeder reactor, which Carter hoped would prompt other countries to stem a tide toward nuclear proliferation. Characterizing Carter's reasoning as most noble, Baker found no evidence that his intentions would come to fruition. As five European nations had formed a consortium to keep open a market for plutonium, Carter's decision effectively removed a U.S. check upon nuclear proliferation and potentially allowed foreign producers to use their fuel as blackmail. As GAO and Senate attorneys maintained that Carter could not end the project without congressional approval, Clinch was safe for a time, and Baker got the Senate to ban Carter from acting indirectly to end the program. With the Senate opting to provide half the original amount, thus allowing construction to continue while it studied Carter's ideas, an impasse developed.[18] But a delay portended trouble, as cost overruns and inflation emboldened those who believed Clinch too expensive. At the time, the debacle was just another symbol of a perception that Carter's working relationship with Congress was less than harmonious.

If there was a campaign promise that rung home with the people but flummoxed congressional veterans, it was Carter's pledge to make the U.S. government "as good and decent as the American people." When Carter appointees came under fire for less than simon-pure practices, it was Baker's practice not to moralize, but to lament a double standard. Characteristic was his response to news that prosecutors were investigating several House members, most of them Democrats, for accepting bribes and campaign contributions from South Korean financier Tongsun Park. "Simple fairness," he said in a press conference with John Rhodes, "says . . . Democrats ought to be willing to investigate this situation . . . as . . . Republicans were willing to investigate Watergate." He responded likewise upon learning of allegations of improprieties against Office of Management and Budget Director Bert Lance. Not personally critical of Lance, Baker guessed that "they would have hung him from a lamp post" were he a Republican. Lance's biggest problem was his boss's moral posturing. "A man who holds himself out as a paragon of virtue," he noted, "always suffers when something goes wrong." Lance's eventual resignation from his OMB post, Baker felt, was a lesson to Carter to "not moralize so much."[19]

Baker took a harder line when he feared Carter's commitments might lead to bad policy. Particularly abhorrent to him was Carter's cargo preference bill tripling the amount of foreign oil being imported in ships flying the American flag. Long demanded by maritime unions, it was opposed by Treasury Secretary Michael Blumenthal, who figured it would cost consumers $800 million a year by 1985. While other guesses limited costs to between $110 and $240 million per annum, Baker termed the bill a blatant political payoff that helped no one but a few unions. While a House panel dominated by members loyal to maritime interests approved the measure 31–6, members outside that panel examined the overall impact. Two hundred fifty-six joined Rhodes, convincing Senate Democrats not to bring the bill to the floor.[20]

Baker was pleased that he would not have to lead his forces against the measure, as adding such a matter would delay more important business and sharpen tensions. He had fought a similar battle when Carter tried to extend public financing to Senate elections. Believing "public financing diminishes the chances we can throw the rascals out" and "threatens the extinction of the Republican Party," he decried "incumbent protection" and another step towards making the Senate a "full-time bureaucratic institution." Assessing his determination, Robert Byrd filed a cloture petition the next day, alarming Republicans who recalled predecessors waiting a week. With Carter phoning colleagues to urge the adoption not of the bill, but of the cloture resolution, even advocates of public financing like Jacob Javits labeled such tactics a "Democratic attempt to roll over . . . Republicans with raw power" and joined all but two Republicans in voting with Baker and Hatfield. Byrd was thus left eleven votes short of the sixty needed to close debate. Javits, having promised to support the final cloture bid, repeatedly asked if the next cloture move was it. Not getting an answer, he and six other pro public financing Republicans voted with Baker, thus rendering certain that Byrd would not muster the requisite sixty votes.[21]

To Baker, the action was significant, as a bad bill had not become law. To Common Cause vice-president Fred Wertheimer, the chief lesson was that Republican moderates had been broken. Indeed, the episode served notice that Republicans would unite whenever Democrats engaged in practices they believed tore away at their rights. To be sure, such debates were relatively few. Baker and Byrd, a fiddle-playing West Virginia moderate with slicked-back gray hair, tried to ensure that partisan squabbling did not render the Senate's work impossible by meeting several times each day the Senate was in session to devise arrangements to conduct business and initiating a ritual handshake on the floor to open each day. Neither man being one to ignore tradition or overlook a potential ally, each saw the other as a formidable opponent who could be a valuable partner on relatively nonpartisan matters.[22]

Early Attention to Carter Energy and Arms Policy

Baker adopted a relatively detached view toward Carter's domestic centerpiece, his energy bill. While voting with Carter to stimulate coal use, reform utility rates, and give tax breaks to those conserving energy, Baker allied with Lloyd Bentsen and James Pearson on a substitute to Carter's plan to phase out controls on the price of natural gas produced in the United States or off its coast. While only seventeen senators voted against cloture, liberals James Abourezk and Howard Metzenbaum perfected a new obstructive tactic, the postcloture filibuster. Forbidden to speak for more than an hour, the two introduced more than five hundred amendments, forcing senators to sleep on cots off the floor for days so they could answer quorum calls. While Baker and Byrd agreed they would have to break the filibuster, they, lacking a precedent, could not agree how. Byrd wanted to suspend the rules. Baker resisted, fearing "Democrats might get to liking it," and deliberated with Byrd until they found a solution in a rare Sunday session. With Rule XXII prohibiting dilatory motions, the two opted to use their right of preferential recognition. Baker needed one concession. "If we're going to do this," he told Byrd, "you have that Vice President in the chair" so Carter would share in the blame. Walter Mondale assumed his chair the next day and recognized Baker, who said that an amendment that was ruled out of order was no longer the business of the Senate. Mondale agreed and recognized Byrd, who began a litany, whereby Mondale ruled each of the addenda out of order. While the tactics aroused concern, most recognized that unusual means were necessary. Once such matters were settled, the Senate approved the substitute.[23]

While the Senate version completely removed price controls, the House bill merely phased them out. A compromise might have been reached under normal circumstances, but neither side was certain what Carter would accept. While his original proposal gradually phased out controls, he had supported complete deregulation in his campaign and delighted in telling low- and middle-income voters that the natural gas companies were nearly omnipotent. His stand encouraged Abourezk and Metzenbaum but annoyed potential allies. If Carter "could address himself to the real issues, we could get a grip on it," Baker said. "Instead he set up . . . the strawman of a rip-off by oil and gas companies." While conferees agreed on all measures but the natural gas bill by December, House negotiators, at Carter's behest, would not accept the three bills save as part of a comprehensive package.[24]

While monitoring energy policy, foreign and defense matters became Baker's priority no later than June 1977 when Carter announced a reduction in U.S. troop levels in South Korea. Appalled, Baker berated Carter for not consulting America's Pacific allies or any member of Congress. Japanese and South Korean leaders reacted angrily, as did General John Singlaub, the American commander on the peninsula. Once George McGovern moved for the Senate to back Carter's policy, Baker rallied sufficient bipartisan support to cause Robert Byrd to draft a substitute measure declaring Congress a partner in formulating policy toward South Korea. As Byrd's plan implied a criticism of Carter but avoided a clear test, fifteen GOP conservatives voted no. Baker, however, joined twenty other Republicans in supporting Byrd. Merely drafting his measure had made his point, and he saw no reason to press the matter further, as the outcome seemed to imply a larger Republican role in making foreign policy in the near future.[25]

Just as uneasy about Carter's slowness in cementing relationships that his predecessors had built in troubled areas of the world, Baker came to fear that foreign governments would have to rely upon press dispatches, as they did when a June 1977 State Department paper termed peace impossible in the Middle East without Israeli concessions. Terming it "an astonishing example of diplomacy by publicity," Baker saw the timing as unfortunate, as new Israeli Prime Minister Menachem Begin was to meet Carter for the first time three weeks later. He likewise expressed outrage in November at a Carter plan to reconvene the Geneva Conference, fearing it recklessly reinvolved the Soviets. Warning that Carter was playing "Russian roulette" with Israel's security, he said he did "not want to see the United States . . . ever try to buy peace by sacrificing Israel on the altar of American policy."[26]

While Baker's warning was unnecessary because an impatient Egyptian President Anwar Sadat accepted Begin's invitation to fly to Jerusalem to begin the peace process, Carter's invitation to the Soviets so bothered him that he came to fear that Carter, in his desire to complete a SALT-II Treaty, might be giving away the store. Troubled by Carter's decision to halt construction of the B-1 bomber, seeing it as a needed replacement for an obsolete fleet of B-52s, he thought Carter might be overrelying upon the cruise missile as the airborne leg of the strategic triad. Unbeknownst to most, the Defense Department was developing a stealth bomber that, unlike the B-1, could escape radar. But the lack of an identifiable alternative meant that the B-1 would appeal to defense-minded members of Congress and a few liberals whose constituents it employed. Baker was queasy that Carter's decision was meant to induce the Soviets to conclude a SALT-II pact. If so, he found Carter's logic faulty, for if the B-1 were as worthless as its detractors claimed, it still could serve as a bargaining chip to force the Soviets to suspend one of their systems. While Baker had backed Carter's earliest attempts to reach an accord, he grew less certain that the pact would be equitable and began to study the terms of the treaty and their consequences. Before 1977 ended, he retained hardliner Fred Ikle and arms-control advocate Alton Frye to advise him and made it known that he had hired Frye to "know what the other folks are thinking."[27] While reserving judgment, Baker hoped that a SALT-II debate would provide an opportunity for a wide-ranging debate on the full scope of U.S.-Soviet relations, a debate that never occurred.

In fact, some of the other folks were already concerned that Carter had not exerted a bit of the capital available to him at the outset of his administration in trying to reach a SALT-II accord. While applauding moves like the B-1 cutoff that seemed to limit arms, many Republicans and Democrats alike came to regret both the lack of reciprocal Soviet moves and the symbol of retreat by the leader of the Free World. Here was the crux of the debate that Baker sought but never got, albeit it was hardly for his lack of trying. Unfortunately for him, the foreign policy debate that engulfed the nation in late 1977 and early 1978 was not one over an issue that, if handled badly, might, as Russell Long said, "cost our lives and our very freedoms." Instead, what ensued concerned a far more powerful image that signified to the Third World what Tennessee GOP chairman Tom Beasley called "the nearest purest colonialistic experience that this country had had" and evoked to Baker's usual allies the most vivid symbol of an America in retreat in the face of the most accelerated arms buildup in history.[28]

Baker at age eight with sister, Mary.

Lieutenant Howard H. Baker Jr., c. 1945–46.

Howard and Joy Baker on their wedding day, 1951.

Howard, Joy, and Darek Baker visiting Congressman Howard Baker Sr.

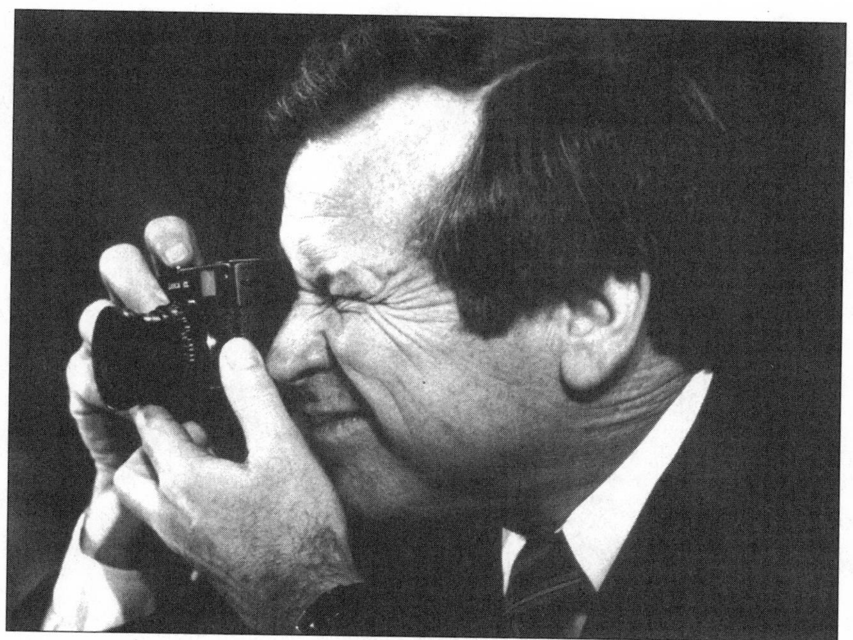

Baker at play. *National Journal* photo by Rick Bloom, courtesy of Howard H. Baker Jr.

Reenactment of Baker being sworn in as senator by Vice-President Hubert Humphrey as Mike Mansfield and Everett Dirksen look on, 1967.

Richard Nixon with Baker at Independence Hall, Philadelphia, after signing the bill creating a revenue-sharing program. White House photo, courtesy of Howard H. Baker Jr., 1972.

Darek, Joy, Howard, and Cissy on the *Rose Bud* in the final days of the 1978 campaign.

Baker flanked by colleagues, 1978. *Clockwise,* Malcolm Wallop, Richard Lugar, Bob Dole, Jesse Helms, John Tower, S. I. Hayakawa, and Orrin Hatch.

Baker announcing his candidacy for president, flanked by Karyn, Darek, Joy, and his stepmother, Irene Baker, November 1, 1979.

Ronald and Nancy Reagan visit Baker's hometown, Huntsville, Tennessee, 1982.

The Reagan National Security Team—Reagan, George Shultz, Colin Powell, and Baker, 1982. White House Photo, courtesy of Howard H. Baker Jr.

"My work is done": Baker congratulating successor Kenneth Duberstein as President Reagan looks on, June 1988. White House photo, courtesy of Howard H. Baker Jr.

Baker and his grandmother and heroine, Lillie Ladd Mauser, the first woman sheriff in Tennessee, on her one-hundredth birthday, 1979.

Baker took this picture of President Jimmy Carter and predecessors Gerald Ford and Richard Nixon at a reception he held in his Capitol office in January 1978 prior to memorial services for Hubert Humphrey.

Howard and Nancy Kassebaum Baker, 1996. Photograph by John Rice Irwin.

CHAPTER 8

A PROFILE IN COURAGE, VANDENBERG STYLE 1977–1978

"Your representative owes you not his industry only, but his judgment," the oft-quoted British conservative Edmund Burke declared in 1774, "and he betrays, instead of serving you, if he sacrifices it to your opinion." Virtually every senator of national stature over the course of American history has had to face an issue where he has had to put his view of the national interest ahead of myopic demands from vocal partisan or constituent groups that have long supported him. Growing calls for disunion led Henry Clay and Daniel Webster to proffer the Compromise of 1850 and thus preserve the union for ten years over the objections of fire-eating southerners and abolitionist northerners. Aiming to stimulate trade and employment across America, John F. Kennedy backed Dwight D. Eisenhower's plan to build a St. Lawrence Seaway over the howls of constituents in Massachusetts ports. Simple egalitarianism compelled Lyndon Johnson in 1957 to abandon an alliance with segregationists and lead the first of many fights to guarantee basic rights to black Americans. Not one, but three such emotion-laden issues faced Baker in 1977 and 1978. To be sure, Carter proposals to sell jets to Egypt and Saudi Arabia and restore military aid to Turkey aroused fervor only among committed but well-financed and vocal ethnic blocs. But treaties long in negotiation with Panama reverting control of the Panama Canal Zone to the country that retained sovereignty over that ten-mile-wide strip provoked a vehement reaction from committed American nationalists. Three generations of American students had grown up scanning history texts featuring, as Richard Scammon noted, "an American flag, a snapshot of Teddy Roosevelt and an image of gallant engineers overcoming the mosquito." It was hardly true that most Americans were acquainted with the nuances of U.S. policy in Panama. "Eighty percent of Americans agree . . . that we must keep the canal," a Zone official joked in 1976. "Unfortunately, half of those . . . are not sure where the Panama Canal is." But rooted within this ignorance was a sense that to conservative activist David Keene it "said more about the . . . people's feelings about where the country was . . . and their frustration about the incomprehensibility of foreign policy over the last couple of decades."[1]

A Stalwart's Perspective on Foreign Policy

It was not lost upon Baker that many of the disillusioned nationalists identified with his party and that this issue encapsulated their anxieties more clearly than any other in recent memory. "You can doubt their judgment," he had often said, "but you better never doubt their authority." While the numbers of the irate were never as large as right-wing leaders liked to claim, they did provide much of the activist core of the GOP, and their wrath could be politically fatal to anyone who took them too lightly. "Conservatives can't elect you to anything," one conservative former senator told the author, "but they sure as hell can lick you." While Baker's voting record can only be termed conservative, he was a conciliator, preferring to dispense with issues rather than create them. And often, "it is . . . the compromisers and conciliators," John F. Kennedy wrote, "who are faced with the severest tests of political courage as they oppose the extremist views of their constituents."[2]

Immediately, Baker saw merits in positions of both the proponents and opponents of the treaties. But his instincts were not those of the group A. James Reichley calls fundamentalist Republicans. Rather, he identified with the fiscally conservative small businessmen and socially conservative mountain Republicans of his native East Tennessee, the primary cogs in his state's strand of stalwart Republicanism.

Since 1945, stalwart Republicans had generally followed the path laid by one-time isolationist Arthur Vandenberg, who asserted in breaking from former America First allies that "our oceans have ceased to be moats which automatically protect our ramparts." The father of the bipartisan foreign policy, Vandenberg helped the Roosevelt and Truman administrations to create the United Nations, long the bane of isolationists, and was indispensable in 1947 and 1948 when Republicans held the majority in the Senate in securing enough GOP votes to approve the Marshall Plan for the economic recovery of Europe and extend economic and military aid to Greek and Turkish governments then fighting to stave off leftist threats to their existence. While Vandenberg warned Democrats that he would not help with "crash landings unless I'm in on the takeoff," he, once involved, would return to the GOP caucus and the Foreign Relations Committee to brief the wary, listen to their concerns, and then kill them with kindness by seeing that amendments they forwarded that did not gut the substance of Truman-Vandenberg initiatives were approved. This way, both sides benefited politically and a process was set in motion that resulted in a bipartisan consensus to contain Soviet expansionism that lasted until George Bush declared the Cold War over in 1990.[3]

The stalwart leader whose example Baker was most familiar with was Everett Dirksen, who had proven steadfastly loyal to John Kennedy during the Cuban Missile Crisis if more reluctantly so on the Nuclear Test Ban Treaty, as well as an unbending supporter of Lyndon Johnson's handling of the Vietnam War. It thus came naturally to Baker to tell Jimmy Carter in early August 1977 that he "owed any President . . . who asked me to consider an important foreign policy matter . . . the obligation to consider it." Here was a posture at odds with his long-held visceral sympathies with opponents of any change in the existing relationship with Panama. He had taken the Senate floor in 1967 to praise a retired general for asserting that any cession of sovereignty to Panama would bolster Communist aims in the Caribbean. Six years later, he signed a petition criticizing a set of principles developed by Henry Kissinger and a Panamanian counterpart for a new treaty. But his perspective changed after Ronald Reagan raised the issue in 1976 and he remembered that each president since Eisenhower had wanted to revise the relationship. When negotiators Ellsworth Bunker, a tough-minded career diplomat, and Sol Linowitz, a former ambassador to the Organization of American States, told him a new treaty was likely, Baker asked to be kept posted. While Carter was encouraged, Baker also vowed not to expedite Senate consideration. Remembering with Spark Matsunaga that "the first concern of every senator is to get elected and the second is to get reelected," he told Carter he needed to educate the American people before the Senate would even contemplate such a move, as an August poll showed 78 percent did not want to give up the canal, while only 8 percent favored the idea.[4]

Indeed, preliminary discussion of the Panama Canal Treaties, the historian Walter LaFeber wrote, was "shaped more by gut feeling than by historical knowledge." This was implicit from the question, for the phrase "give up" was fundamentally inconsistent with the 1903 Hay-Bunau-Varilla Treaty, which gave America the right to build the canal and exert "the rights, power and authority within the zone . . . it would possess and exercise if it were the sovereign." Panama owned the land, a fact established in *The Truth about the Panama Canal*, the most cogent contemporary monograph about the treaties by no less a conservative than Denison Kitchel, Barry Goldwater's 1964 campaign manager. But more conservatives were convinced by rhetoric like Reagan's statement that the Zone was "sovereign United States territory just the same as Alaska is," and thinking patterns seemed immobile. While no one had gone so far lately, Democratic Congressman Daniel Flood had threatened in 1960 to initiate impeachment proceedings against Dwight D. Eisenhower because he ordered officials to fly both the American and Panamanian flags everywhere in the Zone.[5]

The importance of the canal in the Panamanian consciousness took on a new complexion after 1964 when violence resulted in twenty-eight deaths. Coupled with Panama's resentment of an imperialist mentality among Zonians that led some who had not been to Panama in twenty years to be proud of it was a dearth of training programs for Panamanians aspiring to high-wage positions, and a preference for Americans in the two-thirds of the positions in the Zone that did not require skilled labor. Skillfully manipulating such resentment was Panama's "Maximum Chief," Omar Torrijos-Herrera, who came to power in a 1968 coup. A product of the National Guard, the debonair Torrijos posed as a champion of the peasantry with an extensive program of land reform coupled with generous funding for schools, housing, water systems, roads, and health centers in impoverished rural Panama. But backing from the urban poor and students came harder, as Panama's economy was festering. To placate leftists, the anticommunist Torrijos emulated the style of Fidel Castro, even to the point of chain-smoking cigars while limiting his contact with Castro to occasions when he could use Castro's apparent friendship to quell discontent. In fact, many Panamanian leftists lost their jobs and more than a few lost their lives, tendencies that became known when the UN Security Council met in Panama in 1973 and Torrijos assigned a Hungarian participant in the 1956 uprising to the Soviet delegation as its interpreter. More vividly than any Panamanian, Torrijos knew how to exploit Panama's classic alibi—America controlled its most valuable resource and deprived it of money and jobs. If anti-government sentiment was transformed into a crusade to take the Zone, a mob might form that Torrijos could smash or lead, and he vowed never to smash it.[6]

Torrijos's warning coincided with an increase in anti-American sentiment in Latin America. Disturbed by reports of CIA plots, Latin heads of state wanted signals that the United States saw them as equals. By 1973, Torrijos had them behind the idea that the requisite gesture should be a U.S. acceptance of Panama's negotiating position. Prompted to reassess America's role, Richard Nixon found that the canal's geopolitical importance was diminishing. Built before the day of the aircraft carrier and the supertanker, it could not accommodate ships with cargoes of more than 65,000 long tons. While submarines had to resurface before passing through, producers had to transport their wares around Cape Horn. Only 17 percent of U.S. oceangoing commerce and 3 percent of U.S. intercoastal trade passed through the canal by 1977. As the canal's strategic value was receding, it had begun operating at a deficit, but remained important, if less so than in the past, as it continued to service many support and supply ships.[7] Like each postwar president, Nixon concluded that America's interest lay in the use of the canal, not its operation. He would negotiate on the basis of his answers to the questions of the best means to guarantee that the canal remained open and how best to defend it.

America, it was agreed in February 1974, would retain its rights to operate and defend the canal during the transition, but Panama's role and share of the toll revenues would increase gradually until the termination date, when it would assume full responsibility. Panama, moreover, refused to allow any American presence after 2003, the centennial of its independence. Enough support arose to block a move to ban further spending for negotiations in 1975, but Ronald Reagan's exploitation of the canal issue caused Gerald Ford and Jimmy Carter to forgo the question for the duration of 1976.[8]

Opponents of revision thus won the initial upper hand. In the forefront of the respectable opposition were groups and individuals with ties to Americans in the Zone. Many in the military lobbied against the treaty within groups like the American Legion and the VFW. Some wanted to keep the headquarters of the U.S. Southern Command in the Zone, an oft-ridiculed aim as the Southern Command was notoriously top-heavy in brass and deficient in firepower. Others, such as veteran *New York Times* military analyst Hanson W. Baldwin, believed that transferring control was "evidence that the United States is a paper tiger" and would "encourage penny dictators and minor aggressions everywhere." But some conservatives such as William F. Buckley had concluded that America should "get out—while the initiative is . . . ours. That is the way great nations should act." Agreeing completely, Jimmy Carter announced in August 1977 that America had agreed to two accords with Panama. A Neutrality Treaty stipulated that Panama would manage the canal and ensure that it remained secure and open to peaceful transit by the vessels of all nations. While allowing the U.S. to help Panama defend the canal from external threats, it gave Panama alone the right to maintain defense installations after 2000 and U.S. warships the right to cross the canal expeditiously in wartime. The Panama Canal Treaty extended until 2000, save for a provision letting U.S. workers keep their jobs until they opted to leave. Until then, America would be the primary operator and defender of the canal. But the Zone would begin to be integrated into Panama thirty months after the treaty entered into force, with a new Panama Canal Commission paying Panama $20 million a year for salaries and maintenance and 30 cents per ton of the revenues from canal tolls.[9]

While many dignitaries attended an elaborate signing ceremony, only 39 percent of the people were behind the pacts. Forty-six percent opposed them. Although this represented a substantial gain for Carter, Baker feared that the president had overplayed his hand by heightening expectations. Realizing optimistic supporters could find but fifty senators who were certain to vote yes, Baker "decided not to decide . . . until I know what I'm talking about," but to do his best to make his view prevail when he decided. All recognized the pivotal role he would occupy. The American Conservative Union (ACU), outlined a "Southern Strategy" to kill the treaty by focusing on southern Democrats and Baker. "Howard has been . . . teetering on the brink," ACU chairman Phil Crane said. "We want to make sure Howard gets religion, too."[10]

While Baker never experienced the conversion Crane sought, it was not for the lack of preaching. Full page ACU ads in Tennessee newspapers read "Senator Baker Alone Can Save the Panama Canal—Write, Telephone or Visit Senator

Baker Today." Some of their allies were clever. The University of Tennessee Young Americans for Freedom, for instance, hired a blimp to fly over a football game Baker attended with a banner reading "Save Our Canal: Write Senator Baker." Others, like the Conservative Caucus, threatened to finance a Baker opponent if he backed the pacts. The National Conservative Political Action Committee (NCPAC) sent 10,000 letters urging recipients to tell Baker that a vote for either accord would end his chances to be president. Unfortunately for them, aides to many senators found their bosses less and less impressed with such lobbying. One treaty opponent declared that 99 percent of his likeminded correspondents did not seem to know what was in the pacts.[11]

The rhetoric of treaty opponents prompted much of the confusion. Opponents who dubbed the accords a giveaway were hardly struck by the inconsistencies between their words and those in the 1903 pact. For some, the canal had other implications. While Howard Phillips of the Conservative Caucus said the question was one of patriotism, Gary Jarmin of the ACU declared it "not . . . the issue . . . we're fighting for," but control of the GOP. To their chagrin, several notable conservatives, among them James and William F. Buckley, James Burnham, James J. Kilpatrick, George Shultz, John Wayne, and George F. Will, were actively supporting the accords. Curiously enough, however, when pro-treaty conservatives were mentioned while the pacts were considered, it was less often by the administration than by irate rightists charging that Wayne had been overly influenced by his close ties to Latin America or that the Buckleys were backing the pacts to protect Caribbean investments.[12]

With charges of "giveaway" and "traitor" flowing liberally from the right, Baker came to fear that the public would not hear the real issues. Believing reporters less likely to cover the reasoned analysis of retired generals who opposed the pacts on national security grounds than the shouts of extremists who claimed they were a bid to ensure that loans from the Chase Manhattan and Marine Midland banks to Panama would by repaid, he urged the televising of the proceedings to guarantee a less emotional view. While Senate elders knew this to be a limited restatement of his plan to televise all floor proceedings and remained opposed, the issue's volatility prompted Robert Byrd to allow radio coverage. Baker congratulated him, commended radio as a means of linking representatives and constituents, and declared that the people, once informed of the implications of new laws, proved "remarkably right."[13]

While opinion among Tennessee Republicans ran heavily against the treaties, opposition was never as strident as some claimed. Typical was the tone of GOP chairman Tom Beasley, who had been stationed in the Zone for two years and recognized Panama's concerns but believed that Carter should have extracted more concessions. Formally, the state Democratic executive committee approved a resolution backing the pacts. State party secretary Will T. Cheek wrote Baker field coordinator Bill Hamby that the vote made it virtually impossible for a Democrat to use if Baker voted yes. Cheek's message interested Baker but did not sway him, for he knew most Tennesseans remained opposed to the treaties.[14]

While Jesse Helms thought Baker was "squirming like a worm on a hot brick," proponents agreed with a Baker friend who observed that "he can't be with Reagan and Helms and against Ford and Kissinger if he wants to be President." Baker convened several meetings to discuss the implications, and his staff generally agreed with Helms. Backing the pacts "may be the right thing," one said, "but it may mean that you can never be nominated." To this, Baker responded, "If I start doing everything based on how it would affect such a race, I'm going to bomb out . . . before I ever get to be President."[15]

For substantive advice, Baker came to rely upon William D. Rogers, the assistant secretary of state for Latin American affairs under Nixon and Ford, who provided arguments for the accords, and Roger Fontaine, a professor at the Georgetown Center for Strategic and International Studies, who countered Rogers. Through careful study of their papers, Baker concluded that ratification would more closely link the United States and Panama and rejected the notion that reversion of control to Panama would lead to a Soviet or Cuban takeover. "If there's going to be a standoff with Russia," he said later, "it's not Panama where the real danger is." Indeed, the canal was more susceptible to sabotage from internal extremists than from any external force. Joint Chiefs of Staff Chairman George Brown, in fact, had concluded that the canal could not be defended adequately without 100,000 troops present. Certain that the canal was "more efficiently and effectively defended in partnership with Panama," Baker was not yet convinced that these pacts adequately protected American security. Indeed, Romulo Escobar Bethancourt, Panama's chief negotiator, had said that Panama did not have to keep the canal open if it ceased to be profitable or give America preferential passage in wartime or allow it to defend the canal against an attack from a third country. When Secretary of State Vance appeared before the Foreign Relations Committee, Baker asked him to explain the discrepancies with Carter's public statements and provide the cables and memoranda to let members determine what each side meant. Unless Panama gave written assertions that Escobar was mistaken, Baker warned that the chances of ratification would be very much diminished.[16]

To the chagrin of many senators, Vance never released the communications. But Bob Dole obtained a cable saying that Panama disputed U.S. assertions that expeditious passage gave its warships the right to proceed to the head of the line in wartime, and worried that the right to intervene to defend the canal might allow America to interfere in its internal affairs. Praising Dole, Baker warned that ratification would be next to impossible without clarifications. After Robert Byrd advised Carter likewise, Torrijos flew to Washington to clarify matters before Panama's October 23, 1977, plebiscite. With Baker being regarded as a question mark by Carter lobbyists as late as a month and a half later, Carter had to tell Torrijos that an optimistic reading was that fifty-five senators supported the treaties and twenty-five could be persuaded, but Escobar's remarks had made it necessary to clarify America's right to defend the canal and the rights of its warships. Torrijos agreed, contingent upon the inclusion of a ban upon U.S. intervention in Panama. Nine days later, the people of Panama approved the treaties by a better than two-to-one vote.[17]

Escobar's interpretations and lingering confusion were shown in an October poll revealing "four in ten . . . aware that the United States has the right to defend the canal, . . . one in four aware that the canal is . . . to be turned over in . . . 2000, and . . . one in seven aware that aircraft carriers and supertankers cannot use the canal." Ignorance reflected a general acceptance of giveaway rhetoric and the absence of a response from Carter until October, when he created a broad-based Committee of Americans for the Canal Treaties to educate the public about the treaties.[18]

Baker now had considerable leverage over the pacts, and he was not tipping his hand. As autumn drew to an end, he concluded that continuing the status quo would inflame an already tense relationship, but ratifying the treaties as negotiated would be equally abhorrent. Finding the Carter-Torrijos statement far too easily renounced, he demanded that the language clarifying U.S. rights be amended to the text of the Neutrality Treaty to bind future Panamanian governments and notified Carter and Robert Byrd of his assessment in early December. While Carter feared that additions might prompt Torrijos to abandon the accords, Byrd was even more certain that the treaties could not be ratified without Baker. Aiming to show support for his position, Baker commissioned a survey of Tennessee sentiment. As he expected, 23 percent of those polled in mid-December backed the treaties as they stood, while 45 percent were opposed. But a reversal occurred when respondents were asked where they stood on pacts as he planned to amend them by granting America the right to defend the canal and its ships the right to move to the head of the line in wartime. Fifty-six percent said they would back such accords, while only 29 percent said they would be opposed.[19] The results were hardly a godsend. Thousands who backed the pacts in any form were Democrats who had voted against Baker three times and would stick with their party regardless of who they nominated. Many opposed were Republicans and too many for Baker's comfort were making vows similar to these:

> To attest to my sincerety [*sic*] and grave concern about the dangers of the present Treaty [*sic*], I am signing the pledge . . . below.
>
> I PLEDGE ALLEGIANCE TO THE UNITED STATES OF AMERICA.
>
> I PLEDGE NEVER AGAIN TO VOTE FOR ANY ELECTED OFFICIAL WHO SUPPORTS THE SURRENDER OF THE U.S. SOVEREIGN

JURISDICTION AND CONTROL OVER THE AMERICAN CANAL AND ZONE AT THE ISTMUS [*sic*] OF PANAMA.

I WILL NOT BE FOOLED BY COSMETIC UNDERSTANDINGS, RESERVATIONS, OR AMENDMENTS TO THE PANAMA CANAL TREATIES. *THE ONLY ACCEPTABLE VOTE IS A "NO" VOTE.*[20]

Baker Makes Up His Mind

Enough of a southerner to recall John C. Calhoun's doctrine of concurrent majorities, Baker weighed the passions of the most vehement opponents before making a final decision. But he was not certain what to do until he visited Huntsville at Christmas and found neighbors more interested in Social Security deduction increases and care for black-lung victims. When the issue arose, almost always when he raised it residents generally suggested that he do what he thought was right.[21]

These soundings convinced Baker that his course was the correct one. His polls strengthened his hand, as the results indicated widespread public support for his position, but not Carter's. When he told Carter that he wanted to meet with Torrijos, Carter authorized a plane to fly him and colleagues John Chafee, a supporter of the treaties, Jake Garn, a staunch opponent, their wives and several aides to Panama, where they met Torrijos at a high school on January 4, 1978. There, Torrijos, in combat gear with bloodshot yellow eyes and quivering hands, spoke in what Garn recalls as a "subdued sickly way" until he took a belt from his canteen and his hands "steadied right down." Torrijos led his guests through a staged demonstration in the streets of Panama City, then flew them on a tour of Panama in his helicopter before reaching Farallon, his villa on Contadora Island, near dusk. When they arrived, Torrijos excused himself to change clothes. Mrs. Torrijos looked to Mrs. Garn and pointed to a "little, pock-faced man over there. That's Lt. Col. Noriega. I keep telling my husband someday he will kill him. But my husband doesn't believe me."[22]

Recalling the incident today, Garn guesses that Noriega may have had something to do with the 1981 plane crash that took Torrijos' life. Carter aide Frank Moore, who accompanied the party, remembers Baker and Senate minority counsel Howard Liebengood having been especially concerned about Noriega's rapid rise within the Panamanian National Guard. Liebengood maintained modestly that he and Baker were merely more vocal about their objections to a lengthy threatening diatribe from an enormously cocky Noriega about the canal's vulnerability to sabotage, a possibility no senator needed to be reminded about. While scattered reports linked Noriega to drug trafficking, Baker had nothing concrete on which to base anything. With the treaties as Baker hoped to amend them binding the United States and Panama and not individual leaders, Noriega's presence played no role in the decisions of Baker or any other senator, although most vowed privately to continue to monitor events in Panama.[23]

Torrijos went upstairs to change, then invited Baker to join him, which Baker found strange, as Torrijos was not supposed to speak English. Baker led that he could not support the treaties without amendments. "What do you need?" Torrijos asked in very clear English, before sending for his interpreter. Starting over, he looked Baker in the eye and asked if the Senate would pass the treaties. "Not without . . . amendments, they won't," Baker replied. Stung, Torrijos responded, "What can I do to pass them?" "I'm not sure you can do anything other than agree to these amendments," Baker replied. "You're being very tough," Torrijos replied. "No," Baker shot back, "I'm being realistic, and I came here to tell you the treaties won't pass unless we can amend them." "Would you support them," Torrijos asked. "If you do these two amendments," Baker replied. Torrijos peered down before raising his eyes and saying, "You're trying to negotiate new treaties." "I have no intention of negotiating new treaties," Baker insisted, "but . . . the Senate will not ratify the treaties unless these amendments are attached. President Carter knows my judgment."[24]

When the two returned, Chafee and Garn supported Baker's estimates, leading Torrijos to ponder his options while Baker, Chafee, and Garn spent the next three days meeting with Panamanians from all walks of life and U.S. officials in Panama and the Zone. What they saw reinforced their preconceptions. American commanders warned that a rejection of the pacts might further anti-Yanqui sentiment and propel sabotage against the canal. Zonians, in contrast, seemed unconcerned with the effect of a rejection upon U.S.-Panamanian relations and moved more by fears about their jobs and salaries. But Carter and Torrijos, at the insistence of AFL-CIO chief George Meany, had included language letting American workers keep their jobs as long as they wanted. Garn, while more opposed to the treaties than ever, declared that some Zone land should be returned to Panama. After Torrijos assured another delegation that Baker's amendments merely restated principles in the October Statement of Understanding, thus vitiating any need for a second plebiscite, Baker drove to the White House on January 16 and told Carter that he would support the treaties if the Senate agreed to his amendments. Torrijos, he said, had shown enough flexibility.[25]

Baker's decision infuriated a sizable bloc of Republicans. By mid-March, he had received 64,000 letters, 98 percent of them from treaty opponents. While Senate opponents like Orrin Hatch and Paul Laxalt hailed his "courage," even while seeing the pacts as an abysmal mistake, external opponents were less charitable. A rumor arose in Tennessee that Baker had traded his vote for Jimmy Carter's promise that he would not receive substantial opposition in his bid for reelection. Amused, Baker denied the story but quipped that he might talk to him about it. Such frivolity contrasted sharply with the bombast of twelve House Republicans, who demanded that Baker step down as Leader until the Senate acted. "You have no right," they wrote, "to use that office as a means of advancing the treaties against the wishes of our party and the American people." Most heavy-handed was the claim that their position had the support of the people. Polls of early February indicated that Americans favored the pacts by a 45–42 margin, and those who knew of Baker's amendments and their likelihood of incorporation backed the treaties by a better than two-to-one margin. The assertion that the GOP opposed the pacts as Baker aimed to mold them was incorrect, albeit confusing enough to seem plausible. The Republican National Convention had in 1976 opposed an accord with Panama that jeopardized the security of the United States and the Western Hemisphere. A year later, the Republican National Committee passed a resolution opposing the treaties Carter and Torrijos had signed. But the GOP never took a position on the amended treaties. And, while the twelve boasted of Barry Goldwater's and Ronald Reagan's opposition, Gerald Ford, the party's titular head, and many other luminaries backed the pacts with or without amendments.[26]

What concerned the twelve was Baker's effectiveness. "Your . . . cooperation with a Democratic President . . . has lent significant help in giving away the Panama Canal," they wrote. Lloyd Bentsen, John Glenn, Richard Stone, and Charles Percy declared that the clarifications allowed them to back treaties that they would have opposed otherwise. Noting the popularity of the two amendments, Baker and Byrd announced that they would introduce them jointly and let each member cosponsor them and thus be credited for strengthening American defenses.[27]

The Senate Acts

Carter had but forty-eight commitments by February 8, the day debate opened on the floor, with but twelve from Republicans. For the first time since Baker assumed the leadership, a serious rift had developed. Having been the primary target of the treaties' most vitriolic opponents, he acted to ensure that Senate proceedings did not become riddled with the same kind of passion. He saw to it that opponents had access to relevant documents and joined them in requests for drafts of bills implementing the pacts and evidence on Torrijos's alleged involvement in a heroin-trafficking ring. Waverers of both parties trusted him enough that they informed him of their intentions before anyone else. To facilitate intraparty harmony, he swapped desks with antitreaty manager Paul Laxalt for the duration of the debate and kept him appraised of his headcounts, a courtesy Laxalt returned by agreeing to Baker's request to address the Shelby County Lincoln Day dinner. But these concessions masked a rare determination to see that the treaties were approved. What a failure to ratify the treaties would signify, Adam Clymer wrote, was that Baker "couldn't even do wrong right."[28]

"The country is overwhelmingly opposed to the treaties as submitted," Baker acknowledged when debate opened, "but . . . the public will support the treaties as I hope they are amended." The night before, he had addressed Tennesseans via a television hookup and told them that he could not vote for the treaties Carter and Torrijos had signed, as they did not adequately protect American security. But, he pointed out, the Constitution empowered the Senate to give its advice and consent to the president. In the past, he said, the Senate had given very little advice, a state of affairs that would have to change if the Senate were to approve these accords. He would not vote for the pacts without amendments guaranteeing America's right to defend the canal and the privileges of its warships to pass through first in wartime. Terming his decision a close call, he described meetings with Carter and Torrijos and said the 1903 pact was a good treaty in its time, but no longer, as conditions demanded the establishment of a community of interests for the canal to stay open, secure and accessible.[29]

Baker spoke often in Tennessee the next week. His audiences generally took his messages in stride, even though VFW representatives frequently asked how they could change his mind. When opponents asked why America should give up the canal, he turned the question around and asked why America should risk losing it. To his delight, audiences seemed more interested in local issues, such as when a highway would be built from Erwin, Tennessee, to Asheville, North Carolina; if construction would begin on the Clinch River breeder reactor; and if Ray Blanton could be stopped from pardoning convicted murderer Roger Humphreys. Only in Sevierville, a town where most GOP candidates receive more than 70 percent of the vote, did his position become the focus of discussion. There, someone asked him to poll those present and Baker was shocked to find better than half of his audience fully behind him.[30]

While Baker's amendments had transformed sentiment in Tennessee, the hard-line antitreaty position had wide residual appeal nationally. With opponents trying to defeat the treaties with dozens of killer amendments, some of which seemed innocuous enough, Baker and Byrd opted to try to lure votes by letting undecideds amend the resolution with reservations acceptable to Panama, and joined waverers in meetings with Panamanian Ambassador Gabriel Lewis and Deputy Secretary of State Warren Christopher to find language that encompassed their concerns without provoking Torrijos.[31]

Supporters received an important boost on March 1, when defense-minded Democrat Thomas McIntyre took the floor to deliver an impassioned endorsement of the pacts, replete with vehement denunciations of the "bully boys of the radical right." The almost universally favorable response stiffened the resolve of those backing Carter, but only John Danforth among GOP undecideds announced his support by March 7. With Henry Bellmon, Edward Brooke, and John Heinz professing indecision, Baker met with each and prompted Carter as to the best talking points. Certain of only fifty-nine votes, Carter knew that a pivotal senator was Sam Nunn, a defense expert who, while not inclined to embarrass him, wanted to see how Herman Talmadge, Georgia's senior senator, would vote. While Talmadge had told Carter that he might hold his nose and vote yes, he did not decide until Carter declared his support for a pet farm-subsidy bill. To sway Dennis DeConcini, Carter announced that the government would buy 25,000 tons of Arizona copper, which, if anything, deterred converts. Edward Brooke left a White House meeting angry, while DeConcini termed the concessions too late to help the copper industry. What undecideds wanted were clarifications. As some feared that the canal could not be defended without U.S. help, Carter, Baker, Byrd, and Christopher arrived at a reservation with Gabriel Lewis declaring that nothing precluded the two countries from agreeing to allow U.S. forces to remain in Panama, leading Baker to declare himself optimistic for the first time.[32]

Nunn and Talmadge introduced the amendment and added their endorsements. Only Russell Long fell in line right behind, however. John Heinz held out for a reservation forcing Panama to help pay to maintain the canal before using its money for social welfare programs. Democrats Jennings Randolph and Edward Zorinsky told Carter they believed the pacts were in the national interest but feared retribution. Others who were up for reelection in 1978 took the same path. Even more unpredictable was Henry Bellmon, who was discussing the issue with only Baker, Lloyd Bentsen, and Paul Laxalt. Strictly political were the conditions of Montana Democrat Paul Hatfield, who demanded that Carter get from ambassador to Japan Mike Mansfield an endorsement of the pacts and a pledge to remain neutral in Hatfield's upcoming primary. Of more consequence was Dennis DeConcini's reservation giving America the right to "take such steps as it deems necessary, including . . . force . . . to reopen the Canal or restore the operations of the Canal," an addition that almost caused Torrijos to renounce the accords. But Carter had to back down, as Edward Brooke had told him that his vote depended upon the inclusion of DeConcini's reservation and an understanding of his own. While Carter wanted to add a reservation reiterating the ideal of nonintervention, Baker and Byrd warned that DeConcini might renege. Henry Bellmon soon announced his support, saying he knew how he would feel if Panama owned a strip of land along the Mississippi. Paul Hatfield followed, prompting Howard Cannon, who opposed the pacts, to announce that he would vote aye to ensure that no member would be stigmatized with the notion that he had cast the final vote to give away the canal.[33]

The Senate adopted the DeConcini reservation, 75–23, and then the Neutrality Treaty as amended by Baker and Byrd, 68–32. Reaction was hardly ecstatic in Panama, where students, who had heard many insults of their leader, burned copies of the accords. Torrijos flew to Farallon to decide whether or not to renounce the pacts. Equally irate were U.S. opponents. While Henry Bellmon was called a communist traitor and a buzzard, the main target was Baker, who an inscription borne by a plane that flew over Washington during the vote said could still save the canal. In the traditional usage of the phrase, Baker was the senator most responsible for saving the canal from sabotage, as five more Republicans would have voted no had he not worked to persuade them. "I got to like the guy," one Carter aide said of Baker after the vote. "The son of a bitch scares me, if you want to know the truth."[34]

Action still awaited on the Panama Canal Treaty, on which Paul Laxalt found it possible that the public might find their side with thirty-eight or thirty-nine votes. While Henry Bellmon and John Heinz held firm, Edward Brooke and Paul Hatfield wavered until Baker and Byrd mollified them by securing approval of a series of reservations they had drafted to the resolution of ratification. Such pledges seemed to guarantee approval of the second accord, but events converged to place the pacts in danger of renunciation by Panama and rejection by the Senate. Panama's concern was the DeConcini amendment, which Torrijos found a violation of the OAS and UN charters. "The United States didn't demand as much from Japan," he grieved. While his course alarmed Baker and Carter, who advised restraint, it prompted Edward Kennedy, George McGovern, and Daniel Patrick Moynihan to announce that they would not support the Panama Canal Treaty unless the principle of nonintervention was reiterated. DeConcini wanted to amend the second accord with a reservation similar to his earlier addendum, but Carter aides told him that such a provision must also restate America's intention not to intervene in Panama's internal affairs. When DeConcini and the State Department could not agree on specifics, Byrd and Baker got Carter to step aside and relayed drafts to Gabriel Lewis, adding to DeConcini's original understanding a pledge that action assuring that the canal would remain open, neutral, and secure would not be taken as a U.S. right to intervene in the internal affairs of Panama.[35]

DeConcini's acquiescence assured proponents of the votes of the shakiest supporters of the Neutrality Treaty. But James Abourezk, angry because conferees on the natural gas deregulation bill had not invited him to participate, asked Carter to assure him that cabinet members would not attend closed-door meetings. Carter refused, saying he had no time to police the Senate. S. I. Hayakawa was concerned about broader questions of foreign policy, especially after Carter opted not to produce the neutron bomb. While agreeing with Baker that it was another in a long line of national defense mistakes, Hayakawa feared that the treaties projected an image even more symbolic of national weakness. Not wanting to vote against modernizing a relationship with a potential ally, he saw no other way to influence Carter. Only when Russell Long convinced Hayakawa that he could only influence future decisions if he voted right this time did Hayakawa reconsider and tell Carter that he feared that policy toward Africa did not protect American friends from Soviet-funded subversion and that Carter needed his advice on foreign policy.[36]

Having been noncommittal toward Hayakawa, Carter awoke the morning of the vote two votes short. Howard Cannon's late morning pledge to back the pacts led Carter to spend the rest of the day phoning mutual friends to see if they could sway Abourezk. Late in the day, he took a call from Baker, who led, "Mr. President, do you need to meet with Sam Hayakawa from time to time" on foreign affairs? Assuming Hayakawa was listening, Carter fibbed, "I really do," and assured ratification, leading Carter aides Hamilton Jordan and Frank Moore to term Baker's help "absolutely crucial" and opposition manager Paul Laxalt to credit the result to "the effectiveness of the . . . Leadership."[37]

New Arrangements in the Middle East

While Baker might have liked to spend time in Tennessee mending fences, he had little time once Carter notified Congress that he planned to sell sixty F-15 fighter jets to Saudi Arabia, fifty F-5E jets to Egypt, and seventy-five F-16s and fifteen F-15s to Israel. Carter aimed to further an already cooperative stance by the Egyptians and Saudis in the Middle East peace process, but an outcry arose from American Jewish organizations, spurred by Menachem Begin's objections to the sale of military equipment to the Saudis. With Congress able to block any such sale by a majority vote of both houses, Joseph Biden's move to do just that attracted support from RNC Chairman Bill Brock and Senate GOP Campaign Committee Chairman Bob Packwood, who feared that a sale might be detrimental to Israel's security and hoped that a large GOP vote against the transfer might dislodge Jewish votes from the Democrats. Brock and Packwood could not convince Baker, who, while a longtime supporter of Israel, feared that the Saudis might abandon their moderate position and that America might "breach a trust" with Anwar Sadat, who had repeatedly demonstrated his commitment to peace. Afraid what might happen if America abrogated an agreement with friends, Baker made it known that he would back a deal, but only if it contained some concessions to Israel.[38]

Baker's ideas appealed to Abraham Ribicoff, a Jewish Democrat from Connecticut, who took him off the floor and told him that he had the making of a solution. Once they agreed upon principles, they convinced Frank Church and Jacob Javits, two of Israel's strongest supporters, to explore the matter further. Baker then took soundings within his caucus, found a majority of Republicans in support of a modified version, and informed Carter that the sale would not be approved in its original form. "If you want to work this out," he said, "I'm willing to try." Carter demurred, but had to call Baker back later that week and promise changes. Believing Baker's suggestion to double the number of F-16s he planned to sell to Israel excessive, Carter let him know that Israel had tentatively agreed to a plan letting them buy twenty additional F-15s and banning the Saudis from transferring the jets to a third country without U.S. approval, using the F-15s against Israel or buying jets from another country, thus blocking them from buying Mirage F-1 fighters from France, which did not restrict the use of the planes. Only then would Baker say publicly that he would support a package that he had played the largest role in crafting.[39]

While Baker and other opponents of the resolution figured on eleven certain votes in the Foreign Relations Committee, Begin proclaimed later that day that the sales violated America's special relationship with Israel. American Jewish groups flooded Senate offices with messages opposing any transfer, even though Foreign Minister Moshe Dayan conceded that sales with restraints were in Israel's best interest. Three members reneged, leaving an 8–8 tie, but twenty-five GOP colleagues were convinced that the sales were in America's and Israel's interests, and the resolution blocking them was rejected 44–54 when it reached the floor.[40]

Baker invested as much time securing approval of a Carter move to lift the arms embargo upon Turkey that had been in place since 1975. Baker had joined Hubert Humphrey in fighting the initial embargo at Gerald Ford's behest in recognition of the importance of Turkish bases and monitoring stations so close to the Soviet border. His primary consideration was "what is best for the United States, within the limitations of general . . . moral conduct." For many Greek Americans, the issue was a fear that Turkey would attack Greece, and their trepidations had mounted in 1974 once Turkey invaded Cyprus after a long-bumbling Greek junta deposed that island's ethnic Greek leader, Archbishop Makarios. The subsequent fall of the Greek autocracy, restoration of peaceful democratic forces, and subsiding of conflict in Cyprus did nothing to alleviate Greek American fears. Indeed, it seemed to many Ford and Carter aides that each member of Congress had a Greek constituent who owned a restaurant and hosted fundraisers for them without ever asking for anything in return—that is, until the issue of the Turkish arms embargo arose.[41]

With Turkish diplomats as tactless as Greek American innkeepers were generous, no compromise seemed possible until George McGovern devised one in July 1978 allowing revocation if Turkey withdrew from Cyprus. Baker, aware of the strategic benefits of Turkish goodwill, quickly lined up more of the Senate's thirty-eight Republicans than Carter had of its sixty-two Democrats to vote to end the embargo. Once again, Republicans had to pull Carter's feet from the fire while Democrats pandered to a single-issue constituency, Baker, having watched this occur in the F-15 debate, warned reporters that several proponents of ending the embargo would change their minds unless half the Democrats cast their lots with Carter. Only when Democrats split evenly did Baker and five others cast their votes to repeal the embargo. Republicans overall supported the measure by a 26–11 margin, giving it an unexpectedly large 57–42 count.[42]

For the third time in four months, Baker had rescued Carter from certain defeat on a major foreign policy issue. That Carter was appreciative is indicated by his handwritten postscripts to letters to Baker after each of the debates describing Baker's leadership as "invaluable," "very important," and "crucial." Carter's aides went even further, hailing Baker in several anonymous comments as "one of the greatest bipartisan statesmen in recent decades."[43] As with the postwar Truman-Vandenberg collaboration, the meeting of the minds of Baker and Carter brought innumerable benefits. The resumption of military aid to Turkey prompted the Turks to reopen bases and listening bases, which became incalculably more important with the fall of the pro-American Shah and the rise of the xenophobic Ayatollah Khomeini. The sale of jets to Saudi Arabia and Egypt boosted the confidence of moderate Arabs in America's integrity as an honest broker and catalyzed negotiations that within a year culminated in Carter's historic mediations. Events of 1988 render an evaluation of the effects of the Panama Canal Treaties more problematical, but those pacts ultimately resounded to America's benefit, too. In the short run, they averted a potentially lengthy conflict and stabilized a long tenuous American-Panamanian relationship to the point that Omar Torrijos offered a safe haven in 1980 for the Shah's exile. In the long run, they defused long-smoldering anti-Yanqui sentiment, gave an impetus to Panama to aid U.S. efforts to limit left-inspired expansionism in Central America, gave George Bush a legal justification to invade Panama in 1989, and limited Panamanian opposition to that operation to the minuscule minority loyal to the ever more tyrannical Manuel Noriega.

As with Vandenberg, however, the benefits to American security and interest abroad did not transfer to domestic political benefits for Baker. Some not-so-charitable Republicans grumbled that he had "pulled Carter's chestnuts out of the fire" too often. Here was a concern Baker tried to defuse by saying that these three issues represented merely isolated areas of agreement with Carter. In fact, Baker saw the perception that America had lost its national will that was so vividly reflected in the virulent opposition to the Panama Canal Treaties as quite aptly indicated in Carter's abandonment of the B-1 bomber and neutron bomb, his cuts in naval construction, military manpower and troop strength in South Korea, as well as in his failure to link a SALT-II Treaty to America's perception of Soviet behavior around the world. But even as responsible treaty opponents concede it was the Baker-Byrd amendments that clarified and preserved American rights in the Canal Zone, the passion aroused in that debate intensified the identification of nationalists with the candidacy of Ronald Reagan.

It was always Baker's belief that Carter might be swayed to limit cuts to defense programs he deemed vital if he spent more time consulting with himself and other influential Republicans. Such a working relationship with the president himself, as well as a host of executive branch back channels, were the means Arthur

Vandenberg and Harry Truman had used to build a working relationship to rebuild Western Europe and contain Soviet expansion. If there were no such arrangement of mutual give-and-take that Baker, Vandenberg, and Everett Dirksen so cherished, however, there was another strain of stalwart Republicanism from which Baker could draw strength, the strain embodied by Robert A. Taft.

CHAPTER 9

AN HEIR TO ROBERT TAFT EMERGES 1978–1979

It would seem that two more divergent personalities never existed than the intense, often aloof Robert A. Taft and the laid-back, friendly Howard Henry Baker. Taft, a scholar with a rarely paralleled understanding of legal theory whom liberals liked to call "the best eighteenth-century mind in America," could dominate his party in the hierarchical Senate of the 1940s and early 1950s through the sheer awe Republicans and conservative Democrats shared for his intellect. Baker, a small-town lawyer with an approach rooted in institutional lore whom George McGovern called "one of the best combinations of personality and intellect in the Senate," preferred to exercise his prerogatives in the more individualized upper chamber of the 1970s and 1980s through a brand of cajolery and good-natured appeals to party loyalty.[1]

Yet while the styles of the two were diametrically opposite, the ideological continuity linking Baker with Taft is readily apparent. Although Baker took more of a lead in foreign policy debates than Taft, both distrusted Soviet intentions enough to scrutinize any deal that American presidents concluded with Communist leaders that did not seem fair and equitable to the United States. Both also recognized a role, albeit a limited one, for the federal government in solving domestic problems, especially those they believed could be alleviated by expanding opportunities available to those whose standards of living had been historically limited by laws rooted in injustice. While neither made a habit of being in the forefront of civil rights measures, Taft favored the abolition of the poll tax and anti-lynching bills, opposed education measures that did not raise standards for black schools to white levels and led the fight to prevent Mississippi racist Theodore Bilbo from taking his seat in 1947 because he had intimidated black voters with virulent racist appeals in his 1946 campaign. Baker had by 1978 shown considerable sensitivity to black concerns. As Taft, in the eyes of one education lobbyist, had "crammed his mind with more facts and figures than any man I've ever seen" before introducing a bill giving federal aid to states spending a declared minimum percentage of their revenues for school funding, Baker, like many from poorer states long strapped for education aid, championed a federal Department of Education. Fully in line with Taft's view that "the entire basis of American life is opportunity" and that the federal government had a "secondary interest to see that there is a basic floor," Baker saw a need for Washington to take steps to assist businesses in helping defuse the "social dynamite" in America's cities. Here was a proposal not terribly different in tenor from the public housing plan Taft advanced in 1946 and defended by stating a need to "put a floor under essential things to give all a minimum standard of living, and all children an opportunity to get a start in life." But to both Taft and Baker, the proper federal role was as a secondary agent of such action, with the forces of private enterprise being the most desirable catalysts of change. While both enjoyed some support from union members and defended the rights of labor to strike and the National Labor Relations Board (NLRB) to adjudicate union complaints against management, a landmark law allowing states to enact right-to-work laws bears Taft's name, while Baker was just as quick to resist those union-demanded measures that he believed put businesses, especially small ones, at disadvantages.[2]

A Taftite Agenda for 1978

It was the Taftite strain in his philosophy that Baker emphasized in his campaign for reelection in 1978. In line with Taft's doctrine of responsible parties, he made his disagreements with Carter not just his platform for reelection but also national party policy. With GOP Policy Committee Chairman John Tower, he released a statement in May 1978 signed by all but two members of his caucus condemning the broad direction of a foreign policy that projected an image of weakness and invited Soviet expansion. While not taking an explicit position, members pledged not to vote for a SALT-II agreement that did not adequately provide for a strategic balance, limit Soviet deployments of its Backfire bomber, and ensure that Soviet compliance could be verified. If anything, Baker was more resolute than his colleagues, saying that "the world thinks the United States no longer has the will nor the determination to make the right decisions." Well known was his plan to link his vote on SALT-II with his assessment of Soviet behavior, and he vowed to oppose the pact unless the Soviets ended the involvement of their Cuban surrogates in African civil wars and stopped persecuting dissidents. Several times, he called upon Carter to suspend SALT talks to demonstrate America's concern about Soviet "adventurism."[3] But Carterites who relied on him to carry votes on more controversial matters ignored him on more fundamental questions. Not once in his first eighteen months did Carter side publicly on a controversial question with those who warned of the consequences of U.S. military decline. Thus disillusioned, Baker adopted his disagreements with Carter on foreign policy as one of the primary themes of his reelection campaign.

Baker's other main arguing point was that statism was hindering the productive capacity of the American free-enterprise system and adding to an intolerable inflation rate. While praising Carter for singing a Republican song in emphasizing the desirability of a balanced budget, he berated him for pursuing policies he believed antithetical to growth and full employment. Stressing the burdens of overregulation and excessive taxation, he liked to cite figures showing that small businessmen were paying $18 billion a year to comply with regulations requiring them to file reports, thus adding to prices and preventing investment for expansion or hiring the unemployed. He joined a bipartisan bid to cut the corporate capital gains tax to 25 percent and a more partisan effort by Congressman Jack Kemp and Senator William Roth to reduce individual rates by 30 percent over three years that proponents claimed would reinfuse the economy with $43.4 billion and 1.2 million jobs. Realizing Carter rejected such an approach, Baker continued to urge its adoption in the hope Carter might expand relief to the middle class.[4]

Likewise proposing a series of tax incentives for firms moving to depressed areas and for the unemployed who relocated to find work, Baker called upon Carter to create a jobs commission to devise ways to employ the chronically unemployed and subsidize locally and privately run training centers for the unskilled and those starting their own businesses. Believing that the welfare system in place had "locked the poor into a recurring cycle of dependency," he introduced a bill with Henry Bellmon, John Danforth, and Abraham Ribicoff that extended tax credits to firms hiring the hard to employ and financial incentives for unemployed fathers to stay with their families. In some respects, their measure resembled a Carter bill, and HEW Secretary Joseph Califano suggested that the differences were negotiable. But Carter concluded that enacting such a bill would damage his image as a budget-minded president and let key Democrats know in mid-1978 that he would not be angry if Congress let it slide. While recognizing Carter's inattention also effectively precluded action upon his bill, Baker knew that his proposal would convey his desire to catalyze employment and a stable dollar by stimulating private investment.[5]

Baker announced for reelection on May 17 from his front yard. Aiming through these arrangements to portray himself as a man appreciative of his roots, he directed his campaign more against Carter than any opponent. With most key Tennessee Democrats wanting no part of such a race, it was hard to determine for what to prepare.[6] With Tennessee House Speaker Ned Ray McWherter, Carter's preferred nominee, opting not to run, the primary field opened to seven largely unknown contenders, only two of whom—former State Representative Bill Bruce and Jane Eskind, a wealthy party activist from Nashville—were taken seriously.

Foil of Big Labor and Small Fish

Debate had opened on a bill to expedite the process the National Labor Relations Board (NLRB) used to adjudicate disputes by stripping from it the right to hear any but labor complaints in nonunion shops. Knowing unions would not act until sure they would win recognition, small firms also opposed requirements that the NLRB seek court orders forcing management to rehire workers the unions claimed were fired for organizing and reimburse them with 150 percent of their back pay. A few objected to strengthening the right of organizers to meet workers on the job, a provision directed at the J. P. Stevens textile company, a firm notorious for union busting. On this count, Baker sympathized with labor. "If they wanted a J. P. Stevens bill," he said, "I'd give 'em a J. P. Stevens bill." But fearing that the bill's main provisions would "take small business down the tubes," he joined Orrin Hatch and John Tower in promising a filibuster. The NLRB had served America well, he said, by providing a mechanism to maintain a desirable equilibrium between labor and management. While polls indicated that a majority of the public opposed the measure, many senators backed it, as several unions were making support a litmus test. While few groups openly threatened supporters of revision with electoral revenge, small businessmen, most of whom members guessed had never written them before, inundated the Capitol with mail opposing revision. Buoyed, Baker and Hatch drafted five hundred amendments and met daily with the Senate parliamentarian to ensure that they would not be surprised. The first attempt to shut off debate won but 42 votes. Byrd waited a week and found his position ahead in a second bid, 49–41. Eleven votes short, Byrd opted to buy time by withholding further petitions until he deemed sixty votes likely. Sensing victory after getting fifty-eight ballots on a fourth vote, he forced a fifth one the next day. But opponents held firm. Baker, while having promised Hatch he would be with him through the end, hoped that a compromise was possible. But Hatch "felt it . . . better to . . . let people know what they were facing" and used a week to rally small businessmen and pick away at senators not obliged to the unions. When proponents won but fifty-three votes on a sixth ballot, Byrd moved to return the bill to committee with instructions to report one opponents might accept. But union leaders found the J. P. Stevens bill Baker wanted a token measure not worth fighting for, thus killing labor law revision for 1978.[7]

From a strictly political standpoint, Baker was more vexed by conflicts between groups that had supported him in the past. Such a struggle had developed between TVA and environmentalists over the desirability of a dam near the confluence of the Tennessee and Little Tennessee rivers. When Congress originally authorized the dam in 1966, planners envisioned it as a flood control and recreation project that would also supply enough power for 20,000 homes. While environmentalists had joined the *Knoxville Journal* and a bevy of small groups in questioning whether the benefits justified the costs, perceptions changed when planners came to see a 40,000-acre stretch of land near the dam as an ideal site for a model town that would bring 11,000 new jobs. After the Boeing Company announced plans in 1969 to work with TVA to develop Timberlake, as the new town would be known, polls showed three-quarters of area residents behind the plan. Many, like Tellico Plains Mayor Charles Hall, thought that the project might stem the outmigration of the area's youth. Others concluded after a 1973 storm that another flood control project was needed while still others like Governor Winfield Dunn believed that the jobs to be created in the new town now justified a dam that they had at one time opposed. Opponents were far from mute. Loudest were those whose land would be immersed, but most were placated by a measure Baker coauthored requiring TVA to compensate them for their homes, land, and relocation expenses. Many fishermen also opposed construction, fearing they would lose a choice stretch on the Little Tennessee well stocked with large trout, notwithstanding studies showing that the dam would remove very few of the prime spots.

On behalf of the fishermen, the Environmental Defense Fund sued in 1971 to cease construction, claiming the amount of water stored would threaten the extinction of several species of fish and fowl and destroy a rare recreational and environmental resource and that Chota, the onetime capital of the Cherokee nation, and Tenassee, the Indian village from which the state took its name, would be immersed. As no Cherokee had lived near either site for decades, a federal court held for TVA. But opponents of the dam at the University of Tennessee had promised Baker they would "find something that'll stop this dam . . . under the body of environmental law," and their position improved with the passage of the Endangered Species Act that required the government to list all species in danger of extinction and banned projects that might jeopardize their habitats. Once it was learned in 1973 that a school of less than a thousand heretofore unknown three-inch-long fish was swimming a mile from the site, the snail darter was put on the endangered species roster, and the Environmental Defense Fund sued for the dam's cessation. While TVA arranged to transfer the school to a comparable spot three miles downstream, that action coincided with congressional intentions, but not the letter of the law, and an appeals court ruled in January 1977 for the dam's opponents.[8]

When construction stopped, the dam was 90 percent complete, $135 million had been invested, and the prospect of 11,000 jobs was delayed. Tennesseans prescribed a variety of remedies. John Duncan proposed exempting the dam from the Endangered Species Act. Robin Beard suggested exempting projects from termination provisions if construction began before a species was listed. The General Assembly declared the dam vital to Tennessee and that it would not result in the extinction of any species. Convinced that "the prospects for human growth" were being "sacrificed in the name of an absolute principle that was not . . . being violated,"

Baker, a cosponsor of the Endangered Species Act, feared that the extreme applications some environmentalists demanded would eradicate support for its principles. Thinking it could be made more flexible, he joined Iowa Democrat John Culver in convincing the Senate to pass a measure creating a seven-member interagency review council, henceforth known as the "God Committee," which could exempt projects from coverage.[9]

The Long Road to Reelection Begins

Despite his success, Baker's reelection was not as certain as many assumed it would be. To begin with, he had to deal with the State Election Commission, which by a 2–1 vote declared his signature on his qualifying petition a forgery. The "H, o and d in Howard and the J in Jr.," said executive director David Collins, looked different from those on earlier petitions. "Maybe," said member Tommy Powell, a union leader with a vendetta, "Mr. Baker was too busy giving away the Panama Canal and fighting labor reforms to . . . sign his petition." Powell's vindictiveness was coupled with Collins's failure to notify a GOP member that a meeting would be held, ensuring a disqualification, as the chairman, a Democrat who sided with Baker, had no vote save in case of a tie. Jim Harpster, the one Republican present, was angry, as Collins had done nothing between the day the petitions were filed and the deadline to notify anyone of a problem. After calling it "one of the most despicable things" ever, Harpster phoned Baker, who assured him that he had "signed that petition in front of a whole raft of witnesses." "I thought I'd seen a new low," former state GOP chairman Dortch Oldham added, "but this is the lowest of the low."[10]

Baker responded by lecturing that "politics is rough enough without people playing childish games." Ron McMahan phoned Fred Thompson in Nashville and begged him to get over to the election commission office. The six-foot-five wisecracking attorney rushed to the State House, found Collins, and asked what was going on. Once Collins replied, Thompson left, phoned a calm but mad Baker, and discussed all options. "Keep your eye on the ball," Baker instructed Thompson, "and . . . get it straightened out . . . and the easiest way . . . the better." After telling reporters that "Mr. Collins's . . . handwriting expertise could prove costly," Thompson strode into the room and told Collins, "If it were me, I would play this for all it was worth and sue you guys and . . . get you thrown out of office. . . . Fortunately for you, it's . . . him and he's going to let you get out of this . . . gracefully if you're smart enough to do it." Scrambling to certify Baker with what Thompson called the "least amount of egg on their face," Collins's associates qualified Baker when he affirmed in writing that he had signed his petition on May 26. "I'm trying to get the commission to question my signature," one publicity-starved Democrat quipped. For Baker partisans, the incident became a rallying point, as the most popular Baker campaign item that fall was a bumper sticker featuring his signature.[11]

Baker's challengers in the primary dwelled upon the Panama Canal treaties. Harvey Howard, a John Birch Society member who was his best-funded opponent, claimed that the votes proved Baker was a closet liberal anxious to bail out big banks and his actions reflected his membership in the Council on Foreign Relations, who he termed a "bunch of criminals . . . with the goal of World Government." Tom Anderson, another JBS member running as an independent, declared that Baker had "complained he has cast 6,000 votes. Pontius Pilate may have rendered 6,000 votes, too—but he's only remembered for one." To stem the possibility the attention to Howard and Anderson might allow their message to take hold, state GOP chairman Tom Beasley assured county chairmen that Baker's overall record coincided with their outlooks. Far Right leaders, in turn, tried to paint their concerns as broader than merely the single issue of the Panama Canal, and attacked Baker for supporting the Gun Control Act of 1968, which they said meant support for further restricting the sale and ownership of guns. The distortion prompted National Rifle Association lobbyist Neal Knox to praise Baker prior to the primary for having been a big help in fighting further limitations. The misfiring of the gun issue sealed the fate of Harvey Howard to an 8.8 percent showing.[12]

Jane Eskind won by a closer margin in the Democratic primary, but her victory embarrassed many who saw her of insufficient stature to challenge Baker. To facilitate defections, Baker established an adjunct committee dubbed "Tennesseans for Baker" and installed State Senator Ed Blank of Columbia as chairman and Henry Hooker, the brother of former gubernatorial nominee John J. Hooker, Frances Hooks, the wife of NAACP Executive Secretary Benjamin Hooks, and former State Representative Harold Sterling, a conservative who Baker protégé Lamar Alexander trounced in the GOP gubernatorial primary, as vice-chairmen. That Blank, a former majority leader, risked sanctions to endorse Baker signified that several Democratic leaders and thousands of their followers would cross over in the privacy of the voting booth. For Eskind, the news indicated that her chances of winning rested upon her success in limiting further defections and Tom Anderson's ability to pull GOP opponents of the Panama Canal Treaties away from Baker.[13]

The Taftite Returns to Washington

If there was a figure in conservative iconography who symbolized a descendance from Robert Taft, it was the often obstinate but always forthright Barry Goldwater. With civil rights the central moral issue of American life in the 1950s and 1960s, liberals sensed negligence in Taft's opposition to a Fair Employment Practices Commission and Goldwater's vote against the Civil Rights Act of 1964. But such an appearance rests upon a narrow reading of these positions, as the keys to the philosophies of Goldwater and Taft were grounded in a strict constructionist view of the Tenth Amendment, which reserves for states those powers not granted to the central government. Implicit within Taft's advocacy of Supreme Court decisions opening southern graduate and professional schools to blacks and his 1946 aid to education bill were reliances upon orderly procedures of law and the use of financial incentives to encourage the South to institute practices treating all races equally. For Goldwater, local control was an unbending principle that he promoted regardless of the political consequences. No sharper symbol of the crusty Arizonans determination to empower people to control their own destinies exists than in his 1978 alliance with Edward Kennedy behind a constitutional amendment giving the District of Columbia voting representation in Congress for the first time, a move that all recognized would add two seats to an already powerful 62–38 Senate Democratic majority.[14]

Baker's grounding in Taftite principles was as strong as Goldwater's. Like Goldwater, Baker was attracted by the democratic principles of the D.C. representation amendment and encouraged by its endorsements in both the Republican and Democratic platforms of 1976. But as both a floor leader and one who wanted to see justice done, he had to consider elements of timing. Sensing that the civil rights lobby had not developed support for the measure outside the black community, he advised proponents to wait until closer to the election when blacks might make it a litmus test for all candidates for federal office. While his warnings were prescient, as only sixteen states voted to ratify the amendment, the House's approval of the measure forced the issue upon the Senate. Baker gained hope when he noticed southerners like Strom Thurmond, John Sparkman, and Herman Talmadge, who had opposed all previous civil rights legislation, backing the amendment with chairmen Bill Brock and John White of the Republican and Democratic National Committees. While ratification was far-fetched, Baker saw the resolution's defeat would be even more harmful and declared the day before the vote that the 700,000 residents of the district had a "right not only to a voice but to a vote."[15]

Right after the 67–32 vote, Baker shook hands with Edward Kennedy, whom many credited with the victory. But Kennedy's task was easy, as Democrats were accustomed to solid blocs of black votes. Only five GOP senators had ever won a majority of black votes, but nineteen voted to give the district voting representation, leading Kennedy to praise GOP leaders, as they had provided the margin with little hope of a payoff at the polls. The seemingly permanent alliance between blacks and Democrats confounded Baker. The GOP had "been so far out, so long," he said, "that we don't even have any sensing mechanism." While he in part had made his reputation through his work in removing discriminations, his focus had shifted to the development of programs within the free-market model to upgrade the quality of life for minorities. His welfare reform model reflected this, as did his sponsorship of a bill creating a center to train minority workers involved in building the Tennessee-Tombigbee Waterway. Looking at things purely politically, he told the Black Republican Council that the GOP could not succeed unless it involved blacks.[16] While Bill Brock was supportive, the idea of appealing to blacks was resisted by GOP pols in states without large black populations and by others whose past sins were too many to hope for electoral atonement. As such, an opportunity for the GOP to make inroads into the black vote was lost. Even in Baker's home state, the Tennessee Voters' Council, the state's largest black organization, endorsed Jane Eskind, who, never having been elected to office, had no concrete record of support for their group or any other.

One liberal group where Baker did find friends was the education lobby. Like Robert Taft, he saw education as a means to opportunity and long had cosponsored bills granting tax credits to those paying college or vocational school tuition, believing such incentives would provide relief for low- and middle-income families. He found less meritorious the idea of extending similar credits to parents of elementary and secondary school children in private schools, deeming them stimuli to "segregation academies" and invitations to parents to take their children out of public schools. While appreciative, teachers' groups were more interested in 1978 in creating a separate Department of Education. Baker cosponsored their legislation and joined twenty-three other Republicans in voting aye when the bill reached the floor in September 1978. Two days later, he flew to Nashville to receive the thanks of the Tennessee Education Association (TEA). While mentioning his support for the voluntary prayer amendment and the back-to-basics movement, he focused upon hailing the Senate's action and declaring that no other duty of government was as "closely bound . . . to the lives of the people." Immediately upon his departure, the 40,000-member group gave him their endorsement.[17]

One Final Campaign Thrust in Tennessee

While Baker was again making inroads into generally Democratic groups, Jane Eskind, whose liberalism was reflected in her preprimary endorsements of the Kennedy national health insurance plan and some Carter defense cuts, was trying to wage a vigorous campaign as what some reporters called an "Archie Bunker conservative." In ads, she proclaimed her disgust with Baker's votes for the Panama Canal Treaties and her support for a voluntary prayer amendment to the Constitution. But Baker had surrogate Ed Blank reveal that she had moved at a September 1977 Democratic Executive Committee meeting to suspend the rules to allow that body to endorse the accords. Baker then recalled her speech against including a voluntary prayer plank in the 1972 Democratic platform, to which she replied that most Tennessee religious leaders opposed him because he backed government-mandated prayer. Astonished by her misrepresentation of his support for voluntary prayer, Baker declared her "as liberal as any politician in the state." Harold Sterling, his link to right-wing groups, went him one better by calling her a wolf in sheep's clothing, as she backed the Panama Canal Treaties, amnesty for draft dodgers and deserters, defense cuts, and federally funded abortions.[18]

The abortion issue was no godsend for Baker. With opponents, he believed the *Roe v. Wade* decision a mistake, as it removed from states, whom he deemed the proper arbiters of the question, the right to permit abortions. But he found it increasingly difficult to listen to either lobby with sympathy and meditated that abortion was "freighted with all of the moral, cultural and religious weight a single issue can bear." In 1977, he had voted against a bill eliminating all restrictions on the use of federal money for abortions. More often, he had backed measures allowing Medicaid funding in cases of rape, incest, and danger to the mother's life or health, leading Monsignor Leo G. Siener of Nashville to chastise him as "a leader of the pro-abortion forces." Here was a charge that won few votes for Eskind. Not only had Siener overstated Baker's role and ignored his discomfort with the issue, he had also failed to note confusing and conflicting statements from Jane Eskind.[19]

Even though Eskind's ardor disturbed some Democrats who were "offended that a Democratic candidate is attacking Howard Baker, conservative as he is, from the right," her candidacy remained viable. Not only was the Democratic base in Tennessee strong, but Tennessee blacks were generally in her corner, and union leaders were more determined than ever to defeat Baker. It thus became incumbent upon her to attack Baker as a creature of the establishment, and her strategy worked while business kept him in Washington. One mid-October poll showed that she had cut his lead to six points.[20]

But Baker had a few secret weapons. One was Joy, who had always been reticent about speaking before groups. But this time her friend Frances Hooks was pushing her in her firm but cheerful manner. "My participation with my husband has meant that I might forgo any shyness or inhibitions," the first lady of the NAACP counseled. "You've got to do the same thing." Joy fought the idea for a while, then gave in and spoke to a small group Mrs. Hooks assembled in Memphis. "Her honesty goes over," Mrs. Hooks noted, and her success added to her confidence in her ability to deal with people.[21]

Not until October 16 could Baker return home knowing that no further Senate business would be conducted. He resumed campaigning as he landed. While generally blasting the policies of Jimmy Carter, he did commend Carter for persuading Egypt and Israel to agree upon the framework for a peace treaty. Limiting his attention to Eskind, he had aides document that he had spent 142 days in Tennessee in 1977 while answering more than 80 percent of that year's roll calls, thus negating Eskind's logo—"She Hasn't Lost Touch with Tennessee"—and prompting her to dig deeper to discredit him. Hardly surprised, Baker remained confident. Accustomed to support from Tennessee's metropolitan dailies,[22] he found even more encouraging boosts from rural Middle Tennessee. Baker, said the *Sparta Expositor*, had done "more for the good name of Tennessee . . . than anyone since . . . Senator Kefauver and Secretary Hull." More blunt was the *Clarksville Leaf-Chronicle*. "He possesses just about every qualification," it said. "Lacking just about every qualification . . . is his . . . opponent, Jane Eskind."[23]

Desperate, Eskind attacked Baker for his work in creating the Big South Fork National River and Recreation Area, saying his friends would benefit and his vote to override Carter's veto of a bill funding it was a conflict of interest. This Ron McMahan dubbed irresponsible, noting that environmentalists had instigated the park's creation. Eskind then declared it the fault of Baker, "the only man who can straddle a snail darter," that the Senate rejected an amendment exempting the Tellico Dam from the Endangered Species Act. His sending John Chafee to a conference committee in his stead, she said, had allowed extremists to block completion. Baker extolled the merits of his amendment, telling several audiences it was inconceivable that a reasonable body would block completion of the dam. Angry that she was not scoring points, Eskind said Baker was "lying" when he said his amendment would save the dam, a charge that confounded Baker, who could not recall a statewide candidate calling an opponent a liar. Appalled by the course of her campaign, Baker urged her to "calm down." Hardly dissuaded, Eskind clung to the low road and charged him with a trail of financial dealings and conflicts of interest. Focusing on his 1977 measure allowing TVA to operate its coal-fired, steam-powered Kingston plant without scrubbers, she said it was designed to benefit him, as TVA bought some of the highly sulfurous coal it burned from strip-miners who leased some of the Brimstone land in which he had once held an interest. But the TVA board of directors and the Tennessee General Assembly had cleared him before he ever advanced the measure, knowing three of his friends—Don Stansbury, Bill Swain, and Bob Worthington—had bought his interest from his blind trust. With little emotion, he noted that the $375 million cost would force the plant's closing and thus, a 17 percent increase in customer rates and a rise in unemployment among East Tennessee coal miners.[24]

It was Eskind's hope that a Carter visit to Nashville on October 26 would lend her a boost, as Carter, while earlier under fire for cutting funds from Tennessee projects, had seemed to revive his fortunes with his triumph at Camp David. Greeted by thousands of Democrats and a few Republicans with signs like "Miz Lillian was right, Billy is smarter," Carter did find time to hail Eskind as a champion of "the little people." But he resisted the temptation to attack Baker, not wanting to incur the wrath of someone who might help him in the future and looked certain to win reelection. Aides made clear that Carter had come to help Democratic gubernatorial nominee Jake Butcher, who was enmeshed in a close race with Lamar Alexander, and not Eskind.[25]

While only Eskind considered the Senate race close, Baker took no chances, reserving the campaign's last week for a whistle-stop tour of the state. He began in Bristol with Joy, Darek, Cissy, Roy Acuff, Ed Blank, Robin Beard, John Duncan, and Jimmy Quillen, a host of local candidates and even more reporters, and the train picked up Lamar and Honey Alexander later in the tour. While using the trek to shoot nearly one thousand rolls of film of his beloved Tennessee, Baker took the time between shots to work the caboose platform and introduce each of his ticket mates to each of his audiences. In some respects, he was out of place, as he was cast at the tender age of fifty-two as his state party's elder statesman. While spooning out disagreements with Jimmy Carter and ignoring Eskind, save to tell those who encouraged retaliation that he "didn't stoop to name calling when I ran against Ross Bass or Frank Clement or Ray Blanton, and I sure ain't gonna have to do it against Jane Eskind," he also took time to address local concerns. In Knoxville, the home of TVA, he condemned the Carter energy program as "an impenetrable maze of regulations" that would result in "the same . . . dependence on imported energy this policy was to reduce." In Cowan and Sweetwater, he vowed to see the Tellico Dam to completion. In Lenoir City, he recited his votes against bids to restrict gun ownership by law-abiding citizens and called upon Eskind to end confusion about her positions on prayer, gun control, and tax reduction.[26]

By the time the *Rose Bud* reached Memphis, Baker was certain that he and Alexander would win. Crowds had been enthusiastic even in towns with long Democratic traditions. Save for the Chattanooga stop, where union members met him with signs carrying the middle-finger salute and caption, "This Is For You, Howie," the trip proceeded smoothly. Certain this would be his last Senate race, he returned to Knoxville to make a Saturday-before-the-election trip to Huntsville along a path through the winding roads of East Tennessee that his father had carved out nearly thirty years earlier.[27]

Three days later, Tennesseans gave Baker 55.5 percent of their votes. His showing was down, reflecting the presence of Tom Anderson, who won 4.2 percent from the hard core of those opposed to the Panama Canal Treaties. Baker carried solid majorities in seven of the state's eight congressional districts, losing only in the black majority Eighth, a pattern resembling that of Lamar Alexander, who actually won 19,315 votes more than he. Not threatened, Baker took as much pride in his protégé's victory as in his own and boasted only that he had "kept a civil tongue."[28]

A Firm Break with Carter

Even while contemplating a campaign for president, it was not Baker's desire to blindly obstruct matters that Carter deemed vital. Always a believer in a strong presidency and that presidential strength flows in part from congressional confidence in his judgment, he had suggested to Carter in the same meeting where he told him that he would support amended Panama Canal Treaties that the two work together, as Everett Dirksen had with Presidents Kennedy and Johnson, to develop a bipartisan foreign policy. Some Carter aides liked the idea enough to hail Baker as one of the greatest bipartisan statesmen in recent decades. But Carter, with no close friends in either chamber and, having carved no back channels as governor of Georgia, would not develop them as president, not even with Baker, a man chief congressional liaison Frank Moore found a "joy to work with" and one he "would have voted for" for president.[29]

Carter's style seldom impacted legislation in the House, which Democrats held by nearly two-to-one margins throughout his tenure. But what partisans deemed proper for the House was hardly the best practice for the Senate, especially on foreign policy. Never in Carter's tenure did Democrats enjoy the two-thirds majority necessary to pass treaties by themselves; by 1979, their ranks had fallen to fifty-nine, one less than the number needed for cloture. And Democrats were divided. Many like Sam Nunn and Henry Jackson believed Carter's defense cuts had been harmful to American security and questioned the wisdom of a SALT-II Treaty. But they were consulted before Carter abandoned the B-1 bomber and the neutron bomb and reduced funds for naval construction. Most Republicans had not been consulted, and comments like Baker's "another in a long line of national defense mistakes" dotted newspapers. As Carter had made each decision on his view of the merits, he took angrily news that some senators would link their SALT-II votes to their perception of the state of American defenses. To him, the issue was partisan politics, a notion shaped by some who had overheard talk that some Republicans would vote no to please rich extremists. But, while anti-Soviet rhetoric flowed liberally throughout the 1976 campaign, some of it from Carter's own mouth, talk of opposing a SALT-II Treaty was limited to a handful of senators until Carter stopped production of the B-1 bomber in July 1977. Thereafter, such discussions became common, even among those like Baker and Daniel Patrick Moynihan, who had long defended the SALT process.[30]

Believing Baker was the one Republican whose help it was imperative to get to secure ratification, Carter encouraged Baker, John Danforth, Jake Garn, S. I. Hayakawa, John Tower, and Malcolm Wallop to fly to Moscow to meet with Soviet President Leonid Brezhnev. Before leaving, Baker told Carter that he would inform Brezhnev that the Senate would consider any accords in the overall context of Soviet American relations and that he considered the idea of concluding a SALT agreement as an executive agreement unwise. While Carter took this as a sign of opposition, Baker left open a possibility that he might support an amended pact. "I don't want you and me to get in the same situation as Henry Cabot Lodge and Woodrow Wilson," he said.[31]

Baker's party met with their Clemenceau in early January and found Brezhnev old, domineering, and intransigent. Confounding to them was a predictable

Brezhnev lecture that ratification was necessary to ensure that the world did not return to the dangerous atmosphere of the 1950s and 1960s. Baker, the highest-ranking member, opened the response by describing an imperative for America and the USSR to "continue to negotiate, no matter how long it takes, to bring about a reduction . . . in the nuclear arsenals of both countries." But, he said in a way "so . . . skillful . . . and yet so diplomatic" that Jake Garn thinks that he "could elect . . . Baker president" if he had a videotape, that the Senate was unlikely to ratify the agreement without changes. Too many Senators, he added, feared that Carter had been outtraded. Brezhnev stormed the room, bent paper clips, and demanded that he outline his concerns. Baker cited verification and said he would oppose SALT-II unless America could verify Soviet compliance. "Talk to your own people," Brezhnev responded. "They can verify anything." To Brezhnev, verification was a small issue. To Baker, it was one of many, although its importance grew once America abandoned its monitoring stations in Iran. Just as troubling to Baker was a portion counting U.S. B-52s as strategic weapons but not more modern Soviet Backfire bombers. Brezhnev termed these concerns as inconsequential as protests from others that it was hypocritical to allow the Soviets to point SS-20 missiles at Western Europe while America could not transfer cruise-missile technology to its NATO allies.[32]

Such inequities Baker took as evidence that the Soviets aimed to secure a military advantage. Having learned that the Soviet Defense Ministry had theorized that "by means of powerful nuclear strikes, strategy can obtain its objectives directly," he took these words to mean "first strike no matter what . . . language." Knowing Soviet leaders feared retaliation from U.S. air- and sea-based forces and were unlikely to launch a first strike, he believed that a SALT-II accord might serve America poorly if the USSR could divert resources to non-nuclear pursuits. When Baker noted that Cuban troops were increasingly active in southern Africa and that the Soviets were concentrating more troops and missiles in Eastern Europe, Brezhnev responded that the Eastern bloc had "not added one thing to . . . our Warsaw Pact in ten years," and "you . . . have done nothing but stream an endless reinforcement of NATO power." When Tower interrupted, "That is exactly contrary to our understanding" and "something both of us can verify," his colleagues were left guessing if Brezhnev was bluffing or merely ignorant of the practices of his Defense Ministry.[33]

Baker returned to Washington more determined than ever to delay SALT-II until it was substantially revised. Other senators who had visited Moscow, including some Carter expected to support the pact, were angered by a Soviet posture Carter found "heavy-handed, abrupt, rude and argumentative." Arms control exponent Jacob Javits complained that the Soviets were not willing to give up anything. Even in the face of such bluster, however, Carter continued to insist that a rejection of SALT-II would brand America as warmongers, a posture Baker found wrongheaded. While reserving room to maneuver if Carter took his concerns to heart, Baker took his case to a February assembly of GOP-elected officials in Easton, Maryland, and won near unanimous approval for a resolution declaring the SALT-II debate a time to reexamine the U.S.-Soviet relationship. While some saw the resolution as a rejection of a bipartisan foreign policy, Baker declared "Vandenberg . . . right in his time . . . but we . . . right in ours." In his Lincoln Day addresses, Baker vowed to fight for an America "so strong no nation would ever dare challenge us" and warned of a "gap in our ability to defend . . . against a first-strike." Of more immediacy were problems arising from a revolution in Iran that had toppled the government of the Shah and installed a loosely organized mob structure accountable only to the Ayatollah Khomeini. Declining comment when asked what course the revolution might take, Baker hoped that Carter had made adequate provisions for evacuating U.S. citizens, a prophetic warning, as mobs seized the embassy the next day. More ominously, Afghan terrorists assassinated Ambassador Adolph "Spike" Dubs in the streets of Kabul. "A view is growing around the world that America is a patsy," Baker told Massachusetts Republicans. "We do more with someone who shoots a cop than someone who shoots an ambassador." The Middle East's volatility, he said, necessitated a signal that U.S. emissaries were off-limits so as not to leave Americans as sitting ducks.[34]

Equally troubling to Baker was a unanimous decision by the "God Committee" not to exempt the snail darter. Having cowritten the law creating that panel, he was appalled that it had justified its decision on economic grounds it had no authority to use. Certain that TVA had complied with the spirit of the act by transferring schools of snail darters from the Little Tennessee River to pools nearby, he introduced bills exempting the dam and abolishing the committee. Few wanted to terminate the panel, but exempting the dam appealed to enough to prompt environmentalists to make an exemption a litmus test. Once they convinced the Environment and Public Works Committee to vote down a Baker move of early May to exempt the dam by a 3–8 margin and the full Senate to reach a similar 43–52 verdict, Baker vowed not to "stand by and see a stultification of common sense." He and Jim Sasser aimed to attach a reauthorization for the dam to a water development bill scheduled to be considered in July. While the House approved the exemption, John Culver moved to delete it, saying it would subvert the review process. Baker disagreed, holding that the process was designed to resist the extremes of well-intentioned environmentalists. Again, the Senate rejected his arguments, this time by a 45–53 margin, leaving a deadlock that conferees could not break. Once the House again voiced its approval, Baker warned that the extremism surrounding proposals to give the snail darter "ultimate veto power" over its habitat might doom their movement. This time, colleagues, by a 48–44 margin, voted with him, more out of a desire to accelerate the flow of money to their states than anything else.[35]

While Carter reluctantly signed the bill, the victory was a truly Pyrrhic one for Baker in both the long and short runs. Although discoveries of snail darters in several Tennessee streams in the 1980s rendered bogus the claims of environmentalists, the promised economic harvest from the planned Timberlake community never appeared either. At home, the God Committee's decision had embarrassed him on a matter he considered one of simple common sense. Three Senate debates had reduced the time he could devote to his presidential campaign and to more substantive matters like the bill creating a Department of Education that conservatives, buoyed by a rare alliance with HEW Secretary Joseph Califano, hoped to kill with amendments purporting to tackle ticklish issues like sex education and prayer in the schools. Most controversial was a proposal to end the agency's charter in 1985, which only Baker and six other Republicans joined most Democrats and Carter in opposing. But their votes were crucial, as the amendment was killed by just two votes, making passage certain.[36]

The Education Department debate marked the end of a once-productive Baker-Carter working relationship. Save for the bill implementing the terms of the Panama Canal Treaties, virtually no proposal thereafter bears their joint imprint. In part, Carter, who later told interviewers that he valued it that Baker told him the truth, was becoming sensitive to the jealousies of some senators in his own party, chiefly Majority Leader Robert Byrd, about the considerable productivity of his work with Baker. By summer, Carter aides were saying that their boss believed further cooperation with Baker might further his image as a bipartisan statesman and render more viable a presidential candidacy Carter deemed the most formidable of any. Instinctively a populist and a Wilsonian, Carter saw himself as a trustee for the national interest and took to adopting unbending positions on the issues he deemed priorities. Later, Baker termed Carter a man of "too much substance and too little politics." At the time, he chided the detail-absorbed Carter as a "yellow-pad President." So frequent was it that Carter urged him to do the right thing without building support among Republicans, affected groups, or the public that Baker told Carter he would lose the next election if he voted right many more times, and he told friends that "deep down" he'd like to tell Carter to "go to hell." Submerging such feelings, he offered to help Carter on SALT-II to the point of providing regular whip checks of GOP senators.[37]

It was Baker's fervent hope that his objections could be incorporated through a series of amendments, as had happened during the Panama Canal debate, and he volunteered his services as an amendment broker to senators skeptical of a new arms agreement. SALT-II proponent Gary Hart had been to Geneva, knew some negotiators were opposed to the pact, and suggested to Carter aides that Carter might be best served by taking Baker up on his offer and not putting all its eggs in the basket of Henry "Scoop" Jackson, a patron of the dissidents. While getting the message, Carter soon took to declaring that addenda would doom the pact, a stance allowing the Soviets to harden their position. While his lobbyists knew it would be virtually impossible to approve the pact without Baker, Carter continued to put him off, fearing that the Soviets wouldn't stand for change.[38]

Of greater political concern was the cost of gasoline, which had risen since mid-1978 from sixty cents a gallon to nearly a dollar, reflecting a doubling of the price of foreign crude, even bigger hikes on the spot market, and an interruption in exports from Iran, where a workers' strike had halted production. Mile-long gas lines were common near most cities. To forestall occasionally violent discontent, governors in hard-hit states imposed a variety of programs, the most prevalent being an odd-even system of distribution. Wide differences in orientation were evident. Stressing a need for conservation, Carter called for a ten-cent tax on each gallon of gasoline and a windfall-profits tax on producers, from which an energy security fund would be created to develop alternative energy sources and public transportation systems. He would use his authority to decontrol oil prices and seek new power to mandate gas rationing and other conservation measures in the event of emergencies. Consumer groups targeted Carter's decontrol plan, believing it would increase prices, but their aim to maintain the same artificially low prices attracted almost no support in Congress, as most members believed controls would perpetuate America's dependence on foreign oil.[39]

"The only way the United States . . . is going to get out of this energy crisis," Baker said often, "is to produce its way out." Like Carter, he desired a phased decontrol program and a windfall-profits tax to prevent oil companies from gouging the public. But unlike Carter, he wanted incentives for firms to plow back profits into production and exploration. While encouraged by a Carter plan embodying many tenets of his own, Baker found inexplicable Carter's vacillation between schemes of control and decontrol and cringed at his straw man of a massive effort by the oil companies to defeat the windfall-profits tax. Guessing Carter could have it virtually for the asking, he said he had not been lobbied by the oil companies save after he had given them a friendly warning that they risked nationalization if they were found profiting excessively during shortages. Here again, Baker and John Rhodes offered to work with Carter on a bipartisan energy policy. Not getting a response, he said all he and Rhodes could do was assume "Jimmy Carter was not interested."[40]

Baker had a few ideas to alleviate such problems. He drafted a bill creating a Home Heating Fuel Stamp Program to be administered with the food stamp program. More often, he stressed production, backing proposals adding funds for research and development for geothermal and solar sources and stimulating the coal and nuclear industries. Coal, he acknowledged, had an inherently superior position because of psychological fallout from an accident at the Three Mile Island nuclear plant, where "things happened . . . that I'd been assured couldn't happen." Suggesting that authority to license reactors, train operators, and protect facilities be centralized in a single federal agency, he urged the nuclear industry to take steps like clustering ten to twenty reactors in parks away from population centers that would make its product more politically and socially acceptable. While the issue had little potential as few Republicans questioned the use of nuclear energy, Baker argued it with relish. The one time the issue was the focus of a debate, Baker espoused his idea of nuclear parks and California Governor Jerry Brown, a long-shot Democratic presidential aspirant, attacked it, declaring future accidents likely. "You can't put the genie back in the bottle," Baker replied. "It is wrong to frighten the people with the concept of a nuclear priesthood." The debate meant little, as it was not broadcast. But crowd response indicated that the winner was Baker, a surprising verdict as most present were Democrats.[41]

Another facet of the nuclear issue preoccupied Baker. With the SALT-II Treaty not limiting Soviet deployment of SS-18s or counting its Backfire bomber as a strategic weapon, Baker told Carter on June 21 that he would not support the treaty without amendments.[42] Two days later, Robert Byrd told Brezhnev that the Senate was not required to ratify SALT-II and that amendments would help. To this, Foreign Minister Andrei Gromyko replied that any addition would mean the end of negotiations, thus convincing Baker that the chances that his doubts would be alleviated were nil.[43]

Pundits had long speculated about the political fallout of Baker's SALT-II stance. Proponents said he would be considered a statesman if he sided with them and be seen as pandering to the New Right if he opposed them. But their assessment of the imagery was a bit convoluted, as their position was supported by large majorities. Many were surprised when he declared that SALT-II would give the Soviets substantial strategic superiority and vowed to work to defeat it unless it were amended. With the Soviets unwilling to consider addenda, he believed it counterproductive to try to ratify an amended agreement. Carter, he said later, had brought SALT-II to the Senate before he "was ready to bring it to the Senate. Once you do that you can't do much about it because you've already got the Soviets on the line." Determined to have the Soviets reduce its force of 308 SS-18 missiles for which America had no equivalent, he also wanted the Soviets to count the Backfire bomber as a strategic weapon and ensure that Soviet compliance could be verified. Approving the treaty as submitted, he said, would send an unfortunate signal that America accepted the status quo, a perception he feared would invite the Soviets to abandon the "continuum of reducing arms."[44]

Baker's position hardened over the next few weeks as he grew more confident of his knowledge of the issues involved. Accepting Carter's position that the question was "whether we are better off with this treaty than without it," he met Carter's prediction of grave consequences if the Senate rejected the pact by warning of equally dire prospects if it were approved. Troubled by Defense Secretary Brown's guess that Soviet ICBM strength had grown to triple or quadruple the

U.S. number under SALT-II, he suggested that America's power of deterrence was much weaker than in 1972.[45]

Many others were questioning Carter's judgment. A June poll revealed that fewer people approved of Carter's performance than had approved of Richard Nixon's at his lowest point. Upon returning from the annual summit of leaders of the Western democracies, Carter canceled a planned address on the energy crisis and began parading political advisors, governors, members of Congress, and other opinion shapers to Camp David. The only GOP governor invited was chairman Otis Bowen of the National Governors Conference. While three GOP senators were there, congressional Republican leaders were excluded. And all were surprised when Carter announced that he had amended earlier plans with a new $80 billion Synthetic Fuels Corporation, and an Energy Mobilization Board to cut through red tape.[46]

While opposed to a Synthetic Fuels Corporation, Baker vowed not to "nickel and dime these proposals to death." But Carter's real message, Germond and Witcover wrote, "was an attempt to shift blame from himself to the people." In describing a "crisis of confidence" that posed a "fundamental threat to American democracy," Carter said the government had become "isolated from the mainstream of our nation's life" and that the people had been given "false claims . . . and politics as usual." Two days later, Baker promised Carter he would decide each program on its merits and warned that if he wanted to speak to a Senate Republican, he should talk to him, the party's elected leader. Carter promised candor in the future, and Baker left the Oval Office with a grin that faded when reporters asked him what he thought of Carter's request of his cabinet that each member submit his or her resignation, a step Carter had told him nothing about. But the joke was on Carter, for his firings of Secretaries Brock Adams (Transportation), W. Michael Blumenthal (Treasury), and Joseph Califano (Health, Education, and Welfare) and the resignations of Attorney General Griffin Bell and Energy Secretary James Schlesinger conveyed an image of a government under siege, and his ratings fell by the end of the week to where they were before his speech. Thinking "malaise" a phony issue and finding it hard to believe that Carter was still espousing anti-Washington themes, as the only possible scapegoats were a Democratic Congress and administration, Baker told one audience that he was astonished to hear Carter tell the American people that they have lost confidence in themselves. "The fact is the people have lost faith in Jimmy Carter."[47]

The Breaking Point Hardens

Baker's breaking point with Carter had been the SALT-II Treaty, which was jeopardized even further when it was learned in August that the Soviets had stationed a 2,600-man combat brigade in Cuba. Foreign Relations Committee Chairman

Frank Church, long an exponent of arms control, postponed deliberations and declared ratification unlikely until the troops were removed. While Carter pronounced the situation unacceptable, Baker saw the brigade as another example of the Russians "thumbing their noses at us" as they had by stationing pilots in Cuba, Cuban combat units in Africa, and East European fighting forces in Afghanistan, South Yemen, and Yemen. While Baker called upon Carter to make public intelligence confirming the brigade's presence, Carter, who was dismayed by the decision delaying the hearings, accepted explanations that the unit was there to train Cuban troops. This hardly placated Baker. "In a toe-to-toe confrontation," he said, "we blinked." When asked what would save the treaty, he responded that a Soviet agreement to allow an addendum requiring it to count its Backfire bomber toward its limit would probably be enough to sway enough senators, albeit not him.[48]

To Baker's chagrin, the Backfire issue was nonnegotiable to the Soviets and to Carter. Not only were fellow Republicans S. I. Hayakawa, Jesse Helms, and Richard Lugar aligned against the accord, but John Glenn, who had been an expert on satellite photography since his days as an astronaut, believed that the portions relating to verification made it impossible to detect Soviet cheating. Their votes were but five of the fifteen needed to delay considering the accord, but Democrats Richard Stone and Edward Zorinsky let it be known that they would also vote against the pact without amendments. When markup sessions opened, Baker, fully cognizant of the ramifications of a failure to approve the accord, declared the operative question as whether America got a good deal or a bad deal and whether the treaty was fair and equitable. With Henry Kissinger and Andrei Gromyko having agreed in 1976 that the Soviets would constrain the deployment of Backfires if the United States counted cruise-missile-carrying bombers against its MIRV subceiling, the Backfire bomber provisions failed both tests. To counter such disadvantages, Baker introduced an amendment requiring the Soviets to count Backfires against their ceiling of strategic weapons and allowing the United States to count its less powerful F-111 bombers as half of a weapon toward its limit, but it failed in committee by a 5–10 vote.[49]

Debate proceeded in a civil fashion until Baker raised the matter of the Soviet heavy ICBMs. Believing "we could have gotten rid of the SS-18s," he introduced an amendment on October 23 granting America the right to build a similar system, which failed, 7–8. The next day, he tried an alternative. If America could not develop such a system, the Soviets should dismantle its SS-18 launchers. SALT-II, he lectured, was merely a means and not an end in itself, and Carter had been out-bargained. His words drew the wrath of White House special counsel Lloyd Cutler, who lectured that Carter did not have the luxury others had of rejecting any portion of a treaty that did not seem ideal. While Carter aides always aimed to portray Baker's skepticism as politically motivated, they had always been more subtle. With Cutler, Carter's top SALT-II lobbyist, making such charges openly,

Baker let loose his own barrage. "The nation is in great peril," he lectured, "because you did a bad job negotiating this treaty and . . . left in place these monstrous . . . weapons . . . and gave us no corresponding right . . . to build such a system." Even so, the panel rejected this amendment and another abrogating the pact if the Soviets did not dismantle their SS-18 launchers.[50]

The first formal test for SALT-II came on November 9, when the Foreign Relations Committee voted 9–6 to report it. But even this was illusory, as Edward Zorinsky said that he would not support the pact without amendments. A month later, the Armed Services Committee declared SALT-II not in the national interest, by a 10–0 vote, meaning only fifteen of the thirty-two senators on panels with jurisdiction over SALT-II were behind it. If anything, Baker's effectiveness in leading the opposition made the debate he had long sought less certain. Carter's one hope was that he could pick off enough recalcitrants with amendments crafted to alleviate the concerns of moderates and conservatives in both parties about the pact's equitability. This would have been difficult. By October 1979, the anti–SALT-II lobby counted forty solid votes against the pact if it came to a vote, some of them from senators like Russell Long, who, while loyal to Carter, believed it "horribly ridiculous" to suppose that Soviet compliance with the treaty could be verified completely with satellite photography.[51]

Here in effect was another Pyrrhic victory for Baker. If SALT-II was not desirable, and the removal of the SS-18s in the 1987 INF Treaty, an action Brezhnev declared out of the question in 1979, lends some credence to that view, then it may be correct to cite the axiom of Edward Gibbon that "progress is made not by what goes on the statute books, but by what comes off." To be sure, Baker would never go so far as to hold with Taft that the purpose of the opposition is to oppose. If Baker's view of the national interest coincided with or even resembled Carter's, he did not hesitate to push legislation to see that their sources of agreement were made law. But herein lay the largest part of Baker's strength as a legislative leader and his weakness as a national candidate. Inasmuch as his success stemmed from the meticulous personal attention he gave to each of his colleagues' concerns and their faith in his word, it also rendered negligible the time he could spend wooing the grassroots activists who so dominate the process of nominating a president.[52]

Nor was it to Baker's benefit that the national clientele of the GOP had changed somewhat since the days of Taft. The dominance of those A. James Reichley calls stalwarts over Republican affairs had given Taft readymade blocs of delegates of small-town professionals and merchants from the Midwest and the South at the GOP conventions of 1940, 1948, and 1952. Stalwarts still played a large role in the GOP, but the best-organized GOP groups by the late 1970s were those Reichley deemed fundamentalists. Never as numerous as their leaders claimed, they mitigated this deficiency with their intensity and their capacity to get their supporters to the polls. Were Baker to have a chance, he would have to combine his stalwart compatriots with majorities of less-organized moderate and progressive Republicans, not to mention a few fundamentalists. Here was a feat Baker had accomplished three times in Tennessee, where voters were familiar with his record and character. Those outside of Tennessee were not so exposed, and the GOP voters who did know of him knew of his stature as a leader of the Senate. If approval ratings are any indication, they respected him. But respect in political terms is not love, and love rarely comes on the basis of a reputation. In troubled times, as 1979 seemed to be, voters look for potential presidents from those who can evoke dreams of monumental change. It was Baker's hope that the electorate would opt for an experienced candidate who knew Washington well enough to change Washington. To be sure, Baker's work on issues like the environment, the Fair Housing Act, and the Panama Canal Treaties guaranteed him audiences of often dispassionate progressives and moderates. He, too, could hope that word would spread of his aloofness from the ways of Washington, thus allowing him inroads among stalwarts and fundamentalists outside of Tennessee. But fundamentalists were already devoted to a candidate who had risen in Horatio Alger fashion from roots in Dixon, Illinois. It was a tall order for the five-foot-seven Baker to supplant Ronald Reagan and a monumental one in the short amount of time before the caucuses and primaries.

Chapter 10

A PRESIDENTIAL CANDIDACY DIES; A MAJORITY LEADER IS BORN 1979–1980

Until Bill Clinton's election, it was standard for a generation of successful non-incumbent aspirants to the presidency to engage in a four-year marathon of campaigning. Curiously enough, Baker did not initiate his bid for the presidency until after his reelection in 1978. With polls showing him a solid but distant third behind Gerald Ford and Ronald Reagan, Baker had a potentially strong base if Ford did not run. But his seeming foundation in the center of GOP thought was a vacuum that several—Senators Bob Dole, Larry Pressler, and Lowell Weicker, ex-CIA Director George Bush, and Congressman John Anderson—sought to fill. Save for Dole, Baker was the best-known of the aspirants to Ford's crown as champion of the wing of the GOP most pundits deemed the moderate one. Yet even that distinction is misleading, as an early poll showed only 44 percent of the Republicans who responded knew enough about him to comment on his qualifications.[1]

Lesser-known candidates aimed to raise their name recognition by spending most of their time in Iowa and New Hampshire, hoping a win in either would draw enough attention to bring money rushing in from new donors and votes following in subsequent contests. Philip Crane used his time after announcing his candidacy in August 1978 trying to convince rightists that Reagan was too old or too soft to warrant their support. More successful was Bush, who copied the Carter strategy of developing strong organizations in the early states while avoiding clear stands on the issues.[2] Baker, in contrast, did not set foot in New Hampshire in 1978 until December 1. Somewhat limited throughout 1978 by the time he gave to his own reelection and his duties as Leader, he was the only one of the major contenders—the others being Bush, Reagan, and former Texas Governor and Treasury Secretary John Connally—with a full time job. By the time he got started, rivals had substantial head starts in co-opting the support of key workers in states with early caucuses and primaries.

While others waged individual campaigns, Baker acted as a party spokesman, telling audiences that any of his GOP rivals "on a bad day is better than Jimmy Carter on his best." He avoided personal attacks and expected the same from his opponents. Quick to draw his ire was an article in the *Manchester (N.H.) Union-Leader* alleging that Crane's goal in life was to sleep with a thousand women. Seeing some charges, but not these, as inevitable but inappropriate, he advocated the creation of a panel of elder statesmen to enforce Reagan's "Eleventh Commandment—Thou Shalt Not Criticize a Fellow Republican."[3]

"You Have to Be Unemployed to Run for President"

Baker ignored the conventional wisdom that elections are won and lost on questions of bread and butter and made his role in the SALT-II debate the cornerstone of his campaign, believing that the Senate's decision might determine the survival of the republic. Rivals focused upon the safer issue of inflation, which Baker decried in secondary appeals as the "biggest unpunished crime in the country today." Finding its roots in America's overreliance upon foreign oil, he said this did not exculpate Carter, who had resisted calls to deregulate prices and give incentives to U.S. firms to produce enough to relieve demand for foreign petrol. Attributing equal responsibility to extravagant spending, Baker proclaimed his support for a constitutional amendment requiring a balanced budget unless both houses of Congress voted by two-thirds margins for deficits. Less often, he boasted of having cosponsored bills limiting federal spending to 21 percent of the gross national product and requiring the president to submit an alternative balanced budget if his request contained a deficit. He buttressed such calls with blasts at the centralization of government, pleasing crowds with calls for "more revenue sharing and a lot less HEW."[4]

Baker made a positive impression on his six-state stint on the Lincoln Day circuit, but this was his first extended tour, and his organization was primitive, to say the least. Not until March 14 did he announce that Indiana Senator Richard Lugar would chair his committee. While the choice of the scholarly Hoosier was widely heralded, Lugar's time, like Baker's, was limited by his dedication to his senatorial duties. National issues coordinator John Danforth, a bright young Missouri senator, was equally preoccupied. As Baker and Danforth had as solid a grasp of issues as any candidate or issues advisor in the race, this did not hurt. What did was Baker's inattention to the details of his campaign, a trait others had found in his senatorial races. Pols, like Tennessee GOP chairman Tom Beasley, who applauded his focus on the big picture, rued that he was not thorough enough. Consultant Doug Bailey, who found Baker's instincts the best he had ever seen, recognized that he was no administrative dynamo. Baker's disinterest in the tedious tasks of organizing put off several who had considered working for him,[5] and dictated that he choose less experienced hands like Don Sundquist, a Memphis businessman and former national Young Republican chairman, as his campaign manager and Fred Smith, the founder of Federal Express, as his finance chairman. But Sundquist agreed only to stay long enough to open a Washington office, and Federal Express could not spare Smith the time he needed to raise enough money to make Baker competitive.[6]

Worker recruitment proceeded equally slowly in key caucus and primary states. At the time of the Lincoln Day tour, the highest-ranking New Hampshire officeholder whose support Baker could claim was a county commissioner. While Baker aimed to co-opt the support of the state's moderate GOP establishment in the hope that the rank-and-file would follow, George Bush was devoting much more time to courting the grassroots of the same bloc. Bush's strategy was faring even better in Iowa, the state with the first caucus, which Bush was visiting regularly. Baker did not make his initial foray into Iowa until March 17 and then spoke but twice. While Des Moines attorney David Belin, who had been the staff director of the Rockefeller Commission, was on board, neither Baker nor his staff bothered to ask most prominent Iowa Republicans for their support until late in the year. The absence of a credible Baker team left Bush, who remained an asterisk in most polls, substantial room to maneuver.[7]

Baker's principal problem was time. He had opted to remain Minority Leader and allow Ted Stevens to assume his duties during his absences. But Rebecca Cox, then a top Stevens aide, termed Baker "such a responsible Minority Leader that . . . it really hurt his campaign." Baker premised his original schedule on a guess that a verdict on SALT-II some time in the first half of 1979 would allow him to announce his candidacy at his annual Fourth of July picnic. But with SALT-II unsigned until June 18, Baker remained a weekend warrior, spending most of his time attending to Senate duties. By September, Crane had spent forty-five days in New Hampshire; Bush, twenty-four; Dole, twenty-one; Anderson, fifteen; and Baker but seven. Iowa figures were even more lopsided. While Bush had solid organizations in both states, Baker's lagged, especially in Iowa, where he had operations by October in only fifty-four of the state's ninety-nine counties, and their ineffectiveness was so notorious that the governor's staff was joking that the only precinct they had organized was the one adjacent to the Rusty Scupper bar in Des Moines.[8]

Central to Bush's success was his status as the best-known alternative to Reagan who could spend all of his time campaigning. As Baker's campaign floundered, more and more Iowans signed up with Bush, in spite of frequent suggestions that Bush was light compared to Baker. Many moderate Republicans like Robert Ray, the Hawkeye State's popular five-term governor, privately saw Baker as a better alternative. Incredibly, neither Baker nor his staff had asked for Ray's help. Doubting both Baker's viability and Bush's ability to handle the presidency, many welcomed the entry of Gerald Ford, who did not rule out a candidacy until October.[9]

In this context, Baker stressed his electability. Apologetically, he reminded listeners of the Tennessee saying that "he that doesn't tooteth his own trumpet doesn't get his own trumpet tooteth" and showed potential backers polls indicating that he would defeat Carter handily, but unfortunately for him, that Ford and Reagan could also win. He told the rank-and-file that he would reach beyond the GOP and attract Democrats, independents, and blacks as he had in Tennessee and that he was the only one of the four major Republicans who had won an election since 1970. He had no preference for a Democratic opponent. "Carter," he said, "would be easier, but Kennedy would be more fun. If there's a man . . . who represents the tired old theories of the 1930s and the Depression mentality, it's Teddy Kennedy and we'll beat the socks off him." While Carter trailed Kennedy two-to-one in September, Baker saw a contest between the two as likely to "spill blood on the floor."[10] His scenario proved insightful, but it spelled trouble. If the nomination was worth having, it stood to reason that GOP voters would support the candidate they were most familiar with or the one with the best organization. Those candidates were Reagan and Bush, and Baker still had to deal with SALT-II.

Only when SALT-II was stalled did Baker feel free to announce his candidacy with no harm to his credibility in the Senate. Urging him even further was Doug Bailey, his chief political advisor, who wanted him to resign from the Senate and show an absolute commitment to the race by making a psychological break from the reflective role of a senator which runs counter to the decisive image Americans seek in a president. The idea appealed to Baker, but Joy believed it too slick and convinced him. "How . . . am I going to explain to all those folks that . . . they elected me to the Senate," he kept thinking, "and then I resigned?"[11]

Full-time Candidate

Having seen George Bush gain credibility through several Iowa straw-vote victories, Baker concluded that a similar win at a November 3 GOP forum in Maine would attract a similar degree of new attention to his campaign. Expecting victory, he moved up the date of his scheduled announcement to two days prior to that psychologically important if electorally meaningless contest. Present on November 1 in the Caucus Room of the Old Senate Office Building were a sizable portion of the Tennessee GOP leadership—Lamar Alexander, Robin Beard, John Duncan, Lewis Donelson, Winfield Dunn, Dan Kuykendall, Jimmy Quillen, Harold Sterling, Fred Thompson, and others, and Democratic State Senator Ed Blank. Between the podium and the door were Senate Republicans as different as Barry Goldwater and Jacob Javits. Paul Laxalt, Ronald Reagan's national chairman, was there as was Henry Bellmon, his counterpart to John Connally. Baker entered with Joy to a long round of applause, strode to a point behind a podium on the green-felt table from whence he rose to national prominence, and announced his candidacy.

Vowing to "nurture the national unity needed to govern with purpose and launch a new generation of confidence," he said this could only be accomplished only by "a President who knows Washington well enough to change Washington." "Washington," he said, "needs a President . . . to curb useless regulation and spending, assure energy independence, . . . help our people cope with inflation, and . . . set in motion a . . . program of tax relief to cut inflation and assure a generation of economic resurgence." But his focus remained SALT-II, the terms of which he labeled "outrageous." Saying the Soviet buildup had left America no margin for error, he declared that rejecting SALT-II would signal that "we intend to be masters of our fate again." "America," he added, "needs a President who will face up to the realities of a Soviet foreign policy that probes every weakness and fills every vacuum—a President to insist on defenses strong enough . . . to give us the confidence to stand tall again." His message differed little from those of his GOP rivals, save for his focus upon SALT-II, which disheartened some supporters, and his stress upon his electability. The GOP, he said, needed "a President who can win—in the South and the North . . . with white and with black Americans—with the old and the young." "I am ready to be that President. I do not ask you to trust me; I ask you to judge me." Not certain he could "beat Jimmy Carter and Teddy Kennedy on SALT-II," he felt certain he could beat either in 1980. "Watch me. Judge me. Then come with me. Let's reach for the future and make it ours."[12]

Initial response was overwhelmingly positive. Six supporters hailed his candidacy on the Senate floor within thirty minutes and six others hinted that they might add their endorsements. Baker drew consistently impressive audiences the next day, which former Governor Walter Peterson, his New Hampshire chairman, credited to positive curiosity. "I think I'd like to be for him," people said, "but I'd like to meet him." While Baker's message was generally well received, Peterson warned that there wasn't a great deal of time.[13]

A victory in the Maine straw poll, Baker hoped, would allow him to make up for some of the lost time. Senator Bill Cohen, the state's most popular Republican, was in his camp, as were three former state GOP chairmen and incumbent Hattie Bickmore. Cohen and executive director John "Jock" McKernan, a future congressman and governor, had co-opted the support of much of the party hierarchy. While one Bush aide suggested that Bush, Connally, and Reagan pull out to minimize the value of a Baker win, calmer Bushites raised the stakes. "If Baker doesn't win with at least fifty percent," one said, "it will be a loss," leading Baker to believe that he could appear in Vermont the morning of the vote without repercussions. But Baker's prospects were never so rosy. A November 2 poll showed 33 percent of the delegates for Baker and 24 percent for Bush, who summered in Kennebunkport and installed New Hampshire state legislator Josie Martin in an office six weeks earlier to secure pledges from uncommitted delegates not to decide until they had heard all of the candidates.[14] Having more than countered her work, Cohen had the upper hand. Introducing Henry Kissinger the night before the vote, he tried to transfer Kissinger's popularity to Baker, who delegates knew less about. Baker aides set up a hospitality suite, allowing Baker but a half-hour there before taking him away, leaving seven hundred activists muttering in the hallways. Once delegates started drinking, complaints that Baker was taking Maine for granted became as frequent as claims that Cohen had twisted arms and called in IOUs, charges suggesting that a southerner had disdain for Yankee independence.

Cohen awoke the next morning worrying that a dense fog might prevent Baker's return. He began meeting with undecideds but could not dissuade them from thinking that Baker was taking them for granted. Only twenty minutes before Baker was scheduled to speak did he arrive. Connally had "had the place rocking," Cohen remembers, and Bush was beginning "one of his better speeches." "You better give the speech of your life," Cohen warned. Baker listened to conflicting advice about the acoustics, then followed with a speech on the essence of governance that Cohen found eloquent but not the raw meat delegates came to hear. To Lewis Donelson, the content of Baker's address was superior to Bush's, but Baker came off flat because "Bush shouted and he didn't." Surprising everyone, Bush carried the day with 466 votes to Baker's 446, while six others split 424 ballots. While Baker lost some votes because of his overconfidence, Reagan supporters, in fact, had swung the vote to Bush to deny Baker, whom they deemed a worthier challenger, any burst of momentum.[15] But the result, Germond and Witcover wrote, confirmed "whispers about the ineptitude of his campaign." While Baker tried to get the press to "Forget the Maine," he guessed privately that it might not be possible for him to recover.[16]

Baker quickly replaced campaign manager Don Sundquist, who had taken the job with the understanding that he would hold it long enough only to open an office with Wyatt Stewart, the longtime executive director of the House GOP Campaign Committee, and installed as his finance chairman Ted Welch, who had turned down similar offers from Bush and Reagan. But he attended to normal Senate duties until the end of 1979, hoping press coverage of the SALT-II debate, which he figured to dominate, would give him an advantage over rivals who would be engaging in relatively frivolous activities like attending tea parties in Iowa and New Hampshire.[17]

Indeed, SALT-II was still alive, but Carter was preoccupied with securing the release of sixty-two American diplomats who had been hostage outside the U.S. embassy in Tehran in the early hours of November 4 by students outside the U.S. embassy in Tehran protesting Carter's decision to allow the Shah to be treated for cancer in America. As images appeared showing diplomats being blindfolded, Carter worried little, having been assured that the son of the Ayatollah Khomeini would be at the embassy the next day. But the younger Khomeini promised the kidnappers that his father would approve of their holding of hostages until the United States expelled the shah and returned his assets.[18]

While outraged by Carter's earlier refusal to let the Shah take up exile in the United States, seeing it as a sign that America was an unreliable ally to a willing host to American interests, Baker resisted temptations to criticize Carter, seeing the crisis in Vandenbergian terms as a time for Americans to rally behind their president and a rare opportunity for Carter to demonstrate leadership.[19]

Baker rejoiced in a rekindled spirit of international responsibility. Believing the episode held up a mirror of an America in retreat, he found it "time to recognize that where America overreached it did so in the cause of justice; if some of our . . . allies had hands that were unclean by the standards of liberal democracy, their replacements have almost uniformly been bloody tyrants, whether . . . dressed as . . . ayatollahs, or in the olive drab of Latin American dictators." When thousands of Americans converged on the Iranian embassy on November 11, he drove to watch, took pictures, and later mounted a photograph of denim-clad youths carrying flags and signs "demanding the most extraordinary actions against the Ayatollah Khomeini." That "the . . . flag was in such prominence" symbolized to him that a new generation had "come home to the . . . belief that America must be strong and outgoing."[20]

While such words struck responsive chords, insiders knew that the Bush and Reagan organizations were more advanced. To counter this impression, Baker sought to score a coup among GOP governors, most of whom were moderates who feared that Reagan would lead the party to disaster but were unwilling to go out on a limb if they believed him unstoppable. Generally finding Baker preferable to Bush, whose résumé they believed "a mile wide and an inch deep," many questioned his viability, as he seemed wedded to his Senate duties. A case in point was Robert Ray, whose endorsement Baker commissioned John Deardourff to secure at the Republican Governors' Conference. While Ray was gravitating toward Baker, he declined. "I will do some things to help you," he said. But "what you've done is come in so late that . . . my . . . friends are . . . split. If I had heard from you four months ago, . . . not only could I have endorsed him but I could have encouraged these people . . . to come along . . . and we might have been able to put the whole thing together."[21]

Minutes later, Ray told Baker that he was thirteenth in a field of twelve and that his campaign would keep sliding until he began spending most of his time in Iowa and invigorated his organization. Baker hired Ray's daughter to a lower-level position and Ray associates Marvin Pomerantz and Dick Redman soon thereafter. His standing had dropped since August, when an Iowa Poll showed him second, with 23 percent to Reagan's 48. Reagan's 50 percent was well ahead of Bush's 14, Connally's 12, and his 11. Baker began focusing on the early contests, fired his chief advance man, and replaced the head of his Iowa operation with Dick Redman, under whom he installed a ten-person paid staff. While a deputy campaign director resigned, this was offset by a perception that Ray had laid the groundwork for a three-man race. Baker picked up an immediate endorsement from the GOP members of the Iowa PAC for Education, who remembered his support for a Department of Education. To make further headway, Baker launched an intensive media campaign. Some spots had been produced long before, showing him asking what Richard Nixon knew and when he knew it and espousing an expanded revenue-sharing program. A biographical spot called him the "most respected man in the Senate," a designation he won in a poll of senators, heralded him as vice-chairman of the Senate Watergate Committee, and said that he had "stopped SALT-II and started revenue sharing." These spots were supplanted by scenes of Baker's discussions with Iowans, a tack aimed at conveying an image of a well-informed senator and calling attention to Reagan's absence and Bush's image orientation. As inflation far above commodity prices was forcing thousands of foreclosures while production was never higher, Baker said the problem was one of too few markets and promised that his vice-president would embark upon a trade offensive the day he took office. Vowing to choose someone experienced in promoting the sale of farm produce, he clearly inferred that he would consider Governor Ray, whom he had already invited to be his running mate.[22]

To capture Baker's ideas on foreign policy, Bailey traveled to the University of Iowa to film an address billed as major. As before, Baker asked his audience to give Carter their unqualified support for his efforts to win the release of the hostages. But he attributed the crisis itself to America's perceived weakness. Declaring a need for an "unmistakable symbol of our . . . strength and our confidence," he called for a 50,000-man mobile First Brigade trained in counterterrorism that could move at a moment's notice to protect Americans from any threat. After telling a questioner that "America must resolve that she's not going to be pushed around anymore," Baker pointed to Mohammed Tavacoli, an Iranian student on a full scholarship who, in accusative tones, asked why he was concerned about Iran violating international law but had not been so disposed "when the Shah was killing Iranian people with U.S. weapons." As the question reached the twenty-five-second mark, Baker's face reddened. When Tavacoli took a breath, Baker arched his brows, looked the young Iranian in the eye, pointed at him, and exclaimed, "Because, my friend, I'm interested in fifty Americans, that's why, and when those fifty Americans are released, I'm perfectly willing to talk about it." With a burst of applause drowning out the last half of Baker's response. Doug Bailey was certain that he had struck gold. A thirty-second ad featured the question, Baker's response, and the fade-out "Baker-Republican-President-Now." A five-minute film included scenes of Baker at his most forceful, his quieting of Tavacoli, and choruses of "Welcome Back, America," his campaign song. The patriotic appeal of these ads, run twenty times a week for three weeks, allowed Baker to cut into both Bush's and Reagan's constituencies.[23]

The appeal of patriotic themes mounted on December 28, the day Soviet troops invaded Afghanistan. Jimmy Carter labeled the threat "the most serious . . . since World War II," recalled America's ambassador from Moscow, embargoed grain sales to the Soviets, deferred most cultural exchange programs, and grumbled about Leonid Brezhnev's lie that the Soviets had invaded at the behest of the existing government. Baker believed Carter naive not to suspect Brezhnev of habitual lying in the past and saw the invasion as one more reason not to ratify SALT-II. With many heretofore quiet senators now saying the same thing, Carter checked, found Baker's assessment that the invasion was "the straw that broke the camel's back" accurate, and asked Robert Byrd to delay consideration. SALT-II, which Carter once found passable assuming that he would have to at some point come to terms with Baker, was now unmistakably dead, as were the last vestiges of Baker's strategy of using the debate to examine Soviet-American relations.[24]

Baker at last could give full time to his campaign. While his advertising alleviated his organizational deficiencies somewhat, he would not use the other prescription for a catch-up race. "I am not going to climb over the dead bodies of my opponents . . . or chew at their ankle or bite them in the back." This was characteristic, but also reflected a guess that rejoinders, particularly at Reagan, might lose votes in the general election. With it being a high-risk game, an aide confessed that Baker was willing to let somebody else take the shot.[25]

Reagan's one serious strategic mistake came when he declined to participate in an Iowa debate, saying it might polarize the GOP. Iowans saw instead six attractive candidates engaged in a civil exchange of ideas. All but John Anderson reiterated calls for tax cuts for individuals and businesses, regulatory reform, cuts in domestic spending, and increases in defense. No one faulted Carter's handling of the hostage crisis. Terming it a symptom of a failed foreign policy, Baker cited a need for deterrence and called for a First Brigade and renewed production of the B-1 bomber. The embargo he termed ineffectual, as "we almost always starve the wrong people . . . I doubt that we will . . . even inconvenience the leaders of the Soviet Union." Dole said Carter had taken "a poke at the Russian bear and knocked out the American farmer." Bush, quoting Yogi Berra, said Carter's was the "wrong mistake." But Anderson dissented that a "clear . . . signal" was needed to show the Soviets that "we will not tolerate the kind of conflict they have just engaged." With the debate otherwise unmemorable, most saw the GOP and the people of Iowa as the winners and absentee Reagan as the loser.[26]

The national audience saw a different picture from one- or two-minute snippets on news programs the next day in reports that placed a premium upon conflict. Many got the impression that Anderson had won, as he alone defended the embargo and questioned if a balanced budget could emerge from tax cuts, defense increases, regulatory reform, and waste elimination, responses appealing to liberals, even though he won little support from Iowans or Republicans.[27]

A January poll indicated that those who saw the debate found Baker and Crane the winners and Connally and Dole the losers. Reagan, moreover, had fallen to 26 percent and Baker and Bush had climbed to 18 and 17 percent, respectively, showing that Baker and Bush were much stronger than anticipated. Bush's staff sent anyone they believed a prospective supporter a letter giving the time and place of each precinct meeting and a list of neighbors who would be voting for Bush. Bush and Reagan alike noticed movement toward Baker, whose radio ads featured the message "The hostages can't vote, but we can" in a last-minute bid to drive up turnout. "In terms of popular opinion on the day of the caucus," Doug Bailey guessed, "if it had been a primary, we would have had a three way tie." But popular opinion carries little weight in caucuses. While Dick Redman had done much in six weeks to rescue Baker, he could not match Bush's yearlong effort. Even in the week before the caucuses, some Baker aides could not tell voters where their precinct meetings would be. While Reagan campaign manager John Sears thought turnout would be three times that of 1976 and assigned his chairmen quotas to meet the 30,000 votes needed, turnout was five times higher and Reagan won but 29 percent. The presence of Bush workers at each precinct and the absence of Bakerites at many allowed Bush to take most of those convinced that either was preferable to Reagan. Bush thus amassed a total of 33,530, slightly less than double the 16,773 won by Baker, his main contender for the moderate vote.[28]

Bush became a household word overnight, jumping from the choice of 6 percent of Republicans to 27 percent in national polls. While Baker remained constant at 11 percent, Reagan fell to 27 percent. Newsmen began focusing almost exclusively upon the themes of Reagan's vulnerability and Bush's momentum. Stories recounted Bush's record as a bomber pilot, an oilman, a congressman, ambassador to the United Nations and China, CIA director and RNC chairman on TV news reports, magazine covers, and page-one stories all over America. Many hoped that he was, as his ads suggested, "the man America turns to when a tough job has to be done." The situation spelled trouble for his opponents. Now that Bush was out as the frontrunner, Baker's New Hampshire coordinator John Michels noted, "the rest of us have been shut out."[29]

Bush christened his new selling point "the Big Mo" and pushed new literature featuring pictures of him jogging ahead of a crowd. Knowing Reagan remained popular with many who had doubts about his age and vigor, Bush spin doctors, hoping to attract Anderson and Baker supporters, began saying that they expected Anderson and Baker to take more votes from Bush than Connally and Crane would from Reagan. Bush also aimed to peel away voters who liked Reagan but were concerned about his age by addressing issues in generalities. It mattered little that Carter aides said their slogan for a Carter-Bush race would be, "Why change wimps in the middle of the stream?" His strategy seemed to work, as his six-point lead in New Hampshire grew to thirteen.[30]

Baker and Reagan both needed a concrete demonstration of their strength to halt "the big mo." Their first chance came in Arkansas, where Republicans entrusted three hundred party leaders to pick their delegates. All four major candidates had some support. Baker, Bush, and Connally had traveled to Arkansas often to speak for local GOP candidates, while Reagan had a following from 1976. Bush was backed by Congressman John Paul Hammerschmidt, the man who foiled Bill Clinton's initial bid for office in 1974. Baker was backed by loyalists of the late Winthrop Rockefeller. But no one had a majority. Surrogates for each candidate "would go to meetings where two delegates would be available," said Tom Beasley. "I felt like I was back running a legislative campaign."[31]

The tenuous atmosphere placed a premium on wheeling and dealing. Three delegates would be chosen one-by-one at four district meetings and seven at-large delegates would be elected later. Reagan left unchallenged the election of two Baker delegates and one uncommitted delegate in Winthrop Rockefeller's Second District stronghold and one Baker delegate in both the Third and Fourth Districts. Bakerites did not fight two Reagan supporters in the Third and the Fourth. Baker deemed his showing a shot in the arm, having beaten the front-runner, gained his first four delegates, and at one point led the national delegate count, 1–0. The results angered Bush, who decried such deals, but what happened was a mere repeat of tactics Reagan had used to give Bush his first shot of the "big mo" in Maine.[32]

Tired of the Byzantine politics of Arkansas, candidates returned to New Hampshire's more predictable confines where Baker had been saying all along he had to perform. While he had a solid if limited base, all was not well. Undecideds were disappointed with his staff's slowness in sending literature while they were barraged by Bush and Reagan. "I liked him during Watergate," one Reagan backer said, "but he hasn't been pushing hard enough." Such a notion grew as footage from his speeches failed to appear on television. Baker's rhetoric was ill tailored to draw the media to cover him. Typical was an address at Dartmouth College where he called for defenses "of Cadillac quality, but not gold-plated," an appeal leaving potential supporters unsure of the direction a Baker presidency might take. Advised to "mix it up" by press secretary Tom Griscom, who knew that a reasoned statement by the third-place finisher was not news, but an attack on the front-runner was, Baker relented, charging Bush's plan to cut revenue sharing would cost New Hampshire $25 million a year and render likely a state income tax. Later, he hit at Bush's opposition to the Panama Canal Treaties and a balanced budget amendment and his support for the Nixon pardon and tax indexing. Even these tame attacks made him uncomfortable. "I've been a human being longer than I've been in politics," he said, "and if you have to slash . . . the other guy, they can . . . find some other candidate." Stressing similar themes in a five-minute ad featuring his pictures, he, clad in a flannel shirt, vowed to continue to pursue his hobby if elected. "I am not driven to be President," he said. "If you have . . . such a burning desire to be President, you'll probably fail on the job. If you have to be pathological in your pursuit of it, skip it." He was running because "The Presidency is the one place where we can change this country," and "I believe I can do a better job than anybody else." Designed to contrast his easygoing nature with Bush's intensity, Doug Bailey hoped the ad would project the idea that Baker might be "less of an ideal candidate" and "more of an ideal President."[33]

It was Baker's hope that the February 17 winner-take-all Puerto Rico primary would give him a much-needed boost. In the early 1970s, he and Hubert Humphrey had won a four-year fight to transfer weapons testing operations on the island of Culebra to uninhabited isles that effectively derailed arguments for separation and allowed a statehood movement to flourish. With Gerald Ford having embraced that cause while president, every candidate but Edward Kennedy endorsed Puerto Rico's entry into the Union, the one issue that mattered. Cissy Baker made several trips and addressed gatherings in broken Spanish. Jeb Bush, in contrast, was fluent in Spanish and moved with his Mexican-born wife to the island. While Baker had an advantage in the outlying areas, Bush's organization was potent in San Juan and "the big mo" carried him to a 3–2 margin.[34]

Bush's win strengthened his image as the frontrunner and convinced him to emphasize his résumé. Having invited the public to judge him on his style, Reagan aides and William Loeb, the publisher of the *Manchester Union-Leader,* were glad to oblige. No longer did Loeb demonize Baker for backing the Panama Canal Treaties or declaring Chappaquiddick "not a valid issue." Bush, now Loeb's sole target, was accused of slowing down the count in Iowa in the style "of a CIA covert operation" and telling a pro-lifer to perform an impossible sex act. Common were blasts at Bush's ties to an elite and depictions of him as a "spoiled little rich kid who has been wet-nursed to succeed and . . . thinks he is entitled to the White House."[35] Few but the truly fanatical took Loeb seriously, but Reagan's theme of the people against the elite appealed to far more. Even so, that perception was slow in taking hold. One-on-one, Bush cut an impressive figure, and his criticisms of Carter effectively refuted charges that he was too liberal for most Republicans.

Bush's approach prompted Baker to urge him to discuss the issues with more particularity. Bush's waffling was most evident in a debate involving all seven candidates on February 20, where he waved position papers when asked where he stood on the Equal Rights Amendment and abortion. Baker focused upon his disagreement with Bush on revenue sharing, saying its expansion would allow Congress to cut billions in overhead. While reporters believed the affair bland, instantaneous polls showed that Baker and John Anderson had swayed some votes from Bush. But the big winner was Reagan, who in many eyes won by merely showing up and not erring, thus ending doubts about his age and capacity, and dropping Bush, who some had expected to be a supercandidate, twenty points behind in polls taken thereafter.[36]

One debate remained that was originally designed to include only Bush and Reagan. Bush insisted that it be held in Nashua the Saturday before the primary under the sponsorship of the *Telegraph*, whose publisher, J. Herman Pouliot, and editor, Jon Breen, were close to Hugh Gregg, his state chairman. This scarcely bothered John Sears, who saw Bush as an unworthy challenger not only to Reagan, but also Baker and Connally, and he gave the encounter his blessing. Believing the debate would reinforce the idea that the contest was a two-man race, he figured the others would object, but thought they would blame the *Telegraph*. Unfortunately for Bush, Baker and Dole convinced the Federal Election Commission that the cost was an illegal contribution to the Bush and Reagan campaigns. When Reagan aides suggested that the campaigns split the cost, Gregg refused, forcing Reagan to cover the charges. Knowing Reagan did not relish excluding the others, Sears figured including them would limit the chances of a Reagan gaffe and end any possibility that the five might be "bad-mouthing us the last three days." Reagan press secretary Jim Lake mentioned the idea the day before the debate in passing to Breen, who contacted Bush aides and told them that Sears might try to include the others. If that happened, Breen vowed to recite the agreement and Bush would affirm his intention to keep his word.[37]

Sears and Lake phoned the other candidates and told them that they might be able to participate if they came to Nashua the next evening. When Reagan arrived, Baker, Anderson, Crane, and Dole were with Sears. Sears then dispatched Reagan political director Charles Black to tell Bush that he would like to see him. When Bush campaign manager James Baker arrived instead, Sears told him that Reagan wanted to open the debate. Jim Baker noticed Reagan with the "Nashua Four" and rushed to Bush's room to warn of an ambush. When it became clear that Bush was not coming, Reagan sent Senator Gordon Humphrey to try and get Bush to speak to his opponents. An annoyed Bush shouted that he had "worked hard for this and they're not going to take it away." Humphrey ran back and recounted what had happened. Reagan wanted to walk out if the four were barred, but aides advised against it. "We'll all stand behind you," Baker followed. "I've been thrown out of better places than this," Dole agreed. With Humphrey on one side, Lake on the other, and the Nashua Four right behind, Reagan encountered Bush near the door. "I'm not going on unless this goes as planned," he announced. Calm, Reagan marched in and waved the four inside to loud cheers. An alarmed publisher Pouliot told the crowd that they sounded like a circus and that the Nashua Four had not been invited. Boos ensued until a woman screamed, "Get them chairs," and a man cracked that the vertically challenged Baker could "stand on the table." Still uncertain what Reagan would do, Lake sent him a note telling him that "everybody's with you." Reagan winked.[38]

With Breen sitting stoically and Bush refusing to acknowledge the four, Reagan tried to make his case. "Turn Mr. Reagan's microphone off," Breen ordered. Flabbergasted, Reagan leaned forward, grabbed the mike, and uttered indignantly, "I am paying for this microphone, Mr. Green." While getting Breen's name wrong, Reagan sparked the loudest roar of the evening. Once it was clear that Breen would not yield, the four thanked Reagan and moved to the band room. Among them were the highest-ranking GOP officeholder in America (Baker), the GOP's titular vice-head (Dole), and the third-ranking Republican in the House (Anderson). And Bush refused even to meet with them. Primed for an hour and a half, Baker declared the event "the most flagrant attempt to return to the closed door I've seen." Dole quipped that Bush's performance was so bad that he would announce his own candidacy again.[39]

Bush in turn complained about being sandbagged. Aides cut a radio spot, explaining, "At no time did George Bush object to a full candidate forum." This rivals knew was false and his airing of it led many to question his capacity. As no media outlet carried the debate live, the ads led listeners to watch news clips of Breen's attempted silencing of Reagan and the Nashua Four, and Bush's stony acquiescence. Anger grew as film footage showed Bush's departure for the sunny climate of Houston. Conservatives returned to Reagan, who also picked up the votes of some Anderson and Baker supporters who were mad at Bush. While many moderates switched to Baker or Anderson, others who were inclined to switch but feared a Reagan nomination stuck reluctantly with Bush.[40] The result was a Reagan rout with a full 49.7 percent over Bush with 22.9 percent, Baker with 12.9, and Anderson with 9.9.[41]

Reagan, said a headline in the next *Newsweek*, was "back in the saddle," but Sears, Black, and Lake were replaced by a team headed by William Casey. Baker aides contacted the three, hoping to add them and signal contributors and voters that Baker was still a factor. But the three told Wyatt Stewart that they remained committed to Reagan and left Baker with little hope of scoring the kind of quick public relations coup that might revive his candidacy. While reporters judged him the victor of a South Carolina debate two days after the New Hampshire primary, southern moderates, save in Tennessee and Arkansas, had joined in the march to Bush. Nor was he a factor in Massachusetts and Vermont, where Bush and Anderson were well organized. In fact, onetime Kennedy backers crossed over and gave Anderson surprise second-place finishes in both states. Left behind in fourth place, Baker saw no state in the next month where he could turn things around and no reason to linger in the campaign. "Why," he asked aides, "am I going to borrow a million dollars to come in fourth in Illinois?" With reports surfacing that a better known "moderate," Gerald Ford, was considering entering the race, Baker knew that this, if true, would dissipate any remaining support.[42]

Having promised himself that he would stop if he "faced . . . economic ruination or political embarrassment," Baker, with his campaign $1 million in debt, spoke at length with Joy and Cissy, called Darek in Murfreesboro and many supporters across the country. The next day, flanked by Joy, Cissy, and Richard Lugar, he acknowledged in his Capitol office that his campaign "isn't going anywhere." "I want to be President," he said, "but I don't think that's in the cards right now." The last contender to enter, he was the first to leave. "Had Howard been in Bush's shoes," John Sears argued, "he might have made more of his position." Baker was not certain. "It may be a late start," he said, "but if it is, that is a mistake because this country doesn't need two- and three-year campaigns for the Presidency." The results were Baker's only regret, as he found the experience unrivaled in public life, having learned that the country has a clearer perspective than most in Washington, a lesson he vowed to carry into the legislative process. As for the future, he said little, save to joke that he would keep a promise to Cissy not to challenge her for the GOP nomination in 1992 and would campaign as hard as time and energy would permit to elect a GOP Senate. He had begun the race with all of his opponents his friends, he concluded, and hoped he had ended it that way.[43]

Surrogate for a GOP Majority

Baker saw the March 18 Illinois primary, where Bush ran thirty-seven points behind Reagan, as Bush's last gasp and notified Reagan that he would have his support once the details could be worked out. Baker wanted assurances that Reagan would campaign on themes that united Republicans—the worldwide decline of American prestige, big government, extravagant spending—and not the bugaboos of his more conspiratorial-minded supporters. William Casey assured Baker representative Lamar Alexander that this was Reagan's intention and that Reagan, as a sign of good faith, would eliminate a Panama Canal joke from his standard speech. Casey, too, got Alexander's assent for Baker to speak in Reagan's stead at fundraisers that Reagan would have to cancel in return for Baker's pledge to appear at a series of unity dinners whose proceeds would be used to pay off his, Bush's, and Connally's debts.[44]

Nursing a bad cold, Baker flew to Philadelphia two days before the April 22 Pennsylvania primary to keep his pledge. While heaping praise on Bush, he said voter response had made it obvious that Reagan would be the nominee. "Ron, I'm for you," he said, looking Reagan in the eye, and added that only intraparty bickering could keep Reagan from winning. Such remarks were directed less toward Pennsylvania than Tennessee, a state where Reagan feared a loss would be embarrassing. Realizing his comment about selling TVA bothered Tennesseans, Reagan brought Baker with him to Johnson City to affirm that he would not consider selling TVA under any circumstances. His message signaled a massive switch of onetime Ford supporters, which added to those of longtime Reagan supporters spelled a landslide.[45]

Reagan's win furthered speculation that he would pick Baker as his running mate. Key Reagan aides told Godfrey Sperling that Reagan saw Baker as a particularly intelligent and articulate representative of the New South and believed that he and Baker shared in essence the same philosophy, even if they disagreed upon the Panama Canal Treaties and a few other issues. While Baker and Bush held the support of most who had backed them in the primaries, Baker drew broader backing from many who had not supported his presidential bid like Governors Albert Quie and Jim Thompson and Senators Nancy Kassebaum, Ted Stevens, and Strom Thurmond. And they were joined by Richard Lugar and William Simon, who made a published list of eight finalists but commended Baker as a better choice. But Baker was no longer interested. Never having seen a happy vice-president, he did not think he enjoy a support position. Not anxious to relive his ordeals of 1968 and 1976, he also feared that he would have less influence in formulating policy than he would as Leader. If Reagan asked, it would be his duty to accept, but he hoped that Reagan would choose a moderate who had earned less resentment than he. Clarifying his position, he said there was "no draft for Baker" and it was "the hardest bill of goods" he had ever tried to sell.[46]

The vice-presidential choice alone awaited Reagan, who had decided to choose only from those well known to the country, thus eliminating all but Baker, Bush, and Gerald Ford, his dream partner. For Baker, this did not matter. He declared during a June 29 *Face the Nation* appearance that he would accept the nod but would prefer to stay in the Senate. Reagan was watching and phoned Baker to ask if his statement should be taken at face value. Baker assured Reagan that it should, leading Reagan to promise to honor his wish, but not to tell Baker that he had already decided that he would be of more use to him in the Senate.[47]

Having had doubts about Bush since the Nashua debate, Reagan vowed to do everything he could to convince Ford to accept the slot. When Ford stopped short of no the first time Reagan broached the subject on Tuesday, July 15, Reagan tried to prod those close to Ford to help convince him to join the ticket. Bill Brock enlisted Baker late that night and Baker told Reagan the next morning that Ford would be ideal. "If it isn't Ford," he asked, "is it Dick Lugar?" It was not, Reagan replied. Having been in Lugar's shoes, Baker asked to break it to him. Reagan was amenable and Baker found his campaign chairman "crestfallen," just as he had been.[48]

Baker had little time to console Lugar, however, as he had to meet with Ford that afternoon. Baker and others told Ford that his presence would guarantee the elections of Reagan and a GOP Senate and that Reagan would substantially increase the powers of the vice-president if he accepted the nod. Reagan aides took the same line later in the afternoon. The idea that presidential powers were being surrendered did not set in until Ford, having been told by Henry Kissinger and others that he might become the equivalent of a chief executive officer of a business to Reagan's chairman of the board, did not disabuse Walter Cronkite of the idea of a co-presidency. While the comment set a red flag in front of Reagan, all three networks picked up on enough rumors to report that Ford and Reagan would come to the convention for Reagan to announce his choice of Ford. Here were thoroughly unfounded reports. While Cronkite reported that they were cast in stone, Bill Brock learned that the deal was not final and recruited Baker and Bob Dole to salvage the situation. As the two were leaving the arena, Ford was entering Reagan's suite to tell him "this . . . isn't right." Baker and Dole arrived at Ford's suite minutes later, learned that their dream team would not be taking the field, then rode the elevator down seventy stories, where they were besieged by autograph hounds and reporters. Both kept tight-lipped, even when they found their taxi gone. John Warner emerged from another meeting and the three eventually hitched a ride from a policeman who recognized them, but the lateness of their effort became most vivid to them when they spotted the Reagan motorcade in front of them en route back to the convention where Reagan would announce that he had picked Bush.[49]

Baker's principal role in the fall was as an apologist for Reagan misstatements. After Reagan said that he believed in an official relationship with Taiwan, for instance, Baker declared that Reagan was merely saying that Carter had treated the Taiwanese shabbily. But such apologies were less frequent than barbs at Carter. After Defense Secretary Harold Brown announced that America had developed technology to make U.S. planes invisible to Soviet radar, Baker joined John Tower and John Warner in calling the disclosure a violation of the public trust. Just as distasteful to him was Carter's aim to paint Reagan as an extremist who could not be trusted to keep America out of nuclear war, maintain the Social Security system, or pursue a rational tax policy. But Carter was safe for a time, as he had raised doubts about Reagan, and surrogates were airing most of the truly irresponsible rhetoric on his behalf. Only on September 23 did he begin to lose his image as a decent man trying his hardest, after he declared that the election would determine "whether we have peace or war." Less than two weeks later, he told Democrats that they would "determine whether or not . . . America will be unified or, if I lose . . . , whether Americans might be separated, black from white, Jew from Christian, North from South, rural from urban." Civility had been an everpresent side issue in Baker's own bid, and he found such shrill attacks "below the dignity of the Presidency." With Carter striking with such abandon, he made a need to "recivilize politics" and "get back to discussing the issues" his primary talking point. Aiming to see enough Republicans elected to allow control of the upper chamber to revert to his party, he succeeded in most of the twenty-five states he visited in legitimizing his party's nominees, most of whom were more conservative than he, and reassuring compatriots that Reagan recognized a duty to represent all the people. Characterizing Reagan's appeal as broad-based and deep, Baker declared that his election would create a new spirit of optimism.[50]

Few were so sure until October 28, the night Reagan demolished Carter on style points in their one debate. Having predicted since June not only a Reagan landslide but a GOP takeover of the Senate, Baker told reporters the day before the election that each candidate for a GOP controlled seat would be elected and be joined by new GOP senators from Alaska, Colorado, Florida, Georgia, Indiana, New Hampshire, South Dakota, Washington, and Vermont. The election materialized almost as he surmised. Reagan's victory, a 489–49 electoral college margin and a plurality of 8.3 million votes, was so one-sided that he raised the totals of countless Republicans across the country. Baker's predictions were a mite off, as Democrats Gary Hart and Patrick Leahy narrowly averted losses, but these defeats were more than offset by GOP takeovers of Democratic seats in Alabama, Idaho, Iowa, North Carolina, and Wisconsin.[51]

Baker's likely ascension to Majority Leader rankled New Right chieftains, who began talking up plans to replace him with someone attuned to their agenda. Jesse Helms was interested, but his position on the fringe scared away most of the caucus. Paul Laxalt thought the job "dull, boring work" and himself without "the personality to conciliate . . . ninety-nine other" senators. Believing Baker had done a good job and "was one of the best consensus achievers," he agreed to Baker's election night request to nominate him. New senators appreciated Baker's aid to their campaigns and pledged their support as they took his calls of congratulation. Especially anxious to help were conservatives James Abdnor, Charles Grassley, and Dan Quayle, who were angered by last-minute NCPAC and Moral Majority smears on their opponents that they believed had recklessly jeopardized their elections. Reagan, when asked if he had confidence in Baker, replied that he not only had confidence in Baker, but had been told that there was "no friction and . . . no move . . . to change." Reagan's response should have ended the discussion, but it did not. Right-wing PAC leaders Paul Weyrich and Terry Dolan, apparently unaware of exit polls showing that only 11 percent of Reagan voters had cast their ballots for him because he was a "real conservative" and most saying they wanted either a new leader or a change, took full credit for the Reagan victory, called Baker a "roll-over-and-play-dead leader" and made a last-ditch bid to replace him with someone more compliant with their demands. But Weyrich and Dolan had to face reality. "The first thing they need to learn is how to count," said Richard Lugar, "and I have 41 votes for Howard Baker."[52]

Having long since stopped worrying, Baker spent much of his time after the election planning the transition of his caucus from minority to majority status. The main task of the 1980 lame-duck session was securing the creation of a superfund to clean up toxic wastes. Here again Baker played a key role, helping negotiate its charter, then making it public that Reagan welcomed the creation of such a fund, thus rendering futile a filibuster that Jesse Helms was planning. While the bill's enactment constituted the start of a campaign to eradicate hazards from the dumping of toxic chemicals, it was just as significant for Baker in that it marked the start of a historic working relationship with Reagan, who he believed would be pragmatic. Reagan left the same impression upon many in his first post-election visit to Washington and the caucus soon confirmed that Baker would occupy the point position. Vowing to try to help Ronald Reagan on the commitments he made, he warned GOP colleagues that it had become their duty and Reagan's "to perform."[53]

CHAPTER 11

RONALD REAGAN'S POINT MAN 1981–1984

Baker's central challenge in 1981 lay in re-creating for Republicans the role of the Senate's majority party. History had taught him that the principle-at-any-cost, compromise-be-damned approach William Knowland had used the last time Republicans held the White House and the Senate had served neither party nor country. Like Robert Taft in 1953, Baker knew that his party would be held responsible for making the government work, and that its fortunes were intertwined with those of Ronald Reagan. Having retaken control of the upper chamber for the first time in a generation, they no longer had the luxury of blind opposition. But if they acted in ways the people deemed wise, they had their best chance in half a century to regain the role of Congress's governing party. In Reagan, the caucus gained an articulate spokesman dedicated to principles embodied in statements it had made since 1977. As Baker had molded these consensuses, it was he Reagan trusted to lead fights for bills incorporating caucus edicts. Shortly after the inauguration, he told Reagan there were "things on what you and I may disagree and . . . if I must take a separate position, I will try to let you know in advance. But you should also know that on every . . . close call, I'm going to resolve the issue in your favor."[1]

One disagreement emerged early. When Education Secretary Terrell Bell came to lobby for a plan to abolish his department, Baker smiled and commended him for a good pitch. "You've done your part," he said, "but I don't think you believe it." Stunned, Bell took the message to Reagan and was told not to worry. Over the next two weeks, Bell found that he would get no more than nineteen votes. When he asked why, Reagan responded that he had never seen Baker so stubborn.[2]

Ronald Reagan's Year

On virtually all other issues, Baker proved a staunch Reagan ally. While seeing Reagan's proposed spending and tax cuts as a solid blueprint for reversing such trends, he remained cognizant that very few presidential prescriptions are adopted without modification and that dosages would be altered contingent upon prognoses for recovery. To facilitate harmony, he hosted a get-acquainted dinner on January 4, 1981, for Reagan appointees entrusted with the recovery program and committee chairmen with jurisdiction over the economy. Diverging sharply from the Carter path, Reagan and his associates patterned a solid basis for cooperation with Congress by Inauguration Day, for which Baker was as responsible as Reagan. Relying upon Baker's judgment, Reagan had aides install hot lines in Baker's Capitol office to both the Oval Office and to chief of congressional liaison Max Friedersdorf.[3]

Within the Senate, Baker instituted other lines of communication. Republicans had always held policy luncheons each Tuesday, where the leadership would inform members of decisions about upcoming business and likely pressures. While these sessions were useful, they also created the image of a hierarchical party, an undesirable perception in the individualistic Senate of the 1980s. With this in mind, Baker involved more senators in regular meetings of the Leadership. On Mondays, he met with Whip Ted Stevens, Reagan liaison Paul Laxalt, one or two senators managing upcoming bills, and a first-term member chosen on a rotating basis. Every other Tuesday, Baker and Stevens went with House leaders Robert Michel and Trent Lott to meet with Reagan. Upon returning, Baker met with his chairmen, two freshmen, and occasionally George Bush. After Baker's presentation, each member described measures under their control and matters likely to arouse controversy. What resulted were closer ties among senior members and an added sense of involvement among junior ones.[4]

While Senate Democrats today bemoan the results of the Reagan tax- and budget-cutting blitz of 1981, they speak in admiration of Baker's skill in holding together his GOP troops. They, too, appreciated that Baker had fashioned a workweek where debate would end by 6:30 P.M., except on Thursdays, when members knew sessions would be lengthy if Friday roll calls could be obviated, letting members schedule engagements and know they were likely to be able to attend. As problems tended to be modulated, rather than exacerbated, in contrast to the previous Byrd regime, where members were less certain and were often more fractious, it was said that an "Era of Good Feelings" had entered the Senate, in no small part because Baker had made everybody feel wanted.[5]

Baker's first substantive task as Majority Leader lay in shepherding Reagan's cabinet nominees to confirmation. The only brouhaha originated when it became known that Alexander Haig was being considered for secretary of state. When Robert Byrd warned that confirmation would be difficult because of Haig's alleged involvement in Watergate, Reagan took this as a test of strength. Baker advised Haig to retain counsel, then got Foreign Relations Committee Chairman Charles Percy to hire Fred Thompson as his panel's special counsel. The faith of a counsel to the Ervin Committee in Haig's innocence effectively rendered these charges moot. While a few Democrats insisted that the answers could be found on the Nixon tapes, no one questioned Haig's qualifications, leading many to believe the charges were motivated by partisanship and all but six to vote aye.[6]

Jesse Helms, in turn, aimed to fight the confirmation of any nominee he believed a "Kissinger retread" to a top State or Defense Department position, and he tried to make Defense Secretary designate Caspar Weinberger, a Reagan loyalist once considered a liberal Republican, his first victim. When just three senators backed Helms, Baker did nothing. A more serious challenge loomed when Reagan named Frank Carlucci, the CIA's deputy director in the Carter years, as Weinberger's chief deputy. Angered by Reagan's failure to appoint a hardliner, Helms urged Carlucci's replacement by Fred Ikle, whose ideas meshed with his own and who Reagan intended to name as Carlucci's deputy. Recognizing Carlucci faced a more formidable challenge, Baker withheld Carlucci's name and got Paul Laxalt to tell Helms that Carlucci and Ikle would come as a package or not at all.[7]

The fact that Carlucci's selection was controversial illustrated the difficulty of a caucus making the transition from minority status to governing, an image pointedly evoked in early February when the Senate took up a routine measure to raise the federal debt ceiling. In the past, Democrats had routinely backed such requests, only to find GOP challengers using their votes as evidence that they were big spenders. Thus, when Reagan had made the request, Robert Byrd declared that no Democrat would back a hike without the simultaneous support of most Republicans. But several Republicans were just as determined to keep vows not only not to vote to raise the debt ceiling but also to supplement them by voting for a move by Colorado freshman Bill Armstrong and veteran Russell Long to let Reagan unilaterally reduce spending and his cuts to stick unless Congress overruled him within forty-five days. Thinking the plan would give Reagan control of the budget process and bring the budget closer to balance, Armstrong made his case to Baker and George Bush. "It doesn't matter what I think," Bush replied. "The President wants a clean debt ceiling bill." Armstrong backed off, but many Republicans were unconvinced. When appeals from Reagan, Barry Goldwater, Jesse Helms, and John Tower did not sway newcomers, Baker called in the eldest conservative statesman, Strom Thurmond. "Gentleman," the spry South Carolinian lectured, "Some of you served in the House and you never voted to increase it. Well, neither have I. But I never had Ronald Reagan for President before, so I'm going to vote for it and . . . you should, too."[8]

"I never owed a greater debt of gratitude to anybody than I do to you," Baker told Thurmond after the Senate increased the debt ceiling. But Reagan and many of his aides credited Baker, for he had orchestrated movements toward their position and saw to it that the Senate held off volatile social issues until such debates would not impede the passage of Reagan's economic recovery package. Baker, said

Kenneth Duberstein, then Reagan's deputy congressional liaison, "knew the institution of the Senate . . . and his fellow senators like a book, . . . had a keen insight into what was . . . doable and what the opposition was likely to do," and could "cajole without getting people upset at him or . . . Reagan." "Before we do anything," added chief of staff James Baker, "we pick up the phone and get Howard Baker's judgment on what will or won't fly." Knowing each victory added to public perceptions of a successful presidency, Howard Baker let it be known that he would not use Reagan's early days as president to push quixotic crusades for issues that some of Reagan's core supporters deemed priorities. Recognizing that discord would rise if such issues tied up his caucus, and indeed the Senate, for the duration of the Reagan presidency, he said that he wanted 1981 to be "Ronald Reagan's year" and announced that debates on the social issues would be delayed until 1982. While Paul Brown, the chairman of the Life Amendment PAC was angered enough to declare Baker "incapable of being the Senate Majority Leader," pro-lifers like Orrin Hatch, Paul Laxalt, and Edwin Meese had approved his course as early as January 4.[9]

Budget issues dominated the calendar for the first half of 1981. While Baker shared Reagan's goal of reducing Carter's projected budget by $41 billion, the two occasionally differed on specifics. Privately, Baker defended Tennessee interests, disabusing OMB officials of plans to end TVA's ability to borrow money from the Federal Financing Bank and end funding for the Big South Fork National Recreation Area, and prevailing upon Reagan to overrule OMB Director David Stockman's objection to the Clinch River breeder. But Tennessee projects were hardly untouched. Big South Fork's allotment was less than half of what Carter deemed proper. Baker also acquiesced in Reagan's plan to eliminate the Appalachian Regional Commission (ARC), saying it "did a good job in its time, but . . . has outlived its time." To symbolize a need for across the board cuts, Baker led the Senate to disapprove hefty salary hikes for top officials in all three branches of the federal government. And instead of making loud pronouncements for Tennessee projects, he took to lobbying members of appropriate committees privately, a course letting Democrat Jim Sasser take much credit for federal works in Tennessee, but adding to the impression of GOP unity behind the Reagan program. To secure the same end, he persuaded chairmen Bob Dole and Mark Hatfield of the Finance and Appropriations Committees to step aside and allow Pete Domenici and the Budget Committee sole jurisdiction over proposed cuts.[10]

The instrument Baker and Domenici settled upon with OMB Director Stockman was reconciliation, which required committees to impose targets and cut programs to meet them. This stratagem afforded a chance to maintain all cuts in a single package and for the GOP caucus to treat attempted restorations as attacks on Reagan. "With the majority," Baker explained, "every time they stick together it makes it . . . a little easier to stick together the next time." They deemed GOP cohesiveness important enough that Reagan and Baker prompted chambers of commerce in Iowa and other states with conservative senators like Charles Grassley with reservations about reconciliation to press them to vote with their new president, as that instrument seemed the most readily manageable as any which might be pursued to limit spending. Indeed, lobbyists for shorn programs were swarming the Capitol in search of the largesse to which their clients were accustomed, and most had Democratic allies. In the first two days of voting on instructions to the Senate Budget Committee in late March, the Senate rejected several proposals to add funds for veterans' hospitals and school lunches, with never more than two Republicans voting against the Baker-Domenici levels, and always more defectors from Democratic ranks than from the GOP. With Democrats forcing votes on popular programs and attempting to brand supporters of cuts as antagonists of large groups, Baker, who believed the Reagan budget protected "the truly needy" by ruling out Social Security cuts and major cuts in Medicare, veterans benefits, school lunches, and summer youth programs, pronounced that "the poor . . . are being cruelly used."[11]

Debate was under way just after 2:00 P.M. on March 30 when Baker learned that shots had been fired at Reagan and that press secretary James Brady, a policeman, and a Secret Service agent had been wounded. Baker jumped in, reported what he knew, yielded to Edward Kennedy, who echoed his wishes for Reagan's safety and the recovery of the three men stricken. But Baker's information was wrong. Reagan had been hit. Once this was confirmed by Paul Laxalt, who was comforting the First Lady, Baker retook the floor, called on ordained Episcopal priest John Danforth to lead the Senate in prayer, and moved to adjourn. Reagan's condition soon stabilized. Reporters narrated the saga of a man serene in the presence of death, detailing his use of quips to calm those around him. The next morning Baker reported on Reagan's condition and commended his strength and courage and personality. Democrats picked away at the cuts in the meantime, but only nine voted against the bill. While some attributed the victory to public sympathy, insiders credited Baker. "If you had predicted the extent of the . . . cuts," said conservative James McClure, "you would have been told you were . . . on pot."[12]

The degree of Baker's success allowed Reagan and his aides to concentrate upon lobbying members of the House, which Democrats controlled by a 243–192 margin. While House Republicans were just as united behind the Reagan program, it took a dramatic address from Reagan to a joint session of Congress four weeks after the shooting and dozens of calls from Reagan to uncommitted Democrats. Alarmed, David Stockman urged Baker to push senators to accept the House version. But Baker refused categorically, knowing that the Senate would produce a similar measure and that members would not take kindly to being told to yield to the House. And, just as he had expected, the Senate approved the conference report with just twenty dissenting votes.[13]

But all was not well, for the thorny problem of Social Security had arisen. While a 1977 bill seemingly assured solvency by increasing payroll deductions, the old age and survivors benefit fund was nearly bankrupt. Reagan wanted to restore solvency by cutting $82 billion in benefits over five years by penalizing early retirees and eliminating the $122 minimum monthly benefit. But the Social Security lobby rose in anger when this idea was floated. Tip O'Neill labeled it "despicable." While Reagan saw such charges as demagogic, he could do little. As senators decried "unfair" cuts, Baker and Robert Michel told Reagan that his bill could not be passed. Uncertain of another way to restore solvency, Reagan read a speech to the two. "It's a magnificent speech, but you ought not to give it now," Baker said before recommending that Reagan create a bipartisan panel comparable to the Water Quality Commission, on which he once served. Finding top aides favorably disposed, Reagan agreed, named five members, and asked Baker and O'Neill to choose five members each.[14]

Reagan's move defused fallout from his only major faux pas in his first eight months. Not only had Congress passed the budget cuts, but it had also adopted a revised version of the Kemp-Roth tax cut he had pushed so ardently. While Orrin Hatch found Baker's role so vital that the cuts wouldn't have gone through without him, Baker respected the prerogatives of Finance Committee Chairman Bob Dole and limited his own role to lobbying those senators whose votes Dole told him were shaky. In truth, Baker had never supported the bill's provisions indexing tax rates. On the whole, he believed the bill a "riverboat gamble," albeit one likely to catalyze long-dormant business activity. Having been raised at the altar of the balanced budget, he worried that the deficit growth sure to ensue might harm the economy in the long term. With Dole and Domenici, he relayed his concerns to Reagan and helped convince him to restrict the first year reduction to 5 percent and delay its effective date to October 1. Democrats had begun to condemn deficits in their rhetoric, but the alternative their members forwarded in the House was even more costly over the first two years. While adding relief to low- and middle-income taxpayers, it made the third-year cut dependent on a trigger fired by a favorable prognosis of the economy and led to a bidding war to make the bill more generous. Although Reagan had opted not to reduce the top marginal rate on unearned income to 50 percent or remove a marriage tax for two-earner families, as Democrats might use them to paint him as a tool of the rich, he felt justified in incorporating these parts of the Democratic bill as well as cutting the corporate capital gains tax, increasing the business depreciation allowance and giving relief to savings and loan institutions.[15]

Baker opened debate on the Senate version on July 15. While unable to act until the House voted, the Senate, in view of the long period needed to consider tax measures, started two weeks earlier to allow 118 amendments to be considered. Relief went to firms hiring the disabled and poor, utilities converting to coal, and those hard hit by home heating oil price hikes. Other concessions, like cuts to small oil producers, were made to attract "Boll Weevil" Democrats. But House passage was assured only on July 27, the night Reagan delivered a nationally televised pitch that prompted thousands to call their congressmen. Following a 238–195 victory in the House, the Senate approved the bill by an even larger 89–11 majority. While Baker heralded Bob Dole, from whom he said he had never seen a "more sterling" performance, he deserved equal credit, having forged a united Senate GOP front behind tax reduction in the Carter years and maintained that cohesiveness once Reagan entered office.[16]

A different fate seemed to await Reagan's revival of a Carter plan to sell five Airborne Warning and Control Systems (AWACS) jets to Saudi Arabia, which America had leased to the Saudis since war erupted between Iran and Iraq in 1980. Finding the AWACS invaluable in monitoring developments in the Persian Gulf, the Saudis wanted to buy the planes, a gesture they hoped would signal U.S. protection to its enemies. But Israel let its allies in Congress know that it did not want the United States to be tied to any of its neighbors. "We've got twelve votes," Baker warned Reagan in April, "and that's counting me, and I don't want to vote for it." To Menachem Begin, such a sale would violate Israel's "special relationship" with the United States, even though his intelligence chief conceded to aides to Foreign Relations Chairman Charles Percy that "it doesn't change the balance of power . . . in the Middle East," but Israel didn't like the symbol of America doing business with Saudi Arabia. Although some like Bob Packwood thought that the best political posture was to oppose a sale, Baker saw Saudi concerns as legitimate in light of the instability of the region, but found the chances of the sale being approved as nil and convinced Reagan to delay formalizing it until Congress enacted his economic program.[17]

Even in the face of inept lobbying from Reagan national security advisor Richard Allen, Baker became convinced that the sale could be approved, if only because he had acted with Percy and Armed Services Committee Chairman John Tower to see that Reagan had a chance to make his best case, hosting Alexander Haig, Undersecretary of State James Buckley and Saudi Prince Sultan in Huntsville for strategy sessions in August. The first break came at a Foreign Relations Committee luncheon for Menachem Begin, who had promised Reagan that he would not lobby his hosts. But when time came for questions, Percy led, "Setting aside the AWACS sale and our relationship with Saudi Arabia . . . , don't you feel if the United States is to be instrumental in achieving peace in the Middle East . . . , it would strengthen our hand if we had a . . . strong relationship with the more conservative Arab countries?" Saying Percy had mentioned AWACS, Begin made a five-minute case against the sale. Ranking Democrat Claiborne Pell followed with an unrelated question that Begin answered with what Percy calls another ten-minute dissertation on AWACS. Baker found it obvious that "no matter what . . . we ask the prime minister, he's going to answer AWACS," and opted to let the "prime minister . . . get the story off his chest." Begin called on his intelligence chief to bring in charts and expounded at length. Word got out that he had violated a pledge not to lobby, and Saudi lobbyists began painting the issue as Reagan vs. Begin. Once Baker told Reagan that Senate anger with Begin had made the fight winnable, Reagan, said Baker, was "raring to go."[18]

While a House defeat was certain and a Senate loss looked just as likely, as fifty-four members had signed a petition condemning the sale, Baker guessed that some members might switch if assured that the planes would not be used against Israel. He arranged for seventy-five members to speak with Reagan on the issue, forty-four of them in one-on-one sessions. When groups went to the White House, Baker outlined the seating arrangements of each limousine and joined James Baker in briefing Reagan as to the best talking points to use with each. When lobbying Republicans, he stressed that a significant foreign policy victory in Congress would add credibility to Reagan's diplomacy. He spoke of bipartisanship to Democrats and targeted David Boren, an Oklahoman who headed an informal caucus of conservative Democrats, and John Glenn and Sam Nunn, who were respected for their expertise on defense matters. Although Glenn was disturbed enough by Saudi refusals to allow U.S. personnel on each flight to remain opposed, Boren privately began arguing in the sale's favor. Nunn, with John Warner, arranged for Reagan to send Baker a letter just before the vote assuring the Senate that the Saudis would not use the AWACS against Israel. Until that time, the letter would be revised to address concerns of doubtful members. Little progress seemed apparent until October 6, the day fanatics assassinated Egyptian President Anwar Sadat. While Baker and forty-two others had intended to spend the next day discussing the Warner-Nunn letter with Reagan, all were bitterly reminded of the murder of America's best Arab friend. Alluding as well to a recent Iranian attack upon Kuwaiti oil fields, Reagan argued that a rejection would lend credence to radical Arab claims that America could not be trusted and thus serve to destabilize friendly regimes. Some were impressed, but only three members switched by the end of the week.[19]

With but thirty-one votes committed publicly, most still pronounced as slim chances that the deal might be saved. Not disheartened, Baker began circulating the Warner-Nunn letter and found many prepared to switch if their concerns were addressed, particularly after former Presidents Nixon, Ford, and Carter endorsed the package. Dan Quayle, who was canvassing freshman senators, added his endorsement and was joined by Mack Mattingly and Ted Stevens. A short time later, Foreign Relations Committee members S. I. Hayakawa and Charles Mathias privately committed their votes. Larry Pressler, another member, was more difficult to sway. Unable to determine what might move him, Baker phoned U.S. Ambassador to Italy Maxwell Rabb, a close Pressler friend, and learned that Pressler needed a plea from Reagan and a guarantee in writing that radar-jamming equipment would be sold to Israel. Reagan phoned Pressler just as Baker began arguing for the sale in a Foreign Relations Committee meeting. Hailing Reagan for the extraordinary amount of time he had spent consulting senators, he said those who believed Israel's security would be "enhanced by reducing our influence in the Arab world . . . fundamentally wrong." Pressler arrived soon and his vote reduced the margin for the resolution blocking the sales to 9–8, a boost as the narrowness of the margin shocked proponents. While the Armed Services Committee provided a bigger surge with a 10–5 vote against the resolution, even these counts were deceptive, as the only shaky votes belonged to some who had voted against the sale.[20]

Indeed, Baker was swaying converts from among those AWACS opposition leader Packwood thought would never break. Russell Long told Baker that he would vote with him if the vote was close. John Heinz and Robert Kasten pledged their ballots if they were needed. Montana Democrat John Melcher switched when Baker showed him a letter from U.S. Ambassador to Japan Mike Mansfield, his predecessor, endorsing the sale. Each time someone declared with Reagan, Baker was on the floor commending him. When freshman Warren Rudman made his intentions known, Baker hailed him for handling AWACS like a veteran. More effusive was his praise for Democratic converts like David Boren, whose careful, methodical approach led him to say that the Senate often converts "good men . . . into great men."

While Baker was telling his staff that the fight was won five days before the vote, he continued to shuttle senators into the Oval Office. "How can I convince foreign leaders . . . I'm in command," Reagan asked several, "when I can't even sell five airplanes." The public breakthrough came the day before the vote with the conversion of Roger Jepsen, not an influential senator but one whose rhetoric had approached the bombastic, who brought with him fellow Iowan Charles Grassley. Their switches facilitated conversions by Democrats Exon and Huddleston and Republicans Dole, Murkowski, and Schmitt, giving Baker enough votes to block the resolution, but only he knew it. Resolution managers continued to believe they would prevail until the day of the vote, when their hopes were wounded with the defection of Edward Zorinsky and shattered by the switch of Bill Cohen, who Reagan mollified by promising to maintain Israel's quantitative and qualitative military edge. With GOP Senators Mark Andrews and Slade Gorton declaring that they too were convinced that the pledges protected Israel's security, Baker could release Heinz and Kasten and prevail, 52–48.[21]

Justifiably, Reagan received much of the credit. In the view of senators like David Boren, however, the man "who got this passed was Howard Baker." Indeed, Baker's performance in 1981 won him kudos from every band on the political spectrum. North Carolina New Right leader John East said he had "nothing but the highest praise" for Baker, who had "carried a great deal of water for Ronald Reagan."[22] Many liberals marveled at the way he let the right fringe of his caucus "blow off steam and then reason[ed] with them." Indeed, each time someone tried to add an antiabortion rider to an unrelated bill in 1981, Baker objected, always vowing to guarantee free-standing debate once regular appropriations bills were passed in 1982.[23]

Reaganomics on Trial

To Baker's chagrin, the recovery Reagan promised did not materialize as quickly as the White House expected. Although inflation had declined in half, unemployment jumped to 8.9 percent and interest rates were rising. "We made the first massive cut . . . in my political lifetime," he said in amazement, "and . . . the first major adjustments in tax law targeted to savings and investment in a long time." And what was the response, he asked. "Interest rates went up." To an extent, Baker blamed Fed chairman Paul Volcker's tight money policy and suggested that Reagan prod Volcker to "get his foot off our neck." Publicly, he called upon Reagan and Volcker to "get away . . . from . . . acting . . . so . . . independent that they never communicate." Reagan and Volcker soon met, but Volcker delayed loosening his policy until July 1982 when he concluded that the inflationary momentum had been broken. High deficits, traditionally the cause Republicans cite for inflation, persisted, with OMB Director Stockman estimating the likely shortfall for 1982 at $84 billion. Reagan responded with a budget just $32 billion more than that he had projected for 1982, with just $7 billion in added taxing authority, but a $33 billion increase in defense and hikes in debt service and entitlements. These figures dictated another round of domestic cuts, hardly a popular approach in an election year. Baker was disappointed, having joined chairmen Dole, Domenici, and Hatfield since September 1981 in advising Reagan that Congress would not accept a second round of domestic cuts without concurrent reductions in defense.[24]

The budget stood a good chance if modified, Baker told reporters. Privately, GOP senators were grumbling. "Keep your powder dry," he urged them in February 1982, although his warnings hardly hid his concern. "Every fiber in my . . . body," he said, "resonates against a $90 billion deficit," and he forwarded his own proposal to increase some excise taxes, make minor cuts in defense projections, and close some loopholes to signal members that alternatives would be heard. Upon learning that Ernest F. "Fritz" Hollings, the ranking Democrat on the Budget Committee, shared some of his goals, like limiting defense and cost-of-living adjustment increases to 3 percent in real terms, he was conspicuously present when Hollings introduced a bill which he calculated would lead to a surplus by 1984. When Treasury Secretary Donald Regan declared Hollings's plan ridiculous, Baker blamed himself, thinking he should have sent word that Hollings had some good ideas. His chagrin did not last long. When he could not persuade Reagan not to reject alternatives, he brought Paul Laxalt to convince him that his original plan would not fly. Days later, Reagan aides declared a Domenici alternative interesting.[25]

Reagan's interest was short lived, as he was blasting alternatives within a week as "documents designed for saving . . . legislators' hides." Angry, Baker lodged protests with James Baker and George Bush, and he got a call from Reagan within the hour. "You're talking about us," came the reply, and Reagan soon accepted Baker's invitation to mend fences at the next caucus luncheon. The optimism of his pronouncement that Reagan would listen prompted stockbroker Bernard Lasker to phone him to say that he had brought a seventeen-point increase in the Dow Jones industrial average, and another similar statement would have them all "wearing diamonds."[26]

Negotiations involving Baker, Laxalt, Dole, Hatfield, Domenici, and Budget Committee Republicans ensued nightly and produced a package with $100 billion in tax hikes and $80 billion in spending cuts over three years, which all but two GOP Budget Committee members endorsed. While Reagan saw the document as only a centerpiece for discussion, he realized that his plan would be rejected and had aides open talks with Tip O'Neill that were expanded to include the joint congressional leadership of both parties, the chairmen, and ranking members of the money committees and White House counterparts. While some progress followed, Democrats would not share blame for revising entitlement formulas and cost-of-living increases without curtailing the third year of the tax cut. Believing it absurd to surrender their issue of Reagan as the scourge of senior citizens while allowing him to keep his image as the great tax-cutter, some Democrats also distrusted Reagan pledges to promote a compromise reducing cost-of-living adjustments.[27]

The denouement came on April 28, when Reagan, James Baker, Edwin Meese, Donald Regan, and David Stockman met with the House and Senate leadership of both parties. House Rules Committee Chairman Richard Bolling opened the session by charging that Reaganomics had caused much suffering. More followed until Reagan offered to split the differences with Democrats on unresolved issues. With the idea arousing little enthusiasm, Baker argued in a recess for a final proposal to demonstrate Reagan's flexibility and suggested that Reagan delay the third year of the tax cut in return for a similar deferral of cost-of-living adjustments, a compromise he hoped might draw other concessions from O'Neill, and one which, if rejected, would result in the public blaming the Speaker. Reagan acquiesced and Baker aired his proposal when the meeting reconvened. But Reagan insisted that the idea had come from the Senate, leading O'Neill to declare Social Security off the table. While Reagan protested that he would accept the deferral as part of Baker's package, Democrats were not interested. When House Majority Leader Jim Wright urged abandoning the third installment of the tax cut, Reagan blurted, "You can get me to crap a pineapple, but you can't get me to crap a cactus."[28]

Both sides rose in anger. While Baker declared that Reagan had gone the extra mile, the principals were intemperate. O'Neill stood near a pile of "VOTE DEMOCRATIC—SAVE SOCIAL SECURITY" bumper stickers and declared that Reagan continued to offer a "raw deal" that had brought "hardship . . . and historic rates of unemployment and . . . bankruptcy." Reagan claimed that the dispute revolved around a Democratic desire for "more and more spending and more and more taxes" and appealed for a constitutional amendment requiring a balanced budget. As no one addressed the problem, the Senate Budget Committee confirmed by a 20–0 vote on May 5 that most senators saw his original budget as irrelevant. That afternoon, James Baker, Richard Darman, and David Stockman went to Howard Baker's office. In return for Reagan taking a lead in trimming some entitlements and agreeing to some defense cuts, Baker, Dole, and Domenici would reduce the total they were asking in taxes. Few were pleased. At a meeting with Budget Committee Republicans, Baker commanded, "We will offer no amendments . . . and we will vote down all amendments from the Democratic side." While Democrats protested that Reagan would not be able to push through the tax hikes, the Senate divided along a near party-line basis to approve the deal.[29]

Not quite as controversial was an extension of the Voting Rights Act. Seemingly, strife had ended when Bob Dole crafted a compromise extending the law for twenty-five years and defining the criteria for areas to escape coverage as an absence of discriminatory results shown in their history of facilitating the right to vote. Not all some desired, it was acceptable to civil rights groups and embraced by Reagan, who had been indisposed toward a House bill he feared would mandate proportional representation. When Baker returned from a trip to the Peoples Republic of China, debate had been under way for four days. Having rendered null notions that the extension was not being considered thoroughly, he moved for cloture. But Jesse Helms and John East, seeing the extension as a slap in the face, did not concede. Members of Helms's Congressional Club received letters urging them to demand that the right to vote and the right-to-life be protected in the same bill, a mailing that mobilized far fewer abortion opponents than Helms hoped. Many Republicans, including some anxious to reverse *Roe v. Wade*, told Helms they would block the move. More tactfully, Baker suggested that it would be hard to find time to debate a balanced budget amendment if riders were added and settled matters by vowing to object to any unanimous consent request until the voting rights extension was acted upon, thus derailing the filibuster.[30]

Perturbed, Helms and East pointed to Baker's edict that social issues would get a hearing once the recovery program was in place and got him to promise that an upcoming debt ceiling bill would be a proper vehicle for their school prayer and antiabortion amendments. More immediate to Baker was a need to enact the $98 billion in tax increases and $17 billion in spending cuts for Medicare and food stamps mandated by the new budget. To win the votes of Helms and East, Baker had to limit a cigarette tax to three years. This time, Baker needed a solid GOP front, as Democrats resented being excluded from the negotiations. Only after Baker stood at the door of the GOP cloakroom and reminded Helms three times of his pledge did a 50–47 margin appear for the bill. As the bill was titled the "Tax Equity and Fiscal Responsibility Act of 1982," the name given a minor House measure, a conference committee was in order that produced a startling shift in party roles.[31]

House Democrats accepted the Senate measure virtually without change. Eighty-four-billion dollars of the $98 billion tax hike involved closing loopholes, some of which were opened in the Reagan tax-cutting blitz. While others were of longer vintage, all conflicted with the fairness doctrine Democrats espoused. If a Democrat voted against the package saying the $14 billion tax hike on tobacco, phone calls, airplane tickets, and tip income placed excessive burdens upon ordinary citizens, then he or she risked surrendering the deficit issue. But the deficit question was less important to some House Republicans, who argued that a tax increase would stunt economic growth when unemployment was rising. "This," said Newt Gingrich of Georgia, "is a fight over the heart and soul of the Republican Party."[32]

While Reagan agreed to Baker's request to lobby for the bill, the ardor of Gingrich and his allies forced him to get Tip O'Neill's cooperation and promise GOP waverers that George Bush would campaign for them if they supported the bill. Democrats used their television time to respond to Reagan's presentation to let Majority Whip Tom Foley argue for the bill, and secured the win by enlisting enough Democrats to counteract eighty-seven House GOP defections. Conservatives blared that Reagan's alliance with O'Neill was a sellout to liberalism. With such claims legitimized when Edward Kennedy announced his support, Baker got a list of fourteen Democrats who backed the plan from Bob Dole and got those he could find to temper their statements and thus facilitate GOP votes. Forty-three GOP votes were certain by the time of the balloting, enabling Dole to release six Democrats and still win.[33]

Although irked, New Right chieftains did not want to alienate members they deemed persuadable on the abortion issue. Baker had finally convinced pro-choice senators to allow votes on antiabortion amendments to the federal debt limit bill. Debate would occur on measures by Orrin Hatch and by Jesse Helms, and no amendments would be permitted to either. First was the Helms measure, which extended to fetuses the protections accorded persons, let states bar spending for abortions or abortion research, and gave pro-life groups alone the right to appeal directly to the Supreme Court. Discerning that the Senate would not approve his proposal, Helms attempted to alter it. Bob Packwood saw this as an abrogation of the agreement that Baker had forged, broke in, read a history of abortion into the record, and yielded to allies when he tired. Now before the Senate was the talkathon Baker had tried to avert. Acting as an honest broker, he did not support the Helms amendment, which went farther than his preferred course of barring funds, save in cases of danger to the mother's life, rape, or incest. But, anxious to get the abortion debate out of the way, he sided with Helms five times for cloture. With Helms unable to muster more than fifty votes, Hatch saw further debate as counterproductive and withdrew his measure in return for Baker's promise that the issue would be considered in 1983. Once the Senate tabled his amendment, Helms introduced a measure stripping jurisdiction from federal courts over school prayer. Baker voted four times for cloture. With Helms's amendment garnering no more than fifty-four votes, Baker got Barry Goldwater to move to table it. The motion was upheld, but debate did not end. As Robert Byrd wanted votes on Democratic alternatives to Reagan programs and others saw the bill as a vehicle for their ideas, Baker, finding these measures would require more debate less than a week before the government ran out of borrowing authority, pushed through a motion recommitting the bill with orders to eliminate all amendments but his proposal to end construction of the Hart Senate Office Building gym. With time to spare, the bill and a continuing appropriations resolution were on Reagan's desk.[34]

Another Politician in the Family

Not up for reelection himself, Baker traveled and appeared for GOP candidates from coast to coast under the auspices of his political action committee, the Republican Majority Fund. He took particular interest in the races of protégé Lamar Alexander, who was headed for a landslide reelection, and daughter Cissy, who was making her initial foray into politics as a candidate for the House in a new district created when Tennessee gained a seat after the 1980 census. Spanning four hundred miles from the southwestern tip of Virginia to the Alabama border, the Fourth held twenty-three counties, none of which had a city of more than twenty thousand. Even with Scott and six other GOP counties, the Fourth was comprised largely of turf that had been Democratic since the days of Andrew Jackson. But there had been some erosion and Lamar Alexander, Doug Bailey, and state GOP chairman Charles Overby believed their gains could be made permanent under the right circumstances. Their choice was Cissy, then an assignment editor at Cable News Network, and she agreed to make the race almost as soon as the reapportionment plan reached Alexander's desk.[35]

Like any aspiring Tennessee Republican, Cissy scheduled a meeting with Baker in his Capitol office, leading him by her formality to be concerned, as any father would be, if she might be making a good career move or maybe marrying someone he did not like. His relief was evident once Cissy described her preparations. Before announcing her candidacy, she would spend a week in each county and bunk each night in a different home, thus allowing her to reassert her Fourth

District roots and plant organizations in each county. To overcome the Democratic advantage, she planned blitzes of the five media markets serving the Fourth that she hoped no Democrat could match. Having always trusted Cissy's judgment, Baker was even prouder now. "What can I do to help?" he asked. "For starters," came the response, "you can stay out of my district."[36]

While even *Human Events* reported that "her grasp of issues and her rapid-fire speaking style has won her high marks," 1982 was not Cissy's year. Instead of drawing an underfinanced good old boy as she had hoped, she wound up with an opponent with an equally distinguished pedigree who was willing to mortgage his family's farm to make his campaign competitive. The son of former Governor Prentice Cooper, Jim Cooper had degrees from the University of North Carolina and Harvard Law School, and had practiced law in Nashville. Needing every possible break, Cissy incurred primary opposition from Marianna Frost, a farmer and Methodist minister whose laissez-faireism was so pure that she declared a law banning miners from carrying cigarettes and lighters into mines an example of overregulation. An advocate of traditional values, Frost hit what she called Cissy's support for resolutions advocating abortion, the Equal Rights Amendment, and lesbian rights at the 1977 National Women's Conference. While Cissy, who had been elected by her student body, was visiting George Bush when the votes were taken, Frost continued to blast her for attending a "federally funded feminist fiasco."[37]

This barrage had minimal impact upon the primary—Cissy defeated Frost two to one—but it called attention to the traditional role of women in rural areas. "You ought to be home making babies," voters told Cissy when they weren't lecturing that "a woman's place is in the home and not in the House." Nor did it help that the president presiding over the ongoing recession was of her party. While she could argue for stimulating growth by creating enterprise zones in rural areas and restoring federal funds for Appalachian and rural programs, Cooper could and did advocate even more aid.[38]

Cissy was behind in September and had the one wild card of her father's aid that many Republicans mumbled that she should have invited sooner. Baker recognized the trend but declared the race "eminently winnable." In his first venture into the Fourth, he sought to paint Cooper as out of touch with the mindset of rural Tennessee by declaring "Reaganomics" better suited to solving the area's problems than "Tipponomics" and blasting Cooper's promises to vote with the House Democratic leadership. This might have worked in another year, but few Democrats questioned the ideology of their nominees in 1982. This was especially true of Cooper, whose father older voters remembered as a conservative. With unemployment rising, conservative Democrats would allow Cooper a temporary alliance with Tip O'Neill until the economy picked up. By no means did most intend their votes as a repudiation of Cissy or her father. Indeed, crowd enthusiasm kept Cissy hopeful until October 27, when she met an elderly man who told her he shared her philosophy, liked her even more personally, but would vote for Cooper. "Why?" she asked. "Because the Bible says to," came the reply. Smiling resignedly, Cissy knew enough others felt the same way to end any chance of her winning in 1982. Truly prepared, she congratulated Cooper minutes after the polls closed. "We beat the best," Cooper told his backers, and Cissy was equally quick to praise the man who defeated her for a "clean, aggressive campaign." Baker observed his daughter on election night and took pride, as she "lost with class and style."[39]

Jobs and User Fees

While Baker took solace in Lamar Alexander's landslide and in the narrow takeover of a West Tennessee congressional seat by longtime associate Don Sundquist, their victories were the exception. Republicans lost twenty-six House seats and picked up none in the Senate, even though two-thirds of those up for reelection were Democrats. "The Democrats scared people to death" on Social Security and the economy, Baker explained. But he would not engage in bickering that might result in gridlock, signaling "my good friend Tip" on election night that "we can't permit . . . the House and Senate to be in conflict." His message prompted O'Neill to open communications with Reagan, who wanted to convey the image that he was determined to end the recession. Had he had his way, Congress would have moved up the third installment of the tax cut by six months. But Baker and Robert Michel, aware that concern about the deficit made such a move impossible, suggested a program to repair highways and bridges that would create 320,000 jobs and be financed by a nickel-per-gallon hike in the gasoline tax. O'Neill assented, with the Baker-Michel proposal the only vehicle available to put thousands back to work. Once Baker and O'Neill let Transportation Secretary Drew Lewis make a few changes, Reagan added his support.[40]

O'Neill could term the measure a jobs bill, Baker a highway-jobs measure, and Reagan a highway repair bill and a user fee. Pessimistically, Baker thought it would be an accomplishment of major magnitude if Congress approved the gas tax and a continuing resolution. As he expected, delaying tactics materialized from John East, Jesse Helms, Gordon Humphrey, and Don Nickles. While Edward Kennedy believed the tax too regressive to justify voting for a mere 320,000 jobs and Barry Goldwater opposed it for the same reasons as Helms, both supported cloture, holding with George F. Will that "proper filibusters . . . were waged over more epochal issue(s) . . . than . . . that taxes were yucky."[41] But the initial votes hardly dissuaded Helms, who found propitious the wish of Democrats to extend unemployment benefits, strip benefits from the rich, and keep the job creation aspects of the bill while eliminating the tax increase. Such debates, all resolved on a party-line basis, bought time for truckers to make a case against a part of the Baker bill increasing the tax on heavy trailers. While their pressure prompted

Reagan to reduce the hike, thus mitigating trucker ardor, Baker still had to pull the bill to allow action on a continuing appropriations resolution necessary to keep the government operating after midnight, December 17.

After persuading the Senate by a one-vote margin to continue funding the Clinch River breeder, Baker rechanneled his energy into breaking an East filibuster on the appropriations resolution aimed at using enough time to block passage of the gas tax bill. His timing aggravated S. I. Hayakawa, who asked East if "his own wisdom is so great . . . , why . . . he demean(s) himself by associating . . . with clods and peasants . . . like us?" More irate was Reagan, who had to consider furloughing federal workers. Baker's warning of presidential ire did not sway East, nor did his keeping the Senate in session for thirty-eight straight hours. Only when Baker exploited a parliamentary gaffe to retake control of the floor at 2 A.M., December 19 did this filibuster end. A dozen hours later, the Senate approved the continuing resolution, thus rendering any furloughs unnecessary. But the four kept objecting to unanimous consent requests, forcing Baker to file cloture petitions every step of the way. Once the Senate passed the continuing resolution, it invoked cloture on a motion letting Baker substitute his bill. A day later, it approved the substitute and the gas tax bill. Taking the results to mean that the conference report would be approved by the same count, some left town.[42]

But Helms again kept the Senate late, even after the House voted its approval, in a last-ditch bid to block the conference report. Baker aimed only to "get this . . . concluded" but had little precedent to guide him. While talkathons on unpassed bills were common, repeat performances on conference reports of similar substance were rare. Baker let both sides make their case, then moved for a vote after midnight. Helms's objection to his unanimous consent measure annoyed many. "We ought to have a showdown," Robert Byrd blared, "or we ought to go home." Ted Stevens explained the difficulties of arranging flights to Alaska, said he would like to spend time with grandchildren he had never seen, and a vote later in the day would be the finest Christmas present ever. If members only wanted to get home, Helms replied, they should abandon the tax or take the time to read the report. As all knew what was included, many took offense. Loudest was Alan Simpson, a hard-nosed six-foot-seven-inch freshman who hailed Baker before 2 A.M. for his patience and good humor and then expounded upon the intent of the rules to protect a large minority, not a handful of obstructionists. Then, he peered down and "let 'er rip." "Seldom have I seen . . . a more obdurate and obnoxious performance. I guess it is called hardball. In my neck of the woods we call it stickball and children play it."[43]

"Creeping maturity" suggests to Simpson that frustration got the best of him. Under normal circumstances, he would have been ordered to sit down. Baker deemed this the proper time to file a cloture petition, even if enough senators had left Washington that he doubted he could win. Equally alarmed, Reagan spent the next day phoning senators and offering them a round-trip flight on an Air Force jet.

Few refused. "When you're whipped, you should quit," said Barry Goldwater, who was recuperating from hip surgery in an Arizona hospital but returned at Baker's request. The Senate invoked cloture and reapproved the gas tax by a 54–33 count, a verdict *Time* credited to Baker's "reservoir of good will."[44]

The Citizen-Legislator as Lame Duck

The travails of 1982 led many to believe that Baker had grown tired of the Senate. In truth, he had never intended to spend his entire career in the Senate. "No one," he told a friend in 1966, "should serve in the Senate for more than three terms." Determined to be true to his ideal of a citizen-legislator, Baker had warned many times of the dangers of America being run by career congressmen who adopted the mindsets of "elected bureaucrats" and "tourists in our own constituencies." The sole elective office that still interested him was the oval one sixteen blocks northwest of his Capitol quarters, and Baker had urged Ronald Reagan to seek reelection. If Reagan opted against running, consultant Doug Bailey had prepared a "1 percent plan" that mandated Baker resign anyway. But those who knew Reagan's thinking saw this as far-fetched. Baker's eyes were on 1988, and he had concluded that "you have to be unemployed to run for President," thus dictating that he resign no later than January 1, 1987, to stand a chance of being nominated. If he left the Senate and took a job with an established law firm, he could have more control over his time, replenish the fortune he had sacrificed, be free of the task of mending fences in Tennessee, and have a chance to experience a perspective more attuned to the country at large.[45]

Baker's intentions became known on January 11, 1983, when former press secretary Ron McMahan revealed plans in the *Knoxville Journal* that he had known of since Baker had told him the day after his reelection that "we're not going to ever do this again." By 1982, Baker was confiding the same to close Senate associates, but some were astounded that he might follow through. "SAY IT AIN'T SO, HOWARD," Bob Dole wired. After being harassed about the reports at Lamar Alexander's inauguration, Baker shortened his vacation in Florida, where he took pictures while Joy recuperated from the removal of a lung tumor, and flew to Knoxville on January 21 to announce that he would not seek reelection. Professing a belief in "life after the Senate," he said that he would not challenge Ronald Reagan in 1984 and that his timing was dictated by his wish to allow his party time to groom a successor. Content to hint that he would run in 1988, he admitted that he would consider an earlier bid if Reagan opted against a second term.[46]

While Baker remained Reagan's principal ally on Capitol Hill, Reagan's influence there had diminished. The majority comprised of Republicans and Boll Weevil Democrats that had surfaced in the House for Reagan programs in 1981 and 1982 had been decimated. While the Senate GOP count remained at fifty-four, members were more divided. Baker was afraid that the body might become a battleground of agendas. Were this to happen he left no doubt which side he would take, but he, more so than during his first two years, had to couple his partisan duties with his duty to make Congress work. Save for a pet resolution to televise Senate debates, each of the proposals he cosponsored—a constitutional amendment establishing a commission to set congressional pay rates and bills extending revenue sharing, making the birthday of Martin Luther King Jr. a federal holiday, removing statutory discriminations against women, implementing the recommendations of the Greenspan Commission for the solvency of the Social Security System and revising the federal criminal code to, among other things, transfer the burden of proof for insanity from the prosecution to the defense—enjoyed support from both parties.[47]

Recession Recovery and Social Security Solvency

While Baker sought economic stimuli both Reagan and the Congress would accept to deal with those deficits, action would be delayed. With unemployment at 10.8 percent, Baker believed that Congress needed to signal a determination to alleviate suffering. Paul Laxalt had seen a depressing news clip detailing the travails of those laid off at a Minnesota factory and went with Baker to convey to Reagan the sense of the caucus that a moderate public works program would be a proper symbol of a commitment to end the recession. Although Laxalt led by saying "this doesn't run . . . consistent with our . . . philosophy," he and Baker convinced Reagan to add $4.3 billion for a jobs program to a spending bill that had to be passed in March.[48]

Aiming to complete action on the jobs and Social Security bills before Easter, Baker opened debate on the jobs measure on March 9 and asked senators to offer amendments quickly as the fund for unemployment benefits would soon run out. Once a Democratic bid to add $1.3 billion for 200,000 more jobs was rejected, Robert Kasten introduced an addendum repealing the part of the 1982 tax bill requiring banks to withhold 10 percent of customer earnings from dividends and interest. The American Banking Association followed with enough prepaid postcards to backlog the Senate post office for weeks and sway enough senators for Kasten to claim enough votes to override a veto, even though Baker told the Senate that Reagan would veto any bill that included Kasten's amendment. After unsuccessfully prodding Kasten to find another vehicle, he adjourned the Senate to buy time for Reagan and the AFL-CIO to make a counterstrike. The next Monday, Baker filed for cloture and facilitated Kasten's bid to end debate on his amendment. His motion fell ten votes short, but the Senate also failed to end debate on Kasten's addendum. With only five days before reserves for unemployment benefits ran out, Baker got Kasten to withdraw his measure and pledged to give him a chance to attach his plan to a bill due in April. Having asked Reagan for "absolutely straight dope" on the reserves, he warned that the time had passed "where we can avoid any dislocation." The approval of the jobs bill soon thereafter led Carl Levin, a sponsor of the Democratic alternative, to observe that he had rarely seen Baker "fail once he has expressed the kind of determination that he has in this."[49]

Next was the bill restoring solvency to the Social Security system, a mixture of benefit reductions and tax increases that a member said was not a "work of art," but an "artful work" that was the one package twelve members could agree upon. Behind the package of chairman Alan Greenspan were unlikely combinations, such as Bob Dole and Daniel Patrick Moynihan and Lane Kirkland of the AFL-CIO and Alexander Trowbridge of the National Association of Manufacturers, diversity indicating the accord's fragility were it stained by any revision. Thus intent to keep the bill as clean as possible, Baker and Dole rallied the Finance Committee and then the Senate against each proposed change. But the package came close to being unraveled on March 21, when John Melcher introduced an amendment delaying the requirement that banks withhold 10 percent of earnings from dividends and interest. Thinking this had been settled, Dole railed that the bankers "almost beat the homeless . . . and now they're after the senior citizens." Baker, declaring that the addition would "blow this package apart," moved to table it. Unsuccessful, he then convinced Reagan to use his voice to condemn the selfish obstructionism of the bankers. His words had some effect. Melcher needed the Senate's permission to get a vote, as the amendment exceeded revenue targets for fiscal 1983. This allowed members to vote against the bankers and keep images as fiscal conservatives, a chance many relished. Fifty-three sided with Baker to kill the ploy and remove a last roadblock to Social Security solvency. A lopsided vote for the bill, Baker said, marked "a successful conclusion of another chapter in the . . . greatness of the American system . . . the subordination of our . . . ambition in favor of the greater good."[50]

Symbols of a New South

More certain was the fate of a bill making the third Monday each January a holiday commemorating Martin Luther King's birthday. Once the House passed the bill, Baker put it on the calendar and helped convince Ronald Reagan to add his support. While this usually guaranteed a quick verdict, Jesse Helms wanted to discredit King as a proponent of "action-oriented Marxism." Two decades earlier, his aim would have ignited the passions of southern traditionalists. By 1983, such a course was embarrassing even to those who deemed another holiday too expensive or Jefferson or Lincoln more worthy honorees. Especially disturbed were southerners anxious to remove doubts that their homeland had cast aside its past and Republicans confounded by their inability to win black votes. Fitting both categories, Baker filed a cloture petition as soon as Helms took the floor, and promised

Helms that action on a dairy and tobacco bill vital to North Carolina would only be expedited if Helms allowed a vote on the holiday on October 19.[51]

After losing a lawsuit for the release of King's wiretapped conversations, Helms compiled a dossier of documents condemning King, set copies on each senator's desk, denounced King's opposition to the Vietnam War, reiterated allegations linking King to the Communist Party, and said that the Senate had not done its homework. Edward Kennedy, having held hearings in 1979, declared Helms's charge "inaccurate" and "false," prompting Helms to complain that the rules prevented one member from impugning another's motives. While Baker mitigated this breach of decorum by expunging the word "false," the exchange indicated that the behavior of Helms and John East would become as much a point of discussion as the holiday. Especially vocal was Daniel Patrick Moynihan, who picked up a dossier, lectured that the Senate would be "sick . . . to pay attention to the filth in this . . . binder," flung it to the floor, and stormed from the chamber. Republicans, in contrast, distanced themselves from Helms. Those who admired King but opposed another holiday took pains to explain themselves. Proponents carefully echoed the sentiment of new Senator Daniel Evans that Helms and East "don't represent the majority of Republicans." One step further, Bob Dole noted that the holiday's sponsor (Charles Mathias), its manager (himself), the majority leader who guaranteed its approval (Baker), and the president who had promised to sign it into law (Reagan) were all Republicans.[52]

Baker as majority leader had the right to close any important debate. Virtually alone among members, he had been at the Lincoln Memorial two decades earlier when King had spoken of his dream, not as a participant but as a lawyer en route to the airport so struck by the mass assembled that he ordered his cabdriver to stop so he could watch. Remembering King's impact, he said the holiday should not be seen as a monument to King's oratory or even his martyrdom. "We owe this special recognition to black Americans, who have suffered so much, contributed so much, and with whom we all can celebrate the continuing redemption of America's first and foremost promise of liberty and justice for all." Passage, he said, would be "proof positive that the country and the Senate have a soul." Democrats divided 41–4 for the holiday, an expected count. Few Republicans ever enjoyed majorities from blacks, but they opted for the bill, 37–18. Support from senators from the eleven Confederate states was even more glaring. Seventeen joined Baker. Only three voted with Helms.[53] It could not be said that the vote signified the dawn of the state of interracial brotherhood King envisioned. But Helms, while appealing to unreconstructed whites, had been defeated largely because of the work of southerners Baker and Strom Thurmond. In and of itself, the outcome was a monument to the notion that white southerners had largely accepted King's ideal of racial equality and that the focal points for southern politics had shifted from racial venues to social and economic ones.

Still the most controversial Tennessee project was the Clinch River breeder reactor, which Congress had continued in 1982 with the proviso that no more money would be provided without a new financial arrangement. A new plan did not satisfy the House, which provided only enough funds to end the project. Six months later, Baker and Jim Sasser convinced the Appropriations Committee to add $1.5 billion for the breeder to $1 billion from private sources, a plan opponents estimated would cost more than the one it replaced. While West Virginia's senators shifted in favor of the new arrangement, they were offset by many Republicans disconcerted by the cost. Once it was clear fifty-two senators would vote no, Baker released those with doubts. The result was a 56–40 vote to kill the project, whereupon Baker took the floor, as he had when votes were more favorable, to salute opposing manager Dale Bumpers, but also to lament a fear that "we will regret not having an entry."[54]

Breeder opponents generally attributed their victory to matters of economics. Bob Packwood and William Cohen were not so sure, saying many senators had overcome doubts in the past because "we felt so loving of Howard." His retirement led members to scrutinize Tennessee projects as they would those of any other state, a development paralleling a growing fractiousness Baker called his "wet noodle problem." "I cannot make the Senate do anything it doesn't want to do," he explained. "This place is tied in knots," said Lowell Weicker, "and it's a credit to Baker that it's not even worse."[55]

Grenada and Lebanon

Baker's handling of sensitive foreign policy questions for Reagan particularly supports Weicker's view. After four Marines were killed in Beirut cross fire in August, a review of American policy in Lebanon became necessary. Involvement there did not mesh with Baker's view of America's proper role in the world. He advised Reagan in July 1982 that he did not deem it wise to introduce American fighting men and never lost his distaste. But when an April 1983 bomb killed sixty-three employees of the U.S. embassy in Beirut, he became convinced that a unilateral U.S. withdrawal would signal terrorists that they would be rewarded by retreat. When Reagan asked that protective measures be undertaken to prevent further casualties, Senate Democrats aligned behind a plan requiring the withdrawal of all troops save those authorized by Congress. House Democrats like Tip O'Neill and Foreign Affairs Committee Chairman Clement Zablocki opted to work with Reagan and Baker to limit the number of American troops in Beirut and establish a time frame. While all hoped the stay of the troops would be short, negotiators believed a six-month limit might allow Syria to delay its attacks knowing they could soon resume them. Twelve months would make the Lebanon issue a political football during the 1984 election. Agreeing to revive the Vandenbergian notion that "politics stops at the water line," negotiators scheduled a termination date for eighteen months after Reagan's signature.[56]

O'Neill's intervention produced a bipartisan majority in the House. In contrast, Senate Democrats, who resented being left out of the negotiations, generally held that it was unrealistic to win the withdrawal of all foreign forces. Republicans were equally wary, but most found some basis to back Reagan. Baker admitted that it was a hold-your-nose-and-vote-yes proposition, but said that the troops had "a mission and a role . . . and . . . it would be a mistake of tragic proportions if the Congress were to withdraw them." He changed no votes, but provided cover for all but three GOP colleagues, many of whom shared his doubts. "I don't think . . . any of us knows where this is leading," Charles Percy confessed.[57]

Perceptions changed on October 23, when a bomb killed 241 Americans and wounded hundreds more in the Marine barracks in Beirut. The attack strengthened the arguments of those who wanted to restrict deployments to six months or unilaterally withdraw all American troops. Such sentiment Baker found wrongheaded. "We should not leave at the point of a gun," he said, hoping Reagan could disperse peacekeeping duties among more nations. Believing an informed Senate more likely than one left in the dark to go along, he arranged for senior officials to brief the Senate on the ramifications of all potential responses. Still, a number of members remained impatient. To buy time for Reagan to involve more countries, Baker joined Chairman Percy in blocking all attempts to amend the war powers resolution to limit the duration of the stay of the troops.[58]

Reagan was preparing at the same time to invade the island of Grenada, which had been an irritant since its takeover by a Marxist junta in 1979. While government leader Maurice Bishop indicated in summer 1983 that he would be more independent of Cuba in the future, he and more than a hundred allies were slain by more doctrinaire Marxists. Once a shoot-on-sight curfew was imposed, Reagan came to fear for the lives and freedom of 1,100 American medical students. The presence of 700 armed Cuban construction workers convinced Reagan that Cuban aid might be used to consolidate the new regime's position. On October 24, Baker, Byrd, Robert Michel, and Tip O'Neill were called and asked to be at the White House at 8 P.M. without their cars. Baker and Byrd met at the Madison Hotel, took a cab to the southwest gate, and went to the president's living quarters, where Reagan, Secretaries George Shultz and Caspar Weinberger, National Security Advisor Robert McFarlane, and Joint Chiefs of Staff Chairman John Vessey briefed them about a request from the Organization of Eastern Caribbean States (OECS). Baker asked enough questions to concern Shultz that he seemed worried, but remembers a general pattern of friendly wishes from congressional counterparts. The only downbeat note came when Reagan took a call from British Prime Minister Margaret Thatcher. "Judging from his side of the conversation," Baker jokes today, "she didn't sound too happy."[59]

Marines and OECS troops landed within hours. While Austin's troops provided resistance, the students were back on U.S. soil the next day. Some kissed the ground, others praised Reagan, and nearly all had kind words to say about the Marines who liberated the island. Wanting to put the Senate on record in favor of the most vivid symbol of America's renewed resolve, Baker asked the Senate to pass the war powers measure restricting the deployment of troops to ninety days and another commending Reagan and the Marines. "How well I remember the humiliation of America in the streets of Tehran, and the seeming ineffectuality of America to do anything about it," he declared. "America appeared reluctant, confused and uncertain . . . but no longer." A shouting match ensued between Steven Symms, a supporter, and Lowell Weicker, who believed it "one thing to turn your head when the President . . . violates the law" but another to commend him. Seeing Baker's amendment as a ploy to contrast Reagan's action favorably with Carter's handling of the Iran hostage crisis, Robert Byrd figured voters might make this connection anyway and introduced a rider condemning security in Beirut, as embarrassing an appendage as Baker's was congratulatory. Realizing he had been outfoxed, Baker got Byrd to withdraw his amendment by pledging to withdraw his own.[60]

Social Issues

The delay of action on the budget prompted some to demand that their social agenda be considered. While some ardor sprung from guesses that Democrats would be disadvantaged if forced to vote for abortion or against school prayer, moderates and Old Rightists held with Warren Rudman that the social agenda was "not what ails the country." Baker shared their priorities but saw some merit in requests from his right. He had no stomach for another abortion debate, having allowed a vote in 1983 on a constitutional amendment overturning the *Roe v. Wade* decision. Even with his vote, the measure was defeated, 49–50, and he saw no point in airing the issue again. School prayer was another matter. Since entering politics, he had advocated a constitutional amendment overturning rulings banning prayer and Bible reading in public classrooms. He had voted for Jesse Helms's moves to strip federal courts of authority to hear such cases, but reluctantly, as he preferred the direct means of a constitutional amendment. Fundamentalists at both the pastoral and the electronic levels now shared his approach. Supreme Court baiting was no longer the focus of their campaigns. Action was, and polls showed 81 percent behind them. Seeing the best chance in decades to approve a school prayer amendment, Baker set aside early March 1984 for such a debate.[61]

Too many intangibles existed for Baker to be as confident as he would have liked. Opponents with an eye to the Constitution argued that reintroducing organized prayer would violate the separation of church and state. The hierarchies of large Protestant denominations feared that any prayer drafted to appease all would be so devoid of religious expression that it would be a "To Whom It May Concern" prayer. Supporters of school prayer were divided themselves. One group led by Alan Dixon and Orrin Hatch favored a measure authorizing time each day for silent meditation. A larger group led by Baker, Jesse Helms, William Proxmire, and Strom Thurmond congregated behind vocal, voluntary prayers. Differences in approach favored opponents of any sanctioned prayer time in the schools. It would be difficult to rally a majority and next to impossible to garner two-thirds.[62]

Recognizing these debilities, Baker waited to file a cloture petition until all senators had time to make their case. Aiming to devise language that supporters of silent prayer could accept, he added language banning government employees from helping construct any prayer and guaranteeing the voluntary nature of participation. But Alan Dixon was disturbed by the concentration upon vocal prayer and objected to a Baker request for a vote to guarantee that his silent prayer amendment would be considered. Baker then moved to kill Dixon's measure and won an 81–15 verdict from those opposed to any prayer amendment, those who preferred the verbal approach, and those who wanted to give Reagan an up-or-down vote. He set March 20 for the vote and sent Reagan a list of senators he deemed persuadable. But this time, Reagan's appeals fell flat. Some rejected the idea that the theological notions of a president should carry more weight than those of anyone else. Others resented the image that some religious groups were trying to paint of a debate between the godly and the ungodly. Lowell Weicker framed the issue in constitutional terms and denied that previous court decisions had suppressed religious liberty, saying nothing prohibited individuals from praying. As long as exams remained, he kidded, so would prayer, and this amendment would deny freedoms to those indisposed toward prayer and those uncomfortable with particular prayers. Baker disagreed, saying previous rulings had been a tragic perversion of the intentions of the Founding Fathers. As each session of the constitutional convention opened with a prayer and both houses of Congress honored that tradition, denying children the same right had had a "chilling effect" on the guarantee of freedom of religion. No longer was government accommodating religious liberty; it was merely condoning it, and he was merely trying to "restore the neutrality of the state." The question for undecideds was whether the state's neutrality was better protected by a constitutional amendment permitting voluntary prayer or by maintaining the status quo. Fifty-five sided with Baker, leaving proponents eleven votes short.[63] Even so, Baker could tell evangelicals that he had given them ample time and move Senate debate to more important matters.

Election-Year Politics

The most pressing point on Reagan's foreign agenda was a rider to an appropriations bill supplying $93 billion in military aid to El Salvador. Having long believed such assistance necessary, Baker declared in 1983 that America "cannot stand by and see the Soviets export mischief while we stand idly by," a position seconded in the report of the bipartisan Kissinger Commission, which held that America should not allow the export of revolution from Nicaragua or allow El Salvador to fall to Marxist guerrillas. While divided on means, their agreement on purpose let Baker paint Reagan's request as a return to a bipartisan foreign policy. Some saw the amount as overly large when El Salvador's commitment to democracy was uncertain, preferring small sums until they could be sure Jose Napoleon Duarte, a democrat by Central American standards, would defeat a candidate tied to right-wing death squads. While sympathetic, Baker was more convinced of the need for a quick mandate than of all of the funds sought and crafted a compromise providing for two-thirds of the original request, thus allowing the overwhelming defeat of amendments reducing funds and requiring congressional authorization for troops to be sent.[64]

The biggest domestic problem remained the deficit. After talks for a bipartisan budget ended in early March 1984, Baker and his "college of cardinals" agreed on a three-year package reducing the deficit by $143 billion. Forty-eight billion dollars would come from closing tax loopholes and $43 billion from domestic discretionary spending. The only sticking point arose when Baker and Pete Domenici insisted that defense authority for fiscal years 1985–87 be reduced by $57 billion. Although Reagan did not want these cuts, he had to back down when Baker and Domenici told him that he could count on no more.[65]

Democrats rallied behind a three-year, $204 billion reduction imposing $26 billion in new taxes, reducing military spending by $97 billion, and delaying tax indexing, but its partisan packaging sealed its doom. However, a $260 billion reduction of Nancy Kassebaum, Charles Grassley, and Joseph Biden, which delayed indexing, limited defense hikes to 3 percent, and froze other expenditures, appealed to moderate Republicans and many Democrats. It appeared that forty-seven senators would vote on each side until Baker convinced Charles Percy to provide the margin to table the measure. The balance of power remained with the eight GOP proponents of the "KGB freeze," who aimed to cut defense spending by $37 billion and increase by $20.3 billion the total for domestic programs. While John Chafee placed their ideas in an amendment, the Senate remained at a logjam until Baker won the votes of Chafee, likeminded Republicans, and a few Democrats by agreeing to add $2.2 billion for education, environmental protection, and medical research. House-Senate conferees met through the summer and eventually agreed to raise $50 billion attacking tax loopholes and cut $13 billion from domestic costs. Those reductions unaccounted for would be enforced with vetoes. But no defense accord emerged until September 15, when Baker and Tip O'Neill agreed to end the gridlock by recommending that defense outlays for fiscal 1985 be set at $292.9 billion, with savings to come from a delay in building the MX missile.[66]

The Partisan Baker Reemerges

The process had been inordinately long, a delay explained by partisan pressures. Baker's role was still that of an honest broker, but his influence had receded. Senators are always anxious to flex their muscles in an election year, and that tendency was exacerbated by the inevitable strains of a contest between Walter Mondale, a representative spokesman for New Deal liberalism, and Ronald Reagan, the most popular voice of classical conservatism to emerge in the twentieth century. On the campaign trail, Baker adopted the tone of a tough partisan. He was especially visible at the GOP convention, where he presided as temporary chairman over Reagan's second coronation, spent time taking pictures that he hoped would cement political contacts, and delivered a speech pundits billed as an audition for 1988. Contrasting the choice between Reagan and Mondale as one "between a team that has proven it can succeed and a team that has proven it can't," he painted the Carter-Mondale team as one that "gave us double-digit inflation, 21 percent interest rates, a punching bag for an economy and the misery index. Misery has become very important to Walter Mondale. When he's in office, he creates it. When he's out, he invents it, because Walter Mondale has nothing to offer a successful America." Quick to note Democratic attempts to incorporate the celebrated "New Patriotism," he worked in his standard conservative rhetoric. "People," he said, "don't need government to tell them what to do and how to do it. And Walter Mondale can't stand it. So he's trying to invent a trembling . . . miserable America that needs the Democratic Party to come to its rescue. The Democrats are doing their best to rebuild the coalition that elected Franklin Roosevelt so many times, but . . . Walter Mondale is running . . . and he ain't no FDR. And the only rescue America has needed lately was from Carter and Mondale."[67]

Upon returning to Washington, Baker initiated one last bid to televise Senate sessions, a cause he had championed since 1975. Resistance had always been strong among Democrats, who, Robert Byrd wrote, "were trying to adjust to . . . minority status and were not certain how the process would function." Wendell Ford and Russell Long feared that the presence of cameras would cause members to rush to elocution coaches and makeup artists, while William Proxmire saw the plan defective in that it might make compromises more difficult to reach as senators would be seen as reneging on previous positions. Unconvinced, Baker cited Tip O'Neill's view that television had improved the quality of House debate in a *TV Guide* article and a speech on the floor. It, too, gave House members a disproportionate share of media coverage, an imbalance he sought to remove. "Howard," voters had told him, "you're not doing your job. I watched and watched and never saw you up there." Too often, he feared, "debate is stilted, truncated, . . . canned and read into the record with all the conviction of a talking computer. The actual creation of public policy has passed from the . . . chamber to . . . committee rooms and leadership offices, and we file into the chamber only to ratify . . . what we have decided in private." Baker was quick to note that committee attendance was never higher than when television lights were on and suggested "that a . . . debate involving Pat Moynihan, Jesse Helms, Ted Kennedy, Bob Dole, Fritz Hollings and Lowell Weicker . . . would rival the duels of earlier days and make most Presidential debates . . . seem comatose by comparison." Television would also educate voters, who would become more familiar with issues and the thought patterns of their senators. If decisions appeared foolish, voters could better respond. If they seemed wise, a support would be built into the system. "Like it or not, we are what we are. We are elected by our constituents to serve them according to our talents, our disposition, our convictions. . . . We are a composite cross section . . . commissioned to debate the public's business in a public way."

No new arguments emerged when debate opened. Democrats generally followed Ford and Long in insisting that the new technology would cost too much, constitute a breach of tradition, and result in undue pressure on senators to end delaying tactics, thus stripping them of rights they had enjoyed for many years. Their ardor forced Baker to move to invoke cloture on a motion to proceed, a vote he won, but it was hardly a test, as many senators aligned with him out of courtesy. Some made clear that they favored televised sessions in some form, but not gavel-to-gavel coverage. Others allowed that they would permit radio but not television. Thirty-five members aligned with Baker, suggesting that a compromise might have been possible at the beginning of the session, as the Senate approved a compromise two years later. But time was too precious in the waning days of the session for Baker to thwart Ford and Long without adding to inevitable election-year tensions, and he conceded on the spot that his was "an idea whose time has not come."[68]

Election-Year Gridlock

The time had come to consider the year-end continuing appropriations bill. Trouble was certain, as the House passed a bill with $13 billion for new water projects that Reagan and much of the Senate found objectionable. Continuing resolutions had always been vehicles for a bevy of Senate amendments, and 1984 was no different. Civil rights groups wanted a vote on a bill Baker cosponsored overturning the decision in *Grove City College v. Bell,* which said that Title IX of the Civil Rights Act of 1972 applied only to programs receiving federal funds, not to all activities of the institutions maintaining those programs. Reagan opposed it, fearing it might allow never imagined federal intrusions into private matters. Orrin Hatch agreed and introduced 1,300 amendments that Baker asked the Senate to reject. "If we haven't the . . . guts . . . to do . . . things that are unpleasant and politically dangerous . . . to keep this government running," he said, "we have forfeited our . . . responsibility." While the first two addenda were defeated, Baker and Mark

Hatfield drafted a resolution keeping the government funded until October 3 when the Senate would return to the civil rights bill. Twelve hundred ninety-eight amendments remained, leading Baker to ask GOP proponents of the civil rights bill to withdraw their bill in return for the removal of all newly inserted language on social issues. Even with their acquiescence, passage was delayed until the wee hours of October 4. Its inclusion of aid to the Contras infuriated House conferees, and Reagan's anger at the inclusion of the water projects forced a second stop-gap bill that did not pass until Reagan sent half a million federal workers home. With neither side budging, Congress had to approve a third makeshift measure extending funding for another four days, leaving Baker feeling like "the fellow who's about to graduate from college . . . and flunks senior English."[69]

A recess seemed to make members more reasonable. Welcoming another parole from Washington, conferees stripped funding for the Contras and the water projects, and their product won overwhelming support. Only the debt-ceiling bill was unpassed, but this was a tall order, too. No Democrat would back a measure adding credence to GOP charges that he was a big spender. Republicans were no more disposed to vote to increase borrowing authority by $290 billion, as shown in the 14–46 defeat the measure suffered on the first vote. Frustrated, Baker recognized that raising the debt ceiling was a dirty deed that his caucus would have to do. After fourteen hours of debate, he recessed the Senate and decided to enforce party discipline. Any Republican who had used the first vote to make a statement, he decided, could vote responsibly on the second ballot, and those members who had gone home would have to come back. "We're either going to have enough votes that I'm going to win," he said, "or we ain't going to have a vote." To make sure, he found four Air Force jets to return absentees to Washington, and their votes gave him a 37–30 win.[70]

The Great Conciliator Bids Farewell

"We have endured quite a lot," Baker declared in a farewell minutes thereafter. But, quoting Faulkner, he boasted, "We have not only survived; we have prevailed." Again, the Senate had "shown . . . in the clamorous, cumbersome, chaotic way we do business . . . , we do it in the peoples' name and with the peoples' consent and in a manner that reflects . . . the passion . . . and . . . common sense of the American people themselves." Evidence, he said, could be found from the 98th Congress, which had preserved the Social Security system; modernized the banking, criminal, and insurance codes; made a $140 billion down payment on the deficit; and created a holiday honoring Martin Luther King Jr. But Baker was not satisfied. "There is no need to routinely run the risk of shutting down the government . . . for lack of funds. Surely there must be better ways to organize . . . our . . . responsibilities so that the months we pass at leisure in the beginning of a . . . session need not be redeemed in long hours of agony . . . at the end." It was not Baker's aim to recommend specific reforms. This he had done plenty of and would do plenty more of in the future. Instead, he aimed to renew the rule of reason. "The Senate," he said, "cannot fight a guerrilla war over every issue every time. We cannot be sniping at one another . . . while the essential work of government goes undone. . . . If we cannot resurrect the spirit of chivalry that once reigned here, at least we must restore some semblance of civility and commonality of purpose."

Civility was a hallmark of Baker's service and rhetoric, and he spent much of his talk acknowledging seeming debts. Singled out were his "graduating class," Jennings Randolph, John Tower, and Paul Tsongas; the people of Tennessee, "the best people on earth"; Darek and Cissy, in whom he expressed pride; and Joy, a "quiet profile in courage and a source of inspiration and insight beyond value." Not even the press escaped Baker's magnanimity. "I cherish my friends in the fourth estate," he quipped, "as I once cherished a dog that . . . had the single bad habit of biting people in the nose." Marking his final roll call, he asked for the Lord's blessing. "In His care," he said, "the Senate and the Nation it serves will not only endure but prevail in the . . . challenges that define the modern world."

Baker left to a standing ovation, vowing there would be "no more votes." Suppose Ronald Reagan wanted a lame duck session, someone asked. "We'll reason together," he cracked. After a brief stop in his office, rechristened the Howard H. Baker Jr. Rooms, he left and did not return until late November. In the meantime, he withheld comment on his future, save to quote Jesse Jackson.

"God is not through with me yet," he said.[71]

CHAPTER 12

BAKER TO THE RESCUE 1985–1988

It was Baker's aim to use 1985 and 1986 to build a viable presidential candidacy under the auspices of his political action committee, the Republican Majority Fund. Three days a week he would counsel clients of Vinson & Elkins, a Houston-based law firm; one day he would spend working for his Tennessee firm and several corporate boards; and a fifth he reserved for politics. But Baker was soon "running the wheels off the Concorde" advising a global group of clients. And Joy was afflicted with a steady series of ailments. "Bless his heart," longtime aide Ruthie Edmondson Leyen said in a 1986 phone call after describing his trips to the Mayo and other clinics to see Joy treated for a chronic abdominal condition. "We almost lost her." Baker would never publicly cite his wife's health to justify a decision not to run, but close friends noted that he was incredibly understanding and never away from her for more than three days. Only when doctors assured him that her pain was unrelated to a cancer that seemed in remission but eventually took her life did he ask aides to determine if he could raise the $10–14 million he believed necessary to wage a winning campaign.[1]

Baker met sporadically for two years with a group that included Lamar Alexander, Warren Rudman, former New Hampshire Attorney General Tom Rath, and longtime aides James Cannon, A. B. Culvahouse, Tom Griscom, David Spear, and Ted Welch. Rath, Rudman's campaign manager, ran the campaign temporarily and had workers in every New Hampshire precinct by August 1985. But operations elsewhere directed toward Baker's election were so infrequent that an aide joked in 1987 that the "good news is that our strategy hasn't killed us." Baker continued to hold the backing of a steady 9 percent of the Republicans the Gallup organization polled, placing him behind only the much more active Bob Dole, his successor as Majority Leader, and George Bush. As Baker had the best positive-to-negative ratio of anyone in the field, increased visibility stood to raise his standing. When he ventured to Iowa in February 1987, 250 uncommitted activists brought in by 1980 aide Dick Redman gave him a standing ovation after he outlined where he wanted to lead America. In Iowa, Baker's chances rested in the deterioration of Bush's strength from discontent with Reagan farm policy and the Iran-Contra scandal. While Dole attracted the support of many Iowa GOP leaders, there were many Iowans saying that they would "feel good if Howard Baker were in it." Former Governor Robert Ray had no doubt that a viable Iowa Baker team could have been built quickly. But, aware of Baker's disinterest in organizing, he found "whether it would have been done another question."[2]

Baker's chances thus depended upon an array of ifs. If Bush faltered in Iowa, which came to pass, and New Hampshire, which did not, Tom Rath expected Baker to cherry pick the border South on the subsequent Super Tuesday. But this depended upon the projected failure of another candidate to run ahead of Bush. For Baker, this didn't matter. He understood the kind of race he wanted to make and what Rath called "the illogic of the process." If he announced his candidacy, he knew that he had many friends, some of whom might side with him if his campaign seemed to be going somewhere, but few immediate allies. But abandoning the Majority Leadership made it tougher for him to raise money. It was always a problem for Baker that many of his supporters also held Bush or Dole in high regard. What seemed an absence of fire in the belly tipped many workers toward an alternative. Meanwhile, Baker made it known that he would consider any offer from Reagan. It was no secret that he coveted the secretaryship of state second only to the presidency. While George Shultz was not resigning, there was in January 1987 a vacancy in the CIA directorship left by William Casey's retirement. When Donald Regan asked him to replace Casey, Baker replied that he was flattered but didn't really want to do that.[3]

A Reinvigorated Reagan Presidency

By mid-February 1987, it was clear that Regan would be the next high official to go. As loyalists like Orrin Hatch and Richard Lugar had urged Regan's ouster since December, Reagan intimates Michael Deaver and Stuart Spencer brought in former Secretary of State William Rogers and former Democratic National Chairman Robert Strauss to level with Reagan. After recalling how he had felt like a "two-dollar whore" when he could not bring himself to talk straight to Lyndon Johnson about Vietnam, Strauss told Reagan he had a "problem on the Hill, and Don Regan has no . . . allies there. Secondly, you've got a serious media problem and Don Regan has no friends there, either." Reagan appreciated Strauss's candor but resisted his advice for two months. While legend has it that Regan had to go because he hung up twice on Nancy Reagan, what did Regan in was Reagan's finding that he had convinced him to contradict an earlier recollection of when he had first approved the sale of arms to Iran.[4]

The Tower Commission report marked the nadir of the Reagan presidency. Even in historically Republican Knoxville, 48.5 percent of those polled said their faith in Reagan had been shaken. Unbeknownst to Baker, a group of close Reagan associates like Michael Deaver, Paul Laxalt, Attorney General Edwin Meese, GOP National Chairman Frank Fahrenkopf, and pollster Richard Wirthlin determined that he would be the ideal replacement and convinced Reagan. When Reagan reached him in Florida, where Baker and his family were to hold their traditional pre-campaign meeting, Baker agreed to fly to Washington the next day. He was not altogether sure that he would accept the post. When his daughter Cissy, then managing editor at Cable News Network, arrived and asked about rumors that he might be tapped, he promised only to let her know the next day. Even this hint, Joy kidded, was enough to prompt she and her husband to tie a rope around Cissy's neck and hands to keep her from calling the CNN newsroom. The morning of the twenty-seventh, Baker boarded his plane, secured his seat next to *Miami Herald* editor Heath Meriwether, and asked who he had heard might replace Regan. Observing with amusement the foolishness of Regan's tactlessness, Baker told Meriwether that Nancy Reagan "can be a dragon when she gets her hackles up," a remark convincing Meriwether that Baker intended to run for president. But when Reagan told Baker, "I need you to be my chief of staff," Baker heard himself saying, "all right, I will" if he could bring with him the men who would be Reagan's communications director and counsel. Only on the duration of his stay was Baker uncertain, although he did commit his services for a year.[5]

Baker had feared that the news might leak. That indeed happened, prompting Regan to resign in a terse letter. It had not been Baker's desire for Regan to leave in humiliation, and he contacted Regan to express his sympathy as well as to help prepare himself. But much of Washington was ecstatic. House GOP Leader Robert Michel was heard humming and singing in the Capitol. Edward Kennedy, getting in a few digs, guessed that "it would have taken Howard Baker about one second to veto the arms deal with Iran." Bob Dole called his predecessor "the right man at the right time at the right place at this critical period." Calls came to Reagan from British Prime Minister Margaret Thatcher congratulating him on the move and to the First Lady from members of both parties thanking her for her role in restoring credibility to her husband's presidency.[6]

Baker immediately dispatched associates Jim Cannon and Tom Griscom to the White House to take stock of matters. The two interviewed every senior official they could find and were alarmed by the deterioration of the staff work. Assistants had scheduled a major presidential address for the following Wednesday without knowing what Reagan would tell the people. Two Regan aides Baker would not be retaining told Cannon that Reagan was "inattentive, . . . inept, and lazy," and that they had thought nothing of forging Reagan's initials on important documents. "Who had the authority," Cannon asked new press secretary Marlon

Fitzwater, to use Reagan's initials in such a fashion? "Nobody and everybody," came the reply. Cannon now attributes such a chaotic atmosphere to the twin debilities of Reagan's physical recuperation and a notion that Regan's loyalists on the staff seemed infected with that Regan was indispensable as chief of staff. At the time, he was alarmed enough to suggest that Baker consider applying the section of the Twenty-fifth Amendment allowing a majority of the cabinet to declare Reagan unable to continue and George Bush the acting president. Cannon and Griscom reported on their findings to Baker and A. B. Culvahouse, who would be named counsel to the president, at a Sunday night meeting at Baker's home. Baker listened intently, noted that "it doesn't sound like the Ronald Reagan I just saw, but we'll see tomorrow," and was rather adamant that he didn't want to hear anything more of the sort the second time the subject was raised.[7]

It thus became incumbent on Baker to observe Reagan carefully on his first day on the job. "I didn't see an AWOL president," he assured reporters. "I've never seen Ronald Reagan more energetic, more fully engaged and more in command of difficult circumstances." It had bothered Baker that a bevy of reports were referring to him as a regent. Jokes were common that he would be fulfilling his dream of serving as president without having been elected. But Reagan's easy quips and command of his surroundings led Baker to reject the cynicism that Regan's staff had shown Cannon and Griscom, and it came easy to him to tell Reagan that Joy had made him understand "that you are the president and I am not."[8]

Baker's ready acceptance of a staffer's role greatly differed from Regan's conception of the chief of staff's job as a prime ministry. His first duty lay in limiting the damage that might accrue upon Reagan from continuing anger about the sale of arms to Iran. Baker had always believed that Richard Nixon could have averted much of the fallout from Watergate had he stripped his men on the spot. When asked in December 1986 about how Reagan should handle the matter, he urged him not to let it fester. The same advice came from John Tower, who advised Reagan to hire counsel and recognize that "the arms shipment had been perceived as a ransom payment for the release of the hostages, no matter what his real intentions had been." Having been not just out of the loop, but virtually out of politics, Baker was not certain what happened, but saw impeachment as a distinct possibility. To press upon A. B. Culvahouse a need to bear down, he told him that he did not want to be the first counsel to the president to have his client tried and convicted in an impeachment trial. With Reagan's staff behind in their processing of documents, Baker helped Culvahouse and his assistants get some additional resources from the National Archives and other places. Culvahouse then read the documents, cataloged and analyzed them, and tried to understand better than anyone else in Washington what Ronald Reagan knew and when he knew it. What Culvahouse determined from White House logs was that Lieutenant Colonel Oliver North, the principal agent in the arms transfers, never saw Reagan in any group of less than four people and usually was not around him without at least thirty others present. At least one other person was interviewed from each gathering, and Culvahouse advised Baker and Reagan that there was no document indicating that Ronald Reagan knew of the diversion of funds before Edwin Meese discovered it on November 25, 1986, nor was there a legal theory Culvahouse thought would sustain an impeachment conviction. In effect, the question had been framed as what Reagan knew and when he knew it about the diversion. With Baker making access to such sensitive documents as Reagan's private diary available to Iran-Contra Committee Chairman Daniel Inouye and Vice-Chairman Warren Rudman and House counterparts Lee Hamilton and Richard Cheney, considerable faith was restored in Reagan's integrity and senior members of both panels were certain that no smoking gun would point to the president.[9]

This determination came only after weeks of diligent work from Culvahouse and Baker. With political first impressions, like personal ones, often the longest lasting, speechwriter Landon Parvin drafted an address acknowledging that "what began as a strategic opening . . . deteriorated . . . into trading arms for hostages." Baker and Reagan read his draft two days before its scheduled delivery and liked it. But Defense Secretary Caspar Weinberger and Secretary of State George Shultz wanted Reagan to add a paragraph exculpating them because they opposed the transfers. Reagan sympathized, but Parvin found the insertion absolutely horrible. Upon being advised by Baker and then Reagan to include a meaningless defense, Parvin drafted a few sentences, showed them to Weinberger, and then recoiled at his stubbornness. "You should try to deal with him on appropriations," Baker cracked. Parvin suggested the next day that the insert be left out and that Baker tell Weinberger that Parvin was responsible. Certain he would be the one Weinberger blamed and aware of Reagan's loyalty to Weinberger, Baker called in kitchen cabinet members Stuart Spencer and Richard Wirthlin, who agreed with him. "You've got one chance to make an impression," Spencer said. "Don't screw it up." The "Great Communicator" omitted the insertion, and, as usual, rose to the occasion. While most recognized his mistakes, they apparently forgave him, as a majority once again professed a favorable impression of his presidency after his speech. Lou Cannon, thus far Reagan's most astute biographer, took the week's events to mean that Reagan had regained his political footing. A key agent in Reagan's reinvigoration was Baker, who startled nearly everyone at a staff meeting by asking Reagan, "What do you think?" a question unheard of in Regan's tenure.[10]

While much of the luster that had accrued upon Reagan before Iran-Contra would return, he would never again work the magic he had with Congress in his first term. Republicans had lost two Senate seats, including Baker's to Albert Gore Jr., in 1984, and eight more in 1986. As Robert Bork would learn, Democrats controlled not just the chairmanships of all committees but also the process by which testimony was elicited and legislation was considered. It was Baker's belief at the outset that early concessions might bring later ones from Democrats on more fundamental matters. One on which he advised a conciliatory gesture was an $88 billion highway bill, which both houses passed by lopsided margins. After talking with former colleagues, Baker advised Reagan that a veto might endanger his chances for a fresh start. But the cost was $10 billion more than Reagan had requested. His veto dismayed some westerners, who had long sought measures like this one that allowed states to increase speed limits to sixty-five miles an hour, and others whose states would benefit from more funds. Others saw sustaining the veto as self-help for the GOP. John Chafee, Richard Lugar, and Bob Packwood shifted to Reagan's position after low-key Baker appeals. While thirteen others joined them, thirteen more would not budge, not even after Reagan visited Bob Dole's office and begged for votes. The lack of a defection meant that the veto would be overridden by one vote. While some thought that Reagan had wasted valuable capital on a fight that wasn't critical, others at the White House found the near win evidence that they were back in the game.[11]

A new team was in place at the White House, too. Baker's forte had never been in administration. Frank Moore, the Carter lobbyist who found him more helpful than most Democrats, said he was as well informed as anyone but carried it all in his head. Baker's time would be spent negotiating with members of Congress and advising Reagan. To supervise Reagan's schedule and the day-to-day management of the White House, Baker brought in as his deputy Kenneth Duberstein, a tough but amiable forty-three-year-old Brooklyn native who had been Reagan's chief of congressional liaison during the last half of his first term. Longer-range strategy for the use of Reagan's rhetoric fell upon Tom Griscom, Baker's thirty-eight-year-old alter ego whose experience as an army captain and a columnist and rare understanding of the media seemed hidden in the body of a five-foot-six-inch Chattanooga man. While Baker found posts for former aides Patrick Butler, a speechwriter, Dan Crippen, a budget specialist who left a post with the Merrill Lynch Advisory Council, and John Tuck, his executive assistant, he accommodated conservatives by installing T. Kenneth Cribb Jr. and Gary L. Bauer, aides to Edwin Meese and Education Secretary William Bennett, respectively, as chiefs of domestic policy development. Unlike Donald Regan, Baker saw to it that Reagan heard several opinions before making decisions, finding time in his first week for members of the Senate GOP Steering Committee of the body's more conservative Republicans to have a long-sought audience with Reagan and later that month for a group of conservatives outside the administration to meet with him for an hour. Here were opportunities Reagan's most devoted supporters had been denied in the Regan years, and many like Phyllis Schlafly called Baker wonderful.[12]

It was not Baker's intention, however, to act as a mere funnel for the ideas of those who had backed Reagan the longest. While allowing more staff members to make their cases to Reagan personally, he deemed it his duty to "give Reagan reality," regardless of whose advice that reality coincided. Twenty or thirty times a day, he walked down the hall to meet with Reagan, sometimes with Duberstein. He demanded from subordinates that there be no surprises and guaranteed this on foreign policy matters by agreeing with new national security advisor Frank Carlucci that neither would see Reagan alone and that both would accompany George Shultz or Caspar Weinberger when they met with Reagan. Before any document went to Reagan, Baker would read it, then forward it unedited. Here was a course much of official Washington found refreshing, especially after John Poindexter, Carlucci's predecessor, told the Iran-Contra panels that he had not told Reagan or anyone else in the highest levels of the administration about the diversion of profits. On domestic questions, he involved more GOP legislators in formulating strategy. "Phone calls to Howard get returned," explained then House Republican Policy Committee chairman Richard Cheney. "Nobody uses him as the focal point for cloakroom gripes."[13]

Victories for Reagan in Congress would be more difficult, however. A rejuvenated Senate Democratic majority aimed to reassert its muscle after six years in the minority. Likewise, the House regime of new Speaker Jim Wright was also much more aggressively partisan than that of predecessor Tip O'Neill. Such a context led Baker to order aides to seek consensus when possible but never at the expense of Reagan's "central core of convictions." This meant that Reagan would take a generally reactive posture on most domestic questions for the rest of his tenure, choosing the issues he would fight with the help of focus groups that Tom Griscom convened that, as a Clintonite would say, "looked like America." The one initiative in 1987 was a resuscitation of a policy paper of former Reagan aide Martin Anderson outlining an economic bill of rights, which prescribed a constitutional amendment limiting spending, required a balanced budget, banned wage and price controls, gave the president a line-item veto, and mandated two-thirds votes of Congress on most spending bills. With such proposals of little intrinsic value save to the truly committed, their re-airing merely kept Democrats on the defensive on budget and spending issues.[14]

It became Baker's aim to make Reagan rather than himself more visible to the American people, and in situations where the public would not be reminded of Iran-Contra matters. While there would be more presidential addresses outside of Washington and more photo opportunities, there would be far fewer press conferences that might redirect attention toward the Iran-Contra matter. Baker and Griscom knew that the press would resent this, but that was fine, for they were there to serve the people, not please the press. If any revelations were left, they would come from congressional committees. While complying fully with the joint House-Senate investigating committee, Reagan would spend the better part of his time addressing other issues in settings Griscom had the largest role in determining.[15]

Where change would come in the last two years of the Reagan presidency would be in foreign affairs. Planning began at an Easter retreat at Reagan's ranch near Santa Barbara, where Baker mapped out Reagan's schedule day by day for the next two months. Seeing the glasnost policies of new Soviet President Mikhail Gorbachev as offering a chance for a new arms control agreement, Baker assured reporters that "an agreement . . . is not important. A good agreement is important." So was accelerating the move of the Soviet Union under reform–minded Communist chief Mikhail Gorbachev toward a more open and democratic society. Baker chose the Brandenberg Gate that adjoined the Berlin Wall as the site for Reagan to address his hopes to the people of Central and Eastern Europe, and commissioned Tom Griscom and speechwriter Peter Robinson to craft his appeals. Their first draft contained the now famous challenge: "If you seek peace, if you seek prosperity for the Soviet Union and Eastern Europe, if you seek liberalization: Come here to this gate! Mr. Gorbachev, open this gate! Mr. Gorbachev, tear down this wall!" Baker thought the appeal "unpresidential," a misjudgment he kids about today while taking pride in Griscom. Still, Baker and Kenneth Duberstein made sure that the decision was Reagan's, and "the Gipper" aligned firmly with Griscom and Robinson over the lengthy and loud protests of Secretary of State George Shultz that the appeal might ruin any chance for better U.S.-Soviet relations.[16] In fact, the clear, firm stance Reagan trumpeted rippled amongst the peoples of the captive nations of Eastern Europe even if it affected the Communist chieftains of their region little in the short run. Still, those words today perhaps best commemorate Reagan's Truman-like determination to lower the Iron Curtain.

More controversial was Reagan's approach to problems flowing from the Communist Sandinista government in Nicaragua. Baker finds today's functioning non-Communist democracy as emanating in no small part from Reagan's "commitment to support the Contras, . . . his determination to deprive Ortega of a continuing opportunity to subjugate that country in the name of Marxism . . . and his making . . . clear that the way out . . . was free supervised elections." But when Baker took over, support for Reagan's Central America policies had reached its lowest ebb. Fifty-eight percent of those polled by *NBC News* and the *Wall Street Journal* professed to oppose Reagan's policies, while just 29 percent supported them. With losses in the 1986 elections depleting a small margin in the House aiding the Contras and the Iran-Contra hearings focusing disrepute upon administration policies, Baker and others prompted Reagan to make a new departure. In a May address to the American Newspaper Publishers Association, Reagan pledged his full support to any negotiations that could build democracy through Central America without bloodshed while vowing to continue requesting economic and military aid to the Contras to bring pressure on the Sandinistas.[17]

Only after the public testimony of Oliver North, the demonstrably heroic but occasionally dishonest former National Security Council aide, did even a narrow majority of the populace ever favor aiding the Contras, and that majority was decidedly short-lived. Even then, Baker guessed that military aid would fall thirty-five votes short in the House. Recognizing the stakes and that swing Democrats did not trust Assistant Secretary of State Elliott Abrams, whose job it was to sway them, Baker convinced Reagan to appoint former Texas GOP Congressman Tom Loeffler as his principal lobbyist for Contra aid. Loeffler's role was to sway Speaker Jim Wright, who had always opposed Contra aid but had backed aid to El Salvador, and he called upon Wright on July 22 to tell him that Reagan wanted a diplomatic solution. Realizing that Wright distrusted the Sandinistas, who had lied to him that they would allow democratic freedoms, Loeffler invited him to join Reagan in crafting a bipartisan solution. Wright, while trusting Baker, Loeffler, and George Shultz, recognized that most House Democrats vehemently opposed aiding the Contras and that many would resent him even discussing it. Uninterested "unless it is going somewhere," Wright determined after speaking with House GOP Leader Michel and Nicaraguan Ambassador Carlos Tunnerman that an initiative might lead to peace. While recognizing that a failure would renew demands for aid to the Contras, Wright was assured by Baker and senior Democrats on the House Foreign Affairs Committee that there would be no direct linkage between a Wright-Reagan initiative and Contra aid. Baker and Shultz then devised a plan imposing an immediate ceasefire and immediate cessations in U.S. aid to the Contras and Soviet aid to the Sandinistas, if the Sandinistas lifted all emergency laws and gave amnesty to the Contras. All appeared set until the plan leaked and reporters began calling White House sources, most of whom did not know what was going on. Caspar Weinberger was furious. House GOP Conference Chairman Jack Kemp phoned Baker three times and accused him of selling out the Contras. Baker had to explain to Wright that Reagan had had to mollify the right wing with a twenty-one-point interpretation that he had handed him and that he would be doing all a favor if he got rid of the document. While not completely placated, Wright turned on a television and watched Shultz announce that "the President believes in it and the Speaker believes in it. What we need to do now is to do everything we can to bring about peace."[18]

The Reagan-Wright initiative shifted responsibility for the war to forces in Central America. American allies in the region agreed days thereafter to a plan of Costa Rican President Oscar Arias committing them to act toward a ceasefire, grant amnesty to all armed groups, and provide the freedoms embodied in the First Amendment to the U.S. Constitution.[19] While Reagan would later threaten additional Contra aid to compel Sandinista compliance with the plan's premises, little further funding would come from America. A large minority had always backed such aid, but it remained a minority in Congress and among the electorate, albeit one whose size fluctuated with the degree of Sandinista compliance. What Baker and others involved in devising the initiative remembered was that the initial aim of Reagan policy toward Nicaragua lay not in the victory of those Reagan termed "freedom fighters," who represented but a small minority of the

Nicaraguan people. As the 1990 Nicaraguan elections demonstrated, the Sandinistas were also a minority. Contra aid was aimed at deterring the export of the Sandinista revolution and the threat of its revival acted as a catalyst to the Sandinistas to live up to promises they made during their 1979 revolution and only began to deliver a decade later.

More confounding to Reagan were events in Panama, where events came to a head in February 1988, after a Miami grand jury indicted Panamanian strongman Manuel Noriega on drug running charges and Noriega responded by cracking down against his ever more vocal domestic opposition. This time, curiously enough, Baker sensed in Reagan a reluctance, less than five years after the Grenada invasion, to have the United States cast by Latin leftists as an imperial colossus to the North.[20] Even though George Shultz and Central American experts in the State Department spent three months negotiating an agreement whereby Noriega would take up exile in Spain if the charges were dropped, George Bush and Treasury Secretary James Baker opposed such a plea bargain, with their political antennae sensitive to the appearance that the administration might be coddling drug kingpins and to the possibility that Democrats might call further attention to Bush's dealings with the dictator during his tenure as CIA director. In the wake of Nancy Reagan's seven-year campaign against drugs, Baker and Kenneth Duberstein could find no support in Congress for the deal Shultz had been working on, and so advised Reagan. Thus, Reagan had to defer to political pressures from both the Congress and the vice-president, and a move against the Panamanian strongman had to await an even stronger crackdown against Noriega's domestic opposition in 1989.[21]

A Successor to Lewis Powell

For the most ardent proponents of the Reagan revolution, the answer to another prayer appeared just around the corner with the late June 1987 retirement of Associate Justice Lewis Powell, a moderate. It fell upon Baker to ascertain Senate attitudes to twenty potential nominees. While some names drew red flags, that of Court of Appeals Judge Robert Bork, the most renowned academic champion of the doctrine of "original intent" and the man Reagan aimed to choose if he were not presented a compelling reason otherwise, seemed acceptable to Senate Majority Leader Robert Byrd. Senate Judiciary Committee Chairman Joseph Biden's lack of commitment suggested to Baker that Bork might become a lightning rod, albeit a doable one, and the absence of overt opposition led Reagan to announce his choice on July 1.[22]

While Baker expected some dissent, liberals were preparing a far more elaborate fight than had ever been waged against a nominee to the high court. Ralph Neas, the executive director of the Leadership Conference on Civil Rights, told

Tom Griscom that Bork's critiques of many policies and decisions had alienated the civil rights community. Harvard law professor Laurence Tribe warned that Bork's presence might endanger the rights to abortion and birth control, and the Women's Legal Defense Fund and the National Abortion Rights Action League declared their opposition the day the choice was announced. A mere fifteen minutes after Reagan spoke, Edward Kennedy took the Senate floor to condemn "Robert Bork's America" as a land where "women would be forced into back alley abortions, blacks would sit at segregated lunch counters, rogue police could break down . . . doors in midnight raids, school children could not be taught about evolution, writers and artists could be censored at the whim of government, and the doors of the federal courts would be shut on the fingers of citizens for whom the judiciary . . . often is the only protector of the individual rights that are the heart of our democracy."[23]

This characterization of Bork's worldview and many similar ones Alan Simpson termed "pure bullshit." Baker agreed, but believed, as did virtually all interested parties in the White House and the Justice Department, that a response would highlight and perpetuate such charges. Certain like Reagan that Bork would have been an extraordinary member of the Supreme Court, in the mold of Oliver Wendell Holmes, Baker saw the main obstacle to confirmation as the possible growth of a perception that Bork was too conservative to be confirmed. To some Bork allies, this was ideal. Daniel J. Popeo of the Washington Legal Foundation hailed a chance to roll back thirty years of social and political activism. Jerry Falwell heralded "the edge of history." Recognizing such talk effectively and foolishly confirmed liberal suspicions that Bork might be a captive of the far right, George F. Will quoted Groucho Marx's jibe at brother Chico in *Animal Crackers:* "How much do you charge not to play?" The bellowing convinced Baker that Bork would be better served if the White House handled the confirmation, rather than the Justice Department.[24]

Baker brought in Thomas Korologos, who had been the Nixon administration's liaison to the Senate, to shepherd Bork through the hearings. Korologos aimed to accentuate the positive, namely an intellectual agility Baker likened to near genius. Those helping him—Tom Griscom, A B. Culvahouse, and White House lobbyist Will Ball—wanted to humanize Bork to make his brilliance fit better into the political spectrum. But Bork ignored Griscom's advice to highlight his geniality in a televised interview with Barbara Walters as well as Korologos's suggestion that he not talk to print journalists and deny senators with power over his nomination the first chance to ask him tough questions. Korologos wanted to prepare Bork through "murder boards," where he and others would pose tough questions so Bork might better anticipate senatorial concerns and address them in a way that might sway some votes. But Bork had been counseled against these by Justices William Rehnquist and Antonin Scalia, who, having faced them, found them demeaning. Confident he would come off as favorably with the public as Oliver North had a month before, he did just one. To be sure, Bork can be excused to a degree, as the one he did was plagued by questions from a group who Culvahouse termed as "a lot of people trying to show how smart they were."[25]

What Bork never realized was that his confirmation rested upon his capacity to persuade undecideds of his sensitivity to the concerns of their constituents. "It was Bob Bork's to win or lose," Culvahouse said, and Bork could expect no quarter from liberals. While Joseph Biden had earlier promised if a Bork selection did not tip the balance of the court, to "vote for him, and if the groups tear me apart, that's the medicine I'll have to take," and Max Baucus had called him "eminently qualified," both committed against Bork. Two Democrats apologized to Orrin Hatch for voting against Bork, saying "he's the best possible choice . . . a wonderful man . . . a great judge," with whom they couldn't find anything wrong. What had happened was that Edward Kennedy had animated liberals to fight what William Cohen called the caricature of "this Mephistophilean character who was . . . going to be elevated to the federal bench." Some used threats. New York Democratic National Committeewoman Hazel Dukes boasted that she would see that Daniel Patrick Moynihan was defeated in the Democratic primary if he dared vote for Bork, and allies in other states impressed upon their senators similar portraits of their own grandeur.[26]

Had Bork been sufficiently astute politically to address the concerns of swing senators, the pressure may not have mattered. But too many, like Alabama Democrat Howell Heflin, found Bork good on substance but too much the professor. Bork indeed confounded many supporters by never registering the indignation they would have liked when Edward Kennedy and Howard Metzenbaum misstated his record, or when Patrick Leahy callously suggested that he had earned large consulting fees while doing no pro bono work without mentioning that the only years Bork ever earned substantial sums were those where he needed the money to pay medical bills incurred during his first wife's fatal bout with cancer. Even when Metzenbaum accused him of having put women "to the choice of work or be sterilized," Bork was deferential. It was not hard for him to field questions with a brilliance few could match. Unfortunately for Bork, his description of the court's work as "an intellectual feast," when he was asked why he wanted to serve, lent credence to charges that he was insensitive to the plight of justice and the concerns of average Americans.[27]

The swing votes were moderate Republicans and southern Democrats, all of whom Baker had lobbied in mid-July. Key was Arlen Specter, an able GOP constitutional scholar whom Baker took as a special project. After questioning Bork privately and publicly for hours and coming to doubt the propriety of Bork's expansive view of executive powers and his faith in the doctrine of original intent, he phoned Baker the night the hearings ended to tell him that he would vote against

Bork. Knowing wavering senators of all stripes could buttress their decisions on Specter's, Baker asked if a call from Reagan might help. "I don't think there is any need, Howard," Specter replied. Southern Democrats, many of whom Reagan had campaigned against in 1986 and most of whom had been elected with large majorities in the black community, were even tougher to convince. It did not help that Bork was a Yankee intellectual with a frazzled beard or that his detachment from organized religion was longstanding enough for *Time* to term him, inaccurately, an agnostic. Nor were all conservatives behind him. The National Rifle Association, one of the largest right-wing groups, was neutral because it feared that Bork might let state troopers seize unregistered guns they found in vehicles they had searched. While judicial restraint might seem a process southerners would favor, its results were not always to the liking of southern Democratic constituencies, a factor making it marketable only among the already convinced. Some of Bork's more devoted rightwing supporters never understood this. While some wanted Baker to sharpen Bork's conservative image, Baker could not think of a single vote Bork would have gotten had that course been taken. Indeed, Orrin Hatch later admitted that an ad with strident attacks on Democrats Biden, Kennedy, Leahy, and Metzenbaum run by We the People, an outside group lobbying for Bork's confirmation, lost Bork at least three votes. Nor did Baker find it appropriate for the White House to raise money to counter an ad campaign run by Bork's opponents, believing such activities in the Iran-Contra scandal had rendered that approach implausible.[28]

The campaign against Bork succeeded to a far greater degree than anyone imagined. While some say Baker and his subordinates were slow to lobby southern Democrats, Baker spoke to many Republican groups and personally tried to persuade some sixty senators in September. What effect an accelerated effort may have had is difficult to guess, as Bork in many ways was his own worst enemy. While pressing Reagan to appeal directly to the public after the hearings to rally support behind him, Bork refused an offer Joseph Biden had extended him to appear before the committee to rebut some of the testimony of his opponents. Wanting Bork to help himself, Baker, Tom Griscom, and others were also fearful that such an appeal might backfire into a loss of public and congressional support for even more significant Reagan objectives, chiefly an arms-reduction package with the Soviets whose terms were still being negotiated. It may have helped Bork had the administration stressed his credentials as a law-and-order judge or prompted the Senate to put more stock in his rather mainstream record as a judge than some occasionally extreme speculations he had made in law review articles. But right-wing pressure groups were ready to point fingers as early as four days after Reagan's choice of Bork, when direct-mail guru Richard Viguerie promised to hold Baker responsible if conservatives lost the Supreme Court. Some Baker aides found several rightists going after them and not Bork's opponents, actually accusing Baker of mishandling Bork's nomination so he himself might ascend to the high court.[29] Here was the sort of ludicrous charge that flourishes when seemingly sure notions fall to naught. Some blamed Attorney General Edwin Meese for recommending Antonin Scalia in 1986 when Republicans controlled the process. But from the standpoint of conservative ideologues, Reagan was wise to heed actuarial probabilities and select a younger man who could serve longer. While sentiment argued for the elevation of a more influential, more published jurist like Bork, the political realities of 1986 dictated the selection of Scalia, whose Italian heritage was seen as an asset. The realities of 1987 spelled the doom of Bork, a brilliant man who refused to learn how to project his personality and ideas to a public much less legally adept than he.

The search for another nominee began even before the Senate rendered its 58–42 verdict. The field narrowed to Appeals Court Judges Douglas Ginsburg and Anthony Kennedy. Baker preferred Kennedy, deeming him a confirmable conservative. But Charles Grassley, Jesse Helms, and Gordon Humphrey as well as former Attorney General William French Smith were offended that Kennedy had recognized a debate over the applicability of the privacy doctrine to homosexual activity and phoned Reagan to inform him of their displeasure. Allied with them while comfortable with Kennedy was Edwin Meese, who thought Ginsburg one of them and liked it that Ginsburg, at forty-one, might be able to serve longer than Kennedy. The age criteria appealed to Reagan, and he opted for Ginsburg.[30]

Ginsburg had no paper trail, but reporters soon uncovered a series of embarrassing facts. Initial concerns about Ginsburg's business practices took a backseat to what some called "sixties questions." The revelation that Ginsburg's wife had performed abortions during her medical training was followed by disclosures that he had smoked marijuana with students while teaching at Harvard Law School. Many conservatives recoiled in horror that a law-and-order administration would elevate a pot smoker to what some joked might truly become America's highest court. James McClure, after meeting with several conservative colleagues, called Justice Department officials and urged that Ginsburg be dropped. Kenneth Duberstein and A. B. Culvahouse were hardly more sympathetic, having grilled Ginsburg about his background for four hours and not been told about his indiscretions. Aware of general discontent, Education Secretary William Bennett asked Baker and Reagan if he could try to persuade Ginsburg to withdraw. Not discouraged by either, Bennett made his case to the young jurist and evidently swayed him as Ginsburg handed his letter of withdrawal to Duberstein the next afternoon.[31]

Ginsburg's concession to the downturn in his fortunes led Orrin Hatch, his most ardent defender, to blast some in the White House he termed "gutless wonders." Thinking "we could confirm him," Hatch wanted to signal those he thought had done Ginsburg in that "they're going to have to stand up for their people." While Hatch later said that Baker, who had joined Ginsburg on courtesy calls to senators, was not his target, it didn't seem certain at the time. Reagan, however, sharply defended Baker. Even more vocal was William Cohen, who termed the attacks as evidence that "you can get mugged more easily on the . . . stairs of the White House than you can on the streets of any urban ghetto. . . . The focus for the President's fall from grace has now shifted to the very man who rescued him from disaster."[32]

Baker indeed had taken a few blows. "In the Senate," former aide Jim Cannon said, "they fight with boxing gloves; in the White House, they fight with guns and knives." The infighting seemed to affect Baker's health. He had come down with diverticulitis and gained enough weight, and it seemed not just from his passion for blueberry ice cream, for aides to chide him as "the heifer." A former colleague found him worn to a frazzle by the competing demands and interests vying for his attention. Reports abounded that he was contemplating leaving, rumors he dismissed by vowing to lock the door and turn out the lights. But in some respects he had been vindicated, as it was easy for him to convince Reagan that Anthony Kennedy should succeed Lewis Powell. Even *Human Events,* which had urged his ouster, editorialized that he was right to back Kennedy over Ginsburg, and Kennedy was confirmed without dissent.[33]

An Entire Class of Nuclear Weapons Eliminated

It was foreign policy that really interested Baker, and he was certain that Reagan's rearmament had convinced reform-minded Soviet chief Mikhail Gorbachev that there was no way to match the U.S. commitment to the reinvigoration of its military might and thus offered a chance to reduce the risk of nuclear war by facilitating a fair and equitable arms reduction treaty. While never advocating arms control for its own sake, Baker had always been convinced that a fair and equitable pact would limit the risk of nuclear annihilation and predicted to the editors of the *Washington Post* in early 1981 that Reagan would at some point in his presidency engage in successful arms negotiations.[34] In 1984, he and Alton Frye of the Council on Foreign Relations enlisted the unlikely but incredibly formidable tandem of former President Richard Nixon and former Secretary of State Edmund Muskie in a successful pitch to Reagan to nudge him toward tempering his anti-Soviet rhetoric at a time when the four had concluded that Foreign Minister Andrei Gromyko and the rest of the Soviet patriarchy had recognized that Reagan would be reelected and that they would have to deal with him.[35] Only in October 1986 did Reagan nearly complete a treaty with Gorbachev in Reykjavik. Still, negotiations bogged down when Reagan would not yield to Gorbachev's demand that research on the Strategic Defense Initiative be confined to the laboratory. But, having proposed that both sides eliminate their intermediate range missiles from Europe, Gorbachev found it politically feasible to suggest in late February 1987 that this initiative be considered on its own, and he promised to destroy Soviet short range missiles in East Germany and Czechoslovakia. Reagan thereafter found it easy to convince West German Chancellor Helmut Kohl to dismantle Pershing I-A missiles America had installed four years earlier, thus removing the last major obstacle to the completion of the first treaty ever to eliminate an entire class of nuclear weapons and provide for onsite monitoring of the destruction.[36]

To Baker, Reagan's commitment to SDI was the crowning blow that convinced the Soviets that there was no way technologically or economically that they could compete with America. He did everything he could to see that key posts in the foreign policy establishment were staffed by those committed to both SDI and the INF Treaty. When Kenneth Adelman left as director of the Arms Control and Disarmament Agency, Baker joined Frank Carlucci in moving to block Paul Nitze, the candidate of George Shultz, who as Reagan's arms control advisor wanted to put SDI on the bargaining table. While Baker this time backed Ronald Lehman, the choice of Caspar Weinberger, he resisted Weinberger's late 1987 bid to tap deputy William Howard Taft IV as his successor. Taft, Baker argued, was a dedicated public servant, but the ideal choice was Carlucci, who could better cement the improvement of relations among all agencies. Knowing Shultz would agree, Baker persuaded Reagan not to decide until he met with Shultz. Reagan then became concerned about Frank's position. "You've got a perfect choice there in Colin Powell," Baker responded, referring to Carlucci's then-unknown aide who had impressed him with the clarity of his reports when Carlucci was not present. "That's right," Reagan said, and for the duration of his administration, the foreign policy making process was coordinated between Powell, Carlucci, and Shultz at 7 A.M. meetings in Powell's White House office devoid of the rancor which had plagued State-Defense relations over the past seven years.[37]

In 1987, however, that discord was sufficient for Reagan to occasionally express fear that nobody "is for this treaty but me." Albeit Shultz was always supportive, Baker found it necessary to stroke Reagan's psyche. Don't worry, he would reply. "There are millions who support you . . . and if you're ever in doubt about your official family, just remember this. I will back you up on whatever you decide and . . . fight for you tooth and claw." In most cases, the treaty's critics were Reagan's loyalists in the conservative movement, some of whom could never be swayed. "President Reagan," wrote Conservative Caucus chairman Howard Phillips in a *New York Times* op-ed piece, "is little more than a speech reader-in-chief for the pro-appeasement triumvirate of Howard H. Baker, Jr., George P. Shultz and Frank C. Carlucci." But even though Richard Nixon and Henry Kissinger expressed concern that an accord might lead the Soviets to expand their conventional forces, many conservatives had absolute confidence in Reagan and were willing to listen to any case he might make. It thus became Baker's duty to remind them that the Soviets had acquiesced only after Reagan had deployed missiles in Europe in the face of fierce resistance from vocal antinuclear lobbies in both the United States and Western Europe. Aware that he was no favorite of the organized right, he sold the pact as "Ronald Reagan's treaty . . . that the Soviets . . . declared they would never consider."[38]

At the summit itself, Reagan's ego required more stroking. Gorbachev was a master of detail and had learned to manipulate the media, qualities never more evident than in an afternoon meeting in the Cabinet Room right after the two signed the accord. "We were all worn out," Baker recalled, "and Gorbachev was spewing facts all over the place." Reagan met these performances with anecdotes about the Soviet system that Gorbachev found out of place and by deferring to George Shultz on substantive matters. Leaving the meeting discouraged, he told Baker he "had better hit the books tonight." "I wouldn't do that," Baker replied, recalling Reagan's first 1984 debate with Walter Mondale, when Reagan's performance suffered when he overimmersed himself. "Be Ronald Reagan. Remember who you are, what you believe and where you want to go. Let us take care of the facts." Colin Powell spent the evening preparing talking points, which he and Baker gave Reagan the next morning. Reagan stuck to the script and prospects appeared good for the signing of a second strategic arms accord at a summit scheduled for June 1988 in Moscow. But while Gorbachev agreed in April to a U.S. position worked out in January by Reagan, Baker, Powell, and Shultz, wherein America would end its aid to the mujahideen rebels in Afghanistan if and only if the Soviets ended its aid to the puppet government it had installed eight years earlier, negotiations on intricate nuclear issues bogged down when senators returned from meetings in Geneva skeptical of the chances for a breakthrough by June. After hearing this, Baker prompted Reagan to begin lowering expectations by saying that a good treaty, not just any treaty, was his aim.[39]

Still unratified was the INF Treaty. As Senate Democrats generally were quicker to adopt arms control programs as their own, Baker saw the main initial trophy to securing approval as the backing of GOP Leader Bob Dole, who had doubts that Baker believed only Reagan could remove. Tom Griscom suggested that Reagan invite Dole to the White House and then join Dole as the Kansan announced his support for the accord. Reagan was amenable, but George Bush was furious. Alone among the six GOP candidates vying to succeed Reagan, Bush had backed the accord from the beginning and resented the belated backing of his principal rival for a popular treaty being spotlighted. While Bush feared that Baker was trying to tilt the contest toward Dole, Baker reminded him that he alone among the six had met privately with Gorbachev when the Soviet chief visited Washington and was using a picture capturing the moment in one of his ads.[40]

Bush's outburst and the failures of all campaigns but his and Dole's demonstrated the appeal of the treaty. But while polls showed 79 percent of the people in favor of the pact, senators scrutinized the treaty meticulously. Jesse Helms and

Steven Symms introduced amendments rendering the pact inoperative until Soviet compliance with other treaties was verified, but none carried more than fifteen votes. More serious was the insistence by Dan Quayle and Malcolm Wallop that U.S. inspectors be allowed to witness in person the destruction of Soviet missiles and see that their launchers were modified so they could not transport missiles, a matter that was resolved when Shultz agreed to allow reservations incorporating their concerns and notified the Soviets that the INF Treaty could not be ratified without them. Democrats, in contrast, wanted INF provisions to be applied to future weapons like lasers, particle beams, and microwaves. Joseph Biden put their concerns in an amendment barring any president from reinterpreting the pact without Senate approval. Only on May 25, four days before the summit opened in Moscow, did Baker, Shultz, and A. B. Culvahouse find language that Biden, Robert Byrd, and Bob Dole could agree upon, thus easing the quashing of a filibuster and the approval of the treaty two days later by a 93–5 vote.[41]

The lateness of the Senate's action forced Baker to leave for Moscow after Reagan did to deliver the instrument of ratification. Even so, he found the results gold. If there was one policy goal he had set upon entering Reagan's service, it was to see that Reagan did not miss out on the foreign policy opportunities opened by Gorbachev's attempts to stimulate a long-stagnant Soviet economy. With that mission accomplished, he could tell friends that his work was done. He had begun looking for a spot to resign two months earlier, when Joy began experiencing bronchial spasms. More and more, Baker was spending weekends tending to his wife and stepmother in Knoxville hospitals. Aware that Joy had dodged many bullets, Reagan understood but asked Baker to stay on until the first of July, when he would be replaced by Kenneth Duberstein at a point where legislative productivity would be choked by the exigencies of election-year politics, thus rendering his continuation unnecessary.[42]

Baker's departure was less heralded than his arrival, but here in and of itself was a considerable turn of events. Reagan's team again was operating smoothly, following a course Baker had prepared for him months before. He and not his staff would be credited or blamed for any action of his administration. But this is the order of democracy. It said something about a man known as "the great conciliator" that he would subordinate his ambitions to the needs of "the great communicator" and use his steadiness to defuse overcharged political minefields and give Reagan what Tom Korologos called "a third term."[43] But perhaps it said more about the nonconsuming nature of his ambitions, his confidence in a team that he had played the largest role in building, his understanding of the American political process, and his commitment to his family that he would leave a position of great power at a time when he had concluded that his real work was done to attend to the afflictions of Joy and Irene Baker.

Chapter 13

FROM THE CUMBERLANDS TO MOUNT FUJI AND BACK 1988–2006

"I'm happy," Baker invariably liked to say upon leaving Ronald Reagan's service in 1988, "my wife's happy and my banker's happy." As so often happens when top politicos leave public service, his bankroll began accumulating steadily. Baker rejoined the law firm he and his father had created, took on a few lobbying duties, and trekked the country to deliver an occasional lecture. From time to time, he raised money for GOP candidates. While hating that task when doing it strictly for his own benefit, he managed to set new records for cash received while chairing the annual dinner of the National Republican Senatorial Committee in 1990. He served a two-year stint on the President's Foreign Intelligence Advisory Board as well as terms on the corporate boards of Federal Express, Memorex, MCA, Waste Management, Inc., and the Mayo Clinic. Certainly his most lucrative potential opportunity came when the scandal-plagued investment banking firm of Drexel Burnham Lambert, Inc., tried to recruit him to be their chief executive officer, but both sides disengaged from negotiations after that group's public relations crisis stabilized following guilty pleas to previous charges of securities fraud.[1]

Still, Baker's name inevitably entered the fray whenever chatter developed about who would fill key positions in future GOP administrations. Polls taken in the summer of 1988, for example, by the Gannett newspaper chain and amongst Ohio Republican activists indicated that he remained the first choice of those groups queried to be the vice-presidential nominee on the GOP ticket George H. W. Bush would be fielding that fall. Speculation of the sort, he quipped, sounded as if someone "was trying to revoke my parole." While ordinarily commending Lamar Alexander as a better choice or hailing the possibility of the nomination of Colin Powell as an exceptional wildcard possibility, Baker promised an "athletic" effort to avoid being selected and virtually ordered reporters at the GOP convention in New Orleans to take off the "Bush-Baker" buttons they were sporting. Privately,

Baker notified Bush and campaign chairman James Baker that he would prefer not to be selected, but he would fill out forms they provided in the event Bush opted to choose him. That possibility Baker did not anticipate. He knew that Bush and the rest of his team were quite sensitive to his desire to attend to the still-ailing Joy. While an alarmist might be troubled by a temporary seventeen-point deficit in the polls, Baker assumed that a sitting vice-president in the midst of a robust economy would experience a healthy postconvention bounce regardless of the identity of his running mate. Bush then could act upon his preference for a loyalist, and he had never quite felt as close to Baker after Baker endorsed Reagan in 1980 before Bush withdrew from that contest. The only surprise to Baker then could have been Bush's option for Dan Quayle as opposed to Bush's rivals in the spring's primaries or one of Quayle's more senior Senate colleagues, like John Danforth, Pete Domenici, Nancy Kassebaum, or Alan Simpson.[2]

In years to come, Baker's constant political role would be as a mentor for a younger generation of Tennessee politicos. His practice in the Senate was to avoid choosing sides in Tennessee GOP primaries between two or more credible candidates. To be sure, he departed from that policy in 1994 to overtly back longtime associates Fred Thompson and Don Sundquist for senator and governor, respectively. Ordinarily, however, he made time to counsel virtually any hopeful who sought his advice, even a few Democrats. "You go to Mecca to run for almost any office now in Tennessee," said former Congressman Dan Kuykendall. Baker listened more than advised, but did make sure to tell aspirants not to "be afraid of politics," but to go into it "with open eyes." He paid particular attention to those, among them the young Nashville heart surgeon Bill Frist, who he found had the intellectual capacity to contribute to the body politic, laudable reasons for wanting to serve in public office, and solid conceptions about what duties those offices entailed. If he gained an initial favorable reaction, he sought to determine how a campaign might impact that potential candidate's family. Only if that verdict was favorable would Baker give such a race his private blessing.

Baker also counseled those favored to take along on their campaign tours an item which might become a matter of interest. A virtue of carrying his camera, for example, had always been that it gave him an excuse to avoid situations like playing in staff softball games that might highlight a personal shortcoming and focus attention instead on one of his particular talents. One who took heed was Fred Thompson, who recognized that his career as a Lincoln-driving lawyer and lobbyist in Nashville and Washington seemed to set him above the experience of the average Tennessean. In turn, Thompson opted to rent a pickup truck and drive it to campaign stops across Tennessee while wearing blue jeans and boots that reminded voters of his humble origins in Lawrenceburg. The result in that 1994 campaign was a victory whose margin exceeded all but one of Baker's.[3]

Star Witness

Having watched a multitude of clients take oaths over two generations and having administered a few himself, it is indeed surprising that Baker never had to swear an oath to tell the whole truth until his sixty-seventh year. That changed at a hearing of August 1992 held by the Senate Select Committee on POW\MIA Affairs, when Chairman John Kerry called Baker and longtime associate Jim Cannon to testify as to how the Reagan administration responded to suggestions by the mercurial Dallas billionaire Ross Perot that some captured American soldiers might remain in Vietnam. Baker reported to the panel that he sensed anguish in Reagan every time the subject arose and that he and the former president saw Perot, who Baker did not know, as a dedicated and patriotic American who wanted to negotiate the release of any remaining Americans with the Vietnamese. Baker aimed to convince Perot that Reagan's preferred negotiator was General John Vessey. Perot could go to Vietnam as a private citizen, he added, but should avoid any situation which might allow the Vietnamese to play off Vessey against him to the detriment of any of their intended beneficiaries. He spoke with Perot and then sent Cannon, a private citizen who had known Perot for fifteen years, to reiterate his message. Minutes later, Baker convinced Nancy Reagan and former Interior Secretary William Clark, who led fund-raising efforts for the planned Reagan library, not to meet with Perot, as such an encounter might lead skeptics to believe that donations to the library were being traded for unwise policy. Kerry, like committee Republicans John McCain and Bob Smith, treated Baker with deference. Not only did they value his experience and judgment, it was lost upon none of them that Baker's ethical concerns were every bit as valid as Perot's well-known but often quixotic desire to win the release of any American still in captivity was sincere.[4]

Six years later, Baker was downright grateful to the Senate Finance Committee after its staff notified him that David Anthony "Tony" Deaton, a vindictive and corrupt Internal Revenue Service agent, had tried to frame him, Congressman Jimmy Quillen, and District Attorney General David Crockett on bribery charges and boasted loudly and obnoxiously for more than a decade in Johnson City bars that he would see to their convictions. The ire of the alcoholic Deaton stemmed from Crockett's attempt to prosecute him in 1984 after he refused to submit a Breathalyzer test after the car he was driving hit another head on. While managing to be acquitted and continuing to work for the IRS until large amounts of cocaine and scales were found in his car in 1994, this rogue agent succeeded in convincing the local hierarchy to transfer a supervisor who had both encouraged him to seek professional help and sought to fire him for a multitude of other unethical practices. Neither Baker nor Quillen were in any way cognizant of Deaton's vendetta until Finance Committee staffers informed them of it in early spring of 1998. Aide Fred Marcum remembers Baker being concerned enough to pick up the phone immediately and begin making inquiries but considerably calmer than some utterly "volcanic" friends when they learned of the scam. Still, Baker and Quillen told the panel they were grateful to the extreme to two IRS workers who had been denigrated and downgraded and one who had been outright terminated for trying to expose the Deaton frauds. Baker noted that he had the means and the will to aggressively challenge any such fabricated evidence with the best of legal help. Still, he found himself deeply troubled that others in less fortunate circumstances, finding themselves in a similar situation, might not be so lucky. Senators virtually stumbled over each other to profess the greater outrage. "If it could happen to a Howard Baker," declared North Dakota Democrat Kent Conrad, fully in accord with the rest of the committee, "it could happen even more easily to an average American citizen."[5]

The Passing of Joy

Baker's preoccupation for the better part of the five years after his departure from the White House lay in attending to Joy. Like many that endure for four decades, his marriage had its peaks and valleys, but he remained uncommonly devoted to her. Howard and Joy Baker were still "crazy about each other," Darek Baker told a tabloid writer right after his father left Ronald Reagan's service. While Baker was working late nights as Leader, Joy would come to his office a night or two each week to dine with him. It was not unheard of for her to call him late at night after he had had a long day to tell him what she had been doing. Invariably, he lit up, took the call, and listened as intently as he would to any working associate on Capitol Hill. At one point, he even developed a flower in the greenhouse outside their Washington home that he heralded as the Joy Baker pink orchid.

"He loved her," said *Wall Street Journal* Washington bureau chief Al Hunt, a longtime Baker friend who was equally quick to note that the union was hardly one that would commend itself to a Dolly Levi or a Dr. Phil. The Bakers, while both exceptionally astute congressional brats, had several areas of disconnection which might strain the marriages of less committed partners. Baker was invariably dispassionate and friendly; Joy was a highly opinionated, vulnerable, somewhat shy woman with a prodigious memory who much preferred seeking out people to being sought. She loved to cook; he used the freezer to store his negatives. He arose early and was perpetually punctual; she was a bit of a night owl and often late. She was always concerned about her appearance; he on days when it wasn't likely he would be on camera often wore rumpled suits and penny loafers. Home in the minds of both was their mountain spread in Huntsville, but they spent considerable time in their condominium in Bal Harbour, Florida. There, Baker would play tennis and read diversionary material like murder mysteries. Joy would work on her tan, read from more substantive tomes than the whodunits her husband had brought along, or engage in the business of Ford's Theater with her vacation neighbor, Millie (Mrs. Tip) O'Neill.[6]

Still, the Bakers were never closer than in the years after he became Senate GOP Leader. Joy's relationship with Cissy, which had been a bit strained during the years when she was drinking heavily, had been repaired to the point where her daughter was likening her to a sister and calling her regularly merely to refresh herself. She became even more of a beloved fixture within the Senate family as well. To Senate wives like John Warner's then spouse, the legendary actress but political novice Elizabeth Taylor, Joy acted as something of a maternal figure even though they were contemporaries. To interns like Mike Prince, later a Knox County GOP chairman, she was the all-too-rare example of a very considerate political spouse who was always gracious enough to say hello to volunteers and make them feel like they were an important part of the team. To fellow recovering alcoholics like Michael Deaver, the public relations mastermind of the first Reagan term, she was an inspiration and "wonderful" rock of support during the time he worked to overcome their common affliction. And to colleagues on the boards of the Kennedy Center for the Performing Arts and Ford's Theater, she was invaluable, particularly at recruiting talent. One year, for example, members of the Ford's Theater board used a standard formal request to secure a concert by opera star Luciano Pavarotti. Upon being declined, Joy remembered that a manicurist she knew grew up in the same Italian town as Pavarotti and got her to handwrite a personal request in Italian for the board that was air-expressed to the London arena where Pavarotti was singing. That appeal moved the renowned tenor to accept, and the Ford's Gala that he headlined raised millions.[7]

Physically, however, Joy Baker remained frail and battled a constant battery of afflictions. In the 1980s, she experienced lengthy bouts with ulcers, bronchitis, and chronic back pain. Forty percent of her stomach was gone by 1981. The next year, she lost the better part of her right lung to a cancer that had seemed to go into remission. It fell upon Baker to escort her quite regularly from hospital to Huntsville to another hospital to Washington for much of the next decade. Especially fortuitous for Baker was that his hobby was an artistic one that provided a brief but welcome diversion from the troubles at hand. In the eyes of Cissy, an accomplished photo editor herself, the stress he developed as Joy's health declined manifested itself in some of his finest camera work. Several of these pictures are found in *The Big South Fork Country*, a compilation of photos he and the noted nature photographer John Netherton took in the river and recreation area just west of Huntsville. Only in January of 1993 did doctors discern that Joy could not recover. Then, she opted to fly home from the Mayo Clinic to live out the remainder of her days. Death came on Saturday night, April 24. Her funeral a few days later brought George and Barbara Bush, virtually all of the Tennessee political establishment, twenty-two senators, and hundreds of dignitaries and friends to Huntsville.[8]

Nancy

Friends sensed an emotional exhaustion and loneliness in Baker for the better part of the next three years. One was former Secretary of State Lawrence Eagleburger, who loves to tease his wife that she "cannot stand unmatched men." In Baker, Marlene Eagleburger saw a "really nice man" with a "fabulous sense of humor" who had been a "great husband" and could and should be again. They held in equally high regard Nancy Landon Kassebaum, the demure, retiring senator from Kansas who holds the distinction of being the first woman ever elected to a full term in the Senate who was not the widow of a man who had served in Congress. Indeed, the Eagleburgers knew that Kassebaum, whose impending departure from the Senate after three terms they deemed a "real loss" to the institution, admired the way that Baker conducted himself, particularly in adverse circumstances. She, too, shared with Baker some interests, the legacy of being a political brat, she being the daughter of Governor Alf Landon, and overlapping three-term stints in the Senate. While the two were not personally close, they were almost always allied as senators and friendly enough that Kassebaum had attended Joy Baker's funeral. The Eagleburgers invited the two to dine at the Capitol Grille in Washington, seated them next to each other, and noticed the two enjoying each other's company.[9]

Baker indeed felt some chemistry. He had always admired the Landon family. While he as a boy had joined his father in campaigning for her father for president and had given a Landon lecture at Kansas State University while a presidential candidate himself, he particularly enjoyed his encounter with Landon at the governor's one-hundredth birthday celebration in 1987, when he asked Landon if he still rode his horse daily. "Goodness no," came the reply, "that horse is getting kinda old." Baker sensed in Nancy the same brand of humor and the same sense of middle American values, and soon began inquiring among a small group of friends what they knew about her likes and dislikes. He then called and asked her out. Once she said "sure," he donned his best blue suit, then drove to her house in northwest Washington. He walked up her steps and confessed when she opened the door that he felt like he was sixteen years old again. "You don't look sixteen," she responded. Accustomed to being driven around in the heavily trafficked District of Columbia, he then reached to release the emergency brake and wound up opening the hood, thus amusing his former colleague as they proceeded on their first date. It's hardly a surprise that she insisted on picking him up on one of their next dates.[10]

Publicly, the two were first spotted together at the funeral of his close friend and former colleague Edmund Muskie. "Now, there is a great couple," the Illinois Democrat Paul Simon whispered to his wife, Jeanne. Others present, including Republican Olympia Snowe, who holds Muskie's seat, were heard speculating how nice it would be if they got together. For many months, Kassebaum downplayed such talk, even among colleagues and her staff. Baker's instincts were equally private, but he was hinting to a few friends by the summer of 1996 that something special might be in the works. When rain prevented Bill Frist and his family from spending a day rafting on the nearby Big South Fork of the Cumberland River while visiting Baker in Huntsville, Baker opted to introduce Frist's three sons to photography. He showed them his darkroom, then processed a picture that sharpened into an image of Kassebaum, who at the time was Frist's chairwoman on the Senate Labor and Human Resources Committee. A few minutes later, Baker confessed to Karyn Frist that he had felt like a teenager on his first date with his former colleague. The Frists' impressions were confirmed when Baker told them they were double-dating when he invited them to a quiet dinner away from the proceedings at the GOP convention in San Diego.[11]

It hardly was lost upon either senator that they shared an appreciation for rural solitude and a fascination with what Baker describes as "nature and its miracles." Indeed, Morris County, Kansas, the site of the ranch Kassebaum bought from the estate of an aunt, actually has but one-third the population of Baker's native and rustic Scott County. Baker found little unusual when he awoke one morning and observed a herd of cattle staring at him through the window. For him, this was just a prime opportunity to go outside and take some choice photographs as well as an indication that he would be happy spending more time with Nancy in these parts. Even if that were not the case, he explained, "love conquers a lot of things." That Kansans were interested in the progress of their romance can be seen in the quip of Pat Roberts, who was about to be elected to succeed Kassebaum, that he was spending more time that fall explaining the new diamond and ruby ring she was sporting than any program he was advocating. Still, their secret did not emerge completely until late October 1996, when GOP presidential nominee Bob Dole spilled the beans in Knoxville.[12]

The marriage was indeed historic, as it was the first ever to bind a sitting senator and a former colleague. And, as often happens amongst senators, the Baker-Kassebaum union involved a series of compromises. They would keep his condo at the Watergate hotel and divide the remainder of their time between Tennessee and Kansas. His best man was his son Darek; her matron of honor was her oldest daughter, Linda Kassebaum Johnson. The service was jointly conducted by his Presbyterian minister Martha Anne Fairchild, and John Danforth, their favorite clergyman of her Episcopal faith as well as former colleague. But the invitations reflected their common background. "In order to form a more perfect union," they read, "the distinguished gentleman from Tennessee yields the balance of his time to the distinguished gentlewoman from Kansas." Virtually all of official Washington was ecstatic for them, and many, particularly among their contemporaries, were present at the reception. Bill Brock later wrote for most there that his respect for his onetime senior colleague "went off the charts" when he took the hand of this "wondrous, gracious, and truly lovely lady."[13]

Lobbying

Like her husband, Nancy Baker soon found that there was life after the Senate. At first, she joined the boards of trustees of the Robert Wood Johnson and Kaiser Family Foundations and co-chaired a commission on campaign finance reform with former Vice-President Walter Mondale. Baker, too, was adding new responsibilities. He continued to chair a group of telecommunications lobbyists known as the Competitive Long Distance Coalition. By the late 1990s, he had taken on a perch on an International Olympic Committee ethics commission after IOC officials learned that several members of their site selection panel had accepted bribes to locate the 2002 winter games in Salt Lake City.[14]

The most controversial of Baker's clients of the 1990s were the five tobacco companies he signed on to represent in negotiations about their liability to lawsuits brought by victims of smoking-related diseases. For Baker, representing the firms differed little from representing any other clients. His job was not to determine the guilt or innocence of his clients, but to protect their interests as he had with so many others. Indeed, he saw a just settlement as beneficial to the physical health of the public as well as to the overall economic health of the American people. The same considerations affected former Senate Majority Leaders Bob Dole and George Mitchell, former Texas Governor Ann Richards, and several other onetime politicos of both parties who also signed on with the tobacco companies. They, like Baker, knew that most of the firms had interests other than tobacco, and thousands of workers, not just the few top executives of each, would be harmed by a punitive settlement. Baker was quick to point out that he was hardly advocating smoking. Rather, he and his cohorts were engaged in a lawful, legitimate practice. "You've got to register," he pointed out. "You've got to disclose." While the fees Baker and others representing the tobacco firms were considerably less than the amounts collected by some lawyers for the states,[15] they came to be condemned by a bevy of moralists for working with firms commonly seen by the 1990s as less than interested in the public's health. Particularly loud was antismoking crusader John Banzhaf, who bashed him for working with tobacco interests after lung cancer had killed his first wife, Joy, a smoker, and simultaneously serving as chairman of the board of trustees of the Mayo Clinic. Not happy about the personal nature of the attacks and unconvinced by the charges of a conflict of interest, Baker nevertheless resigned his post as the chairman of the Mayo board, thus limiting any potential damage to the clinic's fundraising capacity.[16]

Baker and the Clintons

As might be expected, Baker had less of a presence at the White House during the administration of Bill Clinton, who was both a Democrat and, being the first baby-boomer president, a generation younger. In fact, he was better acquainted with First Lady Hillary Rodham Clinton, whom he had encountered on occasion in Memphis legal gatherings. Still, when Clinton tore his quadruped in 1997, Baker heeded Nancy's suggestion to loan the president a cane he had used after his recent knee replacement surgery that had belonged to her father, Alf Landon. He took the cane to the White House and urged Clinton to use it, saying things would get better. "What gets better," a grinning but skeptical Clinton queried Baker the next time he saw him at a birthday party for Secretary of State Madeleine Albright. "It wasn't meant to be a political statement," Baker shot back.[17]

Generally speaking, however, Baker was disappointed by the Clinton administration, even if he did find the Arkansan "a very talented man." His background with the Watergate and Iran-Contra investigations dictated that he would be called often by reporters once it was determined that Clinton had been less than completely candid under oath about his dalliances with intern Monica Lewinsky. Had the president asked for his legal counsel, his advice would have been simple. "Cover-ups never work," he often pronounced when discussing this, Watergate, or other scandals. But Clinton never called, nor did he ever contact Baker about any potential means of brokering a censure, regardless of a horde of rumors at the time to the contrary. In fact, Baker liked to quip at the time that he hoped in such in instance that he wouldn't be at home.[18]

When commenting for CNN, where he and former Democratic colleague Sam Nunn provided analysis during the Clinton impeachment trial, or other audiences, Baker resisted the temptation to moralize. Rather, his was a voice of a seasoned politico preoccupied with concerns about the long-term health of the Senate and, indeed, the republic. His view differed from that of his wife, Nancy, who preferred that Clinton resign in disgrace. Baker indeed feared that a second presidential resignation in a quarter of a century might swing America closer toward a parliamentary system of government, a trend he believed unhealthy. While Baker did not feel comfortable with the ardor of some Clinton critics and did join former Clinton chief of staff Leon Panetta in decrying a tendency of zealots in both parties to "criminalize" political differences, he was equally quick to warn against improvising outside the processes prescribed in the Constitution. He thus counseled Majority Leader Trent Lott against heeding calls to defuse growing discord by holding an immediate censure vote and thus denying House members, who had impeached Clinton, a trial. The House, he said, had its role and the Senate its. And while the Senate might hold a censure vote after it came to a verdict on the question of whether or not Clinton had committed impeachable offenses, only a ruling of guilt or innocence would provide the closure the American people demanded.[19]

In the remaining two years of the Clinton administration, Baker co-chaired two commissions at the behest of Energy Secretary Bill Richardson. One, undertaken with the venerable Lloyd Cutler, a fixture in several Democratic administrations, looked into the security of the Russian stockpile of nuclear weapons and recommended that the administration of incoming President George W. Bush take all steps possible to prevent any outflow of nuclear weapons, nuclear usable material, or scientists to hostile nations like Iran or terrorists. While Baker and Cutler praised the Russian government and several international police forces for blocking several efforts to acquire some of those materials, they saw the insecurity of such materials as a serious national security matter and thus advocated an eight- to ten-year plan with considerably more funding to help the Russians secure all nuclear weapons material. The second Baker conducted with Lee Hamilton, the respected former Democratic congressman from Indiana, into the curious disappearance of two highly sensitive computer hard drives for more than two weeks at the nuclear laboratory at Los Alamos, New Mexico. The two interviewed Los Alamos officials at every level and found few willing to volunteer information. What they discerned was that many workers had come to fear more the threat of criminal prosecution if they cooperated with internal searches than the loss of the highly sensitive secrets themselves. Accordingly, they urged the Los Alamos hierarchy to design a staff structure geared toward restoring morale amongst workers who had once seen themselves as partners of those at a higher pay level as opposed to subjects of their oversight.[20]

O-Mono

As he had over the previous three generations, Baker did what he could, particularly in Tennessee to elect a Republican president. While he, as he had in 1996, initially supported the candidacy of his protégé Lamar Alexander, he quickly moved over to the camp of Governor George W. Bush once the Alexander campaign fizzled out. While he was generous with his contributions and his time, he at the age of seventy-five never sought nor expected a job when Bush eventually prevailed. Still, early in the Bush administration, White House Chief of Staff Andrew Card phoned Baker and told him that Bush wanted him to consider becoming his ambassador to Japan. Baker told Nancy, who told him that they were in a position in life where he could take the job if he wanted. Unlike many other ambassadorial posts abroad, the perch in Tokyo afforded him as many policymaking duties as social ones. It, too, had been held over the past quarter century by several Americans the Japanese deemed *o-mono*, or a big deal. Mike Mansfield, the former Senate Majority Leader Baker and the Japanese so revered, added distinction to the job in both the Carter and Reagan administrations, while his friends Walter Mondale, the former vice-president, and former Speaker Tom Foley had both served in Tokyo for one of Bill Clinton's terms. Still, Baker gave no answer to anyone connected with the administration of the second Bush until he saw the president motioning him over a few days later at a soiree hosted by

Washington Post publisher Katherine Graham. Baker walked over and heard Bush telling him that he really wanted him to represent the United States in Japan. Baker returned to Nancy and told her that he had accepted the job conditionally, but made it clear that he was not going without her. Ultimately, Nancy concluded that taking the job would afford both she and her husband a chance to stretch their minds and experience new things and indeed be a partnership. The American and Japanese people, Mike Mansfield said, were getting two ambassadors for the price of one.[21]

The Bakers' Senate colleagues were ecstatic. For the Democrats, Joseph Biden jokingly threatened a rigorous confirmation process of all of about twelve seconds. While the Bakers had to be annoyed by the extensive FBI investigation they underwent and the eighty-six pages of questionnaires they had to fill out, they enjoyed the two weeks they spent at a school for ambassadors, where they learned the ethical and legal ropes of the diplomatic corps. Even though Baker later quipped that he would need a corps of translators, his wife began taking Japanese lessons and announced that she would be meeting with the embassy's protocol officer as soon as they arrived in Tokyo to learn the unique customs of the Japanese. While Howard Baker was confirmed unanimously, several senators took the opportunity to show their appreciation for their other former colleague as well. "What a duo," said GOP Leader Trent Lott.[22]

As probably would be the case for anyone who had ever held the Senate seat once distinguished by Cordell Hull, if only for two years, it was Baker's intention as he and Nancy left for Japan to focus upon expanding trade between the United States and Japan. In Hull-like fashion, Baker had long warned of the counter-productive nature that a protectionist crusade against Japanese imports might take. Still he insisted upon reciprocity from the Japanese. As a senator, he and other Tennessee elected officials, especially Lamar Alexander, had experienced considerable success in attracting Japanese firms like Nissan to Tennessee towns like Smyrna. Baker's role, he says, was in identifying Japanese firms he thought might be primary targets for relocation in Tennessee; it fell upon Alexander and his successors to complete the paperwork that would allow them to start operations in the Volunteer State. In no small part because of their work, Tennessee had won more investment from Japanese firms than any state other than California.[23]

The immediate concerns of the Bakers as they arrived in Tokyo lay more in improving the U.S.-Japanese partnership than in addressing matters of mere commercial concern. Anti-American sentiment was rising in Japan in the first year of the twenty-first century. Some ensued from a sense in the Land of the Midnight Sun, particularly among those on the left, that they had long been the junior partner in an alliance that had not always served their best interests. But tension was particularly salient to the Japanese in 2001. In April, the *USS Greeneville*, a submarine, surfaced off the coast of Oahu directly underneath the *Ehime Maru*, a Japanese fishing trawler, thereby capsizing the boat and killing the five students and four adults of the crew. Two months later, an American airman was accused of raping a woman in a parking lot not far from the Kadena Air Force base on the island of Okinawa.[24]

The tone by which Baker took on his new duties thus would not be lost upon the Japanese. Like each of his predecessors in the post–World War II period, he prepared for his installation before Emperor Akihito as if it were a wedding reception. He had donned a morning coat before, for the first Reagan inaugural, but he had never before sported the striped trousers the Japanese require emissaries to wear during their initial bow to their emperor. Then, he waited for the emperor to send a gilded carriage that would carry him to the ceremony. On the way, he was startled by the sight of ordinary Japanese bowing to him and waving rather than honking horns at such a slow vehicle as might have occurred in any American city. But once the rite concluded, he went to work to try and atone for America's most recent mistakes. At a get-acquainted meeting with Junichiro Koizumi, the charismatic, ornately coiffed, heavy-metal-music-listening prime minister, he pledged to do all he could to see that the abuse of Japanese women by American servicemen would never happen again. He hammered out the details by which the offending airman would be turned over to Japanese police in subsequent meetings with Foreign Minister Makiko Tanaka. Upon her pledge that the sergeant would receive a fair trial, Baker saw to his transfer to Japanese custody, thus demonstrating to the Japanese that the United States would maintain tighter control over its troops and to American servicemen that the kind of rowdy nihilism displayed in this incident and several previous ones would no longer be condoned.[25]

It was always Baker's foremost aim to convey upon the Japanese the sense that the United States desired a friendship as opposed to a mere alliance. The impression, he was sure, would come from "human things," which he said "really make up the essences of relationships." There would be no better opportunity for him to show this to the Japanese than at the memorial service for the nine victims of the reckless souls at the helm of the *Greenville*. For him, the question became how to show not just the Japanese people en masse, but the families of the victims in particular, how sorry he and the American people were for their losses. He recognized the Japanese instinct for sincerity, then ruled out any notion of giving a speech. Instead, he took diplomatic steps to be invited to the memorial service for the nine, and brought Nancy, translators, and Japanese officials with him. Upon meeting each grieving relative, he shook their hand, looked them in the eye, and gave each a unique message. "You are very kind to let my wife and I be with you," he told one woman. "Thank you for letting me be here," he said to another. He and Nancy then drifted away quietly to participate in the ceremony with the rest of the mourners, having expressed their sorrow without intruding any further upon the privacy of those grieving the most.[26]

The Bakers left Japan briefly in late summer to address a midwestern U.S.-Japanese friendship partnership as well as spend a bit of time visiting children and grandchildren. On September 11, they found themselves stuck in Chicago waiting to return to Tokyo after nineteen al-Qaeda terrorists who had hijacked planes obliterated the twin towers of the World Trade Center in Lower Manhattan, flew another jet into the Pentagon, and would have hit another high profile target had a corps of fearless passengers not taken control of the plane and flown it into the Pennsylvania ground. Upon their return to Tokyo, they were gratified that thousands of people had gathered in a line surrounding the U.S. embassy, then left flowers, said prayers, and signed a guestbook with their condolences. "In a single, blinding moment," Baker declared, "the world changed." While grateful to Japanese leaders who promised him that they would help the United States in its war against terror, he let the Japanese people know that the United States wanted the government of Japan to decide how they would help. "I'm confident you'll make the right decision," he would say. "It's better to let them do it their way." It thus came naturally for him to hail the Japanese in the hours that followed for dispatching two destroyers to the Indian Ocean to help in the war on terror.[27]

Matters settled into a more comfortable routine in the months after September 11. Baker began meeting almost daily with Japanese businesspeople who wanted to learn more about how they could expand into American markets. He soon learned that the Japanese word for "tourism" translated more closely in English to "visitorism" and quickly let the Japanese know that "I like your term better." He took particular pleasure in saluting Japanese citizens who had excelled in American settings like star outfielder Ichiro Suzuki of the Seattle Mariners, who in 2004 set a new major league record for most hits in a single season. But he devoted every bit as much time to welcoming representatives of American firms to Japan and identifying opportunities for them. Not only did he dine every month with the officers of the U.S. Chamber of Commerce chapter in Tokyo, but he hosted scores of business delegations from the states, and he was particularly glad to receive those led by onetime congressional associates like Governors Frank Murkowski of Alaska and Bill Richardson of New Mexico. And it would be totally out of character for Howard Baker if he did not save some time to photograph some of the scenery of the flora and fauna and landscapes of the islands of Japan, particularly Okinawa, the one he found the most beautiful. In this respect, going to Japan had been a sacrifice as he found it impractical to transport his darkroom equipment all the way to Japan. This dictated that he make the switch he had resisted for years to the technologically advanced but visually inferior mode of digital photography.[28]

Nancy Baker, even without a title, found herself more than occupied. Baker found his wife the instant idol of strong Japanese women who quite naturally gravitated to her because of her stature as a pioneering American female politico. But she took an interest in them as well, speaking in all parts of Japan on a host of topics. A particular interest of hers arose while working with Melanne Verveer, a former aide to Hillary Clinton, on programs to expose and ultimately eradicate the trafficking of women for prostitution or forced labor in Asian countries. She visited shelters that housed the victims of trafficking, then enlisted many influential Japanese women behind a quiet but effective campaign to prompt the Koizumi government to sponsor a conference to educate the public about the persistence of human trafficking and help the Asian law enforcement community devise strategies to combat it. It was her request, however, not Verveer's, which led to the conference's first public relations coup, an opening video hailing the importance of the work that delegates were undertaking featuring U.S. First Lady Laura Bush.[29]

On every other issue, Baker was the public face of U.S. policy toward Japan. Like any successful emissary, he explained the programs of his government to the Japanese government and its people as tactfully as possible and in turn faithfully relayed their concerns to George W. Bush. He demonstrated good will during natural disasters. When an earthquake killed dozens in Niigata, Japan, in October 2004, he immediately authorized the disbursal of $50,000 to aid the victims. After a tsunami killed more than a quarter of a million people in Southeast Asia in the last days of 2004, he announced that the United States had pledged to work with others in Asia and the rest of the advanced democracies to develop a global tsunami warning system that might limit the casualties of a future disaster.[30]

When necessary, Baker worked to downplay sources of potential conflict. He constantly expressed sympathy with the people of Okinawa, who had not asked for a U.S. military presence amongst them, and pledged to work with their government to find a means that would allow the United States to remove some of its forces. More commonly, he hailed Japan for sending $5 billion and 500 troops to aid in the reconstruction of war-torn Iraq. Baker was always quick to note that these were Japan's decisions, not America's. He was just as certain to herald the relationship with Japan as the cornerstone of U.S. security, and not just because the two nations accounted for more than half of the world's gross national product. On its own, he habitually declared, Japan was a scientific and economic superpower. While the United States and Japan had a special responsibility to preserve and extend the stability of the Asia Pacific region, he always acknowledged the centrality to Japan of how it handled its relationship with China and how they and others in the region moved to limit the nuclear capacity of North Korea.[31]

If there was a surreal portion to Baker's stint in Japan, it came in the late summer of 2002 when he arranged for longtime friend and occasional rival George H. W. Bush to visit the site where his plane had been shot down during World War II and two of his crew members had been killed. Baker, along with writer James Bradley, some Japanese officials, and a CNN crew, accompanied the former president as he journeyed back to the scenic island of Chichijima, a small piece of land near Iwo Jima, and traced the route of his flight. They listened to

Bush recount the story of how he and his crew went down, how he tried to save his two companions, and how sailors on the *USS Finback* spotted him as he lay in a dinghy hiding from any Japanese vessels he might encounter. Here for the elder Bush came a form of closure, and a particularly moving tale came from an elderly veteran who said he had observed the rescue of the young flier some fifty-eight years earlier. If the United States cared so much about one flier, he said, they might not only win the war, but also be worthy of winning.[32]

Sayonara, Baker-san

It was always Baker's intention to leave Tokyo after the first term of George W. Bush. That he told the former Texas governor when he agreed to serve as ambassador. While he admired the example of Mike Mansfield, he said, he did not aim to start a new career at seventy-five. His health seemed good, even if he had gained weight, until the latter part of August 2004, when doctors he consulted on a trip home to Tennessee recommended that he allow them to perform double bypass surgery to replace a heart valve. His doctors at Baptist Hospital in Knoxville left him in sufficiently good spirits that he could chuckle when he learned that Secretary of State Colin Powell had joked to a group of Japanese visitors to Washington that "Howard had a double, so [former President Bill] Clinton had to have a quadruple." Not long thereafter, Nancy Baker was telling her husband that if he "felt any better, I don't know what we'd do with you."[33]

So while all medical concerns had been treated, Baker had gotten a bit of a glance of his own mortality. He returned to Tokyo after a month of recuperation and began to ponder his future with Nancy. While his party's president had been reelected, he concluded as he thought he would when he took the job that it would after four years be time to come home. He could take pride in the common observation on this side of the Pacific that U.S.-Japanese relations had never been better. That the Japanese thought equally favorably of his service can be seen in the statement of one of their more astute journalists, Kitamura Fumio. "*Sayonara, Baker-san,* he wrote. "You will be missed.[34]

Baker returned to his ever-expanding law firm and to several corporate boards. He threw himself into the chore of raising funds for the new Baker Center for Public Policy at his alma mater of the University of Tennessee. While not the formulator of its programs, he participates in their direction and insists as a matter of habit that they take on a bipartisan character. The first he spoke at, for example, concerned clean air and water and featured Vice-President Al Gore rendering his now famous PowerPoint presentation on global warming. He also lent his name to several groups with bipartisan objectives and boards of directors. One was Common Good, a body whose leaders ranged from George McGovern on the left to Newt Gingrich on the right, which aimed to create legal reforms that would result in limiting the number of frivolous lawsuits filed in America each year. Another he and Nancy both joined was Partnership for a Secure America, chaired by former Senator Warren Rudman and former Congressman Lee Hamilton, which originally called for a more bipartisan foreign policy making process. Within months, however, members were promoting a tougher line against those U.S. troops in Iraq who employed tactics such as torture, which made America less safe, violated our values, and damaged our reputation in the world. Baker remained busy enough that he and Nancy did not take a full-fledged vacation until a year after their return from Japan. This time, they went to Africa, the continent where Nancy was the better-known Baker, as she had chaired the Subcommittee on African Affairs of the Senate Foreign Affairs Committee. While they met some top leaders of South Africa and Namibia, they also engaged Baker's passion for photography of the flora, fauna, and many landscapes of those countries.[35]

Baker remains in contact with many currently active in government, particularly those in seats he once held. For the most part, his approach is casual. The conversation on a recent flight to Tennessee he took with Bill Frist on a plane the two jointly own, Frist says, related one-third to family, one-third to politics, and one-third to flying. Still, there are special occasions in which Baker will be very direct with Frist or others. After the 2002 midterm elections, the first in American history where, during Frist's tenure as chairman of the Republican Senate Campaign Committee, the party of an incumbent president actually gained seats and recaptured control of a house of Congress, Baker encouraged Frist to contemplate seeking a higher post within the GOP leadership. Once it became clear a month later that Trent Lott would not be able to hold the position of Majority Leader after his ill-considered salute to Strom Thurmond's one-hundredth birthday by hailing his state's support of Thurmond's 1948 "Dixiecrat" campaign, a posture Thurmond himself had abandoned a generation earlier, Baker, on a Christmas visit home from Japan, called Frist to tell him that the time had come to throw his hat in the ring. Within an hour after Lott's statement announcing his resignation from the Leadership, Baker and Lamar Alexander, who had just been elected to the Senate, appeared together in Knoxville and joined a well-orchestrated chorus for Frist. Later that night, December 20, 2002, Baker appeared on *Larry King Live* with fellow former Majority Leader George Mitchell and a few sitting senators who had been active in forcing Lott to resign. While decrying the brutal process that resulted in Lott's departure, he as someone who had long voiced concerns about interracial harmony could hardly fail to note that Lott's comment "really wasn't defensible." In contrast, he heralded Frist as exactly the right man to reinforce the direction of movement in the Republican Party.[36]

For the duration of Frist's two terms in his old perch as Majority Leader, Baker counseled him to take measures that would tend to leave the Senate a more collegial body. Frist is quick to observe that Baker longs for a more bipartisan Senate, even while he recognizes that it has often been a fairly contentious place. In this vein, he had his secretary of the Senate, former Baker aide Emily Reynolds, schedule monthly social gatherings for all senators and their wives, as well as monthly private meetings for all senators in the Tin Can Room on the fourth floor of the Capitol with a rotating high official from the Bush administration.[37]

Still, tempers flared far more regularly than in Baker's Senate. To a degree greater than in any time in memory, denizens of the upper chamber of the early twenty-first century vented especially loudly on judicial nominations. With much prodding from outside liberal interest groups, Democrats took to demonizing a number of able conservatives George W. Bush had nominated for seats on lower federal courts as extremists and then denying up or down votes. Their tool was the Senate rule in effect since 1975 that required sixty votes to close debate, thus allowing their forty-five members a chance to block any nominee with a tinge of opposition from the special interests of the left. While Republicans had used other means to deny able Democratic minds seats on the federal bench in the past, they had never so regularly used their numbers while in the minority to obstruct as they were the confirmations of nominees with the backing of majorities of members of the Senate. GOP leaders at all levels recoiled at the success of increasingly shrill attacks on Bush nominees in raising money for Democrats. In the Senate, they prepared what Frist called the "constitutional" option and critics derided as the "nuclear option" that would grant all nominees an up or down vote but maintain the requirement for cloture on questions of policy. Baker had long lauded the rules of the Senate for protecting the rights of numerical minorities. Still, like most Republicans, he had grown weary of what had become a trivialization of the filibuster, which in previous years had been a tactic of last rather than immediate resort. When Frist called, Baker was quick to emphasize "it's your Senate." Yet Baker was also a friend of and mentor to Frist and he advised him as Everett Dirksen had counseled him when they disagreed on "one man, one vote" questions nearly four decades earlier that he needed to fight to win. As the quintessential Senate institutionalist, however, Baker also implored upon Frist not to do anything that might change the fundamental character of the body. It thus had to please Baker and many others, including Frist, when a bipartisan "gang of fourteen" senators, most either moderates or veterans of many legislative sessions, announced a compromise just eighteen hours before the nuclear option was scheduled to be unleashed. Cloture requirements would remain the same for the rest of the 109th Congress. Some nominees who had been filibustered for years would get an up or down vote. Two of Bush's picks would not, and the fourteen would enforce the notion that there would not be a filibuster on a Bush nominee for the Supreme Court in the next two years except for extraordinary circumstances.[38]

In his ninth decade, Baker does not like to force himself upon those currently holding office. A rare exception came in March of 2006, when he phoned White

House chief of staff Andrew Card to suggest that he inject a bit of new blood into the White House staff after the second Bush administration declined to its lowest point in public approval ratings. Observing the debilitation of the administration in the wake of the thorough mismanagement of relief efforts after Hurricane Katrina, the debacle over the nomination of White House counsel Harriet Miers to a Supreme Court vacancy, and outrage over reports that a firm from Dubai had been awarded contracts to manage six eastern ports, he counseled that bringing in someone of the stature of former Senator Fred Thompson would add credibility to the administration and a new perspective. It would do no good, he continued, for Bush to fire Card or any other key lieutenant without cause. Such a course would merely further the impression of an administration in chaos. What was needed to raise the president's approval ratings above the 35 percent mark where it had slipped was an appearance of action on a well-thought-out game plan. The details of any policies forwarded were less important to the majority of the American people than conveying the perception that the president was changing things for their benefit.[39] Here was advice he had given in 1987 that had catalyzed Ronald Reagan's recovery from the debris of the Iran-Contra scandal. Whether it would propel a less articulate president in the increasingly polarized society of 2006 to the same degree remains to be seen. Even so, he knew that an absence of movement and change would confine any potential future successes of the Bush administration to merely military ones. Even those would be rendered more difficult by the diminishing worldwide stature of a lame-duck president devoid of dynamism and thus any remaining political capital.

For a man who has risen to high ranks within artistic, business, legal, and political communities, Baker remains a fairly humble family man. He loves to regale listeners with the story of what happened after he took the seven-year-old grandson Sam Baker with him on a trip to a Nashville TV station that was producing a retrospective on his career. "Papa," the young tyke asked upon next seeing his grandfather, "did you used to be somebody?"[40]

Still, he occasionally hints that his years of public service may not have ended. "May I remind you," he likes to say, "that my grandmother," the Zeus in his pantheon of heroes, "lived to be a hundred and two."[41]

CONCLUSION

Principal in Baker's conception of his function as chief of staff and as Senate GOP Leader was a duty to make things work. Always an advocate of a strong presidency, he would ascertain the priorities of chief executives and do what he could after Congress made a few changes to give their programs a chance to succeed. Nearly as much as Reagan, Jimmy Carter appreciated his help when their conceptions of the national interest coincided, as on the Panama Canal Treaties and the jet sales to moderate Arab countries, as well as his decisions not to obstruct several programs of deregulation and reorganization that Carter feared might become controversial.[1] His was a course that ran in the family, as Everett Dirksen had pursued the same line with notable results, particularly in the realm of civil rights.

Ironically, Baker's path was hardly suited for the fulfillment of his own aspiration of becoming president. When Baker disagreed with presidents of his own party, he did so quietly, a tack that often denied him publicity garnered by would-be rivals. But such is a course that legislative leaders must take to maintain public confidence and thus save votes in the long run for more significant programs on which their view of the national interest coincides with the president's. From experience, his reading of history, and conversations with colleagues, Baker recognized that Dirksen's predecessor, William Knowland, had followed what George Reedy called a "right must prevail" course separate from a president that rendered the GOP impotent as a legislative force and compelled Dwight D. Eisenhower to yield the initiative on many key issues to Democrats.[2] It served no one, Baker knew, to engage in behavior that promised stalemate. Especially during the four years he served as Majority Leader, Baker sought to guarantee that his party won approval for its most significant initiatives and became the one, in fact, the public saw as the moving force in the upper chamber.

To Baker's detriment, a relatively nonpartisan legislative course has never been the ideal one to use as a springboard to the presidency. Over the past half century, a host of senators known for diligence, records of productivity, and rhetoric in the mainstream—Arthur Vandenberg, Robert Taft, Estes Kefauver, Lyndon Johnson, Stuart Symington, Hubert Humphrey, Edmund Muskie, Frank Church, Henry "Scoop" Jackson, Birch Bayh, Edward Kennedy, Bob Dole, Al Gore Jr., Gary Hart, Robert Kerrey, Paul Tsongas, Richard Lugar, Arlen Specter, Paul Tsongas, Phil Gramm, John McCain, Orrin Hatch, and most recently John Kerry and John Edwards—have been tapped as overqualified for America's highest office, only to find voters opting for men less tied to the enactment of significant public policy. The one senator over the same period who moved directly to the presidency, John F. Kennedy, placed little importance on his legislative output. The others who captured nominations, Barry Goldwater and George McGovern, won less because of what they had accomplished in Washington than because they had attached themselves to movements more dedicated to capturing control of their parties than skillful in capturing control of their government.

Unfortunately for Baker, proficiency in enacting legislation is often a quality voters equate with a compromising, equivocal nature instead of the decisive one they seek in their president. His brand of leadership was not the transformational brand James MacGregor Burns found in Franklin D. Roosevelt and others that resulted in great changes in the way people thought about how governing ought to be conducted. Baker's variety was the transactional form, which in its own way could lead to major changes in the way people lived. Never endowed with the radiant charisma of a John F. Kennedy or a Ronald Reagan, Baker won his followers over time, upon reflection. Baker "could survive the long look," consultant Doug Bailey said, "but he couldn't get there to get looked at." Perhaps his talents were best suited to the legislative arena, where what Richard Lugar called his aptitudes "in bringing together coalitions and in offering . . . pragmatic skills of working out disputes" were invaluable. Baker, who Walter Mondale said was "not one of these guys who enjoy blood," may have been, as Paul Laxalt suggested, "too nice of a guy to be in politics." Baker indeed acted in ways that made potential supporters fear that he would not make the sacrifices that modern presidential politics seems to require. "Howard Baker sets his own schedule," Dan Kuykendall said, and that schedule was often more directed toward executing legislative strategies and keeping family responsibilities than winning votes. He could get away with that in Tennessee, Robert Ray added, because "people came to know him and love him."[3] Voters in states with early contests like Ray's Iowa never had the same opportunity, as Baker never subordinated his legislative duties to thoroughly oversee the operations of his campaigns. Here may be a tragedy, but Baker is hardly the only victim. But candidates, like athletes, must realize that victory often goes to those who concentrate upon one specific aim, and it is hardly unfair to say that Ronald Reagan and George Bush ran ahead of Baker, as the cliché goes, because they wanted it more.

Baker, however, still makes it clear that his happiness has never depended on whether or not he became president. One associate from his 1980 campaign speculated that "he could be just as happy taking pictures." Even so, there is, appropriately, a hallowed place in American history for pragmatic, conciliatory legislators like Baker, whose aptitudes in bringing people together and forging compromises most can accept lead to changes and improvements in public policy. There, too, will be a revered pace in the annals of Eastern Europe for Baker and colleagues like Walter Mondale, Pete Domenici, and Thomas Eagleton, who gave of their free time in the late 1980s and early 1990s to training legislators in those incipient democracies in the means of instituting functioning systems and in securing aid from American firms and taxpayers to make the Polish Sejm and other parliaments, as Mondale joked, "even more complex" than the United States Congress.[4] In this setting, Baker must have felt comfortable, having been indispensable a generation earlier in creating a viable, multiparty democracy in his home state for the first time in a century. But in another sense, the two situations were entirely dissimilar. In Tennessee, Baker found honor in the heritages of Democrats in the middle and western grand divisions, and his success at the polls stemmed to a large degree from his ability to conciliate Democratic voters and convince them that his empathy with their concerns made him a more logical heir than any of his opponents.

Baker's manner was equally conciliatory in Washington. When he expected votes to be close, he frequently asked wavering senators what he could do to make it easier for them. In preparation for such moments, he generally used a collegial approach, allowing virtually all interested Republicans and often many Democrats a voice in developing legislation. Baker "was always willing to listen to the other side and to treat all senators as equals," said Mike Mansfield. "It is a rare thing when Howard Baker attacks the ideology of other people," added John Seigenthaler. "He respects them."[5] Not known for devising bold policy initiatives in original form, he nevertheless exhibited one of the abler analytical minds in Washington and employed a collaborative brand of creativity to fashion solutions to complex problems in many fields of public policy that diverse groups of interested parties found not only acceptable but desirable.

Baker had much in common with a statesman of another century who excelled at reconciling disparate views: Henry Clay, "the Great Compromiser" from Lexington, Kentucky. Both hailed from border states. Both, too, were generally amenable to the interests of business. Conditions in Clay's day dictated that he place as a linchpin of his "American System" a system of "internal improvements" designed to spur economic growth in the newly opened West. Circumstances in Baker's day quite often led him to back Clay-like measures designed by agencies like TVA to catalyze economic growth in underdeveloped parts of Tennessee. Clay said he would "rather be right than President." Critics declared him neither. While the same is true of Baker, there were also important differences between the "Great Conciliator" and the "Great Compromiser." Clay's brashness contrasts vividly with the kindness and consideration many find innate in Baker.[6] Clay's political considerations dictated that he create a party to oppose that of Andrew Jackson while maintaining sufficient leverage as a border state senator to have credibility as an honest broker of solutions to problems that threatened the very Union. Baker's political considerations at the height of his legislative power in the minority necessitated that he, as Robert Taft had done in the 1940s and 1950s, synthesize an economic program around which his party could rally that could win enough support from the other party to allow it the backing of a governing majority in Congress. In part because of the magnitude of the slavery question, the Compromise of 1850, the last of Clay's masterpieces, served to delay a civil war for ten years, but only delayed it, because it did not address the real problems. In contrast, those solutions Baker devised were generally lasting ones or ones giving programs a chance to work. Be it in fair housing or clean air and water or the Panama Canal or arms or education or budget policy, the agreements Baker crafted generally addressed the concerns of all interested parties, limited the problems that might arise, and left all sides in generally good spirits. That both the White House and the Senate were more serene places to be when he left than when he arrived is an eloquent testimony to his success, no small legacy for this introspective yet friendly man. It may be, especially in the television age, that the American people prefer presidents who use uncommon eloquence to chart bold new courses. Yet the divisions and sometimes polarizations that sometimes ensue render invaluable the presence of another kind of leader, the kind who can build bridges between competing interests and their champions, both on an ideological and a personal level.

Here Howard Henry Baker Jr. had no peer.

Appendix

ON HERDING CATS

Howard H. Baker Jr.

I first walked into the Gallery of the United States Senate nearly sixty years ago. My great-aunt Mattie Keen was secretary to Senator K. D. McKellar of Tennessee, and I came here to visit her in July 1939 as a thirteen-year-old boy, and she procured gallery passes for the House and the Senate.

The Senate had only the most primitive air-conditioning in those days. It was principally cooled by a system of louvers and vents and skylights that dated from 1859, when the Senate vacated this chamber and moved down the hall to its present home.

The system did not work well against Washington's summertime plague of heat and humidity, and as a consequence Congress was not a year-round institution in those days.

Anyone who knows me understands how tempting it is to devote the remainder of these remarks to my perennial thesis—that this was precisely the way the national legislature was designed to operate: as a citizen legislature that did its work and went home, rather than a perpetual Congress hermetically sealed in the capital city. In the summer of 1939, in any event, nature and technology offered little choice.

On the same trip in 1939, I traveled even further north—to New York, in the company of the same Aunt Mattie—to see the New York World's Fair. There I had my first encounter with a novel technology that would have even more profound consequences than air-conditioning. It was called "television."

And it was the same K. D. McKellar, my Aunt Mattie's boss, who only three years later would help President Roosevelt launch the Manhattan Project that would shortly usher in the nuclear age. Senator McKellar, by the way, was Chairman of

Leader's Lecture Series, July 14, 1998. *Congressional Record,* 105th Cong., 2nd sess., S8374–77.

the Senate Appropriations Committee at the time, and when President Roosevelt asked him if he could hide a billion dollars to finance this top-secret project, Senator McKellar replied, "Of course I can, Mr. President—and where in Tennessee are we going to build this plant?"

I recite all this personal history not to remind you how old I am but to remark on how young our country is, how true it is in America, that, as William Faulkner wrote, "the past isn't dead. It isn't even the past."

The same ventilation system that Senator Jefferson Davis of Mississippi had installed in the new Senate chamber in 1859—just before leaving Washington to become President of the Confederacy—was still in use when I first came here as a boy, when television and nuclear power were in their infancy.

We enter rooms that Clay and Webster and Calhoun seem only recently to have departed. We can almost smell the smoke of the fire the British kindled in what is now Senator Lott's office to burn down Washington in August of 1814. By the way, you can thank me for whatever smoke you now smell. My late father-in-law, Everett Dirksen, told me that the fireplace in the Republican Leader's offices didn't work since they were sealed when they air-conditioned the Capitol. So when I was elected Republican Leader, I asked the Architect of the Capitol what it would take to make these fireplaces work, and he replied, "A match, I suppose."

My dear friend, Jennings Randolph of West Virginia, with whom I helped write much of the environmental and public works legislation of the 1970s and who passed away recently, came to Washington with Franklin Roosevelt in 1932 and was still here when Ronald Reagan arrived in 1981. He was a walking history lesson who embodied—and gladly imparted—a half-century of American history.

You may be wondering by now what all these ruminations have to do with the subject of Senate leadership. The answer is this: what makes the Senate work today is the same thing that made it work in the days of Clay, Webster and Calhoun, in whose temple we gather this evening.

It isn't just the principled courage, creative compromise and persuasive eloquence that these men brought to the leadership of the Senate—important as these qualities were in restoring political prestige and Constitutional importance to the Senate in the first half of the nineteenth century. (Heretical as it may sound, before these gentlemen arrived, an alarming number of men left the Senate to pursue more influential careers in the House of Representatives).

It isn't simply an understanding of the unique role and rules of the Senate, important as that understanding is.

It isn't even the devotion of the good of the country, which has inspired every senator since 1789.

What really makes the Senate work—as our heroes knew profoundly—is an understanding of human nature, an appreciation of the hearts, as well as the minds, the frailties as well as the strengths, of one's colleagues and constituents.

Listen to Calhoun himself, speaking of the great rival Clay: "I don't like Henry Clay. He is a bad man, an imposter, a creator of wicked schemes. I wouldn't speak to him. But by God, I love him."

It is almost impossible to explain that statement to most people, but most senators understand it instinctively and perfectly.

Here in those twenty-eight words, is the secret to leading the United States Senate. Here, in a jangle of insults redeemed at the end by the most profound appreciation and respect, is the genius and glory of this institution.

Very often in the course of my eighteen years in the Senate, and especially in the last eight years as Republican Leader and then Majority Leader, I found myself engaged in fire-breathing, passionate debate with my fellow senators over the great issues of the times: civil rights, Vietnam, environmental protection, Watergate, the Panama Canal, tax cuts, defense spending, the Middle East, relations with the Soviet Union and dozens more.

But no sooner had the final word been spoken and the last vote taken than I would walk to the desk of my recent antagonist, extend the hand of friendship, and solicit his support on the next day's issue.

People must think we're crazy when we do that. Or perhaps they think our debates are fraudulent to begin with, if we can put our passion aside so quickly and embrace our adversaries so readily.

But we aren't crazy and we aren't frauds. This ritual is as natural as breathing hard in the Senate, and it is as important as anything that appends in Washington or in the country we serve.

It signifies that, as Lincoln said, "We are not enemies but friends. We must not be enemies." It pulls us back from the brink of rhetorical, intellectual, even physical violence, that, thank God, has only rarely disturbed the peace of the Senate. It makes us America and not Bosnia. It's what makes us the most stable government on Earth, not a civil war waiting to happen.

We're doing the business of the American people. We have to do it every day. And if we cannot be civil with one another—if we stop dealing with those who disagree with us or those we do not like, we would soon stop functioning altogether.

Sometimes we have stopped functioning. Once we had a civil war. Once Representative Preston Brooks of South Carolina, who, by the way, was born in Senator Thurmond's hometown of Edgefield, came into this chamber and attacked Senator Charles Sumner of Massachusetts with a cane, nearly killing him. And it is at these times we have learned the hard way how important it is to work together, to see beyond the human frailties, the petty jealousies, even the occasionally craven motive, the fall from grace that every mortal experiences in life.

Calhoun didn't like Clay, didn't share his politics, didn't approve of his methods. But he loved Clay because Clay was, like him, an accomplished politician, a man in the arena, a master of his trade, serving his convictions and his constituency just as Calhoun was doing.

Calhoun and Clay worked together because they knew they had to. The business of their young nation was too important—and their roles in that business too central—to allow them the luxury of petulance.

I read recently that our late friend and colleague Barry Goldwater had proposed to his good friend, then President John Kennedy, that the two of them make joint campaign appearances in the 1964 presidential campaign, debating the issues one-on-one, without intervention from the press, their handlers, or anyone else.

Barry Goldwater and John Kennedy would have had trouble agreeing on the weather, but they did agree that presidential campaigns were important, that the issues were important, and that the public's understanding of their respective positions on those issues was important.

That common commitment to the importance of public life was enough to bridge an ideological and partisan chasm that was both deep and wide. And that friendship, born here in the Senate where they were both freshmen together in 1953, would have served the nation well whoever might have won that election in 1964.

Barry Goldwater and I were also personal friends, as well as professional colleagues and members of the same political team. Even so, I could not automatically count on his support for anything. Once, when I really needed his vote and leaned on him perhaps a little too hard, he said to his Majority Leader, "Howard, you have one vote, and I have one vote, and we'll just see how this thing comes out."

It was at that moment that I formulated my theory that being leader of the Senate was like herding cats. It is trying to make ninety-nine independent souls act in concert under rules that encourage polite anarchy and embolden people who find majority rule a dubious proposition as best.

Perhaps this is why there was no such thing as a Majority Leader in the Senate's first century and a quarter—and why it's only a traditional, rather than statutory or constitutional, office still today.

Indeed, the only senator with constitutional office is the President Pro Tempore, who stands third in line of succession to the Presidency of the United States. Strom Thurmond has served ably in that constitutional role for most of the last seventeen years, and I have no doubt that he has at least another seventeen to go.

In Strom's case I am reminded of an invitation that I recently received to attend the dedication of a time capsule in Rugby, Tennessee to be opened in a hundred years. Unfortunately, I could not attend because of a scheduling conflict so I wrote that I was sorry I couldn't be there for the burying of the time capsule, but I assured them that I would try to be there when they dig it up.

There was a time when even the Vice-Presidency was a powerful office. When John C. Calhoun served as Andrew Jackson's vice-president, he had the power not only to cast tie-breaking votes, but also to appoint whole congressional committees.

There was also a time when Majority and Minority Leaders could keep their members in line by granting or withholding campaign funds from the national parties—the only major source of funds, besides personal wealth, that most senators could call upon.

Even Lyndon Johnson in the late 1950s could wield this power and enforce his party's discipline with cash and committee assignments as well as the famous "Johnson treatment."

Today, every senator is an independent contractor, beholden to no one for fundraising, for media coverage, for policy analysis, for political standing, or anything else. I herded cats. Trent Lott and Tom Daschle have to tame tigers, and the wonder is not that the Senate, so configured, does so little but that it accomplishes so much.

That it does is a tribute to their talented leadership. They can herd cats. They can tame tigers. They can demonstrate the patience of Job, the wisdom of Solomon, the poise of Cary Grant and the sincerity of Jimmy Stewart—all of which are essential to success in the difficult roles they play.

For whatever help it may be to these and future leaders, let me offer now a few rules of Senate leadership. As it happens, they are an even Baker's Dozen.

1. Understand its limits. The leader of the Senate relies on two prerogatives, neither of which is constitutionally or statutorily guaranteed. They are the right of prior recognition under the precedent of the Senate and the conceded right to schedule the Senate's business. These, together with the reliability of his commitment and whatever power of political persuasion one brings to the job, are all the tools a Senate leader has.
2. Have a genuine and decent respect for differing points of view. Remember that every senator is an individual with individual needs, ambitions and political conditions. None was sent here to march in lockstep with his or her colleagues and none will. But also remember that even members of the opposition party are susceptible to persuasion and redemption on a surprising number of issues. Understanding these shifting sands is the beginning of wisdom for a Senate leader.
3. Consult as often as possible, with as many senators as possible on as many issues as possible. This consultation should encompass not only committee chairmen but as many members of one's party conference as possible in matters of legislative scheduling.
4. Remember that senators are people with families. Schedule the Senate as humanely as possible, with as few all-night sessions and as much accommodation as you can manage.
5. Choose a good staff. In the complexity of today's world, it is impossible for a member to gather and digest all the information that is necessary for the member to make an informed and prudent decision on all the major issues.

Listen to your staff, but don't let them fall into the habit of forgetting who works for whom.

6. Listen more than you speak. As my father-in-law Everett Dirksen once admonished me in my first year in this body, "Occasionally allow yourself the luxury of an unexpressed thought."
7. Count carefully, and often. The essential training of a Senate Majority Leader perhaps ends in the third grade, when he learns to count reliably. But fifty-one today may be forty-nine tomorrow, so keep on counting.
8. Work with the President, whoever he is, whenever possible. When I became President after the elections of 1980, I had to decide whether I would try to set a separate agenda for the Senate or try to see how our new President, with a Republican Senate, could work together as a team to enact his programs. I chose the latter course, and history proved me right. Would I have done the same with a President of the opposition party? Lyndon Johnson did with President Eisenhower, and history proved him right as well.
9. Work with the House. It is a co-equal branch of government, and nothing the Senate does, except in the ratification of treaties and the confirmation of federal officers, is final unless the Senate concurs. My father and stepmother both served in the House, and I appreciate its special role as the sounding board of American politics. John Rhodes and I established a Joint Leadership Office in 1977, and it worked very well. I commend that arrangement to this generation of Senate leaders and to every succeeding generation.
10. No surprises. Bob Byrd and I decided more than twenty years ago that while we were bound to disagree on many things, one thing we would always agree on was the need to keep each other fully informed. It was an agreement we never broke—not once—in the eight years we served together as Republican and Democratic Leaders of the Senate.
11. Tell the truth, whether you have to or not. Remember that your word is the only currency you have to do business in the Senate. Devalue it, and your effectiveness as a Senate leader is over. And always get the bad news out first.
12. Be patient. The Senate was conceived by America's founders as "the saucer into which the nation's passions are poured to cool." Let senators have their say. Bide your time—I worked for eighteen years to get television in the Senate and the first camera was not turned on until after I left. But patience and persistence have their shining reward. It is better to let a few important things be your legacy than to boast of a thousand bills that have no lasting significance.
13. Be civil, and encourage others to do likewise. Many of you have heard me speak of the need for greater civility in our political discourse. I have been making that speech since the late 1960s, when America turned into an armed battleground over the issues of civil rights and Vietnam. Having seen political passion erupt into physical violence, I do not share the view of those who

> say that politics today are meaner or more debased than ever. But in this season of prosperity and peace, so rare in our national experience, it ill behooves America's leaders to invent disputes for the sake of political advantage, or to inveigh carelessly against motives and morals of one's political adversaries. America expects better of its leaders than this, and deserves better.

I continue in my long-held faith that politics is an honorable profession. I continue to believe that only through the political process can we deal effectively with the full range of the demands and dissents of the American people. I continue to believe that here in the United States Senate, especially, our country can expect to see the rule of the majority co-exist peacefully and constructively with the rights of the minority. . . .

It doesn't take Clays and Websters and Calhouns to make the Senate work. Doles and Mitchells did it. Mansfields and Scotts did it. Johnsons and Dirksens did it. Byrds and Bakers did it. Lotts and Daschles do it now, and do it well. The founders didn't require a nation of supermen to make this government and this country work, but only honorable men and women laboring honestly and diligently and creatively in their public and private capacities.

It was the greatest honor of my life to serve here and lead here. I learned much about this institution, about this country, about human nature, about myself in the eighteen years I served here at the pleasure of the people of Tennessee.

I enjoyed some days more than others. I succeeded some days more than others. I was more civil some days than others. But the Senate, for all its frustration and foibles and failings, is indeed the world's greatest deliberative body. And by God, I love it.

NOTES

Abbreviations

BP	Baker Papers
CNFP	*Chattanooga News–Free Press*
CQ	*Congressional Quarterly*
CR	*Congressional Record*
CT	*Chattanooga Times*
Chi T	*Chicago Tribune*
CSM	*Christian Science Monitor*
DMR	*Des Moines Register*
FL	Ford Library
HBOHP	Howard Baker Oral History Project
HE	*Human Events*
HHB	Howard Henry Baker Jr.
IS	*Indianapolis Star*
KJ	*Knoxville Journal*
KNS	*Knoxville News Sentinel*
LAT	*Los Angeles Times*
MCA	*Memphis Commercial Appeal*
NB	*Nashville Banner*
NJ	*National Journal*
NME	*No Margin for Error*
NP	Nixon Project
NT	*Nashville Tennessean*
NYT	*New York Times*
OR	*Oak Ridger*
PFC	President Ford Committee
SCN	*Scott County News*
US News	*U.S. News and World Report*
VQR	*Virginia Quarterly Review*
WES	*Washington Evening Star*
WP	*Washington Post*
WS	*Washington Star*
WSJ	*Wall Street Journal*
WSN	*Washington Star-News*
WT	*Washington Times*

Preface

1. Howard Fineman and Richard Wolffe with Holly Bailey, "Flying Blind," *Newsweek*, 11/7/05, 35.
2. Margaret Carlson, *Anyone Can Grow Up: How George Bush and I Made It to the White House* (New York, 2003), 152.
3. Michael Schaller, *Right Turn: American Life in the Reagan-Bush Era* (New York, 2006), 31; *USA Today*, 12/29/05.
4. *Howard H. Baker, Jr.*, video produced by Howard H. Baker Jr. Center for Public Policy at the University of Tennessee at Knoxville.
5. HHB, "Remarks at Reception for Washington Friends of the University of Tennessee and the Baker School for Public Policy," 5/24/06.

6. Several conversations with William H. Frist while writing William H. Frist and J. Lee Annis Jr., *Tennessee Senators, 1911–2001: Portraits of Leadership in a Century of Change* (Lanham, MD, 1999).
7. HBOHP, Box 2, Folder 2, Stephen Bell, 3/3/98.

Introduction

1. *The Tower Commission Report* (New York, 1987), xiii, xviii.
2. Nancy Reagan with William Novak, *My Turn: The Memoirs of Nancy Reagan* (New York, 1989), 326–27.
3. HHB, interviewed on "The Reagan Legacy," aired on C-SPAN, 1/1/89; interview with Paul Laxalt, 5/16/90; *NT*, 2/28/97.
4. Interviews with HHB, 2/9/87, 3/9/90, and Tom C. Griscom, 5/27/87; telephone interview with Bill Brock, 6/24/92; Donald T. Regan, *For the Record: From Wall Street to Washington* (New York, 1988), 75.
5. Interviews with Orrin Hatch, 3/20/90; Daniel Inouye, 5/11/93; and Don Sundquist, 11/15/89; HHB on "The Reagan Legacy"; *NYT*, 12/4/92; *WP*, 7/4/88.
6. Interviews with William Armstrong, 4/24/90; Tom C. Griscom, 7/16/82; Dan Quayle, 6/10/82; and Daniel Inouye, 5/11/93. Undated *Albany (NY) Times-Union* editorial, printed in *CR*, 98th Cong., 2nd sess., S1971–72; Jack Anderson and Tony Capacio, "Jack Anderson Rates the Congress," *Washingtonian*, 10/80, 166–81; Bernard Asbell, *The Senate Nobody Knows* (Garden City, New York, 1978), 114; *KNS*, 10/27/80; "8th Annual Survey: Who Runs America," *US News*, 4/23/81, 38–41; "Even Congress Is Unhappy with Congress," *US News*, 4/23/81, 37–39; Eleanor Randolph, "The Best and Worst of the US Senate," *Washington Monthly*, 1/82, 30–43; Courtney R. Sheldon, "What Congress Really Thinks of Itself," *US News*, 3/15/82, 22–24; Hedrick Smith, *The Power Game: How Washington Works* (New York, 1988), 471; George F. Will, "The Professional," *Newsweek*, 11/12/79, 136.
7. HHB on *Capitol Notebook*, aired on 5/30/93; Robert Mann, *Legacy to Power: Senator Russell Long of Louisiana* (New York, 1992), 354; telephone interviews with Frank Moore, 3/14/91, and Abraham Ribicoff, 10/5/92.
8. *CR*, 96th Cong., 2nd sess., S12791; interviews with HHB, 6/24/93, and John Seigenthaler, 8/14/82; *NYT*, 10/1/1973; James Squires, "HB: What Are You? A) Bland and Passionless; B) Cunning and Fiercely Ambitious," *Chi T Magazine*, 11/25/73, 30, 32; telephone interview with Abraham Ribicoff, 10/5/92; Martin Tolchin, "HB: Trying to Tame an Unruly Senate," *NYT Magazine*, 3/28/82, 17; *WSJ*, 10/23/79.
9. Interviews with HHB, 6/24/93, Orrin Hatch, 3/20/90, and A. B. Culvahouse, 12/17/92; telephone interview with Barry M. Goldwater, 9/24/92; Fred D. Thompson, *At That Point in Time: The Inside Story of the Watergate Investigation* (New York, 1975), 84.
10. HHB, "Address before College Republicans at the Republican National Leadership Conference," 3/8/75, Washington, BP; Michael Barone and Grant Ujifusa,

The Almanac of American Politics: 1984 (Washington, 1983), xxx–xxxix; Larry Light, "HB: Aiming for the Republican Middle," *CQ*, 11/10/79, 2525–26; *WS*, 10/16/78.

11. HHB, "Commencement Address at Graceland College," 5/17/70, Lamoni, Iowa, BP; interview with Hugh D. Scott Jr., 6/21/82.
12. HHB, *HB's Washington*, 20; Russell Kirk and James McClellan, *The Political Principles of Robert A. Taft* (New York, 1967), 175; *NME*, 187–88, 235–36; James T. Patterson, *Mr. Republican: A Biography of Robert A. Taft* (Boston, 1972), 319; *NME*, 187–88; A. James Reichley, *Conservatives in an Age of Change: The Nixon and Ford Administrations* (Washington, 1981), 22–27; telephone interview with Gary W. Hart, 8/15/91.
13. Barone and Ujifusà, *1984 Almanac*, xxxi; *CR*, 95th Cong., 2nd sess., 72457246; Patterson, *Mr. Republican*, 593; interviews with Warren B. Rudman, 6/9/82, and Hugh D. Scott Jr., 6/21/82.
14. HHB, "The View from Both Ends of the Avenue," *Presidential Studies Quarterly* 20 (Summer 1990), 492; *CR*, 98th Cong., 2nd sess., S14610; E. J. Dionne, *Why Americans Hate Politics* (New York, 1991), 332; interview with John Seigenthaler, 8/14/82.
15. Telephone interviews with Frank Moore, 3/14/91, and Robert Dole, 7/8/93; Smith, *Power Game*, 466; *WP*, 2/16/82.
16. Interview with Warren B. Rudman, 6/9/82; William F. Hildenbrand, Secretary of the Senate, Oral History Interviews, 3/10/85–5/6/85, Senate Historical Office, 222; Randolph, "Best and Worst of Senate," 32; telephone interview with George S. McGovern, 10/22/92; *WSJ*, 10/23/79.
17. *Chicago Sun-Times*, 8/13/78; Timothy Crouse, "Senators, Sandbaggers and Soap Operas," *Rolling Stone*, 11/22/73, 40; interviews with Rebecca Cox, 6/24/82, and Robert W. Packwood, 1/13/93; telephone interview with Ted Q. Wilson, 10/28/93; Walter Isaacson, Neil MacNeil and Evan Thomas, "The Floor Is My Domain," *Time*, 4/26/82, 19; *KNS*, 3/9/87; Thompson, *At That Point*, 49; Tolchin, "HB: Trying to Tame Senate," 74; *WP*, 2/16/82.
18. Anderson and Capacio, "Anderson Rates Congress," 166; *Asbell, Senate Nobody Knows*, 338; Barone and Ujifusa, *The Almanac of American Politics: 1984*, xxxi; *CR*, 98th Cong., 1st sess., S15175; Isaacson et al., "Floor Is My Domain," 19; telephone interview with Frank Moore, 3/14/91; interview with John Seigenthaler, 8/14/82; *WP*, 12/24/83; C. Vann Woodward, *The Burden of Southern History* (Baton Rouge, 1960), 24.
19. HHB, "Congress According to Baker," *NYT Magazine*, 4/1/84, 68; *CR*, 94th Cong., 1st sess., 16700–16706; 98th Cong., 1st sess., S8375–76; HHB, "The View"; Richard Reeves, "Why HB Is Leaving the Senate," *Parade*, 8/7/83, 10–11; *WP*, 3/30/77.
20. HBOHP, Box 9, Folder 9, Thomas C. Griscom, 9/8/92, 13–14; HHB, *HB's Washington*, 81; Christopher Buckley, "HB's Capital View," *Architectural Digest*, 8/93, 174; Timothy Cahill, "The Senator from the State of Compromise," *Rolling Stone*, 2/14/74, 27; Federal Writers Project of the Works Progress Administration of the

State of Tennessee, *Tennessee: A Guide to the State* (New York, 1939), 359–60; *KJ*, 4/28, 5/3/82; *NME*, 114; Steven Rattner, "Baker: The Cool Candidate," *NYT Magazine*, 11/4/79, 108; Esther Sharp Sanderson, *County Scott and Its Mountain Folk* (Nashville, 1958), 184–85, 198; telephone interview with Cissy Baker, 12/29/82; *WS*, 10/16/78.

Chapter 1

1. Cahill, "Senator from State of Compromise," 28; *KJ*, 6/8/82; Sanderson, *County Scott*, 213–14; Esther Sharp Sanderson, *Scott County: Gem of the Cumberlands* (Huntsville, Tenn., 1974), 52; *Union Station: Nashville, Tennessee: Hearings before the Committee on Environment and Public Works of the United States Senate*, 95th Cong., 1st sess., 33; *WS*, 10/16/78.
2. Cahill, "Senator from State of Compromise," 28.
3. Ibid.; Sanderson, *County Scott*, 214; Sanderson, *Scott County*; interviews with John Sherman Cooper, 6/15/82, and John J. Duncan, 6/2/82; *KJ*, 4/22/59.
4. *CR*, 88th Cong., 1st sess., 8; interview with John Sherman Cooper, 6/15/82; *KNS*, 1/7, 1/8/64; Ray H. Jenkins, *The Terror of Tellico Plains: The Memoirs of Ray H. Jenkins* (Knoxville, 1978), 97–98; *WP*, 4/18/67.
5. HHB, "Address before the Tennessee Electrical Cooperative Association," 10/18/78, BP; Cahill, "Senator from State of Compromise," 28–29; *KNS*, 1/7/64; *LAT*, 7/1/79; Lydon, "Ambivalent Baker," 95; *NB*, 2/27/80.
6. Ernie Beazley, "The Man Who Would Be President," *Nashville*, 2/80, 78; Cahill, "Senator from State of Compromise," 29; *CT*, 7/29/73, 1/8/78; *CR*, 90th Cong., 1st sess., 33654; *KNS*, 1/7/64; Lydon, "Ambivalent Baker," 94; *NB*, 11/1/79; Sanderson, *County Scott*, 242.
7. Cahill, "Senator from State of Compromise," 94; *KJ*, 11/1/50; *KNS*, 1/7/64.
8. Interviews with HHB, 3/9/90, 6/24/93; *KJ*, 7/11/80; *NB*, 10/11/72, 11/1/79.
9. Lillie Ladd had an eventful life after she left the Baker household, too. She took a job as housemother at the Lambda Chi Alpha house at the University of Tennessee after Howard Baker's remarriage. In appreciation of her services to the chapter, the brothers nicknamed her Mother Ladd. As in Kingston, Lillie Ladd was a force to be reckoned with. A rash of burglaries plagued the university in the 1940s. The Lambda house was no exception. Several hundred dollars and a number of watches had been stolen from the brothers. One night, an intruder entered Mother Ladd's quarters. When he failed to identify himself, Mother Ladd loaded her gun and fired a shot of warning. The astonished burglar tore out of the house and was never heard from again in Knoxville.

   Mother Ladd remained a vibrant figure until her death in 1981 at the age of 101. She severely injured her leg falling down the steps at a dog track after winning fifty dollars on a two-dollar ticket when she was 92. She survived a mastectomy at the age of 97. Friends and relatives made plans to celebrate her 100th birthday, but she would only agree if she could spend the day with her boys at the Lambda house. For the occasion, Mother Ladd made her own dress and spent three hours shaking hands with friends and well-wishers under a scorching July sun. The still-strong centenarian concluded her day by seeking out a friend and sharing a bottle of Cold Duck she had stuffed in her purse. Interview with Cissy Baker, 12/29/82; *CR*, 95th Cong., 1st sess., 22259; 97th Cong., 1st sess., S5925–26; *NB*, 2/27/80; Rattner, "Baker: Cool Candidate," 112; *University of Tennessee Beacon*, 4/21/81.

10. Interview with HHB, 6/24/93; Cahill, "Senator from State of Compromise," 30; Hope Chamberlin, *A Minority of Members: Women in the US Congress* (New York, 1973), 308; *KNS*, 1/26/93; Tolchin, "Baker: Trying to Tame Senate," 30.
11. HHB, *HB's Washington*, 9, 80; Cahill, "Senator from State of Compromise," 30; *NB*, 11/1/80.
12. *CR*, 95th Cong., 1st sess., 28439; Robert E. Corlew, *Tennessee: A Short History*, 2nd ed. (Knoxville, 1981), 485–86; Lee S. Greene, *Lead Me On: Frank Goad Clement and Tennessee Politics* (Knoxville, 1982), 48; C. Alexander Heard and Donald S. Strong, *Southern Primaries and Elections, 1920–1949* (Tuscaloosa, Ala., 1950), 114–28.
13. Cahill, "Senator from State of Compromise," 29; *CR*, 95th Cong., 1st sess., 28439; Corlew, *Tennessee*, 485–86; Greene, *Lead Me On*, 48; C. Alexander Heard, *A Two-Party South?* (Chapel Hill, 1950), 104; Heard and Strong, *Southern Primaries and Elections*, 114–28; *NB*, 11/2/79.
14. *CNFP*, 7/16/89; *CT*, 1/8/78; Wayne Greenhaw, *Elephants in the Cottonfields: Ronald Reagan and the New Republican South* (New York, 1982), 205; telephone interviews with A. Warren James, 6/17/92, and C. Houston Patterson, 6/18/92.
15. HHB, "The View"; HHB, "Address before the Southern Coals Conference," 3/15/79, Cincinnati, BP; Cahill, "Senator from State of Compromise," 30; HHB and John Netherton, *Big South Fork Country* (Nashville, 1993), 21; Gary Clifford, "How Do You Spell Relief for Sen. Howard Baker? It's V-I-C-T-O-R-Y for a Treaty," *People*, 4/3/78, 24; *KJ*, 8/4/66; *NT*, 1/11/78; "Senator-elect HHB (R-Tenn) Shatters Tradition in Sweeping Win," Document Received 12/15/66 by Historian of the United States Senate in HHB File in Office of the Historian of the United States Senate; Lloyd Shearer, "Senator HB: Caught in the Middle," *Parade*, 7/29/73, 6; telephone interview with William H. Swain, 11/23/92.
16. Cahill, "Senator from State of Compromise," 30; *Chi T*, 4/8/79; Lucille Deaderick, ed., *Heart of the Valley: A History of Knoxville, Tennessee* (Knoxville, 1976), 320; "Interview: Howard Baker," *Knoxville*, 10/73, 13; *NME*, 21.
17. *CT*, 7/29/73; telephone interview with Ted Q. Wilson, 10/28/93.
18. *OR*, 8/29/79.
19. *NME*, 90; Cahill, "Senator from State of Compromise," 30; Sanderson, *County Scott*, 242–43; telephone interview with William H. Swain, 11/23/92.
20. CQ, 1/10/64, 46; William Goodman, *Inherited Domain: Political Parties in Tennessee* (Knoxville, 1954), 49–50; *KNS*, 1/7/64; Heard, *Two Party South*, 109.
21. Charges of this sort can be found in Heard, *Two Party South*, 104.
22. Interview with HHB, 2/9/87; CQ, 10/7/72, 2513–14; Goodman, *Inherited Domain*, 50; *KJ*, 1/28/50.

23. 1950 Campaign Pamphlet, Box 18, Howard H. Baker Sr., Papers, MSS 745, Kefauver Collection, James D. Hoskins Library of the University of Tennessee, Knoxville; *KJ*, 1/29/50.
24. *KJ*, 1/29/50; Scrapbook 1, Baker MSS.
25. Cahill, "Senator from State of Compromise," 29; *KNS*, 3/11/64.
26. Cahill, "Senator from State of Compromise," 30; Clifford, "Relief for Baker," 24; Louella Dirksen with Norma Lee Browning, *The Honorable Mr. Marigold: My Life with Everett Dirksen* (Garden City, New York, 1972), 140–41; Scrapbook 1, Baker MSS; Shearer, "HB: Caught in Middle," 6.
27. Neil MacNeil, *Dirksen: Portrait of a Public Man* (New York, 1970), 72–73, 96; Dirksen and Browning, *Mr. Marigold*, 140–41.
28. Dirksen and Browning, *Mr. Marigold*, 80, 140–41, 226; *WP*, 6/24/73, 4/26/93; *WS*, 1/6/52, 8/18/76.
29. HHB, "Address before B'Nai B'rith," 12/19/78, BP; Buckley, "HB's Capital View," 153; *CR*, 93rd Cong., 2nd sess., 8202–5; interview with John J. Duncan, 6/2/82; *KJ*, 5/24/56; *OR*, 8/29/79; Scrapbook 1, Baker MSS.
30. *CT*, 7/29/73; telephone interviews with Donald Stansbury Jr., 10/27/93, and Ted Q. Wilson, 10/28/93; Squires, "HB: What are You," 31; *WP*, 6/24/73.
31. Interview with HHB, 2/9/87; HHB, foreword to Jenkins, *Terror of Tellico Plains;* Albert R. Hunt, *Howard Baker* (Washington, 1979), 14; Lydon, "Ambivalent Baker," 95; *NYT*, 12/28/80; Thomas G. Reeves, *The Life and Times of Joe McCarthy* (New York, 1982), 599–602.
32. Cahill, "Senator from State of Compromise," 30–31; *Chi T*, 7/3/77; Marlys Harris, "The Candidates' Family Finances," *Money*, 3/80, 90; *KNS*, 5/26, 5/27/64; Lydon, "Ambivalent Baker," 95; *NO*, 5/16/73; Squires, "HB: What Are You?" 31; telephone interview with William H. Swain, 11/23/92.
33. Lynn Langway, Janet Huck, Renee Michael, Nikki Finke Greenberg, Jenky Ann Jackson and Jerry Buckley, "Like Father, Like Daughter," *Newsweek*, 1/16/84, 78; telephone interview with Howard Denis, 10/9/89.
34. *CR*, 90th Cong., 1st sess., 19681; *CT*, 7/29/73.
35. *NME*, 19; Cahill, "Senator from State of Compromise," 30; *KJ*, 6/18/59; Lydon, "Ambivalent Baker," 30; Rattner, "Baker: Cool Candidate," 116.
36. *CR*, 88th Cong., 2nd sess., 111–12; Hunt, *HB*, 14; *KNS*, 1/7/64; *NME*, 65.
37. Cahill, "Senator from State of Compromise," 31; Chamberlin, *Minority of Members*, 308; *CQ*, 9/2/60, 1528; 11/16/62, 2169; *KJ*, 5/25/60, 3/9/64; *KNS*, 1/26, 2/23, 3/5, 3/8, 3/11, 3/31/64; *NYT*, 3/11/64.
38. Chamberlin, *Minority of Members*, 303; interview with John J. Duncan, 6/2/82.

Chapter 2

1. *MCA*, 11/10/66; *NME*, 6.
2. Jack Bass and Walter DeVries, *The Transformation of Southern Politics: Social Change and Political Consequences since 1945* (New York, 1976), 26, 286; V. O. Key Jr., "The Erosion of Sectionalism," *VQR* 31 (Spring 1955), 163; Norman L.

Parks, "Tennessee Politics since Kefauver and Reece: A 'Generalist' View," *Journal of Politics*, 28 (2/66), 148; David M. Tucker, *Memphis since Crump: Bossism, Blacks and Civic Reformers* (Knoxville, 1980), 144.

3. Bass and DeVries, *Transformation*, 290–93; V. O. Key with C. Alexander Heard, *Southern Politics in State and Nation* (New York, 1949), 65; Theodore H. White, "The Battle of Athens, Tennessee," *Harper's*, 1/47), 54–61.
4. Interview with Benjamin Hooks, 8/14/90; telephone interview with Lewis R. Donelson III, 6/7/90; David M. Tucker, *Lieutenant Lee of Beale Street* (Nashville, 1971), 167, 181.
5. Telephone interview with Lewis R. Donelson III, 6/7/90; interview with Benjamin Hooks, 8/14/90, and Winfield Dunn, 8/6/82; Neil R. Pierce, *The Border South States: People, Politics and Power in the Five Border South States* (New York, 1975), 306; Tucker, *Lieutenant Lee*, 167–68, 170–72, 183–91.
6. Interview with Dan H. Kuykendall, 3/27/90; telephone interviews with Lamar Alexander, 2/28/90, and John B. Waters Jr., 5/31/90; *NME*, 6.
7. *CR*, 96th Cong., 1st sess., S10716–17; *KJ*, 5/27, 8/20, 9/24/64; *KNS*, 5/26, 9/19/64.
8. Interview with HHB, 6/24/93; *KJ*, 9/4, 8/64; *KNS*, 9/4, 10/28/64.
9. James Chester Coomer, "The Growth and Development of the Republican Party in Tennessee, 1948–1966," master's thesis, Georgia State College, 1968, 90; *KJ*, 8/7/64; *KNS*, 8/8/64.
10. For more on Senators Bass and Walters, see the chapters on them in Frist and Annis, *Tennessee Senators*; interviews with Benjamin Hooks, 8/14/90, John Seigenthaler, 8/14/82, and Robert Clement, 1/31/90; Greene, *Lead Me On*, 139, 199–206, 346–55; Bill Kovach, "Racism Wasn't the Answer in Tennessee," *Reporter*, 9/24/64, 37–38; *KNS*, 2/18, 5/13, 6/14, 6/28, 7/1/64; *NYT*, 11/7/69.
11. Greene, *Lead Me On*, 350–51; David Halberstam, "The End of a Populist," *Harper's*, 1/71, 37; *Maryville-Alcoa Times*, 5/2/63.
12. Hugh D. Graham, *Crisis in Print: Desegregation and the Press in Tennessee* (Nashville, 1967), 289; Greene, *Lead Me On*, 351, 382; *KJ*, 8/8/64; *KNS*, 6/7, 9/13/64; Kovach, "Racism Wasn't the Issue," 37–38; *NYT*, 8/8, 8/9/64.
13. Interview with HHB, 2/9/87; Bass and DeVries, *Transformation*, 27; Albert Gore, *Let the Glory Out: My South and Its Politics* (New York, 1972), 176–77; *MCA*, 9/13, 11/4/64; Tucker, *Memphis since Crump*, 16–18.
14. *KJ*, 11/3/63, 9/17/64, 10/12/64; *KNS*, 7/2, 7/12, 9/16, 10/10, 10/12, 10/16/64; *MCA*, 9/17/64.
15. *KJ*, 9/25, 10/15, 10/20, 10/23, 10/24/64; Pierce, *Border South States*, 306.
16. *CQ* 10/9/64, 2361; *KNS*, 10/13, 10/28/64; telephone interview with Kenneth Roberts, 7/30/90.
17. Telephone interview with Lamar Alexander, 2/28/90; *CQ*, 3/19/65, 504; *KNS*, 11/4/64.
18. Bass and DeVries, *Transformation*, 34–35; William J. Carleton, "Two-Party South," *VQR* 41, no. 4 (1965): 486–87; *CQ*, 3/19/65, 504; interview with Dan H. Kuykendall, 3/27/90.

19. Numan Bartley and Hugh D. Graham, *Southern Politics and the Second Reconstruction* (Baltimore, 1975), 109; Greenhaw, *Elephants*, 62, 207; *KJ*, 11/5/64; *MCA*, 11/5/64; Michael S. Lottman "Tennessee: Close but No Cigar," *Ripon Forum*, 7/70–8/70, 70; interview with Dan H. Kuykendall, 3/27/90; telephone interview with William H. Swain, 11/23/92; Louis Seagull, *Southern Republicanism* (New York, 1975), 118; Squires, "HB: What Are You?" 31.
20. Interview with HHB, 2/9/87; telephone interviews with William H. Swain, 11/23/92, and John B. Waters Jr., 5/31/90; Michael Fred Adams, "A Critical Analysis of the Rhetorical Strategies of Senator Howard H. Baker, Jr. in His 1972 Campaign for Reelection," Ph.D. diss., Ohio State University, 1973, 85; Squires, "HB: What Are You?" 31.
21. Telephone interviews with Bill Brock, 6/24/92, and Kenneth Roberts, 7/30/90; *MCA*, 7/3, 7/30/66; *NB*, 7/3, 7/30/66; Steven D. Williams, "The Direct Primary and Party Politics in Tennessee," Dorothy Olsfski and T. McN. Simpson, *The Volunteer State: Readings in Tennessee Politics* (Knoxville, 1985), 88.
22. *CQ*, 7/22/66, 1517; *NYT*, 2/17/66.
23. *KJ*, 6/25, 7/5, 7/8, 7/12, 7/15, 11/1/66; *KNS*, 6/28/66.
24. *KJ*, 6/30, 7/6, 7/16, 7/22, 10/19/66.
25. Lamar Alexander, *Steps along the Way: A Governor's Scrapbook* (Nashville, 1986), 32; HHB, "The View"; telephone interview with Kenneth Roberts, 7/30/90; *CQ*, 7/22/66, 1517; *NB*, 8/4/66, 6/23/77.
26. *KJ*, 5/24, 6/25, 7/1, 7/7, 7/26, 10/18/66; *KNS*, 7/24/66; *WES*, 11/2/66.
27. *KJ*, 7/22, 7/23, 8/1, 10/14/66.
28. *CQ*, 10/7/66, 2368; telephone interview with Lewis R. Donelson III, 6/7/90; *KJ*, 7/13, 7/20/66; *MCA*, 7/29/66.
29. *CQ*, 8/12/66, 1739; Greene, *Lead Me On*, 360–61; *KJ*, 7/20/66; *KNS*, 6/26/66; *NB*, 6/11, 6/25/66; *WES*, 4/24, 8/5/66.
30. Reports of crossover voting in the primary tend to be confirmed by the results of the general election. Clement actually received 479 fewer votes in November than he had in August. *CQ*, 8/12/66, 1739; Greene, *Lead Me On*, 361; *KJ*, 8/8/66; *MCA*, 7/19/66; *WES*, 8/5/66.
31. *KJ*, 8/4, 8/6/66; *NB*, 8/6/66; telephone interview with Kenneth Roberts, 7/30/90.
32. Greene, *Lead Me On*, 310, 367; *KJ*, 10/29/66; *KNS*, 8/7/66.
33. *CR*, 90th Cong., 1st sess., 23250–51; *KJ*, 7/14/66.
34. *CQ*, 8/12/66, 1739; Greene, *Lead Me On*, 366–67; Steven Hess and David S. Broder, *The Republican Establishment: The Present and Future of the GOP* (New York, 1968), 341; *KNS*, 10/2/66; Lottman, "Tennessee," 70.
35. *KJ*, 8/2, 10/7, 10/22, 10/26, 10/29, 11/2, 11/4, 11/8/66; *WP*, 10/16/66.
36. Alexander, *Steps*, 32; telephone interview with Lamar Alexander, 2/28/90; HHB, "The View"; *MCA*, 10/7, 10/21, 10/26, 10/29, 11/5/66.
37. "Baker v. Clement," *HE*, 10/1/66, 6; Coomer, "Growth and Development of the Republican Party," 94; *KJ*, 9/28, 10/29, 11/4/66.

38. Alexander, *Steps*, 37; *MCA*, 10/27, 10/28, 11/5/66.
39. Interviews with Robert Clement, 1/31/90, and Benjamin Hooks, 8/14/90; telephone interview with Kenneth Roberts, 7/30/90; *CQ*, 5/12/67, 766–67; Greene, *Lead Me On*, 369–81; *NYT*, 11/9/66.
40. "Senator-elect HHB (R-Tenn) Shatters Tradition in Sweeping Win," Document Received 12/15/66 by Historian of the United States Senate in HHB File in Office of the Historian of the United States Senate; Bartley and Graham, *Southern Politics*, 123; *CQ*, 3/14/65, 504; 5/12/67, 766–67; Hess and Broder, *Republican Establishment*, 353.

Chapter 3

1. Samuel Shaffer, *On and Off the Floor: Thirty Years as a Correspondent on Capitol Hill* (New York, 1980), 20–21.
2. HHB, "Address before the National Oil Jobbers Council," 3/19/69, Washington, D.C., BP; *CQ*, 9/26169, 1769; *CR*, 90th Cong., 1st sess., 5972–83, 7216–17, 12122, 15400, 20983–84, 21722; 90th Cong., 2nd sess., 6392, 10865–67, 18233–36; 91st Cong., 1st sess., 36975; *NYT*, 4/22/67; *WP*, 2/2/67.
3. *Air Pollution—1968: Hearings before the Subcommittee on Air and Water Pollution of the Committee on Public Works of the United States Senate*, 90th Cong., 2nd sess., 528; "Senator-elect HHB (R-Tenn) Shatters Tradition in Sweeping Win," Document Received 12/15/66 by Historian of the United States Senate in HHB File in Office of the Historian of the United States Senate; HHB, "Address before the Seven States Air Pollution Control Conference," 5/8/69, Chattanooga, BP; *CQ*, 5/5/67, 725; *CR*, 90th Cong., 1st sess., 19179; 91st Cong., 1st sess., 33029; telephone interview with Gary W. Hart, 8/15/91.
4. *Air Quality Standards—1970: Hearings before the Subcommittee on Air and Water Pollution of the Committee on Public Works of the United States Senate*, 91st Cong., 2nd sess., 1472; *CR*, 91st Cong., 2nd sess., 3103–4; *Economic Dislocation Resulting From Environmental Controls: Hearings before the Subcommittee on Air and Water Pollution of the Committee on Public Works of the United States Senate*, 92nd Cong., 1st sess., 262; *NYT*, 3/4/70; *Water Pollution—1970: Hearings before the Subcommittee on Air and Water Pollution of the Committee on Public Works of the United States Senate*, 91st Cong., 2nd sess., 197.
5. "HB Shatters Tradition"; interviews with John Sherman Cooper, 6/15/82, and Edmund S. Muskie, 4/18/90; *CR*, 91st Cong., 2nd sess., 32920; telephone interview with Thomas Eagleton, 10/2/92.
6. *CR*, 92nd Cong., 2nd sess., 34766; MacNeil, *Dirksen*, 295–96; Stacy Colin Myers, "Howard Baker: A Rhetoric of Leadership," Ph.D. diss., Southern Illinois University, 1973, 7; *WES*, 1/18/70.
7. MacNeil, *Dirksen*, 260, 296.
8. *CR*, 90th Cong., 1st sess., 14016–18, 14782–92; Burton Hersh, *The Education of Edward Kennedy: A Family Biography* (New York, 1980), 343–46; *WES*, 5/26/67.

9. *CQ*, 6/30/67, 1106; *CR*, 90th Cong., 1st sess., 14016–18, 29507–9, 29815–16, 30392, 31700–31702, 31709; Hersh, *Kennedy*, 347, 350; MacNeil, *Dirksen*, 296; *NYT*, 6/12/67.
10. *CQ*, 9/1/67, 1703; *KJ*, 12/25/67; *NYT*, 10/22/67.
11. Paul R. Clancy, *Just a Country Lawyer: A Biography of Senator Sam Ervin* (Bloomington, Ind., 1974), 52; *CQ*, 2/23/68, 315–16; 3/1/68, 441; interviews with Edward Brooke, 11/11/92, and Sam J. Ervin Jr., 5/27/81; MacNeil, *Dirksen*, 320–23; telephone interview with Walter F. Mondale, 2/19/93.
12. *CQ*, 3/8/68, 448, 503; *CR*, 90th Cong., 2nd sess., 4574, 4845; MacNeil, *Dirksen*, 324–25; *NYT*, 3/1/68.
13. *CR*, 90th Cong., 2nd sess., 9137; interviews with Winfield Dunn, 8/6/82, and Ron McMahan, 7/27/82; telephone interview with Walter F. Mondale, 2/19/93.
14. *CQ*, 5/24/68, 1237; 5/31/68, 1277; 9/20/68,2523; *KJ*, 7/29/78; *NME*, 135; *SCN*, 10/26/72.
15. *CR*, 90th Cong., 2nd sess., 13660, 24230–322; 93rd Cong., 2nd sess., 38901; John Lazarek, "Republican Racism: Here We Go Again," *Ripon Forum*, 8/68, 13; "Political Notes: Tennessee," *Ripon Forum*, 10/67, 13; Theodore H. White, *The Making of the President, 1968* (New York, 1969), 274.
16. *CR*, 90th Cong., 2nd sess., 24320–22.
17. HHB, "Commencement Address to the Graduating Class of Westminster School," *Atlanta*, 6/2/74, BP; *CQ*, 7/2/68, 1766; *CR*, 90th Cong., 2nd sess., 24320–22; 96th Cong., 1st sess., S10716–17.
18. *NYT*, 8/8/68; *Official Proceedings of the Twenty-Ninth Republican Convention* (Washington, 1968), 337–38.
19. Cahill, "Senator from State of Compromise," 32; Elizabeth Drew, *American Journal: The Events of 1976* (New York, 1977), 404.
20. Richard M. Nixon, *RN: The Memoirs of Richard M. Nixon* (New York, 1978), 312–13; Ripon Society, *The Lessons of Victory* (New York, 1969), 43; Jules Witcover, *The Resurrection of Richard Nixon* (New York, 1970), 350–51.
21. Lewis Chester, Godfrey Hodgson, and Bruce Page, *An American Melodrama: The Presidential Campaign of 1968* (New York, 1969), 543–45; Ripon Society, *Lessons*, 35–40.
22. *NYT*, 8/17/68; Ripon Society, *Lessons*, 40–41; William Safire, *Before the Fall: An Inside View of the Pre-Watergate White House* (New York, 1975), 56; White, *1968*, 294; Witcover, *Resurrection*, 354.
23. MacNeil, *Dirksen*, 332–34; Shaffer, *On and Off the Floor*, 80–83.
24. *CR*, 90th Cong., 2nd sess., 18874, 22339; MacNeil, *Dirksen*, 332, 334; Shaffer, *On and Off the Floor*, 84; *WES*, 6/26/68.
25. *CQ*, 10/4/68,2668; *CR*, 90th Cong., 2nd sess., 28251–64; Lyndon Baines Johnson, *The Vantage Point: Perspectives of the Presidency, 1963–1969* (New York, 1969), 546–47; MacNeil, *Dirksen*, 335–37; *NYT*, 9/27/68.
26. *CQ*, 10/11/68, 2709, 6/6/69, 915; Bass and DeVries, *Transformation*, 35; Pierce, *Border South*, 323–24.

27. HHB, "Address before the National Youth Mobilization Conference of the NAACP," 4/22/69, Washington and "Address before the Pennsylvania Republican Finance Committee," 3/4/69, Philadelphia, BP; *CR*, 91st Cong., 1st sess., 2340, 2367; *NYT*, 1/7/69.
28. *CQ*, 3/14/69, 389; 8/8/69, 1471; *CR*, 90th Cong., 2nd sess., 18384, 29181; 91st Cong., 1st sess., 9175, 19425, 19443.
29. *CR*, 91st Cong., 1st sess., 1328, 3278, 7180, 7265, 11798, 22671–73.
30. MacNeil, *Dirksen*, 387; *SCN*, 9/12/69.
31. *CR*, 91st Cong., 1st sess., 24284–85.
32. Buckley, "HB's Capital View," 151; Cahill, "Senator from State of Compromise," 32; William H. Honan, "The Art of Oratory in the Senate of the United States," *Esquire*, 5/69, 163; Lance Morrow, "The Decline and Fall of Oratory," *Time*, 8/18/80, 76–78; *NME*, 112.

Chapter 4

1. Interview with Robert W. Packwood, 1/13/93.
2. "Filling the Dirksen Gap," *Newsweek*, 9/26/69, 33; interviews with Robert W. Packwood, 1/13/93, and Ted Stevens, 6/24/82; *NT*, 9/23/69; *NO*, 9/15/69; *NYT*, 9/9, 10/69; *WP*, 9/10/69; *WES*, 9/10/69.
3. HHB, "The View"; *CR*, 91st Cong., 1st sess., 29021; John Henry Cutler, *Ed Brooke: Biography of a Senator* (Indianapolis, 1974), 319; "Filling Dirksen Gap," 33; Myers, "HB: Rhetoric of Leadership," 50; *NT*, 9/13, 9/14, 9/16/69; *NO*, 9/15/69; *NYT*, 9/11, 9/13, 9/21/69; *WES*, 9/10, 9/14, 9/15, 9/23/69.
4. H. R. Haldeman, *The Haldeman Diaries* (New York, 1994), 89; interviews with Robert W. Packwood, 1/13/93, Hugh D. Scott Jr., 6/21/82, and Ted Stevens, 6/24/82; *NO*, 9/15/69; *NT*, 9/16, 9/23/69.
5. *CQ*, 9/26/69, 1761; Cutler, *Brooke*, 320; *NME*, 119–23; *NT*, 9/25/69; *NYT*, 9/23/69; interview with Hugh D. Scott Jr., 6/21/82; *WP*, 9/21/69.
6. *CQ*, 10/17/69, 1978; *CR*, 91st Cong., 1st sess., 29565; 91st Cong., 2nd sess., 2524, 18334–50; *NT*, 10/16/69; *NME*, 122.
7. *CR*, 91st Cong., 2nd sess., 18339–50; *NB*, 5/8/70; *NT*, 10/16/69.
8. *CR*, 91st Cong., 2nd sess., 5503.
9. Interview with HHB, 6/24/93; HHB, "Address at Knoxville College," 3/3/70, Knoxville, BP.
10. *CQ*, 12/19/69, 2669; 3/6/70, 720; 7/3/70, 1710; *CR*, 91st Cong., 2nd sess., 3731–32, 10812, 32368; 92nd Cong., 2nd sess., 34415; Steven Saferin, *HB: Republican Senator from Tennessee* (Washington, 1972), 4.
11. Asbell, *Senate Nobody Knows*, 341; *CR*, 91st Cong., 1st sess., 18241; 91st Cong., 2nd sess., 3731–32, 10812, 32368.
12. *Air Pollution—1970: Hearings before the Subcommittee on Air and Water Pollution of the Committee on Public Works of the United States Senate*, 91st Cong., 2nd sess., 1503; Saferin, *HB*, 9.

13. *NYT*, 3/4/70; Saferin, *HB*, 9–10.
14. Adams, "Critical Analysis," 216; HHB, "Address before the Missouri Bar Association," 9/24/70, St. Louis, BP; *Environmental Protection Act of 1971: Hearings before the Subcommittee on the Environment of the Committee on Commerce of the United States Senate*, 92nd Cong., 1st sess., 218; interview with Edmund S. Muskie, 4/18/90; *NME*, 39.
15. *CR*, 91st Cong., 2nd sess., 2907, 33077.
16. Adams, "Critical Analysis," 83, 86; HHB, "Missouri Bar Association Address"; *CQ*, 12/26/69, 2718; *CQ Almanac 1977*, 634–46, 28-S, 29-S; *CQ Rollcall 1970*, 65-S, 68-S; *CR*, 95th Cong., 1st sess., 17747, 18183–87; *WS*, 6/10/77.
17. *CR*, 91st sess., 2nd sess., 44044; Reese Cleghorn, "High Noon for Tex Ritter," *NYT Magazine*, 7/12/70, 10–20; interviews with Carol Browning and James Frierson, 6/21/82; *WES*, 1/17, 2/8/70; "Tennessee's William Brock," *Time*, 11/16/70, 18–19.
18. *CQ*, 7/24/70, 1875; 8/14/70, 2067; "Moderates and Wallace-voters—to Brock or Gore," *Ripon Forum*, 11/70, 66; *NJ*, 10/10/70, 2210.
19. Bass and DeVries, *Transformation of Southern Politics*, 24; *CQ*, 10/23/70, 2597; interview with Winfield Dunn, 8/6/82; Gore, *Let the Glory Out*, 248; William C. Havard, "Intransigence to Tradition: Thirty Years of Southern Politics," *VQR* 51 (Autumn 1975), 520; *NT*, 11/4/70; "The Republican Assault on the Senate," *Time*, 10/26/70, 18–26; *WES*, 11/4/70.
20. Interview with HHB, 6/24/93; *CQ*, 10/23/70, 2597, 2618; *CQ Rollcall 1970*, 60-S; *CR*, 91st Cong., 1st sess., 19987; 91st Cong., 2nd sess., 36479; "Republican Assault on Senate," 18–26.
21. Cahill, "Senator from State of Compromise," 32; Gore, *Let the Glory Out*, 269, 271; Richard M. Scammon, *America Votes 9: A Handbook of Contemporary American Election Statistics* (Washington, 1972), 315–18.
22. HHB, "The View"; interviews with HHB, 6/24/93, John Sherman Cooper, 6/15/82, and Hugh D. Scott Jr., 6/21/82; *CQ*, 1/15/71, 148; 1/22/71, 182; Barry M. Goldwater, *With No Apologies: The Personal and Political Memoirs of United States Senator Barry Goldwater* (New York, 1979), 236; *NB*, 1/19, 1/21/71.
23. HHB, "News Release," 6/1/71, BP; *CQ*, 3/12/71, 591; 3/25/72, 693, 706; *CR*, 92nd Cong., 1st sess., 271, 363, 793–94, 2140–53, 2408, 2488, 5304, 8065–66; *General Revenue Sharing: Hearings before the Committee on Ways and Means of the House of Representatives*, 92nd Cong., 1st sess., 987–92; *National Economic Development Program: Hearings before the Subcommittee on Economic Development of the Committee on Public Works of the United States Senate*, 92nd Cong., 1st sess., 420–32.
24. *CQ*, 7/2/71, 1454; 5/13/72, 1057; *CR*, 92nd Cong., 2nd sess., 13340–41; *KJ*, 7/7/71; *NME*, 21, 23.
25. *CQ*, 6/11/71, 1289; 7/2/71, 1455; *CR*, 92nd Cong., 1st sess., 32371; *KJ*, 12/4/71.
26. Ethan Bronner, *Battle for Justice: How the Bork Nomination Shook America* (New York, 1989), 230; *KJ*, 7/7/71; *NME*, 21–23.
27. HHB, "Lincoln Day Dinner Address to Knox County Republicans," 2/26/71, Knoxville, BP; *CR*, 92nd Cong., 1st sess., 5544; *Water Pollution—1969: Hear-*

ings before the Subcommittee on Air and Water Pollution of the Committee on Public Works of the United States Senate, 91st Cong., 1st sess., 1969.

28. Criticisms of Baker's role would emanate in future years from anti-stripping groups like Save Our Cumberland Mountains because the new owners had leased 24,000 acres to strip miners. Baker, who had bought a 10 percent share in 1972, received most of the criticism even though the controlling interest had been bought by John W. Rollins, an influential GOP donor from Delaware. In 1975, Baker placed his interest in a blind trust and gave instructions to sell his share. *Chi T,* 3/3/77; interviews with HHB, 6/24/93, and John Sherman Cooper, 6/15/82; telephone interview with William H. Swain, 11/23/92; *CR,* 92nd Cong., 1st sess., 96th Cong., 1st sess., 46687–88; *KJ,* 9/21, 10/16/71; *LAT,* 7/1/79; *NT,* 12/14/71; Squires, "HB: What Are You?" 32; *Surface Mining: Hearings before the Subcommittee on Minerals, Materials and Fuels of the Committee on Interior and Insular Affairs of the United States Senate,* 92nd Cong., 1st sess., 572–89.
29. Adams, "Critical Analysis," 285; *CR,* 92nd Cong., 2nd sess., 34291–92; John Egerton, *The Americanization of Dixie: The Southernization of America* (New York, 1974), 95–96; *WP,* 9/23/71.
30. Adams, "Critical Analysis," 63; HHB, "News Release," 2/14/72, BP; *CQ,* 4/23/71, 955; 4/30/71, 1008–9; 2/26/72, 463; 3/4/72, 471, 512–13; 3/11/72, 568; 5/27/72, 1234; 10/28/72, 2834; *CR,* 92nd Cong., 1st sess., 33930, 42937; 92nd Cong., 2nd sess., 5405; Egerton, *Americanization of Dixie,* 96; *LAT,* 3/18/72; *WP,* 9/23/71, 4/11/72.
31. Despite the efforts of Baker, Tower, Robert Griffin, and William Proxmire, Senate busing foes failed four times to muster the two-thirds majority for cloture. *CR,* 92nd Cong., 2nd sess., 9912, 34291–92, 34732–83; *WP,* 5/28/72.
32. Adams, "Critical Analysis," 211; HHB, "News Release," 9/8/72, BP; *CQ Almanac: 1972,* 643–46; *CR,* 92nd Cong., 2nd sess., 19128–29, 29308; interview with Russell Long, 11/11/92; *Revenue Sharing: Hearings before the Committee on Finance of the United States Senate on HR 14370 to Provide Payments to Localities for High Priority Expenditures, to Encourage the Senate to Supplement their Revenue Sources and to Authorize Federal Collection of State Individual Income Taxes,* 92nd Cong., 2nd sess., 95–105.
33. Adams, "Critical Analysis," 82, 211; Saferin, *HB,* 4.
34. Adams, "Critical Analysis," 202–6; Cahill, "Senator from State of Compromise," 32–33; *CQ,* 8/12/72, 1992; Theodore H. White, *The Making of the President: 1972* (New York, 1973), 169–72.
35. Adams, "Critical Analysis," 118, 174; *KJ,* 11/2/72; *WP,* 10/31/72.
36. *CR,* 92nd Cong., 2nd sess., 34291–92; *KNS,* 11/2/72; Helene Lecar and Catherine Bell, *William E. Brock III: Republican Senator from Tennessee* (Washington, 1972), 12; "Tennessee: Role of Blacks Is Critical to Senate Race," *Ripon Forum,* 8/15/72, 5; interview with John Seigenthaler, 8/14/82.
37. Adams, "Critical Analysis," 59, 69, 99, 102, 104; *NT,* 11/1/72.
38. Adams, "Critical Analysis," 101, 104, 143–44; *NT,* 11/1, 11/6/72; *NYT,* 10/25/72.

39. Adams, "Critical Analysis," 82, 106, 107, 211–13; *KJ*, 10/25/72 *NYT*, 10/25/72.
40. Adams, "Critical Analysis," 112–13, 286; *NB*, 10/18/74; *NT*, 10/17/74; "Politics: Profiles," *Ripon Forum*, 9/73, 10–14.
41. *KJ*, 10/6/72; *NT*, 10/22/72; *WP*, 10/31/72.
42. *KJ*, 11/2/72; *KNS*, 11/3/72, *WSN*, 11/3/72.
43. Adams, "Critical Analysis," 69, 117; *NT*, 12/12/72; interview with John Seigenthaler, 8/14/82.
44. Pierce, *Border South States*, 346.
45. *NYT*, 2/22/73.

Chapter 5

1. Hildenbrand Oral History, 148.
2. *CR*, 93rd Cong., 1st sess., 3555, 3831–46; Sam J. Ervin Jr., *The Whole Truth: The Watergate Conspiracy* (New York, 1980), 18, 20.
3. Memories here differ. Scott recalled Baker volunteering. Baker does not remember volunteering, and Hugh Branson, his top aide, recalls "a great deal of internal discussion" about him taking the job. Interviews with HHB, 2/9/87, and Hugh D. Scott Jr., 6/21/82; telephone interview with J. Hugh Branson, 10/1/90.
4. Telephone interview with J. Hugh Branson, 10/1/90; *Chi T*, 3/5/73; *CR*, 93rd Cong., 1st sess., 16097; Dick Dabney, *A Good Man: The Life of Sam J. Ervin* (Boston, 1976), 263; *NYT*, 4/2/73; *NME*, 128.
5. Alexander, *Steps*, 33; telephone interview with J. Hugh Branson, 10/1/90; Timothy Crouse, "Senators, Sandbaggers and Soap Operas," *Rolling Stone*, 11/22/73, 36; Ervin, *Whole Truth*, 22–23; *Hearings before the Select Committee on Presidential Campaign Activities of the United States Senate*, 93rd Cong., 1st sess., 986–88, 1240–44; *NYT*, 4/9/73; "The Man Who Keeps Asking Why," *Time*, 7/9/73, 19–20; Thompson, *At That Point*, 3–4, 1213.
6. Donald G. Sanders, "Watergate Reminisces," in *Memory in American History*, ed. David Thelen (Bloomington, Ind., 1990), 101; Thompson, *At That Point*, 12.
7. Telephone interviews with Donald G. Sanders, 1/18/93, and J. Hugh Branson, 10/1/90; interview with Sam J. Ervin Jr., 5/27/81; *NME*, 128–30; *Watergate Hearings*, 988.
8. Telephone interview with J. Hugh Branson, 10/1/90; transcripts of 2/28/73 conversation of Nixon and Dean and 3/22/73 conversation of Nixon, Ehrlichman, Dean, Mitchell and Kleindienst, *The White House Transcripts* (New York, 1974), 76, 90, 200–201; *NME*, 130.
9. *Chi T*, 3/25/73; *CQ*, 3/24/73, 654; Samuel Dash, *Chief Counsel: Inside the Ervin Committee—The Untold Story of Watergate* (New York, 1976), 67–68; John D. Ehrlichman, *Witness to Power: The Nixon Years* (New York, 1982), 376; interview with Sam J. Ervin Jr., 5/27/81; Ervin, *Whole Truth*, 67; *NYT*, 3/16, 3/19/73; *WP*, 3/16/73.
10. Dash, *Chief Counsel*, 34–42; Ervin, *Whole Truth*, 59; Thompson, *At That Point*, 15–18.

11. Dash, *Chief Counsel*, 49–51; Thompson, *At That Point*, 22–24.
12. Telephone transcripts, Conversations of John D. Ehrlichman and HHB, 4/13/73 and John D. Ehrlichman and George Bush, 4/12/73, Box 28, Ehrlichman Papers, NP; Goldwater; *LAT*, 4/14/73; *WP*, 4/18/73.
13. *NME*, 128; *Watergate Hearings*, 4–6.
14. Telephone interview with J. Hugh Branson, 10/1/90; Dash, *Chief Counsel*, 102; *KNS*, 5/18/73; *Watergate Hearings*, 55–56.
15. "Man Who Keeps Asking Why," 19–20; *NT*, 6/10/73; Thompson, *At That Point*, 51; *WP*, 6/4/73; *Watergate Hearings*, 307, 337, 365.
16. *Watergate Hearings*, 646–52, 813, 815–17.
17. Dash, *Chief Counsel*, 106–10, 114–19; John W. Dean III, *Blind Ambition: The White House Years* (New York, 1976), 286; interviews with Fred D. Thompson, 8/6/82, and Daniel Inouye, 5/11/93; telephone interview with Terry F. Lenzner, 9/21/90; Thompson, *At That Point*, 60–62.
18. Dash had provided each member with such a summary before the committee voted to grant immunity to E. Howard Hunt and Jeb Magruder. Dash, *Chief Counsel*, 117; interview with Fred D. Thompson, 8/6/90.
19. Dash, *Chief Counsel*, 111–20; Thompson, *At That Point*, 61–62.
20. Baker and Nixon met only three times from the committee's inception until Dean's appearance. The president and vice-chairman did not meet after February 22 until May 1. Nixon, in receiving Baker at a state dinner for West German Chancellor Willy Brandt, asked him when the hearings would begin. After Baker replied, "Soon," Nixon commented, "good." A month and a half later, Howard, Joy, and Cissy Baker flew with Nixon on Air Force One to Pekin, Illinois, for the dedication of the cornerstone of the Everett McKinley Dirksen Congressional Leadership Research Center. The two did not confer in flight or on the ground. In fact, it was Cissy and not Howard Baker who posed arm-in-arm on stage with Nixon. *KNS*, 6/23/73; *NYT*, 6/16/73; Dash, *Chief Counsel*, 154–55; Dean, *Blind Ambition*, 326; interview with Ron McMahan, 7/27/82; Thompson, *At That Point*, 66.
21. Dash, *Chief Counsel*, 155–58. Very likely, Dean's lawyers leaked the honeymoon story to give Dean an excuse not to meet further with Thompson and Baker. "When he laid out his statement," Thompson later said, "the day of his testimony, it was the first time any of us had seen it. For everybody else, we had . . . prepared our questions. So it was very smart strategy . . . , but if there were any immoral overtones, it cut the other way"; interview with Fred D. Thompson, 8/6/90.
22. Ervin, *Whole Truth*, 62; James Hamilton, *The Power to Probe: A Study of Congressional Investigations* (New York, 1976), 273; telephone transcript, Conversation of John D. Ehrlichman and Sam J. Ervin Jr., 4/2/73, Box 28, Ehrlichman Papers, NP.
23. *KNS*, 6/22/73; *NYT*, 6/24/73; interview with Hugh D. Scott Jr., 6/21/82; Thompson, *At That Point*, 65; *WP*, 6/13/73.
24. *Watergate Hearings*, 991–1020, 1465–67.
25. HB in *Capitol Notebook*; James Cannon, *Time and Chance: Gerald Ford's Appointment with History* (New York, 1994), 176; Dash, *Chief Counsel*, 154; *NYT*,

6/29/73; Squires, "HB: What Are You?" 32; Thompson, *At That Point*, 66; *Watergate Hearings*, 1503–4.

26. Michael J. Mansfield to the author, 10/22/92; *Watergate Hearings*, 1507.
27. Lydon, "Ambivalent Baker," 11; Thompson, *At That Point*, 73; *Watergate Hearings*, 1653, 1828–33.
28. The meeting was never held. Dash, Chief *Counsel*, 67–68; Thompson, *At That Point*, 170–71.
29. Dash, *Chief Counsel*, 178–83; Ervin, *Whole Truth*, 209–10; Hamilton, *Power to Probe*, 27.
30. *NYT*, 7/26, 7/31, 8/1/73; Thompson, *At That Point*, 104–5.
31. Interview with Daniel Inouye, 5/11/93; *LAT*, 8/2/73; *Watergate Hearings*, 2263.
32. "Frying Fish with the Folks at Home," *Time*, 8/27/73, 16–18; *KNS*, 8/4/73; *NB*, 7/5/73.
33. *CT*, 6/21, 7/29/73; *Chi T*, 7/20, 8/5/73; *CR*, 93rd Cong., 1st sess., 19797; *CSM*, 7/28/73; *KNS*, 7/23/73; *NYT*, 5/21, 9/13/73; *WP*, 8/2, 30/73; Shearer, "HB: Caught In Middle," 4–8; "The Newest Daytime Drama," *Time*, 5/28/73, 22.
34. *CQ*, 10/13/73, 2782; *The Senate Watergate Report: The Final Report of the Senate Select Committee on Presidential Campaign Activities, Volume I* (New York, 1974), 315–16; *Watergate Hearings*, 4986–94.
35. Ervin, *Whole Truth*, 223, 229; Theodore H White, *Breach of Faith: The Fall of Richard Nixon* (New York, 1975), 335–36.
36. Interview with Sam J. Ervin Jr., 5/27/81; Ervin, *Whole Truth*, 232, 236–38.
37. J. Anthony Lukas, *Nightmare: The Underside of the Nixon Years* (New York, 1976), 391.
38. Dash, *Chief Counsel*, 213; Alexander M. Haig Jr. with Charles McCarry, *Inner Circles: How America Changed the World, A Memoir* (New York, 1992), 419–20; *LAT*, 10/21/73.
39. *CR*, 93rd Cong., 1st sess., 35300, 41023–27.
40. Interview with Edward Brooke, 11/11/92; Memo, Bill Timmons to Richard M. Nixon, 11/15/73, Box 23, President's Office Files, Nixon Project; "Mr. Nixon Comes Out Fighting," *Newsweek*, 11/26/73, 27.
41. Memo, Timmons to Nixon, 11/15/73; *LAT*, 11/16/73.
42. *CQ Almanac: 1974* (Washington, 1975), 613–17; *CQ*, 3/30/74, 855; *CR*, 93rd Cong., 1st sess., 26600; 93rd Cong., 2nd sess., 8202–5, 8774, 9552–55; *WP*, 3/28/74; *WSN*, 9/30/73.
43. *CR*, 93rd Cong., 2nd sess., 8202–5.
44. Conferees later removed this amendment.
45. Conferees did restrict public financing to the presidential election. *CQ Almanac 1974*, 613–27, 18-S-20-S; *CR*, 93rd Cong., 2nd sess., 9537, 9552–55, 9781, 9790, 9799.
46. Interview with Howard Liebengood, 1/25/89; Thompson, *At That Point*, 146–49.
47. *WSN*, 1/20/74.
48. *Chi T*, 4/25/74; Thompson, *At That Point*, 151–62, 169, 171.

49. H. R. Haldeman with Joseph diMona, *The Ends of Power* (New York, 1978), 54; Thompson, *At That Point*, 172–74.
50. *CT*, 1/8/74; interview with Howard Liebengood, 1/25/89.
51. *Chi T*, 3/31/74; *NYT*, 3/28/74; *Senate Watergate Report*, 732–61; "Some Foolish Mistakes," *Time*, 7/15/74, 19; interviews with Howard Liebengood, 1/25/89, and Fred D. Thompson, 8/6/90.
52. Dash, *Chief Counsel*, 248, 250; Thompson, *At That Point*, 248.
53. Interview with HHB, 2/9/87; telephone interview with J. Hugh Branson, 10/1/90; *CQ*, 5/11/74, 1161; Thompson, *At That Point*, 260; *WP*, 8/8/74.
54. Stanley Kutler, *The Wars of Watergate* (New York, 1990), 344–45; Lukas, *Nightmare*, 391; interviews with Howard Liebengood, 1/25/89, and Fred D. Thompson, 8/6/82.
55. Telephone interviews with Terry F. Lenzner, 9/21/90, and George S. McGovern, 10/22/92; *WSJ*, 23 October 1979.
56. Interview with Sam J. Ervin Jr., 5/27/81; Ervin, *Whole Truth*, 25, 57.
57. Interview with Sam J. Ervin Jr., 5/27/81; Ervin, *Whole Truth*, 24–25; Kutler, *Wars of Watergate*, 345.

Chapter 6

1. *Chi T*, 10/13/73; memo, Raymond Price to Richard Nixon, 10/11/73, Folder 7, Box 169, President's Personal Files, NP; "Picking a New Number Two," *Time*, 9/17/73, 16, 21; "Should Agnew Quit: A *Newsweek* Poll," 10/1/73, 27.
2. *CQ Almanac 1973*, 46-S-47-S, 88-S, 92-S-93-S; *CR*, 93rd Cong., 1st sess., 24323, 37361, 41646–49; 93rd Cong., 2nd sess., 1139, 3434; *KJ*, 8/3/72.
3. *CQ Almanac 1973*, 440–43; *CR*, 93rd Cong., 1st sess., 1886, 2979, 6101, 6431–32, 7894–7900, 7938, 22083, 27195, 27200–27203; *LAT*, 3/15/73; *NYT*, 5/29, 8/14/73; *WP*, 3/14, 3/15, 3/16, 6/26, 8/14/73.
4. HHB with Netherton, *Big South Fork*, 25; *Chi T*, 7/3/77; *CR*, 92nd Cong., 2nd sess., 8224; 93rd Cong., 2nd sess., 77, 94, 315, 322; interview with John Sherman Cooper, 6/15/82; *WP*, 3/15/81.
5. HHB, "Undated Address at Wesley College," Dover, Del., and "Keynote Address to the Connecticut Republican Convention," 7/26/74, Hartford, BP; *NT*, 7/5/73, 2/11, 8/11/74.
6. See Ford, *A Time to Heal* (New York, 1979), chap. 3 and 40–41.
7. Boxes 19–21, Robert T. Hartmann Papers, FL; *Chi T*, 8/11/74; *KJ*, 8/15/74; *NB*, 8/14/74; *NT*, 8/13/74.
8. Memo, Patrick J. Buchanan to Gerald R. Ford, 8/12/74, Box 21, Hartmann Papers, FL; *CR*, 93rd Cong., 2nd sess., 29095, 38901; Robert T. Hartmann, *Palace Politics: An Inside Account of the Ford Years* (New York, 1980), 226; *NT*, 8/21/74; *NYT*, 8/8, 8/17, 12/20/74.
9. HHB, "Address before the Michigan Bar Association," 9/11/74, BP; Ford, *Time to Heal*, 158–78; Hartmann, *Palace Politics*, 258; *KJ*, 8/27/74; *LAT*, 9/10/74.

10. *Chi T*, 9/30/74; *CR*, 93rd Cong., 2nd sess., 31777, 33479; 94th Cong., 1st sess., 961; *NB*, 8/23/75; *NT*, 11/11/74, 1/5/75; *NME*, 36; Thompson, *At That Point*, chaps. 6–7.
11. William Colby with Peter Forbath, *Honorable Men: My Life in the CIA* (New York, 1978), 391; *CR*, 94th Cong., 1st sess., 1420–25; *NB*, 1/22/75; *NT*, 1/14/75; *NYT*, 9/20/74, 1/28/75.
12. Colby, *Honorable Men*, 324; interview with Howard Liebengood, 1/25/89; *NB*, 6/11/75; *NYT*, 1/5, 2/2/75; *WP*, 3/27/75.
13. Interview with HHB, 2/9/87; telephone interviews with Gary W. Hart, 8/15/91, and Walter F. Mondale, 2/19/93; *CR*, 94th Cong., 2nd sess., 1452–53, 4754; *KJ*, 4/1/78; *LAT*, 5/25/76; *NB*, 9/18/75, 4/27/76; *NYT*, 1/5/75, 8/10/76.
14. *CQ*, 5/1/76, 1025; 5/22/76, 1266; *CR*, 94th Cong., 2nd sess., 1452–53, 4754; *NYT*, 1/22, 4/27/76.
15. *Chi T*, 5/1/75; *WP*, 5/6/75.
16. *CQ Almanac 1975*, 80-S-81-S; *CR*, 94th Cong., 1st sess., 853, 5781–83, 11359, 18548, 23356–63, 42064; *Extension of the Appalachian Regional Development Act: Hearings before the Subcommittee on Economic Development of the Public Works Committee of the United States Senate*, 94th Cong., 1st sess., 4–9.
17. *LAT*, 3/16/75; interview with Ron McMahan, 7/27/82; *NB*, 4/21/75; *NYT*, 2/3/75; *WP*, 2/5/75; *WS*, 3/19/75.
18. *CQ*, 7/5/75, 1447; *NB*, 7/10/75; *WS*, 8/1/75.
19. Ford, *Time to Heal*, 334, 344.
20. Lou Cannon, *Reagan* (New York, 1982), 213; Memo, PFC to Gerald R. Ford, 2/28/76, Richard B. Cheney Papers, FL; *NT*, 2/7/76; *Ripon Forum*, 2/15/76, 8; Jules Witcover, *Marathon: The Pursuit of the Presidency, 1972–1976* (New York, 1977), 401–22, 438–54.
21. Memos, Brad Hays and John Davis to Rogers C. B. Morton, Stuart Spencer and Ed Terrell, 4/6/76, Box C4, PFC Papers; PFC to Gerald R. Ford, 4/6/76, Box 15, Cheney Papers, and Rogers C. B. Morton to Ford, Box 5, Rogers C. B. Morton Papers and Letter, HB to Rogers C. B. Morton, 4/28/76, Box C11, PFC Papers, FL; *Chi T*, 5/24/76; *CQ*, 5/8/76, 1085–86; Ford, *Time to Heal*, 387; *LAT*, 5/21/76; *NB*, 5/14, 5/26/76; *NYT*, 5/15/76; *WP*, 5/21, 5/31/76.
22. *NB*, 5/26/76; *NYT*, 5/22/76; Witcover, *Marathon*, 455–56.
23. *CQ*, 5/29/76, 1329; *NB*, 5/26/76.
24. Gerald R. Ford to HHB, 5/27/76, HHB File, President's Political Files, FL; *NB*,5/28/76; *WP*,6/26/76; *WS*, 6/12/76; Witcover, *Marathon*, 456–57, 461–68.
25. *Chi T*, 8/16, 8/17/76; *NB*, 8/10, 8/16/76; *NYT*, 8/17/76.
26. *Chi T*, 7/6/76; Ron Nessen, *It Sure Looks Different from the Inside* (New York, 1978), 239; Witcover, *Marathon*, 509–10.
27. Notes of 8/11, 8/13/76, Box 64, Philip Buchen Papers, FL; *NB*, 8/18/76; *WS*, 8/19/76.
28. *Chi T*, 8/18/76, 4/8/79; telephone interview with Cissy Baker, 11/25/83; *WP*, 4/26/93; *WS*, 5/28/73, 8/19/76.

29. Telephone interview with Cissy Baker, 11/25/83; *Chi T*, 4/8/79; Margaret McManus, "Joy Dirksen Baker: The Senate Has Been Her Home, but She Wants the White House," *Detroit News Magazine*, 3/19/78, 10; *WP*, 8/29/76.
30. See Box 5, President's Political Files, FL; *KJ*, 8/13, 8/14, 8/17/76; *NB*, 8/10/76; *NT*, 8/15, 8/16/76; *NYT*, 8/10, 8/15/76; *WP*, 8/11/76.
31. *Chi T*, 8/16/76; *KJ*, 8/19, 8/20/76; *NT*, 8/9, 8/15/76; *NYT*, 7/21/76.
32. HHB, "Keynote Address to the Republican Convention," 8/16/76, videotape, Vanderbilt University Library, Nashville; "Baker's Address," *CQ*, 8/21/76, 2310–12.
33. Baker, keynote videotape; *Chi T*, 8/17–8/19/76; *NB*, 8/17–8/19/76; *NT*, 8/17–8/19/76.
34. For material on the Hooper nomination, see Box 9, William T. Kendall Papers, FL. *Chi T*, *New York Daily News*, 8/18/76; *WP*, 8/18/76; Drew, *American Journal*, 404; *LAT*, 8/20/76; Witcover, *Marathon*, 538.
35. *NB*, 8/18/76; *NT*, 8/19/76; *WS*, 8/19/76.
36. David Hume Kennerly, *Shooter* (New York, 1979), 214; "The Dole Decision," *Time*, 8/30/76, 22–23.
37. Telephone interview with Robert P. Griffin, 7/31/90; interview with Paul Laxalt, 5/16/90; Ford, *Time to Heal*, 399–400; Nessen, *It Sure Looks Different*, 236; Witcover, *Marathon*, 536.
38. Telephone interview with Robert P. Griffin, 7/31/90; interview with John G. Tower, 7/6/82; Ford, *Time to Heal*, 401–3; Nessen, *It Sure Looks Different*, 238; Martin Schram, *Running for President: A Journal of the Carter Campaign* (New York, 1977), 262–63; Witcover, *Marathon*, 538.
39. Telephone interviews with James Cannon, 7/15/94, and Robert P. Griffin, 7/31/90; Ford, *Time to Heal*, 78, 403–4; interview with John G. Tower, 7/6/82; Thomas Kean, *The Politics of Inclusion* (New York, 1988), 28; *NB*, 12/2/76; videotape, Dan Rather report on CBS convention coverage, 8/19/76, Vanderbilt library.
40. Interview with Sam J. Ervin Jr., 5/27/81, and John Seigenthaler, 8/14/82; telephone interview with Walter F. Mondale, 2/19/93; Herman E. Talmadge with Mark Royden Winchell, *Talmadge: A Political Legacy, A Politician's Life* (Atlanta, 1987), 264.
41. *MCA*, 8/18/76; interview with John Seigenthaler, 8/14/82; Tolchin, "HB: Trying to Tame Senate," 75.
42. *KJ*, 8/20/76; *LAT*, 8/20/76; *MCA*, 8/20/76; *NB*, 8/20/76; "Some Soared and Some Sank," *Time*, 8/30/76, 37.

Chapter 7

1. *Chi T*, 10/21/76; Malcolm MacDougall, *We Almost Made It* (New York, 1977), 140; Memo, James Field to Gerald R. Ford, 9/13/76, Box 16, Cheney Papers; Memo, Max Friedersdorf to Richard B. Cheney and James A. Baker, III, 10/11/76, Box C4, PFC Papers, FL; *NT*, 9/14/76; *NYT*, 9/14, 9/23/76.

2. "Brock v. Sasser," *Time*, 10/18/76, 39–40; Larry Daughtrey, "Tennessee," *New Republic*, 10/30/76, 19; *NB*, 10/29/76; *NT*, 10/30/76; *NYT*, 11/4/76; *Politics in America* (Washington, 1979), 289–90; interview with Don Sundquist, 11/15/89.
3. *NB*, 11/5/76; *WP*, 11/5/76; *NT*, 11/6, 11/14/76; interview with Robert W. Packwood, 1/13/93.
4. Daniel L. Balz, "The Senate's Robert Byrd and Robert Griffin: Whipping Their Way to the Leadership," *NJ*, 12/25/76, 1806–7; interviews with Pete Domenici, 7/16/90, Edward Brooke, 11/11/92, and Hugh D. Scott Jr., 6/21/82; telephone interview with Robert P. Griffin, 7/31/90; *Chi T*, 1/2/77; *NB*, 1/7/77; *NT*, 12/20/76; *NYT*, 11/13/76, 1/5/77, 1/6/77.
5. Interview with Pete Domenici, 7/16/90; *NT*, 1/5/77; *NYT*, 1/5, 1/6/77; *WS*, 1/7/77.
6. Telephone interview with J. Hugh Branson, 10/1/90; Peter Goldman with John J. Lindsay and Henry W. Hubbard, "The New Kings of the Hill," *Newsweek*, 1/17/77, 16–18; *KJ*, 1/5/77; *NYT*, 1/6/77.
7. HHB, "The View"; *Chi T*, 1/5/77; *NB*, 1/4/77; Goldman, "New Kings of the Hill," 16–18; *NYT*, 1/6/77.
8. Telephone interview with J. Hugh Branson, 10/1/90; *Chi T*, 1/11/77; *NT*, 1/9/77; *NYT*, 1/5, 1/6/77; Richard Zetterli, *Orrin Hatch: Challenging the Republican Establishment* (Chicago, 1982), 76.
9. *CR*, 95th Cong., 1st sess., 4386–88, 14651; *NYT*, 1/5, 3/28/77.
10. HHB, "News Release," 2/9/77, BP; *CR*, 95th Cong., 1st sess., 14651; Hildenbrand Oral History, 68; Jacob K. Javits with Rafael Steinberg, *Javits: The Autobiography of a Public Man* (Boston, 1981), 269–70; Michael J. Malbin, "The Senate Republican Leaders—Life without a President," *NJ*, 5/21/77, 776–80; Tom Matthews with John J. Lindsay, "Baker Does the Hustle," *Newsweek*, 7/4/77, 14–15; interviews with Russell Long, 11/11/92, and Ted Stevens, 6/24/82.
11. Matthews et al., "Baker Does Hustle," 14–15; Malbin, "Senate Republican Leaders," 776–80; *NB*, 2/9/77; *NYT*, 1/5/77; *NME*, 142–43; *WS*, 4/20/77.
12. Interviews with Carol Browning and James Frierson, 6/21/82; *NB*, 3/28/77; *WP*, 6/4/77.
13. Interview with HHB, 2/9/87; Jimmy Carter, *Keeping Faith: Memoirs of a President* (New York, 1982), 67; Betty Glad, *Jimmy Carter: In Search of the Great White House* (New York, 1980), chap. 21, 414–19; *NB*, 4/28/77; *NYT*, 3/29/77; "Party Outlook in Congress: 'A Very Significant Gain,' Interview with Senator HHB of Tennessee," *US News*, 8/20/77, 23.
14. Glad, *Carter*, 414–19; *NYT*, 1/16, 1/17, 1/18/77.
15. Victor Lasky, *Jimmy Carter: The Man and the Myth* (New York, 1979), 332–33; *NYT*, 1/18/77.
16. *CQ*, 2/26/77, 348–49; 3/5/77, 405; 3/12/77, 431; telephone interview with Frank Moore, 3/14/91; *NYT*, 2/12, 3/10/77.
17. Baker later concluded that his vote had been a mistake, as department regulations served to retard rather than expedite the production of standard forms

of energy and the development of alternative sources. HHB, "News Release," 2/9/77; *CQ Almanac 1977,* 24-S; *CR,* 95th Cong., 1st sess., 475, 1463, 14930, 15199, 15744–49; 95th Cong., 2nd sess., S1818; *NB,* 3/1/77; Reeves, "Why HB Is Leaving the Senate," 11.

18. Carter, *Keeping Faith,* 101; *CQ Almanac 1977,* 683–84, 693–96; *CR,* 95th Cong., 1st sess., 8961, 20753, 22184–86, 22242, 22349, 24843; *NYT,* 5/26/77; "Statement by Senators HHB, Clifford P. Hansen and James R. Sasser," 1/26/77, BP.
19. *NYT,* 6/10, 9/3, 9/12, 9/16, 9/22/77; *WP,* 6/10/77.
20. *CQ,* 8/6/77, 1635; *CQ Almanac 1977,* 534; *LAT,* 8/2/77; *NYT,* 8/2/77; *WT,* 8/2/77.
21. *CQ,* 7/30/77, 1617; *CQ Almanac 1977,* 48-S-50-S; *CR,* 95th Cong., 1st sess., 23066, 24651–58; Javits, *Javits,* 269–70; *NYT,* 7/30, 8/2, 8/3/77.
22. *CQ,* 8/6/77, 1634; *NME,* 29.
23. Carter, *Keeping Faith,* 100; *CQ Almanac 1977,* 53-S-56-S, 58-S-64-S, 75-S, 83-S; *CR,* 95th Cong., 1st sess., 30809, 31927; *NME,* 30–32.
24. Carter, *Keeping Faith,* 101; Glad, *Carter,* 422; *NYT,* 10/14/77.
25. *CQ Almanac 1977,* 33-S; *CQ,* 6/18/77, 1204; *CR,* 95th Cong., 1st sess., 18420, 19444; Glad, *Carter,* 421; Cyrus Vance, *Hard Choices: Critical Years in America's Foreign Policy* (New York, 1983), 129–32.
26. HHB, "Address to the World Jewish Congress," 11/1/77, Washington, D.C., BP; *NYT,* 7/1, 11/2/77; *WP,* 7/1, 11/2/77.
27. Carter, *Keeping Faith,* 81; CQ, 7/2/77, 1354; 12/10/77, 2577; *CR,* 95th Cong., 1st sess., 9605, 37925, 38849; 95th Cong., 2nd sess., S993–94; interview with Ron McMahan, 7/27/82; *NB,* 3/25, 7/1/77; *NYT,* 11/14/77; WP, 12/3/77.
28. Interviews with Tom Beasley, 8/3/82; telephone interviews with Russell Long, 11/11/92, and George S. McGovern, 10/22/92.

Chapter 8

1. Stephen R. Graubard, *Burke, Disraeli and Churchill: The Politics of Perseverance* (Cambridge, Mass., 1961), 49; Walter LaFeber, *The Panama Canal: The Crisis in Historical Perspective* (New York, 1978), viii, 191–92; Witcover, *Marathon,* 429.
2. *CSM,* 10/25/77; John F. Kennedy, *Profiles in Courage* (New York, 1956), 21.
3. Robert C. Byrd, *The Senate, 1789–1989: Addresses on the History of the United States Senate* (Washington, 1989), 1:534, 557; Walter Isaacson and Evan Thomas, *The Wise Men: Six Friends and the World They Made* (New York, 1986), 399–400, 409–10, 424–28, 450; Arthur H. Vandenberg Jr., ed., *The Private Papers of Senator Vandenberg* (Boston, 1952), 135.
4. HHB, "The View"; telephone interview with Russell Long, 11/11/92; Carter, *Keeping Faith,* 159; *CR,* 90th Cong., 1st sess., 29682; 93rd Cong., 2nd sess., 8832–33; LaFeber, *Panama Canal,* 191–92; Sol M. Linowitz, *The Making of a Public Man* (Boston, 1985), 185; *NME,* 194–95; *NT,* 3/20/78; *WP,* 3/20/78.
5. Denison Kitchel, *The Truth About the Panama Canal* (New Rochelle, 1978), 58, 70; LaFeber, *Panama Canal,* viii, 119.

6. Kitchel, *Truth About Canal*, 118, 120–24; LaFeber, *Panama Canal*, 137–42, 160–64, 168, 170–74, 182, 195, 198–201, 211.
7. LaFeber, *Panama Canal*, 150–57.
8. Kitchel, *Truth About Canal*, 25–26; LaFeber, *Panama Canal*, 182–95.
9. Carter, *Keeping Faith*, 158–59; LaFeber, *Panama Canal*, 204–6, 209–14; "Texts of Canal Treaties That Were Initialed by Panama and the U.S. in Washington," in *Surrender in Panama: The Case Against the Treaty*, ed. Philip M. Crane (New York, 1978), 178–206; Vance, *Hard Choices*, 147.
10. HHB, "The View"; Carter, *Keeping Faith*, 161; *Chi T*, 8/21/77; *CQ*, 8/13/77, 1741; *LAT*, 9/13/77; *WP*, 9/12, 9/13/77, 3/19/78.
11. Interview with Lloyd C. Daugherty Jr., 6/3/81; *CQ*, 9/24/77, 2033; *NB*, 9/6/77; *NYT*, 1/9/78; Richard A. Viguerie, *The New Right: We're Ready to Lead* (Falls Church, Va., 1981), 65–68.
12. Carter, *Keeping Faith*, 161; *Chi T*, 8/21/77; *CR*, 95th Cong., 1st sess., 37317–18; 95th Cong., 2nd sess., 5138–39; Alan Crawford, *Thunder on the Right: The "New Right" and the Politics of Resentment* (New York, 1980), 90, 181–82; William Jorden, *Panama Odyssey* (Austin, 1984), 698–701; "Senator Baker Walks on Water," *Economist*, 1/14/78, 25–26.
13. *CR*, 95th Cong., 1st sess., 30788; *Thunder*, 89–90; *NYT*, 9/6/77; *WP*, 9/18/77.
14. Interview with Tom Beasley, 8/3/82; *CSM*, 10/25/77; Letter, Will T. Cheek to Bill Hamby, 9/11/77, BP.
15. Telephone interview with James Cannon, 7/15/94; interview with Ron McMahan, 7/27/82; *NME*, 185; *NYT*, 11/9/77; *WP*, 9/12, 9/18/77.
16. "Address of Dr. Romulo Escobar Bethancourt, Head of the Panamanian Negotiating Team before the National Assembly of Panama," 8/19/77, in Crane, *Surrender in Panama*, 228–36; HHB, "The View"; interview with Ron McMahan, 7/27/82; HHB, "Address to the Southern Baptist Convention," 3/27/78, BP; Ken Bode, "The Hero of Panama," *New Republic*, 1/21/78, 14; *Chi T*, 9/25/77; *CQ*, 10/15/77, 2218; *KJ*, 7/21/78; LaFeber, *Panama Canal*, 224; *NYT*, 9/27/77; Rattner, "Cool Candidate," 104; Vance, *Hard Choices*, 148.
17. HHB, "News Releases," 10/6/77, BP; memo, Douglas L. Bennet Jr., Robert Beckel, and Robert Thompson to Hamilton Jordan and Frank Moore, 12/1/77, Box FO-15, White House Central Files, Carter Library, Atlanta; *LAT*, 10/9/77; *NYT*, 10/12/77; Vance, *Hard Choices*, 149–50.
18. Carter, *Keeping Faith*, 162; *CR*, 95th Cong., 1st sess., 37317–18; LaFeber, *Panama Canal*, 216; interview with Hugh D. Scott Jr., 6/21/82; Vance, *Hard Choices*, 150–51; *WP*, 10/23/77.
19. *CR*, 95th Cong., 2nd sess., S3847; *NT*, 1/10/78; *NYT*, 3/19/78; *WP*, 3/19/78; *NME*, 185–86.
20. Undated, unsigned mass mailed petition, BP.
21. *CT*, 1/8/78; *WS*, 1/16/78.
22. Interview with Jake Garn, 4/19/90; Frederick Kempe, *Divorcing the Dictator: America's Bungled Affair with Noriega* (New York, 1990), 77; telephone interview with Frank Moore, 3/14/91.

23. Interview with Jake Garn, 4/19/90, and Howard Liebengood, 4/2/91; telephone interview with Frank Moore, 3/14/91; Kempe, *Divorcing the Dictator,* 77.
24. HHB, "The View"; Garn; *NME,* 187.
25. HHB, "Press Conference," 1/16/78, The White House, and HHB, John Chafee and Jake Garn, "Press Conference," 1/7/78, Panama City, Panama, BP; *Chi T,* 1/11/78; *CR,* 95th Cong., 2nd sess., S3847; Hildenbrand Oral History, 254; *NYT,* 1/13, 1/14/78; "Squaring Off on the Canal," *Time,* 1/30/78, 31; Vance, *Hard Choices,* 147; *WP,* 1/10, 1/17/78.
26. Other Republicans involved in the pro-treaty lobby included Ford administration officials Philip Buchen, William Coleman, John O. Marsh, and Brent Scowcroft; Nixon aides Peter Flanagan, Peter Peterson, and Joseph Sisco; former Senators John Sherman Cooper and Henry Cabot Lodge and former Congressmen Peter Frelinghuysen and William Maillard. HHB, "Press Conference," 3/16/78, BP; "Baker Asked to Step Aside on the Canal Issue: GOP Congressmen Send Open Letter," *HE,* 2/25/78, 5; Carter, *Keeping Faith,* 162, 167; Clifford, "Relief for HB," 22; *CNFP,* 2/8/78; *CR,* 95th Cong., 1st sess., 37317–18; interviews with Lloyd C. Daugherty Jr., 6/3/81, Orrin Hatch, 3/20/90, and Paul Laxalt, 5/16/90; *KJ,* 1/12, 1/16/78; *LAT,* 1/11/78; *NB,* 2/1/78; *NT,* 2/13/78.
27. "Baker Asked to Step Aside," 5; *CQ,* 2/4/78, 316–18; *CR,* 95th Cong., 2nd sess., S1407, S1633; *NYT,* 1/26, 2/3/78; "Opening the Great Debate," *Time,* 2/20/78, 19.
28. Richard Boeth, John J. Lindsay, Hal Bruno, Thomas M. DeFrank, and Eleanor Clift, "Panama: A Big Win," *Newsweek,* 3/27/78, 42; *KJ,* 3/27/78; *NYT,* 3/19/78; *WP,* 3/19/78.
29. HHB, "Address to the People of Tennessee on the Panama Canal Treaties," 2/7/78, Nashville, BP; *NYT,* 2/10/78.
30. *CR,* 95th Cong., 2nd sess., S3501; NT, 2/15, 16/78; *WS,* 2/15, 16/78.
31. *CQ Almanac 1978,* 7-S-12-S; Vance, *Hard Choices,* 153.
32. Boeth, "Panama: A Big Win," 42–49; interview with Edward Brooke, 11/11/92; telephone interview with Frank Moore, 3/14/91; Carter, *Keeping Faith,* 165, 169; "Carter Wins on Panama," *Time,* 3/27/78, 8–11; *CR,* 95th Cong., 2nd sess., S5132–39; *NYT,* 3/12, 17/78; Vance, *Hard Choices,* 153.
33. Boeth, "Panama: A Big Win," 42–45; interview with Edward Brooke, 11/11/92; Carter, *Keeping Faith,* 11, 165–73; "Carter Wins," 8–11; *CR,* 95th Cong., 2nd sess., S6546–47; telephone interview with William F. Hildenbrand, 4/9/91; Vance, *Hard Choices,* 152–54; *WS,* 3/17/78.
34. HHB, "3/16/78 Press Conference," *NB,* 3/28/78; *NYT,* 3/17, 3/19/78; *WP,* 3/17, 3/19/78.
35. Carter, *Keeping Faith,* 174–75; *CQ Almanac 1978,* 19-S-21-S; "How the Treaty Was Saved," *Time,* 5/1/78, 13–14; *NYT,* 3/18/78.
36. Richard Boeth, John J. Lindsay, Eleanor Clift, Jane Whitmore and Ron Moreau, "Victory on the Canal," *Newsweek,* 5/1/78, 23–25; Carter, *Keeping Faith,* 175–77; *Chi T,* 4/5/78; "How Treaty Was Saved," 12–14; telephone interview with Russell Long, 11/11/92; *NYT,* 4/6, 4/7/78.

37. *CQ*, 4/22/78, 952; telephone interviews with Hamilton Jordan, 3/9/91, and Frank Moore, 3/14/91.
38. *CQ*, 5/20/78, 1263; *CR*, 95th Cong., 2nd sess., S7374; NYT, 5/18/78; telephone interview with George S. McGovern, 10/22/92; interview with Robert W. Packwood, 1/13/93; WP, 6/22/78.
39. *CQ*, 5/20/78, 1264; "How a Deal was Made—and Unmade," *Time*, 5/29/78, 14–15; *NYT*, 5/24/78; telephone interviews with George S. McGovern, 10/22/92, and Abraham Ribicoff, 10/5/92; "The Fight Over Fighters," *Time*, 5/22/78, 17–19.
40. *CQ*, 5/20/78, 1264; *CR*, 95th Cong., 2nd sess., S7374; "Fight Over Fighters," 17–18; telephone interview with Abraham Ribicoff, 10/5/92.
41. *CQ Almanac 1974*, 74-S; *CR*, 94th Cong., 1st sess., 25158–89; Ford, *Time to Heal*, 137, 199; telephone interview with Frank Moore, 3/14/91.
42. *Chicago Sun-Times*, 8/13/78; *CQ*, 7/29/78, 1919; telephone interviews with George S. McGovern, 10/22/92, and Frank Moore, 3/14/91.
43. *CQ*, 5/13/78, 1170; Richard E. Cohen, "SALT-II—Selling the Treaty to the Senate," *NJ*, 6/16/79, 1997; Jimmy Carter to HHB, 3/22, 5/25, 7/28/78, HB File, President's Political Files, Carter Library.

Chapter 9

1. Telephone interview with George S. McGovern, 10/22/92; Patterson, *Mr. Republican*, 324.
2. Byrd, *Addresses on the History of the Senate*, 1:588; *Chi T*, 12/14/77; Kirk and McClellan, *Principles of Taft*, 73–76; *NYT*, 12/18/77; Patterson, *Mr. Republican*, 262, 304–5, 315–26.
3. *Chi T*, 3/6/78; *CQ*, 5/13/78, 1160; *KJ*, 7/15/78; *KNS*, 5/26, 7/12/78; *NYT*, 5/20/78.
4. HHB, "Address before the National Building and Lumber Materials Dealers Association," 10/12/78; HHB, "Local Government Day Address," 10/26/78, Nashville; HHB and John J. Rhodes, "News Release," 10/5/77, BP; *CR*, 95th Cong., 2nd sess., S5464, S7344–46; *NYT*, 10/6/77, 1/27/78.
5. HHB, "Local Government Day Address"; Joseph Califano, *Governing America: An Insider's Report from the White House and the Cabinet* (New York, 1981), 362; *Chi T*, 12/14/77; *CQ*, 4/29/78, 1064; *CR*, 95th Cong., 2nd sess., S4307, S8138; *KJ*, 3/25/78; *NYT*, 9/3, 12/14, 12/18/77.
6. *KJ*, 5/17/78; *NB*, 8/1, 9/20/77.
7. *CQ*, 2/11/78, 330; 6/17/78,1519; 6/24/78, 1599; *CQ Almanac 1978*, 28-8; *CR*, 95th Cong, 2nd sess., 87535–36, 88162–66; interview with Orrin Hatch, 3/20/90; *KJ*, 6/23/78; *KNS*, 5/22, 6/22/78; *NYT*, 5/25/78.
8. William Bruce Wheeler and Michael J. McDonald, *TVA and the Tellico Dam, 1936–1979: A Bureaucratic Crisis in Post-Industrial America* (Knoxville, 1986), 68–71, 107, 142–43, 156, 173; interview with HHB, 6/24/93; *CQ*, 3/12/77, 453; *CR*, 92nd Cong., 2nd sess., 12343; 95th Cong., 2nd sess., 810900; *NME*, 40–41; Pierce, *Border South States*, 384–85.

9. *CQ*, 3/12/77, 453; *CR*, 95th Cong., 1st sess., 23731; 95th Cong., 2nd sess., S5382, S10900; Elizabeth Drew, *Senator* (New York, 1979), 32–33, 49, 138–42, 151–60; *KJ*, 4/13/78; *KNS*, 7/20/78; *NT*, 2/3/77; *NYT*, 4/7/78; *NME*, 41.
10. *KJ*, 6/9, 6/10/78; *NB*, 6/9, 6/10/78; *WP*, 6/9, 6/10/78.
11. *KJ*, 6/9/78; *KNS*, 6/11, 6/13, 7/9/78; *NB*, 6/10/78; *WP*, 6/10/78; interview with Fred D. Thompson, 8/6/82.
12. *CT*, 4/1 /78; *CQ*, 7/22/78, 1861–63; 8/5/78, 2089; *Jefferson Standard-Banner*, 8/2/78; *KJ*, 7/29, 10/5/78; *KNS*, 5/10, 7/30/78; *NJ*, 7/22/78, 1184.
13. *CQ*, 10/14/78, 2896; *KNS*, 8/14/78; *MPS*, 8/31/78; *NB*, 8/16/78.
14. Goldwater, *With No Apologies*, 184; Kirk and McClellan, *Principles of Taft*, 74–75; Patterson, *Mr. Republican*, 304–5.
15. *CR*, 95th Cong., 2nd sess., S13989, S13993; Barry M. Goldwater with Jack Casserly, *Goldwater* (New York, 1988), 96; *WP*, 8/21/78; *WS*, 8/21–23/78.
16. HHB, "Press Conference at Foreign Press Correspondents Association Luncheon," 6/14/78, Washington, BP; *CT*, 6/12/78; *CR*, 95th Cong., 2nd sess., S6699, S13992; *WS*, 8/21/78.
17. HHB, "Address to the Tennessee Education Association," 9/30/78, Nashville, BP; *CQ Almanac*, 48-8, 62-8; *CR*, 95th Cong., 2nd sess., S3149, S13381.
18. *KJ*, 10/3, 10/5/78; *NB*, 9/28/78; *MPS*, 10/5/78; *WP*, 10/22/78.
19. *CQ Almanac 1977*, 39-8, 75-8, 88-8; *CQ Almanac 1978*, 61-8; *CR*, 95th Cong., 1st sess., 21546; *NB*, 10/9/78; *NME*, 135.
20. *CQ*, 10/14/78, 2896; *KJ*, 6/6, 9/1/78; *LAT*, 11/1/78.
21. Interview with Frances Hooks, 8/14/90.
22. The *Chattanooga News–Free Press* was the only holdout in 1978. While pronouncing Baker preferable to the "dangerously liberal" Jane Eskind, the *News–Free Press* refused him its nod, citing many deviations from conservative orthodoxy, with the most notable being his "support of the surrender of the Panama Canal to a pro-red dictator." *CNFP*, 10/15/78; *LAT*, 11/1/78; *NB*, 11/3/78; *WP*, 10/22/78.
23. *Clarksville Leaf-Chronicle* editorial, quoted in *KNS*, 10/12/78; *Sparta Expositor*, 10/12/78.
24. *Chi T*, 7/3/77; *CQ Almanac 1977*, 646; *CR*, 95th Cong., 1st sess., 18480–81; *KJ*, 10/5/78; *KNS*, 10/1, 10/7, 10/20, 11/2/78; *NB*, 3/15/77, 11/2/78, 11/3/78; "Transcript of 6/14/79 20-20," BP; *WP*, 10/22/78, 4/2/79, 7/22/79.
25. Memo, Frank Moore to Jimmy Carter, 10/13/78, Box TR7, White House Central Files, Carter Library; *KJ*, 10/27/78; *LAT*, 11/1/78.
26. *CNFP*, 10/30/78; *KJ*, 10/31, 11/1, 11/2, 11/3/78; *KNS*, 10/31, 11/1, 11/2, 11/3/78; *NB*, 10/31, 11/1, 11/2, 11/3/78.
27. *KNS*, 11/1/78; *NB*, 11/1/78.
28. *KNS*, 11/8/78; Richard Scammon, *America Votes, 13: A Handbook of Contemporary American Election Statistics* (Washington, 1980), 333–36, 516.
29. Carter, *Keeping Faith*, 224; Richard E. Cohen, "SALT-II—Selling the Treaty to the Senate," *NJ*, 6/16/79, 997; Memo, Frank Moore to Jimmy Carter, 1/13/78, Box FO-I8, White House Central Files, Carter Library; telephone interview with Russell Long, 11/11/92, and Frank Moore, 3/14/91.

30. Carter, *Keeping Faith*, 67, 224; *KNS*, 11/29/78; *MCA*, 2/8/79.
31. *NYT*, 5/10/79; Strobe Talbott, *Endgame: The Inside Story of SALT-II* (New York, 1980), 255; *WP*, 1/7, 1/11, 1/19, 6/6/79.
32. Interview with Jake Garn, 4/19/90; *NME*, 197, 200–203; *OR*, 8/27/79; *WP*, 1/11/79.
33. *NME*, 201–4; *WP*, 1/19/79.
34. HHB, "Lincoln Day Address," 2/13/79; Carter, *Keeping Faith*, 236–37; *MCA*, 2/8/79; *NYT*, 2/4, 2/18, 20/79; *WP*, 2/16/79; *WS*, 2/14/79.
35. William S. Cohen, *Roll Call: One Year in the United States Senate* (New York, 1981), 276; *CQ*, 1/27/79, 178; 5/12/79, 888; 6/16/79, 1143; 7/28/79, 1559; *CR*, 96th Cong., 1st sess., S767, S9627, S12274; *NYT*, 9/14/79.
36. *CQ Almanac 1979*, 10-S-14-S; *CR*, 96th Cong., 1st sess., S555; Tom Dunkel, "For One Law, It's a Jungle Out There," *Insight*, 4/25/93, 7.
37. Interview with HHB, 2/9/87; telephone interview with Frank Moore, 3/14/91; Carter, *Keeping Faith*, 88; *Chi T*, 7/1/79; *CQ*,6/23/79, 1211, 1224; Glad, *Carter*, 437–60; HBOHP, Box 4, Folder 3, Jimmy Carter, 12/11/96, 4, 12, 15; Hugh Sidey, "Proud of Being a Politician," *Time*, 8/13/79, 18; Smith, *Power Game*, 464.
38. *CQ*, 6/23/79, 1224; Peter Goldman, John J. Lindsay, James Doyle, Eleanor Clift, "Bakerizing SALT," *Newsweek*, 6/25/79, 43–44; telephone interview with Gary W. Hart, 8/15/91; *NYT*, 4/12, 5/10, 5/14, 5/17, 6/7/79; *WP*, 6/6, 6/17/79.
39. Carter, *Keeping Faith*, 110–11, 122; White, *America in Search of Itself*, 152, 262–63.
40. "HB: Right for the 80s," 1979 Campaign Pamphlet, Baker Committee; *CQ*, 7/14/79, 1391; *CR*, 96th Cong., 1st sess., S2984; *CSM*, 4/24/79; *LAT*, 5/17/79; Transcript of "Good Morning America," 7/16/79, BP.
41. "HB: Right for the 80s"; *CT*, 6/10/79; *LAT*, 5/17, 7/26/79; *OR*, 8/27/79.
42. Brezhnev did promise to limit Backfire production. Carter responded that America reserved the right to build a similar system, but he had not informed the public that such a bomber was being planned. Carter, *Keeping Faith*, 252.
43. HHB, "White House Press Conference," 6/21/79, Washington, BP; *NYT*, 6/22, 6/24, 6/27/79.
44. 1993 HHB; HHB, "Press Conference," 6/27/79, Washington, D.C., BP; *CSM*, 6/28/79; *NYT*, 6/28/79; Cohen, *Roll Call*, 240; *CQ*, 6/30/79, 1330; *CR*, 96th Cong., 1st sess., S8607–8; *WP*, 6/28/79.
45. Glad, *Carter*, 431; *NYT*, 7/10, 11/79; Edward Rowny, *It Takes One to Tango* (Washington, 1992), 128; *The SALT-II Treaty: Hearings before the Committee on Foreign Relations of the United States Senate*, 96th Cong., 1st sess., pt. 1, 263–65; pt. 3, 190–92.
46. Califano, *Governing America*, 262–65; Carter, *Keeping Faith*, 114–25; Glad, *Carter*, 444–47; Theodore H. White, *America in Search of Itself* (New York, 1982), 266–68.
47. HHB, John J. Rhodes and George F. Will, Transcript of Appearance on "The Energy Program: Other Views, *CBS News Special Report*," 7/18/79, BP; Cali-

fano, *Governing America*, 269; *Chi T*, 8/8/79; *CQ*, 7/21/79, 1437; Germond and Witcover, *Blue Smoke*, 36; White, *America in Search of Itself*, 269.

48. HHB, "Press Conference," 10/2/79, BP; Carter, *Keeping Faith*, 263–64; *CR*, 96th Cong., 1st sess., S11793; S14214–16; *NB*, 10/1/79; *NYT*, 10/2, 10/3/79; Talbott, *Endgame*, 285.
49. *CQ*, 10/20/79, 2317; *NYT*, 10/13/79; *SALT-II Hearings*, Part VI, 74–75, 98–99, 108.
50. *CQ*, 10/27/79, 2387; *LAT* 10/25/79; *NYT*, 10/25/79; *OR*, 8/27/79; *SALT-II Hearings*, Part VI, 253–55.
51. Telephone interviews with Russell Long, 11/11/92, and Frank Moore, 3/14/91; *NYT*, 11/10/79; Rowny, *It Takes One to Tango*, 131; *WP*, 12/21/79.
52. Telephone interviews with James Cannon, 7/15/94, and Lewis R. Donelson III, 6/7/90; MacNeil, *Dirksen*, 1; David McCulloch, *Truman* (New York, 1992), 531.

Chapter 10

1. *LAT*, 1/8/79.
2. *Chi T*, 2/27/79; *NYT*, 3/21/79.
3. *CSM*, 11/29/78; *NB*, 11/28/78; *NYT*, 11/29/78, 3/10/79; *WP*, 3/10, 3/12, 8/12/79.
4. HHB and Richard G. Lugar, "Press Conference," 2/8/79, Washington, BP; *CR*, 96th Cong., 2nd sess., S1277, S1935; John W. Mashek, "HB Takes Aim at Carter's Southern Turf," *US News*, 7/30/79, 51; *WS*, 2/14/79.
5. John Sears, Baker's consultant in his 1978 race, accepted Ronald Reagan's offer to serve as his campaign manager. Stuart Spencer, Gerald Ford's deputy campaign manager in 1976, resisted feelers from Baker so that he could serve as the former president's eyes and ears in 1980. Bill Timmons, Richard Nixon's chief of congressional liaison, likewise declined, opting to develop business for his consulting firm. Interviews with Douglas Bailey, 12/29/82, Tom Beasley, 8/3/82, and Ron McMahan, 7/27/82; Lou Cannon, *Reagan*, (New York, 1982), 237; *WP*, 3/15/79; *WS*, 4/15/79.
6. HHB, John C. Danforth and Richard G. Lugar, "Press Conference," 4/30/79, Washington, D.C., BP; interview with Don Sundquist, 11/15/89; telephone interview with Ted Welch, 8/2/82.
7. HHB, "Addresses at Des Moines and Waterloo, Iowa," 3/17/79, BP; HHB, Lugar and Danforth, "4/30/79 Press Conference"; Lou Cannon and William Peterson, "GOP" in Richard Harwood, ed., *The Pursuit of the Presidency* (New York, 1980), 132; *Chi T*, 3/13/79; Jack Germond and Jules Witcover, *Blue Smoke and Mirrors: How Reagan Won and Why Carter Lost the Election of 1980* (New York, 1981), 113; *NT*, 4/9/79; *NYT*, 2/18/79; WP, 4/28/79; WS, 4/15, 5/1/79.
8. "Baker Makes His Move," *Business Week*, 8/27/79, 133; Jon Bowermaster, *Governor: An Oral Biography of Robert D Ray* (Ames, Iowa, 1987), 246; Cannon and Peterson, "GOP," 134; *DMR*, 12/1/79; *Detroit Free Press*, 9/27/79; *NYT*, 9/27/79; interview with Rebecca Cox, 6/24/82; *WP*, 2/1/79.

9. Interview with John Deardourff, 4/17/82; Germond and Witcover, *Blue Smoke,* 107–9, 117–19; *NYT,* 7/9, 10/20/79; *WSJ,* 11/27/79.
10. HHB, "Dallas Address," 5/31/79, BP; Germond and Witcover, *Blue Smoke,* 55; *NYT,* 9/30/79.
11. Interview with Douglas Bailey, 12/29/82; Germond and Witcover, *Blue Smoke,* 103–4.
12. HHB, "Declaration of Candidacy," 11/1/79, Washington, D.C., BP; *WP,* 11/2/79.
13. *Chi T,* 11/3/79; *Concord Monitor,* 11/3/79; *CR,* 96th Cong., 1st sess., S15622–25.
14. Cohen, *Roll Call,* 296, 298; Germond and Witcover, *Blue Smoke,* 104–6; *LAT,* 11/4/79; *NT,* 11/5/79; *WP,* 11/5/79; *WS,* 11/5, 12/12/79.
15. Reagan workers admitted to shifting for this reason. Interview with William S. Cohen, 6/13/90; telephone interview with Lewis R. Donelson III, 6/7/90; Cohen, *Roll Call,* 297–300; Elizabeth Drew, *Portrait of an Election: The 1980 Presidential Campaign* (New York, 1981), 32; Germond and Witcover, *Blue Smoke,* 105; *KJ,* 12/19/79; *NYT,* 11/4/79; WSJ, 12/12/79.
16. HHB, "Address to the National Press Club," 11/5/79, Washington, D.C., BP; Germond and Witcover, *Blue Smoke,* 105.
17. Interviews with Rebecca Cox, 6/24/82, John Deardourff, 4/17/82, and Don Sundquist, 11/15/89; telephone interview with Ted Welch, 8/2/90.
18. White, *America in Search of Itself,* 11–12.
19. *CQ,* 12/8/79, 2775; *CR,* 96th Cong., 1st sess., S4401, S5929, S16495–96, S16581, S19335; *NYT,* 11/19/79.
20. Cohen, *Roll Call,* 305; *DMR,* 11/18/79; *NME,* 164–65.
21. Interview with John Deardourff, 4/17/82; *DMR,* 12/18/79; Germond and Witcover, *Blue Smoke,* 118; *NT,* 11/23/79; *NYT,* 11/20/79; telephone interview with Robert D. Ray, 3/30/90.
22. Baker later elaborated on the method he would use to choose his vice-president. Having been in the forefront of speculation in 1968 and 1976, he had come to see the process as degrading and promised to announce his choice before the convention or follow an idea being advanced of allowing the convention to select from among three names he would present delegates. Bowermaster, *Governor,* 247–48; *DMR,* 11/19, 12/1, 12/4, 12/5, 12/6, 12/8, 12/9, 12/16/79, 1/8/80; *NYT,* 12/8/79; "Tapes of 1980 Baker Ads," Bailey, Deardourff and Associates, McLean, Virginia; telephone interview with Dick Redman, 2/6/89; *WSJ,* 11/30/79; *WP,* 12/4/79.
23. Interview with Douglas Bailey, 12/29/82; "Baker 1980 Tapes"; Aram Bakshian, *The Candidates: 1980* (New Rochelle, N.Y., 1980), 216; Lou Cannon and William Peterson, "GOP," in Harwood, *Pursuit of Presidency: 1980,* 129; *DMR,* 12/5/79, 1/14/80; Germond and Witcover, *Blue Smoke,* 115; Jeff Greenfield, *The Real Campaign: How the Media Missed the Story of the 1980 Campaign* (New York, 1982), 135–37; *NYT,* 12/8/79; *WP,* 12/20/79, 1/17/80.
24. Glad, *Carter,* 461; telephone interview with Walter F. Mondale, 2/19/93; *NYT,* 1/3, 1/18/80; Talbott, *Endgame,* 289–90.

25. Tom Morgenthau, Gerald C. Lubenow and James Doyle, "Mr. Stay at Home," *Newsweek*, 1/14/80, 40; *WP*, 12/18/79.
26. *CQ*, 1/5/80, 4; *DMR*, 1/6, 1/7, 1/17/80; Greenfield, *Real Campaign*, 100; *NT*, 1/9/80.
27. Ten percent more Iowa Republicans who saw the debate rated Baker as the winner than as the loser. Eight percent more saw Crane as a winner, and 4 percent more viewed Bush as having given the best performance. The loser was Dole, whom 11 percent more saw as the loser than as the winner. Faring less poorly were Connally, whom 5 percent more saw as the loser than as the winner, and Anderson, whom 1 percent more viewed as a loser than as the winner. *DMR*, 1/11/80.
28. Interview with Douglas Bailey, 12/29/82; Cannon, *Reagan*, 246–48; *CQ*, 1/26/80, 188; *DMR*, 1/11, 1/13, 1/18, 1/19, 1/20/80; Germond and Witcover, *Blue Smoke*, 112; *NT*, 1/21/80; *NYT*, 1/17/80; *WP*, 1/15, 1/18/80.
29. *CSM*, 2/27/80; Greenfield, *Real Campaign*, 36–41; "*Newsweek* Poll: A Big Boost for Bush," *Newsweek*, 2/14/80, 32; *NYT*, 1/16, 1/25/80.
30. Cannon and Peterson, "GOP," 132; *CSM*, 1/30/80; Germond and Witcover, *Blue Smoke*, 95; Greenfield, *Real Campaign*, 114; John F. Stacks, *Watershed: The Campaign for the Presidency, 1980* (New York, 1981), 114.
31. Bakshian, *Candidates: 1980*, 216; interview with Tom Beasley, 8/3/82; Cannon, *Reagan*, 248–50; *NT*, *NYT*, and *WP*, 2/1, 2/2/80.
32. Telephone interview with Lamar Alexander, 2/28/90; interview with Tom Beasley, 8/3/82; *NB*, 2/4/80; *NYT*, 2/3, 2/17/80; *WP*, 2/2/80.
33. David M. Alpern, "A New Hampshire Survey," *Newsweek*, 2/14/80, 40; HHB, "Address at Dartmouth College," 2/8/80, Hanover, New Hampshire, BP; "1980 Baker Tapes"; Greenfield, *Real Campaign*, 44; interview with Tom C. Griscom, 7/16/82; *KNS*, 2/20/80; Tom Morgenthau, Tony Fuller, Stryker McGuire, Gloria Borger and Gerald C. Lubenow, "GOP Shakedown Cruise," *Newsweek*, 2/15/80, 32–34; *NT*, 2/24/80; *NYT*, 1/27, 1/2/7, 1/10, 1/19, 1/21/80; *WSJ*, 2/19/80; *WS*, 2/17/80.
34. HHB, "Press Release," 6/24/73, BP; *Chi T*, 12/28/79; *CQ*, 10/2/70, 2429; 2/23/80, 567; *CR.*, 91st Cong., 2nd sess., 34047–57; 93rd Cong., 1st sess., 81258128, 29638; 37785; 93rd Cong., 2nd sess., 17814; *NT*, 2/14/80; *NYT*, 2/18/80; telephone interview with Cissy Baker, 12/29/82.
35. Greenfield, *Real Campaign*, 44–45; *Manchester Union-Leader*, 2/20/80.
36. Cannon and Peterson, "GOP," 139–40; *CSM*, 2/25/80; Germond and Witcover, *Blue Smoke*, 140; *NB*, 2/25/80; *NYT*, 2/22/80; *WP*, 2/21/80; *WS*, 2/21/80; *WSJ*, 2/19/80.
37. Germond and Witcover, *Blue Smoke*, 125–26; *NYT*, 2/22/80; *WS*, 2/19/80.
38. Cannon, *Reagan*, 251–53; Germond and Witcover, *Blue Smoke*, 127–28; Peter Goldman, Gerald C. Lubenow, Stryker McGuire, James Doyle, Phyllis Malamud, Martin Kasindorf, "Reagan Is Back in the Saddle," *Newsweek*, 3/10/80, 29; *WP*, 2/24/80; White, *America in Search of Itself*, 30.
39. Cannon, *Reagan*, 253; Germond and Witcover, *Blue Smoke*, 129; Greenfield, *Real Campaign*, 46; *NYT*, 2/24/80; *WP*, 2/24, 2/26/80.

40. Thirty percent of New Hampshire's GOP voters made up their minds in the last week. Forty-nine percent opted for Reagan, 21 percent for Baker, 14 percent for Bush, and 12 percent for Anderson. Germond and Witcover, *Blue Smoke*, 130–31; *NYT*, 2/28/80.
41. *CQ*, 3/1/80, 597.
42. *CSM*, 2/8/80; *CQ*, 3/1/80, 599; Goldman, "Reagan Is Back in the Saddle," 29, 34; HBOHP, Box 4; Folder 15, James Cannon, 11/10/92; *NB*, 3/6/80; *NYT*, 2/28, 2/29, 3/1, 3/6/80; Stacks, *Watershed*, 122; *WP*, 2/29/80.
43. HHB, "Press Conference," 3/5/80, Washington, BP; Cannon and Peterson, "GOP," 144.
44. *CQ*, 7/9/80, p. 2003; *KNS*, 4/22/80; *NT*, 4/21/80; *WP*, 6/15/80; *WS*, 4/21, 5/11/80.
45. *CQ*, 4/26/80, 1079; 5/10/80, 1238; *NT*, 4/21, 5/2/80; *WP*, 4/21/80.
46. HHB, "Press Conference," 5/14/80, Washington, and "Tennessee Press Conference," 6/18/80, BP; *CSM*, 3/24/80; *KNS*, 6/30/80; *NB*, 6/16/80; *NT*, 7/13/80; *NYT*, 5/15, 6/18, 7/8/80; *WP*, 7/10, 7/15/80; *WS*, 4/22, 5/15, 6/24, 7/6/80.
47. Cannon, *Reagan*, 262, 264; *NYT*, 7/11/80; *WS*, 7/16/80; White, *America in Search of Itself*, 320.
48. Germond and Witcover, *Blue Smoke*, 172–75, 204; *NB*, 7/18/80.
49. Telephone interview with Bill Brock, 6/24/92; David M Alpern, Martin Kasindorf, Thomas M. DeFrank, Henry W. Hubbard, John J. Lindsay, Gloria Borger, and Deborah Witherspoon, "How the Ford Deal Collapsed," *Newsweek*, 7/28/80, 21.
50. HHB, "News Conference," 9/4/80; HHB, John Tower, and John Warner, "Press Conference," 9/8/80, BP; *Ball State University Daily News*, 10/22/80; Cannon, *Reagan*, 283–84; *CR*, 96th Cong., 2nd sess., S11250–52, S11573, S12120–21; Drew, *Portrait of an Election*, 267–68, 304; Germond and Witcover, *Blue Smoke*, 209, 244–45, 256–57; *KJ*, 10/3, 10/15, 10/29/80; *NYT*, 9/15/80.
51. *NYT*, 11/4, 11/5, 11/6/80.
52. HHB, "The View"; telephone interview with Barry M. Goldwater, 9/24/92; interview with Paul Laxalt, 5/16/90; *CQ*, 11/8/80, 3304, 3350; 11/15/80, 3372; "Eyes and Ears on the Hill," *Time*, 11/24/80, 15; *IS*, 11/8/80.
53. *CQ*, 9/27/80, 2819; 11/15/80, 3379; 11/22/80, 3413; 11/29/80, 3472; 12/6/80, 3509; *Indianapolis News*, 11/10/80; *KJ*, 11/10/80; *NB*, 11/10/80.

Chapter 11

1. Telephone interview with James Cannon, 7/15/94; Smith, *Power Game*, 455; *WP*, 2/16/82.
2. Terrell H. Bell, *The Thirteenth Man: A Reagan Cabinet Memoir* (New York, 1988), 94–96.
3. Cannon, *Reagan*, 333; Richard E. Cohen, "The Senator from Tennessee May Hold the Key to Reagan's Economic Plans," *NJ*, 4/11/81, 597; Isaacson, "Floor Is My Domain," 16–19; James A. Miller, *Running in Place: Inside the Senate* (New York, 1986), 74–75; *WP*, 3/8/81.

4. On fully 30 percent of the votes taken in 1981, Senate Republicans voted as a bloc. Irwin B. Arieff, "Under Baker's Leadership Senate Republicans Maintain Unprecedented Voting Unity," *CQ*, 9/12/81, 1747; Barone and Ujifusa, *Almanac of American Politics, 1984*, xxxi; Cohen, "Senator from Tennessee May Hold Key," 598; interview with Rebecca Cox, 6/24/82; interview with Ted Stevens, 6/24/82; interview with John G. Tower, 7/6/82; WP, 3/8/81.
5. Interview with Richard G. Lugar, 6/7/82; interview with Daniel Inouye, 5/11/93; interview with Howard Liebengood, 1/25/89; interview with Russell Long, 11/11/92.
6. HHB, "Press Conference," 12/16/80, Washington, BP; Cannon, *Reagan*, 308; *CQ*, 1/17/81, 147; *CR*, 97th Cong., 1st sess., S375; Alexander M. Haig, *Caveat: Realism, Reaganism and Foreign Policy* (New York, 1984), 38–46; *NT*, 12/20/80; *WP*, 1/12/81.
7. *CQ*, 5/2/81, 755; 6/6/81, 986; 6/13/81, 1042, 1072; *CR*, 97th Cong., 1st sess., S5850; Evans and Novak, *Reagan Revolution*, 191–97; Tom Matthews and John J. Lindsay, "HB, Point Man," *Newsweek*, 2/23/81, 21; *WS*, 2/23, 4/9/81.
8. Armstrong; interview with Russell Long, 11/11/92; Hildenbrand Oral History, 257; *WP*, 2/16/82.
9. *CQ*, 2/6/81, 323; Evans and Novak, *Reagan Revolution*, 225; interview of Orrin Hatch, 3/20/90; interview with Kenneth Duberstein, 10/26/92; interview with Edwin Meese, 8/14/90; John Lofton, Jr., "Baker Urges Delay of Social Issues Legislative Agenda until Next Year," *Conservative Digest*, 5/81, 2–5; *NYT*, 3/27/81; Smith, *Power Game*, 458–59; *WSJ*, 4/8/81.
10. Arieff, "Senate Republicans Maintain Unprecedented Unity," 1747; Barone and Ujifusa, *Almanac of American Politics, 1984*, xxxi; Cannon, *Reagan*, 332; *CQ*, 3/14/81, 463; *CR*, 97th Cong., 1st sess., S2069, S2107; interview with Rebecca Cox, 6/24/82; *KJ*, 2/20/81; *KNS*, 3/6, 4/12, 9/20/81; NB, 5/11/81; WP, 3/6, 4/12, 5/11/81.
11. *Chi T*, 3/28/81; *CQ*, 4/4/81, 602, 610; *CR*, 97th Cong., 1st sess., S2694; HBOHP, Box 8, Folder 27, Charles Grassley, 3/3/94; *KNS*, 3/13/81; Smith, *Power Game*, 468; Tolchin, "HB: Trying to Tame Senate," 75.
12. Arieff, "Senate Republicans Maintain Unprecedented Unity," 1743; Cannon, *Reagan*, 124–25; *CQ*, 4/4/81, 610–12; 4/11/81, 650; *CR*, 97th Cong., 1st sess., S2694, S2954, S2971; *WS*, 4/8/81.
13. Arieff, "Senate Republicans Maintain Unity," 1747; *CQ*, 5/16/81, 878–79; 5/23/81, 920; Hildenbrand Oral History, 327; *NYT*, 5/12/81.
14. Laurence I. Barrett, *Gambling with History: Reagan in the White House* (Garden City, 1983), 155–58; Cannon, *Reagan*, 380; *CQ*, 5/23/81, 920; *CR*, 98th Cong., 1st sess., S3585; Isaacson, "Floor Is My Domain," 29; *NJ*, 1/2/82, 41; Smith, *Power Game*, 360.
15. Barrett, *Gambling*, 164–69; *CR*, 97th Cong., 1st sess., S8744; telephone interview with Robert Dole, 7/8/93; interviews with Orrin Hatch, 3/20/90, and Robert W. Packwood, 1/13/93.
16. Barrett, *Gambling*, 166–70; *CQ*, 7/18/81, 1312–13; 7/25/81, 1358–59; 8/1/81, 1416–18; *CR*, 97th Cong., 1st sess., S8744.

17. Barrett, *Gambling*, 275; interview with Charles H. Percy, 3/30/90; Tom Morgenthau, John J. Lindsay, John Wolcott, and Milan J. Kubic, "Reagan Faces the World," *Newsweek*, 11/9/81, 23; Smith, *Power Game*, 219–20.
18. Morgenthau, "Reagan Faces the World," 31; *NT*, 9/15/81; interview with Charles H. Percy, 3/30/90; Smith, *Power Game*, 221; *WP*, 9/30, 10/30/81.
19. Barrett, *Gambling*, 275–76; George J. Church, Laurence I. Barrett, and Gregory Wierzynski, "AWACS: He Does It Again," *Time*, 11/9/81, 12–13; *CQ*, 9/19/81, 1783; Walter Isaacson, Joanna McGeary, and Evan Thomas, "The Man with the Golden Arm," *Time*, 11/9/81, 25–26, 31; Morgenthau, "Reagan Faces the World," 31; *NT*, 10/10/81; Tolchin, "HB: Trying to Tame Senate," 75; *WP*, 10/30/81.
20. Barrett, *Gambling*, 275; *CQ*, 10/10/81, 1942; 10/17/81, 2006–7; Richard F. Fenno Jr., *The Making of a Senator: Dan Quayle* (Washington, 1989), 26–27; Tolchin, "HB: Trying To Tame Senate," 75.
21. *CR*, 97th Cong., 2nd sess., S11854, S12171, S12174, S12184, S12190, S12204; Isaacson et al., "The Man with the Golden Arm," 25–26; *KJ*, 10/28/81; interview with Robert W. Packwood, 1/13/93; Hugh Sidey, "The Art of Enticement," *Time*, 11/9/81, 31; *WP*, 9/26, 10/26, 10/30/81.
22. Baker voted with Reagan 88 percent of the time in 1981, second only to Richard Lugar. *CQ*, 1/2/82, 24; Isaacson et al., "The Man with the Golden Arm," 31; *WP*, 2/16/82.
23. *CQ*, 10/31/81, 1891, 2113–14; 11/11/81, 2319; *CR*, 97th Cong., 1st sess., S5459, SI1849; *US News*, 5/24/82, 16.
24. Barrett, *Gambling*, 339, 347, 367; George J. Church, Laurence I. Barrett, and Neil MacNeil, "Blood, Sweat and Tears," *Time*, 9/29/81, 18–19; *CQ*, 9/19/81, 1771; Tolchin, "HB: Trying to Tame Senate," 70; *WP*, 1/30/82.
25. HHB, "News Release," 2/9/82, Washington, BP; *CQ*, 2/20/82, 309; *CR*, 97th Cong., 2nd sess., S690; interview with Ed Allison, 6/16/82; Isaacson, "Floor Is My Domain," 16; James Kelly, Neil MacNeil, and Evan Thomas, "Challenging the Red Sea," *Time*, 2/22/82, 14; Peter McGrath, Eleanor Clift, Thomas M. DeFrank, Rich Thomas, Howard Fineman, Gloria Borger, and Christopher Ma, "The Deficit Rebellion," *Newsweek*, 2/22/82, 22–24; Tolchin, "HB: Trying to Tame Senate," 68, 70.
26. Isaacson et al., "Floor Is My Domain," 16; Tolchin, "HB: Trying to Tame Senate," 68.
27. Barrett, *Gambling*, 352–53; *CQ*, 4/24/82, 901; Richard E. Cohen, "Congress and the White House Play a Waiting Game on the 1983 Budget," *NJ*, 3/20/82, 489; Monroe W. Karmen, "The Budget: When It's All Said and Done," *US News*, 3/15/82, 20–21; Ed Magnuson, "Playing It Cool or Frozen in Ice," *Time*, 3/22/82, 3435; *WP*, 3/10/82.
28. HHB, "Remarks Following Budget Meeting," 4/28/82, BP; Barrett, *Gambling*, 361–62; Smith, *Power Game*, 531; *WP*, 4/29/82.
29. HHB, "Remarks Following Budget Meeting;" Barrett, *Gambling*, 362–64; *CQ* 5/21/82, 1309; 6/26/82, 1555; "Congress' House of Cards Budget May Be Con-

structed on Quicksand," *NJ*, 6/26/82, 1121; Richard F. Fenno Jr., *The Emergence of a Senate Leader: Pete Domenici and the Reagan Budget* (Washington, 1991), 105.

30. HHB, "Statement upon His Departure for China," 5/28/82, BP; CQ, 5/3/82, 1041; 6/19/82, 1491; 6/26/82, 1554; Richard E. Cohen, "Advocates of Voting Rights Say Its Election Results That Matter," *NJ*, 4/3/82, 592–94; *CR*, 97th Cong., 2nd sess., S4467–68; S6714–15, S7139–40; *KNS*, 6/1/82; *NB*, 6/2, 6/3/82; *WP*, 5/31, 6/15, 6/19/82.
31. Barrett, *Gambling*, 364–65; Melinda Beck, Gloria Borger, Howard Fineman, Eleanor Clift, and James Doyle, "Winning One for the Gipper," *Newsweek*, 8/30/82, 25–28; *CQ*, 7/10/82, 1683; 7/17/82, 1705; 7/31/82, 1854; Bob and Elizabeth Dole with Richard Norton Smith, *The Doles: Unlimited Partners* (New York, 1988), 208.
32. Barrett, *Gambling*, 365–67; Walter Isaacson, Douglas Brew, Neil MacNeil, and Evan Thomas, "Scoring on a Reverse," *Time*, 8/30/82, 14–18.
33. Barrett, *Gambling*, 366–67; Beck et al., "Winning One for the Gipper," 25–28; *CQ*, 8/21/82, 2039; Isaacson et al., "Scoring on a Reverse," 14–18; *NT*, 8/5/82.
34. *CQ*, 7/10/82, 1683; 9/11/82, 2279; 9/18/82, 2340; 9/25/82, 2345, 2358; *CR*, 98th Cong., 2nd sess., S10705, S10791, S11237, S11355, S11427, S11495, S11575, S12302–3; Walter Isaacson, "Setback for the New Right," *Time*, 9/27/82, 12–13; *NT*, 8/6/82; interview with Robert W. Packwood, 1/13/93.
35. *CQ*, 11/7/81, 2172–76; *KJ*, 7/7/81; *KNS*, 11/5/81.
36. Telephone interview with Cissy Baker, 12/29/82; *IS*, 10/5/81, 1/3/82; *KJ*, 2/19/82.
37. "A Look at Key 1982 Congressional Races," *HE*, 7/31/82, 12–18; *KJ*, 6/4/82; *NB*, 7/5, 8/7/82; *WP*, 12/24/82.
38. "Cissy,"—1982 Campaign Pamphlet authorized by the Cissy Baker Committee; *KNS*, 3/2/82; interview with Cissy Baker, 12/29/82.
39. *KJ*, 10/7, 11/3, 11/5/82; *KNS*, 11/3/82; *LAT*, 10/25/82; *WP*, 12/24/82.
40. Tom Morgenthau, James Doyle, Gloria Borger, Susan Agrest and Sylvester Monroe, "Will Reagan Change Course," *Newsweek*, 11/15/82, 37; *NYT*, 11/19, 11/30/82; Michael Reese, Howard Fineman and Eleanor Clift, "Guns and Butter in Congress," *Newsweek*, 12/6/82, 36–37; *WP*, 11/4/82.
41. *CQ*, 12/18/82, 3047; *CR*, 97th Cong., 2nd sess., S13437; *Indianapolis News*, 12/8/82; *NYT*, 11/23/82; *WP*, 12/23/82.
42. *CQ*, 12/18/82, 3047; 12/25/82, 3087, 3105, 3120; 1/15/83, 121; *CR*, 97th Cong., 2nd sess., S15060, S15720; Walter Isaacson, Neil MacNeil, and Evan Thomas, "'Not Our Finest Hour,'" *Time*, 1/3/83, 42–44; *KNS*, 12/20/82.
43. *CR*, 97th Cong., 2nd sess., S15969–72; "Helms Plays Hardball," *Newsweek*, 1/3/83, 11; interview with Alan Simpson, 6/15/90; *WP*, 12/23/82.
44. *CR*, 97th Cong., 2nd sess., S16045; "Helms Plays Hardball," 11; Isaacson, "Not Our Finest Hour," 42–44; Tom Morgenthau, Howard Fineman, and Gloria Borger, "A Lame Duck Operation," *Newsweek*, 1/3/83, 11; interview with Alan Simpson, 6/15/90; *WP*, 12/23, 12/24/82.
45. Telephone interview with Lewis R. Donelson III, 6/7/90; interviews with HHB, 3/9/90, and Tom C. Griscom, 3/9/90; *KJ*, 1/11/83; *KNS*, 1/23/83;

"Lost Leader," *Time,* 1/24/83, 26; *NYT,* 1/11, 1/22/83; Mark Starr, Thomas M. DeFrank, Howard Fineman, James Doyle, Christopher Ma, "Who's in Charge Here," *Newsweek,* 1/24/83, 16–17; *WP,* 8/8/83.

46. Interview with HHB and Thomas C. Griscom, 3/9/90; *KJ,* 1/11/83; "Lost Leader," 26; *NYT,* 1/22/83; Starr et al., "Who's in Charge," 16–17.
47. Richard E. Cohen, "Senate Republican Control May Be Put to Test by Tough Issues This Fall," *NJ,* 9/10/83, 1827; *CR,* 98th Cong., 1st sess., S89–90, S493, S1219–20; *NYT,* 5/20/83; interview with Alan Simpson, 6/15/90.
48. *CQ,* 3/26/83, 643; interview with Paul Laxalt, 5/16/90; *NYT,* 1/24, 2/4/83; *WP,* 1/24/83.
49. *Chi T,* 3/18/83; *CQ,* 3/12/83, 491; 3/19/83, 538–39, 588–89; *CR,* 98th Cong., 2nd sess., S2321, S2623, S2901–2, S2997, S2999, S3218, S3231; *WP,* 3/12/83.
50. *CQ,* 1/26/83, 155–56; 3/26/83, 596–97, 643–44; *CR,* 98th Cong., 1st sess., S389, S3585, S4084; *IS,* 4/21/83; Hugh Sidey, "The Buck Stops Here," *Time,* 5/30/83, 19.
51. *CQ,* 10/8/83, 2084; *CR,* 98th Cong., 1st sess., S8265, S14361; *WP,* 8/6/83.
52. *CQ,* 10/22/83, 2176–79.
53. *CQ,* 10/22/83, 2176; *CR,* 98th Cong., 1st sess., S14137–38; *WP,* 10/20/83.
54. *CQ,* 10/22/83, 2173; *CR,* 98th Cong., 1st sess., S14643–44; *NYT* 10/27/83; *WP,* 10/27/83.
55. *NYT,* 11/14/83; interview with Robert W. Packwood, 1/13/93; *WP,* 10/27/83.
56. *CQ,* 9/17/83, 1923; *NYT,* 7/7/82, 9/21/83; *WP,* 4/19, 9/20/83.
57. *CQ,* 9/24/83, 1963; 10/1/83, 2015; 10/8/83; 2095; *CR,* 98th Cong., 1st sess., S13166.
58. *CQ,* 11/12/83, 2359; *CR,* 98th Cong., 1st sess., S14400; *NYT,* 11/27/83.
59. HHB, "The View"; interview with Kenneth Duberstein, 10/26/92; CQ, 10/29/83, 2280; Ronald W. Reagan, *An American Life: The Autobiography* (New York, 1990), 449–55; George P. Shultz, *Turmoil and Triumph* (New York, 1993), 335.
60. *CQ,* 10/29/83, 2280; *WP,* 10/29/83.
61. *CR,* 98th Cong., 2nd sess., S2343; *NYT,* 3/4/84; *WT,* 1/31/84.
62. *NYT,* 2/25/84; *WP,* 3/4/84.
63. *CQ,* 3/24/84, 643; *CR,* 98th Cong., 2nd sess., S2290–92, S2343, S2900–S2901; *NYT,* 3/15, 3/16, 3/20, 3/21/84; *WP,* 3/15, 3/16, 3/20, 3/21/84.
64. *CQ,* 3/31/84, 702; *CR,* 98th Cong., 2nd sess., S2998–99; *NYT,* 3/30/84; *WP,* 6/6/83, 3/23/84; *WT,* 1/11/84.
65. *CQ,* 3/10/84, 535; 3/17/84, 598; *NYT,* 3/17/84; *WP,* 3/16/84; *WT,* 3/15/84.
66. *CQ,* 6/30/84, 1539; *NYT,* 3/25, 5/17, 5/27/84; *WP,* 5/11, 9/21/84; *WT,* 3/15/84.
67. *NYT,* 8/22/84.
68. HB, "We're Losing Historical and Political Treasures," *TV Guide,* 7/21/84, 32–34; Byrd, *Addresses on Senate History,* 2:615; *CQ,* 2/6/82, 208; 9/22/84, 2294; Richard F. Fenno Jr., "The Senate through the Looking Glass: The Debate over Television," in *The Changing World of the United States Senate,* ed. John Hibbing (Berkeley, 1990), 193; *NME,* 142–45.

69. CQ, 4/14/84, 853; 9/29/84, 2356; 10/6/84, 2430, 2469; *NYT*, 9/30, 10/3, 10/6/84; *WP*, 9/30, 10/3, 10/6/84.
70. *CQ*, 10/13/84, 2615; *WP*, 10/6/84.
71. *CR*, 98th Cong., 2nd sess., S14610–11; *WP*, 10/13/84.

Chapter 12

1. *NYT*, 4/29/85, 1/30/87, 2/14/87; *WT*, 4/4/86.
2. *CT*, 8/23/85; *NB*, 12/1/86; *NYT*, 1/7, 2/14/87; telephone interviews with Robert D. Ray, 3/30/90, and with Dick Redman, 2/6/89; WP, 2/13/87.
3. *NYT*, 1/30/87; telephone interview with Thomas Rath, 2/6/89, and Ted Welch, 8/2/90; Donald T. Regan, *For the Record: From Wall Street to Washington* (New York, 1988), 75.
4. Lou Cannon, *President Reagan: The Role of a Lifetime* (New York, 1991), 728; Jane Mayer and Doyle McManus, *Landslide: The Unmaking of the President, 1984–1988* (Boston, 1988), 359, 362; *NYT*, 1/30/87; Nancy Reagan, *My Turn*, 321–22.
5. HHB, "The View"; interview with Edwin Meese, 8/14/90; Cannon, *President Reagan*, 731; *KJ*, 2/26/87; Mayer and McManus, *Landslide*, 383; *NT*, 3/1, 3/2/87.
6. Mayer and McManus, Landslide, 383; *NYT*, 2/28/87; Reagan, *My Turn*, 333; "The Hard Road Ahead on the Comeback Trail," *US News*, 3/9/87, 17; *WSJ*, 3/2/87.
7. Telephone interviews with James Cannon, 7/15/94, and Thomas C. Griscom, 4/5/94; interview with A. B. Culvahouse, 12/17/92; Mayer and McManus, *Landslide*, viii–xi.
8. Telephone interview with James Cannon, 7/15/94; Cannon, *President Reagan*, 733; *KJ*, 3/3/87.
9. Interviews with HHB, 2/9/87, A. B. Culvahouse, 12/17/92, and Daniel Inouye, 5/11/93; Cannon, *President Reagan*, 734; Seymour M. Hersh, "The Iran-Contra Committee: Did They Protect Reagan?," *NYT Magazine*, 4/9/90, 47; *NT*, 3/1/87; Michael Schudson, *Watergate in American Memory: How We Remember, Forget and Reconstruct the Past* (New York, 1992), 168–70, 179–81; John G. Tower, *Consequences: A Personal and Political Memoir* (Boston, 1991), 288; Transcript, "This Week With David Brinkley," 7/5/87.
10. Cannon, *President Reagan*, 736–38; *WSJ*, 3/13/87.
11. Armstrong; John M. Barry, *The Ambition and the Power* (New York, 1989), 194–99; *NYT*, 4/2, 4/3/87; Walter Shapiro, Michael Duffy, Hays Gorey, "Road Warriors," *Time*, 4/13/87, 16–19.
12. Dick Kirschten, "The President's Counselor," *NJ*, 5/23/87, 1335; telephone interview with Frank Moore, 3/14/91; *WSJ*, 3/6/87; *WT*, 3/26, 4/3/87.
13. *CSM*, 4/3/87; interview with Kenneth Duberstein, 10/26/92; *NYT*, 7/24/87; *WT*, 3/26, 5/2, 5/22/87.
14. Anderson, *Revolution*, 180–81; interview with Kenneth Duberstein, 10/26/92; John Anthony Maltese, *Spin Control: The White House Office of Communications and the Management of Presidential News* (Chapel Hill, 1992), 213–14; *WP*, 7/27/87.
15. Interview with Kenneth Duberstein, 10/26/92; Maltese, *Spin Control*, 1, 211–14.

16. Interview with HHB, 3/9/90; telephone interview with Tom C. Griscom, 4/5/94; Cannon, *President Reagan*, 394; *NYT*, 5/12/87; Ronald W. Reagan, *Speaking My Mind: Selected Speeches* (New York, 1989), 348, 352.
17. HHB, "The View"; Dick Kirschten, "After Baker Has Reshuffled the Cards . . . , Managua May Get a New Deal," *NJ*, 5/9/87, 1128–29; *NYT*, 5/4/87.
18. Fred Barnes, "Peaced Off," *New Republic*, 8/31/87, 10–12; Barry, *Ambition and Power*, 327–45; Roy Gutman, *Banana Diplomacy* (New York, 1988), 344–46; *NYT*, 7/20/87; *WT*, 8/12/87; Jim Wright, *Worth It All: My War for Peace* (New York, 1993), 90, 94, 99, 106, 108.
19. Gutman, *Banana Diplomacy*, 349.
20. HHB, "The View."
21. Kempe, *Divorcing the Dictator*, 309–31; Howard Means, *Colin Powell: Soldier/Statesman-Statesman/Soldier* (New York, 1992), 248–52; Shultz, *Turmoil and Triumph*, 1051–79.
22. Fred Barnes, "Bork Talk," *New Republic*, 9/7/87, 10; interview with A. B. Culvahouse, 12/17/92.
23. Bronner, *Battle for Justice*, 98; *NYT*, 7/2/87.
24. Interviews with HHB, 3/9/90, and Alan Simpson, 6/15/90; Bronner, *Battle for Justice*, 193; Gitenstein, *Matters of Principle*, 70; Michael Pertschuk and Wendy Schaetzel, *The People Rising: The Campaign against the Bork Nomination* (New York, 1989), 27.
25. Interviews with HHB and Thomas C. Griscom, 3/9/90, and A. B. Culvahouse, 12/17/92; interview with Kenneth Duberstein, 10/26/92; Bronner, *Battle for Justice*, 194; Anne Edwards, *The Reagans: Portrait of a Marriage* (New York: St. Martin's Griffin, 2003); Gitenstein, *Matters of Principle*, 99; Peter Robinson, *How Ronald Reagan Changed My Life* (New York: Regan Books, 2003); *WP*, 10/5/87.
26. Bronner, *Battle for Justice*, 184; interviews with William S. Cohen, 6/13/90, and Orrin Hatch, 3/20/90; Gitenstein, *Matters of Principle*, 24; "What Biden Really Said About Bork," *HE*, 7/11/87, 3.
27. Bronner, *Battle for Justice*, 227, 235, 275–76; Gitenstein, *Matters of Principle*, 246–47; interview with A. B. Culvahouse, 12/17/92, and Orrin Hatch, 3/20/90.
28. Bronner, *Battle for Justice*, 200–203, 266, 311, 348; Gitenstein, *Matters of Principle*, 69, 276, 298; *WP*, 10/5/87.
29. "Bork Appointment Could Revolutionize High Court," *HE*, 7/11/87, 1, 7; interview with A. B. Culvahouse, 12/17/92; Gitenstein, *Matters of Principle*, 251–53; *NYT*, 10/8/87.
30. Interview with A. B. Culvahouse, 12/17/92; Gitenstein, *Matters of Principle*, 314–15; *NYT*, 10/31/87.
31. Cannon, *President Reagan*, 806; "Conservatives Did in Judge Ginsburg," *HE*, 11/21/87, 4; interview with Kenneth Duberstein, 10/26/92; *LAT*, 11/8/87; *NYT*, 11/8/87.
32. Bronner, *Battle for Justice*, 333; *CR*, 100th Cong., 1st sess., S16040–41; Gitenstein, *Matters of Principle*, 314–15; interview with Orrin Hatch, 3/20/90; *NYT*, 11/12/87; *WT*, 11/6/87.

33. Bronner, *Battle for Justice*, 336–38; Cohen; "Conservatives Did in Ginsburg," 4; *Miami Herald*, 10/16/87; Barrett Seaman, "The Heifer Takes Some Hits," *Time*, 10/19/87, 16.
34. HHB, "The View."
35. The first full-length discussion of this initiative is found in an op-ed piece by Baker and Frye in the *Los Angeles Times* on the occasion of Muskie's death. *LAT*, 4/2/96. See also Leon Billings, "After Dinner Remarks," at "Cleaning America's Air: Progress and Challenges," A Conference of the HB Center for Public Policy, 3/9/05. For more about the circumstances of the meeting, see *NT*, 6/6/85, Reagan, *American Life*, 603, and the oral histories of Frye and Lonnie Strunk at the Baker Center.
36. Cannon, *President Reagan*, 770–75.
37. HHB, "The View"; Lou Cannon, "Antidote to Ollie North," *WP Magazine*, 8/7/88, 38; Means, *Powell*, 244–46; Strobe Talbott, *The Master of the Game: Paul Nitze and the Nuclear Peace* (New York, 1988), 354, 362; *WP*, 3/27/88.
38. Interview with HHB, 3/9/90; Dick Kirschten, "Even before Gorbachev's Arrival . . . The White House Faces a Hard Sell," *NJ*, 12/5/87, 3102; Shultz, *Turmoil and Triumph*, 882, 1007.
39. Don Oberdorfer, *The Turn: From the Cold War to a New Era* (New York, 1991), 262–63, 269, 274–82; Hugh Sidey, "Reagan's End Game Plan," *Time*, 1/18/88, 20; Talbott, *Master of the Game*, 388.
40. Peter Goldman, Tom Mathews, and the *Newsweek* Special Election Team, *The Quest for the Presidency, 1988* (New York, 1989), 215–16; *WP*, 12/23/87.
41. Dick Kirschten, "Summit Caps a Comeback . . . To Staff Chief Baker's Delight," *NJ*, 6/11/88, 1560–61; Rowny, *It Takes One*, 201–2; Talbott, *Master of the Game*, 374.
42. Douglas Harbrecht and Richard Fly, "With Baker Leaving the White House, It's Over before It's Over, *Business Week*, 6/27/88, 41; Kirschten, "Summit Caps a Comeback," 1561–62; *KNS*, 6/15/88; *NB*, 4/12/88; *NYT*, 6/16, 6/19/88.
43. Harbrecht and Fly, "It's Over before It's Over," 41.

Chapter 13

1. *CNFP*, 1/12/89; *CT*, 7/15/88; Memo, Doris Lovett to Lura Nell Mitchell, Addition to HB Papers; MSS227, Box 2, Folder 47; HBOHP, Box 9, Folder 9, Thomas C. Griscom, 9/9/92; George Spencer, "HB: A Life in Focus," *Tennessee Illustrated*, Winter 1990, 14.
2. *CNFP*, 7/20/88; *KNS*, 8/16/88; *NT*, 8/14, 8/16, 8/17/88.
3. HBOHP, Box 1, Folder 27, Cissy Baker, 1/16/96 26; Box 11, Folder 30, Dan Kuykendall, 3/23/95, 30; Box 20, Folder 11, David K. "Pat" Wilson, 11/7/96, 13–14; interview with HHB, 5/26/97; *MCA*, 10/31/93; telephone interview with Fred Marcum, 5/9/06; *NB*, 2/20/95.
4. *US Government's Post-War POW/MIA Efforts: Hearings before the Select Committee on POW/MIA Affairs of the United States Senate*, 102nd Cong., 2nd sess., 296–316.

5. *IRS Oversight: Hearings before the Committee on Finance of the United States Senate,* 105th Cong., 170–93; *KNS* 5/1/98; *NYT,* 5/1/98; telephone interview with Fred Marcum, 5/9/06.
6. Patty Cavin, "Now . . . A Leading Role for Joy Baker," *Washington Dossier,* 4/82, 12–15, 43–44; *KNS,* 12/3/95; *Orlando Sentinel Star,* 10/15/78; *The Star,* 7/12/88; HBOHP, Box 2, Folder 15, Maureen Brink Bates, 11/8/00, 20–23, 28; Box 10, Folder 24, Al Hunt, Box 12, Folder 3, 3/24/94, 7; Timothy Locke, 8/21/01, 11; Box 13, Folder 13, Robert McFarlane, 12/7/94, 3; Box 16, Folder 9, Emily Reynolds, 11/14/96, 31; Box 16; Folder 22, Kenneth Roberts, 10/26/98, 17.
7. Telephone interviews with Cissy Baker, 11/25/83, and Mike Prince, 4/30/06; Cavin, "Leading Role for Joy Baker," 44; HBOHP, Box 6, Folder 3, Michael Deaver, 8/10/94, 15; Box 19, Folder 23, John Warner, 2/2/94, 4.
8. Cavin, "Leading Role for Joy Baker, 43; HBOHP, Box 1, Folder 31, Cissy Baker, 5/9/96, 19; *KJ,* 6/15/88; *USA Today,* 6/15/88; *Oneida (TN) Independent Herald,* 4/29/93; *Star,* 7/12/88.
9. Interview with HHB, 3/21/06; telephone interview with Lawrence and Marlene Eagleburger, 5/24/06.
10. Interview with HHB, 3/21/06; HBOHP, Box 1, Folder 29, Cissy Baker, 3/12/96, 11; *Kansas City Star,* 12/2/96; *LAT,* 11/7/96.
11. Telephone interview with Lawrence and Marlene Eagleburger, 5/24/06; Frist and Annis, *Tennessee Senators,* 157–58; *Kansas City Star,* 12/2/96; *LAT,* 11/7/96; Paul Simon, *PS: The Autobiography of Paul Simon* (Chicago, 1999), 50.
12. *KNS,* 6/23/91, 12/8/96; *WP,* 12/9/96.
13. E-mail, Bill Brock to author, 2/2/06; *KNS,* 12/8/96; "United State: Howard Baker Weds Senate Pal Nancy Kassebaum," *People,* 12/23/96, 88.
14. Interview with HHB, 3/21/06; *MCA,* 5/1/99; *Washington Telecommunications News,* 2/20/95.
15. One Maryland attorney, Baltimore Orioles owner Peter Angelos, settled for merely $150 million of the $1 billion he said the state owed him from its share of the payoff from the settlement. *Baltimore Sun,* 11/18/02.
16. Interview with HHB, 3/21/06; *KNS,* 10/13, 10/29/97, 3/12/98, 9/3/99; *NYT,* 12/15/97.
17. Interview with HHB, 3/21/06.
18. Ibid.; *KNS,* 1/19/99; *New York Post,* 9/13/98; *The News Hour with Jim Lehrer,* 12/21/98.
19. *Face the Nation,* 8/9/98; *KNS,* 1/10, 1/19/99; *The News Hour with Jim Lehrer,* 12/21/98; *New York Post,* 9/13/98; *This Week,* 12/20/98.
20. Interview with HHB, 3/21/06; *Los Alamos News Bulletin,* 9/25/00; *WP,* 9/25/00, 1/11/01.
21. Interview with HHB, 3/21/06; *Oklahoma City Record,* 3/30/01; Millard "Corky"Alexander, "New U.S. Ambassador HB to Arrive Soon," *Tokyo Weekender,* 6/29/01; *Wichita Eagle,* 7/2/01.
22. *KNS,* 3/27/01, 5/24/01; *Wichita Eagle,* 7/2/01.

23. 2006 HHB; *CNFP*, 8/9/02; HBOHP, Box 1, Folder 10, Lamar Alexander, 12/9/97, 37; *KNS*, 5/24/01. See also HHB and Ellen L. Frost, "Rescuing the US-Japan Alliance," *Foreign Affairs* (Spring 1992), 97–113.
24. Alexander, "HB to Arrive Soon"; National Geographic films, *Ambassador: Inside the Embassy*, videotape, 2002.
25. Alexander, "HB to Arrive Soon"; National Geographic, *Ambassador; Stars and Stripes*, 8/1/01; *NYT*, 7/7/01; *WP*, 7/6/01; www.kantei.go.jp/foreign/koizumiphoto/2001/07/09/baker_e.html.
26. National Geographic, *Ambassador.*
27. Dept. of State, Washington File, "Ambassador Baker Says United States, Japan Allied Against Terrorism," 10/05/01; Dept. of State, HHB, "Speech at Japanese Observance for Victims, Office of International Informational Programs," 9/23/01; Duncan Currie, "The Other Special Relationship," *Weekly Standard*, 12/20/04, 15–16; *Japan Policy and Politics*, 10/08/01; *Japan Times*, 1/1/02; *NT*, 8/31/02.
28. Interview with HHB, 3/21/06; HHB, "The US-Japan Relationship in 2004," Japan National Press Club, 12/14/2004; HHB, "Okinawa and the US-Japanese Relationship," Okinawa Federation of Economic Organizations, Naka, Okinawa, 2/28/03; www.accj.or.jp/pages/accjpersonofthe year_ 2004.
29. Interview with HHB, 3/21/06; "Vital Voices Anti-Trafficking Heroines Nancy Kassebaum Baker and Somaly Man, Honored by the U.S. State Department," www.vitalvoices.org/DesktopDefault.aspx.page_id=218, 241; www.vitalvoices.org/files/docs/ta.int-july-2004.pdf.
30. HHB, "US Commitment to Develop a Global Tsunami System," Kobe, Japan, 1/20/05; *Stars and Stripes*, 10/26/04.
31. Bill Hemmer, CNN *American Morning*, 12/14/04; *Boston Globe*, 8/28/05; *Charlie Rose Show*, 3/31/04; HHB, "Address to American Chamber of Commerce, Person of the Year 2004 Luncheon," 1/27/05; HHB, "Farewell Press Conference," Tokyo, 2/16/05; HHB, "Okinawa and the US-Japan Relationship;" *KNS*, 12/8/04.
32. CNN, "George H. W. Bush's World War II Experience," 12/20/03; Hugh Sidey, "One Bush's War and Remembrance," *Time*, 12/20/03, 22;
33. Colin Powell, "Remarks at the Signing of the US Participation in the Aichi, Japan 2005 Exhibition," Washington, 9/7/04; *KNS*, 3/6/05.
34. Kitamura Fumio, "Goodbye, Ambassador Baker," *Japan Times*, 2/9/05.
35. Interview with HHB, 3/21/06; http://cgood.org; *Kansas City Star*, 11/13/05; *LAT*, 8/7/05.
36. Interviews with HHB, 3/21/06, and William H. Frist, 6/12/06; *CNN* report, 12/20/02; *Larry King Live*, 12/20/02.
37. Interview with William H. Frist, 6/12/06.
38. See the op-ed piece by HHB in *WP*, 4/27/93; interview with William H. Frist, 6/12/06; HHB, "Welcome to "Congress and the Presidency: Institute for Teachers," at HHB Center for Public Policy, 6/6/05.
39. Interview with HHB, 3/21/06; CNN, 11/4/05; Gloria Borger, "Them That Brung Ya," *US News*, 3/27/06, 38; *WP*, 3/16/06.

40. HHB, "Remarks at the Groundbreaking Ceremony for the HHB Center for Public Policy at the University of Tennessee, Knoxville, 11/15/05.
41. Interview with HHB, 6/24/93.

Conclusion

1. Telephone interview with Frank Moore, 3/14/91; *WP*, 3/15/87.
2. George Reedy, *The U.S. Senate* (New York, 1986), 149.
3. Interviews with Douglas Bailey, 12/29/82, Dan H. Kuykendall, 3/27/90, Paul Laxalt, 5/16/90, and Richard G. Lugar, 6/7/82; telephone interviews with Walter F. Mondale, 2/19/93, and Robert D. Ray, 3/30/90.
4. Interview with HHB, 3/21/06; telephone interviews with Thomas Eagleton, 10/2/92, and Walter F. Mondale, 2/19/93; *WP*, 9/9/89.
5. Isaacson, "Floor Is My Domain," 16–19; Mansfield to author; interview with John Seigenthaler, 8/14/82.
6. Interviews with Orrin Hatch, 3/20/90, Paul Laxalt, 5/16/90, Richard G. Lugar, 6/7/82, and Warren B. Rudman, 6/9/82.

BIBLIOGRAPHY

Interviews

Alexander, Lamar. Knoxville (telephone), 2/28/90.

Allison, Ed. Washington, 6/16/82.

Armstrong, William. Washington, 4/30/90.

Bailey, Douglas. Mclean, VA, 12/29/82.

Baker, Cissy. Washington (telephone), 12/29/82, 11/25/83.

Baker, Howard H., Jr. Washington, 2/9/87, 3/9/90, 6/24/93, 5/26/97; Huntsville, TN, 8/12/95, 3/21/06.

Beasley, Tom. Nashville, 8/3/82.

Branson, J. Hugh. Knoxville (telephone), 10/1/90.

Brock, William E., III. Washington (telephone), 6/24/92.

Brooke, Edward W. Washington, 11/11/92.

Browning, Carol. Washington, 6/21/82.

Burton, Larry D. Washington, 6/24/82.

Cannon, James. Washington (telephone), 7/15/94.

Clement, Robert. Washington, 1/31/90.

Cohen, William S. Washington, 6/13/90.

Cooper, John Sherman. Washington, 6/15/82.

Cox, Rebecca. Washington, 6/24/82.

Culvahouse, A. B. Washington, 12/17/92.

Daugherty, Lloyd C., Jr. Knoxville, 6/3/81, 7/22/82.

Deardourff, John. Muncie, IN, 4/17/82.

Denis, Howard A. Annapolis (telephone), 10/9/89.

Dole, Robert. Washington (telephone), 7/8/93.

Domenici, Peter V. Washington, 7/16/90.

Donelson, Lewis. Memphis (telephone), 6/7/90.

Duberstein, Kenneth. Washington, 10/26/92.

Duncan, John J. Washington, 6/2/82.

Dunn, Winfield. Nashville, 8/6/82.

Eagleburger, Lawrence. Washington (telephone), 5/24/06.

Eagleburger, Marlene. Washington (telephone), 5/24/06.

Eagleton, Thomas. St. Louis (telephone), 10/2/92.

Ervin, Sam J., Jr. Morganton, NC, 5/27/81.

Frierson, James. Washington, 6/21/82.

Frist, William H. Washington, 6/12/06.

Garn, E. Jacob. Washington, 4/19/90.

Goldwater, Barry M. Scottsdale, AZ (telephone), 9/24/92.

Grenier, John. Birmingham, AL (telephone), 6/5/90.

Griffin, Robert P. Traverse City, MI (telephone), 7/31/90.

Griscom, Tom C. Washington, 7/16/82, 3/9/90; Potomac, MD, 5/27/87; Winston-Salem (telephone), 4/5/94.

Hamby, Bill. Nashville, 8/3/82.

Hart, Gary W. Denver (telephone), 8/15/91.

Hatch, Orrin G. Washington, 3/20/90.

Hawk, Gordon. Washington, 6/24/82.

Heckman, Robert. Washington, 6/2/82.

Hildenbrand, William. Washington (telephone), 4/9/91.

Hooks, Benjamin. Baltimore, 8/14/90.

Hooks, Frances. Baltimore, 8/14/90.

Inouye, Daniel K. Washington, 5/11/93.

James, A. Warren. Ooltewah, TN (telephone), 6/17/92.

Jordan, Hamilton. Ponta Vedra Beach, FL (telephone), 3/9/91.

Korologos, Thomas. Washington (telephone), 11/18/92.

Kuykendall, Dan H. Washington, 3/27/90.

Laxalt, Paul. Washington, 5/16/90.

Lenzner, Terry F. Washington (telephone), 9/21/90.

Liebengood, Howard. Washington, 1/25/89, 4/2/91 (telephone).

Long, Russell. Washington (telephone), 11/11/92.

Lovett, Doris. Huntsville, TN, 7/27/82.

Lugar, Richard G. Washington, 6/7/82.

Marcum, Fred, Huntsville, TN (telephone), 5/9/06.

Mathias, Charles McC. Washington (telephone), 10/19/92.

McGovern, George S. Washington (telephone), 10/20/92.

McMahan, Ron. Knoxville, 7/26/82.

Meese, Edwin. Washington, 8/14/90.

Mondale, Walter F. Minneapolis (telephone), 2/19/93.

Moore, Frank. Chicago (telephone), 3/15/91.

Moore, Steve. Washington, 6/2/82.

Muskie, Edmund S. Washington, 4/18/90.

Packwood, Robert. Washington, 1/13/93.

Patterson, C. Houston. Chattanooga (telephone), 6/18/92.

Percy, Charles H. Washington, 3/30/90.

Prince, Mike. Knoxville (telephone), 4/30/06.

Quayle, J. Danforth. Washington, 6/10/82.

Quillen, James H. Washington, 6/9/82.

Rath, Thomas. Nashua, NH (telephone), 2/6/89.

Ray, Robert. Des Moines (telephone), 3/30/90.

Redman, Richard. West Des Moines, (telephone), 2/9/89.

Ribicoff, Abraham. New York City (telephone), 10/5/92.

Roberts, Kenneth. Nashville (telephone), 7/30/90.

Rudman, Warren B. Washington, 6/9/82.

Sanders, Donald G. Columbia, MO (telephone), 1/18/93.

Scott, Hugh D. Washington, 6/23/82.

Seigenthaler, John. Nashville, 8/14/82.

Simpson, Alan. Washington, 6/15/90.

Stansbury, Donald, Jr. Knoxville (telephone), 10/27/93.

Stevens, Ted. Washington, 6/24/82.

Sundquist, Don. Washington, 11/15/89.

Swain, William H. Oneida, TN (telephone), 11/23/92.

Thompson, Fred D. Nashville, 8/6/82.

Tower, John G. Washington, 7/6/82.

Tucker, David M. Memphis (telephone), 10/10/83.

Waters, John B., Jr. Knoxville (telephone), 5/31/90.

Welch, Ted. Nashville (telephone), 8/2/90.

West, Rich. Washington, 6/24/82.

Wilson, Ted Q. Oneida, Tennessee (telephone), 10/28/93.

Correspondence

Brock, William E., III. E-mail to author, 2/2/06.

Mansfield, Michael J. Letter to author, 10/22/92.

Essay on Sources

Any research on Howard Baker's career should begin with his papers, which are housed at the University of Tennessee at Knoxville. While I, of course, did not have access to all of the Baker papers prior to their opening in 1997, I was lucky to have access to his speeches in 1981 and 1982, when Baker was serving as majority leader and I was researching my Ph.D. dissertation. Also helpful were the papers of Howard H. Baker Sr., assembled as well at the University of Tennessee; Everett McKinley Dirksen, housed at the Everett McKinley Dirksen Congressional Leadership Research Center in Pekin, Illinois; Richard Nixon and aides John Ehrlichman and H. R. Haldeman, stored at the warehouse annex to the National Archives in Alexandria, Virginia, and Jimmy Carter, stored at the Carter Library in Atlanta. Especially valuable to this study were the papers of Gerald R. Ford and aides Philip Buchen, Richard B. Cheney, Robert T. Hartmann, William T. Kendall, and Rogers C. B. Morton at the Ford Library in Ann Arbor, Michigan.

At the national level, any student of politics must stress the importance of weeklies like *Time* and *Newsweek* as well as the *New York Times*, the *Washington Post*, the *Los Angeles Times*, and the *Chicago Tribune*. I've relied equally heavily upon the *Chattanooga Times*, the *Chattanooga News–Free Press*, the *Chattanooga Times–Free Press*, the *Knoxville News Sentinel*, the *Memphis Commercial Appeal*, the *Nashville Banner*, and the *Nashville Tennessean*, but the most important newspaper for my purposes has been the *Knoxville Journal*, which until its demise was the paper of record for Tennessee GOP politics.

Key as primary sources are Baker's words themselves. Most encompassing in scope are those in *No Margin for Error: America in the Eighties* (New York: Times Books, 1980), the reflective but prescriptive tome he drafted in conjunction with his 1980 campaign. But two works featuring his photography, *Big South Fork Country* (Nashville: Rutledge Hill Press, 1993), which he did with John Netherton, and *Howard Baker's Washington* (New York, W. W. Norton & Co., 1982), should also be consulted. For Baker's spoken words, the most thorough compilations are found in the *Congressional Record* and the publications of the Congressional Quarterly Press. And as has been written so often, there are no better political reference works than the eighteen biennial editions of *The Almanac of American Politics* by Michael Barone, Richard E. Cohen, Douglas Matthews, and Grant Ujifusa.

Secondary material devoted strictly to Baker is limited. Easily the longest is my 923-page "Howard H. Baker, Jr.: A Public Biography," Ph.D. diss., Ball State Univ., 1985. Covering Baker's rhetorical style are Michael Fred Adams's "A Critical Analysis of the Rhetorical Strategies of Senator Howard H. Baker, Jr. in his 1972 Campaign for Reelection," Ph.D. diss., Ohio State Univ., 1973, which is a model of a speech dissertation, and the less thorough "Howard Baker: A Rhetoric of Leadership," Ph.D. diss., Southern Illinois Univ., 1973, by Stacy Colin Myers. Outside the academic genre, the two works that attempt a chapter-length analysis are James A. Miller's thoughtful *Running in Place: Inside the Senate* (New York: Simon and Schuster, 1986), which covers a week in the life of Baker and five others associated with the Senate from the perspective of a one-time Baker aide, and Wayne Greenhaw's less accurate *Elephants in the Cottonfields: Ronald Reagan and the New Republican South* (New York: Macmillan Publishing Co., 1982). Extremely brief treatises for an exclusively journalistic audience include Albert Hunt, *Howard Baker* (Washington,

D.C.: Political Profiles, 1979) and Steven Saferin, *Howard H. Baker, Jr.: Republican Senator from Tennessee* (Washington, D.C.: Grossman Publishers, 1972), a project of the Ralph Nader Congress Project.

A more fruitful source of information is a very helpful group of Sunday magazine articles. The best is James Squires's "Howard Baker: What Are You?" in *Chicago Tribune Magazine*, 11/25/73, 30–33, 51, but several others merit attention. Found in issues of the *New York Times Magazine* are David Eisenhower's "Howard Baker: Fighting the President's Battles," 9/6/87, 8, 19–21, 42–45; Christopher Lydon's, "The Ambivalent Senator Baker," 9/30/73, 11, 93–96; Steven Rattner's "Baker: The Cool Candidate," 11/4/79, 30–32, 104–21, and Martin Tolchin's "Howard Baker: Trying to Tame an Unruly Senate," 3/28/82, 17–18, 65–75, 95–96. Especially astute on Joy Baker is Margaret McManus, "Joy Dirksen Baker: The Senate Has Been Her Home but She Wants the White House," *Detroit News Magazine*, 3/19/78, 10–14. Also helpful were Lloyd Shearer's "Senator Howard Baker: Caught in the Middle," *Parade*, 7/29/73, 4–8, and Timothy Cahill's "The Senator from the State of Compromise," *Rolling Stone*, 2/14/74, 24–34, albeit Cahill's piece should be noted for his uncritical acceptance of a contrived tale about the senator's alleged dynamiting of an outhouse as a teenager.

I have scanned a variety of works for information about Baker's early life. For detailed if disorganized material about Baker's native Scott County, see Esther Sharp Sanderson's *County Scott and Its Mountain Folk* (Nashville: Blue and Gray Press, 1958) and *Scott County: Gem of the Cumberlands* (Huntsville, TN: Esther Sharp Sanderson, 1974). For information about Howard and Irene Baker, see Ray H. Jenkins, *The Terror of Tellico Plains: The Memoirs of Ray H. Jenkins* (Knoxville: East Tennessee Historical Society, 1978) and Hope Chamberlin, *A Minority of Members: Women in the U.S. Congress* (New York: Praeger, 1973). For discussions of Tennessee politics in the nascent period of the Republican resurgence in Tennessee, see John W. Kilgo, *Campaigning in Dixie, with Some Reflections on Two Party Government* (New York: Hobson Book Press, 1945), a tract by the unsuccessful GOP gubernatorial candidate of 1944. More elaborate studies circa 1950 are William Goodman, *Inherited Domain: Political Parties in Tennessee* (Knoxville: Univ. of Tennessee Record, Extension Series, vol. 30, no. 1, 1954); C. Alexander Heard, *A Two Party South?* (Chapel Hill: Univ. of North Carolina Press, 1952), and V. O. Key Jr. with C. Alexander Heard, *Southern Politics in State and Nation* (New York: Alfred A Knopf, 1949). More up-to-date are the treatises in Norman L. Parks, "Tennessee Politics since Kefauver and Reece—A Generalist View," *Journal of Politics* 28 (Feb. 1966), 144–69; Numan V. Bartley and Hugh D. Graham, *Southern Politics and the Second Reconstruction* (Baltimore: Johns Hopkins Press, 1975); Jack Bass and Walter DeVries, *The Transformation of Southern Politics: Social Change and Political Consequences since 1945* (New York: Basic Books, 1976); William Carleton, "Two Party South," *Virginia Quarterly Review* 41, no. 4 (1965): 481–98; Harry S. Dent, *The Prodigal South Returns to Power* (New York: John Wiley and Sons, 1978); John Egerton, *The Americanization of Dixie: The Southernization of America* (New York: Harper's Magazine Press, 1974); Dewey W. Grantham, *The Life and Death of the Solid South* (Lexington: Univ. Press of Kentucky, 1988); Neil R. Pierce, *The Border South States* (New York: W. W. Norton & Co., 1975) and Charles P. Roland, *The Improbable Era: The South since World War II* (Lexington: Univ. Press of Kentucky,

1975). More focused studies include Lamar Alexander, *Steps along the Way: A Governor's Scrapbook* (Nashville: Thomas Nelson, 1986); Albert Gore Sr., *Let the Glory Out: My South and Its Politics* (New York: Viking Press, 1972); Hugh D. Graham, *Crisis in Print: Desegregation and the Press in Tennessee* (Nashville: Vanderbilt Univ. Press, 1967); and David M. Tucker's *Lieutenant Lee of Beale Street* (Nashville: Vanderbilt Univ. Press, 1971) and *Memphis since Crump: Bossism, Blacks and Civic Reformers, 1948–1968* (Knoxville: Univ. of Tennessee Press, 1980). First-rate biographies of key Tennessee Democrats of the 1950s and 1960s include Charles L. Fontenay, *Estes Kefauver: A Biography* (Knoxville: Univ. of Tennessee Press, 1980); Joseph Bruce Gorman, *Kefauver: A Political Biography* (New York: Oxford Univ. Press, 1971), and Lee S. Greene, *Lead Me On: Frank Goad Clement and Tennessee Politics* (Knoxville: Univ. of Tennessee Press, 1982).

The best studies of the two senators who most influenced Baker are Neil MacNeil, *Dirksen: Portrait of a Public Man* (New York: World Publishing Co., 1970); Edward L. and Frederick H. Schapsmeier, *Dirksen of Illinois: Senatorial Statesman* (Urbana: Univ. of Illinois Press, 1985); and Robert Schulman, *John Sherman Cooper: The Global Kentuckian* (Lexington: Univ. Press of Kentucky, 1975). Also valuable is Louella Dirksen with Norma Lee Browning, *The Honorable Mr. Marigold. My Life with Everett Dirksen* (Garden City, NY: Doubleday and Co., 1972), although it, like all ghostwritten autobiographies, should be read with an eye for error. Other treatises of use on Baker's colleagues include George Aiken, *Senate Diary* (Brattleboro, VT: Stephen Green Co., 1976); Edgar Berman, *Hubert: The Triumph and Tragedy of the Humphrey I Knew* (New York: G. P. Putnam's Sons, 1979); Paul R. Clancy, *Just a Country Lawyer: The Life of Senator Sam Ervin* (Bloomington: Indiana Univ. Press, 1974); William S. Cohen, *Roll Call: One Year in the United States Senate* (New York: Simon and Schuster, 1981); John Henry Cutler, *Ed Brooke: Biography of a Senator* (Indianapolis: Bobbs-Merrill Co., 1977); Dick Dabney, *A Good Man: The Life of Sam J. Ervin* (New York: Houghton-Mifflin Co., 1976); Bob and Elizabeth Dole, *The Doles: Unlimited Partners* (New York: Simon and Schuster, 1988); Elizabeth Drew, *Senator* (New York: Random House, 1979), which treats John Culver; Richard F. Fenno Jr., *The Emergence of a Senate Leader: Pete Domenici and the Reagan Budget* (Washington, D.C.: Congressional Quarterly, 1991) and *The Making of a Senator: Dan Quayle* (Washington, D.C.: Congressional Quarterly, 1989); Barry M. Goldwater, *With No Apologies* (New York: William Morrow and Co., 1979); Burton Hersh, *The Education of Edward Kennedy* (New York: Dell Publishing Co., 1980); Jacob K. Javits with Rafael Steinberg, *Javits: The Autobiography of a Public Man* (Boston: Houghton-Mifflin Co., 1981); Finlay Lewis, *Mondale: Portrait of an American Politician* (New York: Harper and Row, 1980); Robert Mann, *Legacy to Power: Senator Russell Long of Louisiana* (New York: Paragon House, 1992); Dan Quayle, *Standing Firm: A Vice Presidential Memoir* (New York: Harper Collins, 1994); Hugh Scott, *Come to the Party* (Englewood Cliffs, NJ, Prentice-Hall, 1968); John G. Tower, *Consequences: A Personal and Political Biography* (New York: Little, Brown and Co., 1991), and Richard Zetterli, *Orrin Hatch: Challenging the Senate Establishment* (Chicago: Regnery Gateway, 1982). Useful works on the Senate as an institution include Bernard Asbell, *The Senate Nobody Knows* (Garden City, NY: Doubleday & Co., 1978), which focuses on Edmund Muskie; Ross K. Baker, *House and Senate* (New York: W. W. Norton & Co., 1989); Robert C. Byrd's thorough if partisan *Addresses on the History of the United States Senate, Volumes I and II* (Washington: Government Printing Office, 1989); George Douth, *Leaders in Profile: The United States Senate* (New York: Sperr and Douth, 1975); Steven Hess, *The Ultimate Insiders: U.S. Senators in the National Media* (Washington, D.C.: Brookings Institution, 1986); John Hibbing and John G. Peters, eds., *The Changing World of the United States Senate* (Berkeley: IGS Press, 1990), and Samuel Shaffer, *On and Off the Floor: Thirty Years a Correspondent on Capitol Hill* (New York: Newsweek Books, 1980).

For materials on Baker's first term, I've found especially helpful the hearings of the Public Works Committee, articles in the Ripon Forum, and the previously cited Adams, Asbell, MacNeil and Saferin works. On Nixon's consideration of Baker and selection of Spiro Agnew, see, most important, Richard M. Nixon, *RN: The Memoirs of Richard Nixon* (New York: Grosset & Dunlop, 1978), but also Lewis Chester, Godfrey Hodgson and Bruce Page, *An American Melodrama: The Presidential Campaign of 1968* (New York: Viking Press, 1969); Theo Lippmann Jr., *Spiro Agnew and the Politics of Suburbia* (New York: W. W. Norton & Co., 1972); The Ripon Society, *The Lessons of Victory* (New York: Dial Press, 1969); William Safire, *Before the Fall: An Inside View of the PreWatergate White House* (New York: Belmont Tower Books, 1975); Theodore H. White, *The Making of the President, 1968* (New York: Atheneum, 1969), and Jules Witcover, *The Resurrection of Richard Nixon* (New York: Viking-Penguin, 1970). For material about Baker's relationship to the Nixon White House, see Rowland Evans Jr. and Robert D. Novak, *Nixon in the White House: The Frustration of Power* (New York: Random House, 1971); H. R. Haldeman, *The Haldeman Diaries: Inside the Nixon White House* (New York: G. P. Putnam's Sons, 1994); Richard Kleindienst, *Justice: The Memoirs of an Attorney General* (Ottawa, IL: Jameson Books, 1985); and Jeb Stuart Magruder, *An American Life: One Man's Road to Watergate* (New York: Atheneum, 1974). On Baker's view of what one writer terms "Nixon's good deed," see Daniel Patrick Moynihan, *The Politics of a Guaranteed Income: The Nixon Administration and the Family Assistance Plan* (New York: Random House, 1973). For Baker's work on revenue sharing, see the hearings of the House Ways and Means and Senate Finance Committees. A helpful piece of analysis can be found in A. James Reichley, *Conservatives in an Age of Change: The Nixon and Ford Administrations* (Washington: Brookings Institution, 1981), while the best recent works on Nixon's administration are Jonathan Aitken, *Nixon: A Life* (Washington, D.C.: Regnery Gateway, 1993); Stephen E. Ambrose, *Nixon: The Triumph of a Politician, 1962–1972* (New York: Simon and Schuster, 1989) and *Nixon: Ruin and Recovery, 1973–1990* (New York: Simon and Schuster, 1991); Herbert S. Parmet, *Richard Nixon and His America* (Boston: Little, Brown and Co., 1990); Tom Wicker, *One of Us: Richard Nixon and the American Dream* (New York: Random House, 1991); and the Watergate-related chapters in Alexander M. Haig with Charles McCarry, *Inner Circles: How America Changed the World* (New York: Warner Books, 1992).

Still the fairest and most accurate accounts of the downside of the Nixon administration are J. Anthony Lukas's *Nightmare: The Underside of the Nixon Years* (New York: Viking Press, 1976) and Theodore H. White's *Breach of Faith: The Fall of Richard Nixon* (New York: Atheneum, 1975). Interesting accounts of the enduring American consciousness of the lessons of Watergate can be found in Michael Schudson, *Watergate in American*

Memory: How We Remember, Forget and Reconstruct the Past (New York: Basic Books, 1992) and David Thelen, ed., *Memory in American History* (Bloomington: Indiana Univ. Press, 1989). For this study, the most important works because of the proximity of the authors to Baker during the hearings are Sam J. Ervin Jr., *The Whole Truth: The Watergate Conspiracy* (New York: Random House, 1980) and Fred D. Thompson, *At That Point in Time: The Inside Story of the Senate Watergate Committee* (New York: Quadrangle/The New York Times Book Co., 1975). Both are extraordinarily favorable to Baker, as are Herman Talmadge with Mark Royden Winchell, *Talmadge: A Political Legacy, A Politician's Life* (Atlanta: Peachtree, 1987), and majority staff member James Hamilton's *The Power to Probe* (New York: Random House, 1976). But while Baker had friendly relations with every committee member, he had two enemies on the majority staff, Samuel Dash and Scott Armstrong. Dash's story is told in *Chief Counsel: Inside the Ervin Committee—The Untold Story of Watergate* (New York: Random House, 1976), and it is suspect. Armstrong's conclusions are echoed by liberal historian Stanley Kutler in *The Wars of Watergate: The Last Crisis of Richard Nixon* (New York: Alfred A Knopf, 1990). If the point of the two works is to conclude that Baker would not automatically side against Nixon, then he, like the other members, must plead guilty. But Ervin has said that he made room in *The Whole Truth* to praise Edward Gurney because Gurney asked questions of Dean and Magruder that needed to be answered. So did the others and most insiders found no fault among those who took a nonsycophantic view of Dean's testimony, deeming it the panel's duty to find all of the facts rather than cast judgments.

Material on Baker in the multitude of books by Watergate defendants is generally secondhand. Dean's *Blind Ambition: The White House Years* (New York: Simon and Schuster, 1976) alleges much but proves little. At its conclusion, Dean quotes a conversation with Charles Colson, drawing upon Baker's report on CIA complicity in the break-in. Similar suspicions appear in Colson's *Born Again* (Lincoln, VA: Chosen Books Publishing Co., 1976) and H. R. Haldeman's *The Ends of Power* (New York: Quadrangle/The New York Times Book Co., 1978). It can hardly be said that the Baker report, found in an appendix of *The Senate Watergate Report* (New York: Dell Books, 1974), was complete. Indeed, Baker and the minority staff acknowledged that it raised more questions than it answered. Such questions went unasked while the principal task of investigators was determining what Nixon knew and when he knew it, but were later put by Seymour Hersh in the *New York Times* and former SDS activist Carl Oglesby in *The Yankee and Cowboy War* (Mission, KS: Sheed, Andrews & McMeel, 1976).

What is clear is that the whole truth about the Watergate burglary is not yet out and that material about it will continue to proliferate. Further investigation by Jim Hougan produced *Secret Agenda: Watergate, Deep Throat and the CIA* (New York: Random House, 1984), a work that used the Baker report and FBI reports as starting points and raised even more questions than Baker did. The latest entry is the controversial *Silent Coup: The Removal of a President* (New York: St. Martin's Press, 1991) by Len Colodny and Robert Gettlin, which fingers Dean as the principal culprit in the break-in and characterizes Alexander Haig and Bob Woodward as key players in a military directed plot to oust Richard Nixon from the presidency. For what it's worth, I am convinced by *Silent Coup*'s case against Dean, but disbelieving of its charges against Haig and Woodward.

What *Silent Coup* has done is establish the questions posed in the Moorer-Radford affair as significant and perhaps central to the whys of Watergate. As Colodny and Gettlin have affirmed, theirs is not the last word. They recommend further study, as do I.

Less controversial is material about Gerald Ford. Helpful among memoirs are Ford's *A Time to Heal* (New York: Harper and Row, 1979); *Time and Chance: Gerald Ford's Appointment with History* (New York: Random House, 1994), by James Cannon, an aide to Ford and Baker; Robert T. Hartmann, *Palace Politics: An Inside Account of the Ford Years* (New York: McGraw-Hill Book Co., 1980); David Hume Kennerly, *Shooter* (New York: Newsweek Books, 1979); Malcolm D. MacDougall, *We Almost Made It* (New York: Crown, 1977); and Ron Nessen, *It Sure Looks Different from the Inside* (Chicago: Playboy Press, 1978). Valuable for discussions of Ford's option for Dole are Elizabeth Drew, *American Journal: The Events of 1976* (New York: Random House, 1977); Martin Schram, *Running for President: A Journal of the Carter Campaign* (New York: Pocket Books, 1977); and Jules Witcover, *Marathon: The Pursuit of the Presidency, 1972–1976* (New York: Viking-Penguin, 1977). Helpful primary material on the Carter years is found in Carter's *Keeping Faith: Memoirs of a President* (New York: Bantam Books, 1982); Joseph A. Califano, *Governing America: An Insider's Report from the White House and the Cabinet* (New York: Simon and Schuster, 1981); and Cyrus Vance, *Hard Choices: Critical Years in America's Foreign Policy* (New York: Simon and Schuster, 1982). The best interpretive work on the Carter years is Betty Glad, *Jimmy Carter: In Search of the Great White House* (New York: W. W. Norton and Co., 1980), but Ervin C. Hargrove, *Jimmy Carter as President: Leadership and the Politics of the Public Good* (Baton Rouge: Louisiana State Univ. Press, 1988) and Charles O. Jones, *The Trusteeship Presidency* (Baton Rouge: Louisiana State Univ. Press, 1988) are also noteworthy. Helpful on the Tellico Dam is William Bruce Wheeler and Michael J. McDonald, *TVA and the Tellico Dam: A Bureaucratic Crisis in Post-Industrial America* (Knoxville: Univ. of Tennessee Press, 1986). For a fairly thorough analysis of the SALT-II pact, see Strobe Talbott, *Endgame: The Inside Story of SALT-II* (New York: Harper & Row, 1980). A key dissenter's viewpoint is well summarized in Edward L. Rowny, *It Takes One to Tango* (Washington: Brassey's, 1992).

From Baker's standpoint, the most controversial issue during the Carter administration was the Panama Canal treaties. For the best two treatises available at the time the treaties were signed, see Denison Kitchel, *The Truth about the Panama Canal* (New Rochelle, NY: Arlington House, 1978) and Walter LaFeber, *The Panama Canal* (New York: Oxford Univ. Press, 1978). Instructive on the opponents are Alan Crawford, *Thunder on the Right: The New Right and the Politics of Resentment* (New York: Pantheon Books, 1980) and Thomas McIntyre, *The Fear Brokers* (New York: Pilgrim Press, 1979). Most elaborate of the primary sources is William Jorden, *Panama Odyssey* (Austin: Univ. of Texas Press, 1984), the account of the then ambassador to Panama. Valuable secondary sources include John Dinges, *Our Man in Panama* (New York: Random House, 1990) and Frederick Kempe, *Divorcing the Dictator: America's Bungled Affair with Noriega* (New York: G. P. Putnam's Sons, 1990).

Invaluable on the 1980 campaign are Jon Bowermaster, *Governor: An Oral Biography of Robert D. Ray* (Ames: Iowa State Univ. Press, 1987); Jack Germond and Jules Witcover, *Blue Smoke and Mirrors* (New York: Viking Press, 1981); and Theodore H. White, *America in Search of Itself: The Making of the President, 1956–1980* (New York: Harper & Row, 1982). Other useful works are Aram Bakshian, *The Candidates, 1980* (New Rochelle, NY: Arlington House, 1980); Elizabeth Drew, *Portrait of an Election: The 1980 Presidential Campaign* (New York: Simon and Schuster, 1981); and Jeff Greenfield, *The Real Campaign: How the Media Missed the Story of the 1980 Campaign* (New York: Summit Books, 1982).

Easily the best treatise on the Reagan Presidency so far is Lou Cannon's *President Reagan: The Role of a Lifetime* (New York: Simon and Schuster, 1991), but Cannon's *Reagan* (New York: G. P. Putnam's Sons, 1982) is useful, too. The most readable overview of the American political system during the Reagan years is Hedrick Smith's bestselling *The Power Game: How Washington Works* (New York: Random House, 1988). Helpful primary sources include Martin Anderson, *Revolution* (New York: Harcourt Brace Jovanovich, 1988); Terrell Bell, *The Thirteenth Man: A Reagan Cabinet Memoir* (New York: Free Press, 1988); William S. Cohen and George J. Mitchell, *Men of Zeal: A Candid Inside Look at the Iran-Contra Hearings* (New York: Viking-Penguin, 1988); Michael Deaver and Mickey Herskowitz, *Behind the Scenes* (New York: William Morrow and Co., 1987); Max M. Kampelman, *Entering New Worlds: The Memoirs of a Private Man in Public Life* (New York: Harper Collins, 1991); Edwin Meese III, *With Reagan: The Inside Story* (Washington, D.C.: Regnery Gateway, 1992); Peggy Noonan, *What I Saw at the Revolution* (New York: Random House, 1990); Nancy Reagan with William Novak, *My Turn: The Memoirs of Nancy Reagan* (New York: Random House, 1989); Ronald Reagan, *An American Life: The Autobiography* (New York: Simon and Schuster, 1990) and *Speaking My Mind* (New York: Simon and Schuster, 1989); Donald Regan, *For the Record: From Wall Street to Washington* (New York: Harcourt Brace Jovanovich, 1988); George P. Shultz, *Turmoil and Triumph: My Years as Secretary of State* (New York: Charles Scribner's Sons, 1993); Larry Speakes with Robert Pack, *Speaking Out: Inside the Reagan White House* (New York: Charles Scribner's Sons, 1988); and David A. Stockman, *The Triumph of Politics: The Inside Story of the Reagan Revolution* (New York: Harper & Row, 1986).

Helpful journalistic works on the Reagan years include Laurence I. Barrett, *Gambling with History: Reagan in the White House* (New York: Doubleday & Co., 1983); Howard Means, *Colin Powell: Soldier/Statesman-Statesman/Soldier* (New York: Donald I. Fine, 1992); Jane Mayer and Doyle McManus, *Landslide: The Unmaking of the President, 1984–1988* (Boston: Houghton Mifflin Co., 1988); and Bob Schieffer and Gary Paul Gates, *The Acting President* (New York: E. P. Dutton, 1989). Easily the best weekly coverage of the Reagan presidency during Baker's tenure as chief of staff can be found in the weekly pieces of Dick Kirschten in the *National Journal*. Authoritative in its coverage of the most controversial series of events during the same time is Ethan Bronner, *Battle for Justice: How the Bork Nomination Shook America* (New York: W. W. Norton & Co., 1989). Valuable, too, are Robert Bork's *The Tempting of America* (New York: Free Press, 1990), and *Matters of Principle: An Insider's Account of America's Rejection of Robert Bork's Nomination to the Supreme Court* (New York: Simon and Schuster, 1992) by Mark Gitenstein, the chief counsel to the Senate Judiciary Committee during the Bork hearings. Useful but limited by the uncompromising biases of the authors are Patrick McGuigan and Dawn M. Weyrich, *Ninth Justice: The Fight for Bork* (Washington, D.C.: Free Congress Research and Education Foundation, 1990) and Michael Pertschuk and Wendy Schaetzel, *The People Rising: The Campaign against the Bork Nomination* (New York: Thunder's Mouth Press, 1989).

Dated but still the best work on U.S. Central American policy during the same time period is Roy Gutman, *Banana Diplomacy: The Making of American Policy in Nicaragua, 1981–1987* (New York: Simon and Schuster, 1988). Important case studies of a major player in the development of arms control policy are David Callahan, *Dangerous Capabilities: Paul Nitze and the Cold War* (New York: Harper Collins, 1990) and Strobe Talbott, *The Master of the Game: Paul Nitze and the Nuclear Peace* (New York: Alfred A. Knopf, 1989). The best work thus far describing Reagan's role in ending the Cold War is Don Oberdorfer, *The Turn: From the Cold War to a New Era* (New York: Simon and Schuster, 1991). Many of the same events are covered from Speaker Jim Wright's perspective in Wright's *Worth It All: My War for Peace* (New York: Brassey's, 1993) and John M. Barry's thorough *The Ambition and the Power: A True Story of Washington* (New York: Viking-Penguin, 1989).

Additional Sources for the Second Edition

The largest share of Howard Baker's papers have been opened at the Baker Center for Public Policy at the University of Tennessee, but more have arrived recently and more will be coming. Just as valuable as the senator's papers are the very ably conducted oral histories of Baker's friends and associates. Materials supplementing those in Senator Baker's papers can be found in the papers of his longtime aide Howard Liebengood, located in the Library of Congress. Another display of Baker's and the late John Netherton's photography can be found in Howard H. Baker Jr. and John Netherton, *Scott's Gulf: The Bridgestone/Firestone Centennial Wilderness* (Nashville: Rogue Elephant Press, 2000). Any soul who cares to examine my approach can check the notes I've taken, interviews I've conducted, and materials I've collected that are now in the Baker Center.

Very helpful new materials on southern politics in the 1960s and 1970s can be found in Earl and Merle Black, *The Rise of Southern Republicans* (Cambridge: Belknap Press of Harvard Univ., 2002); and Philip Langsdon, *Tennessee: A Political History* (Nashville: Hillboro Press, 2000). A particularly cogent argument for the notion that the growth of the GOP in the South emanated from concerns of economic development rather than those of class can be found in Byron E. Shafer and Richard Johnson, *The End of Southern Exceptionalism: Class, Race and Partisanship in the Postwar South* (Cambridge: Harvard Univ. Press, 2006).

For more about the roles of Senator Baker and others in investigations of the intelligence community, see Loch K. Johnson, *Season of Inquiry: Congress and Intelligence* (Chicago: Dorsey Press, 1988), and Kathryn Olmstead, *Challenging the Secret Government: The Post-Watergate Investigations of the CIA and FBI* (Chapel Hill: Univ. of North Carolina Press, 1996).

The best book to appéar about the Watergate affair since the first edition has been Fred Emery, *Watergate: The Corruption of American Politics and the Fall of Richard Nixon* (New York: Crown, 1994. But the Watergate mystery that endured the longest was the identity of Deep Throat, Bob Woodward's secret source. Bob Woodward confirmed that Deep Throat was former Assistant FBI Director Mark Felt in *The Secret Man: The Story of Watergate's Deep Throat* (New York: Simon and Schuster, 2005). It must be stated, however, that Howard Baker is not the only figure involved in the Watergate investigation whom suspects that Mr. Felt did not have access to all the information Woodward attributed to Deep Throat.

Various aspects of the political wars of the late 1960s and early 1970s are chronicled in Robert Greenberg, *Nixon's Shadow: The History of an Image* (New York: W. W. Norton & Co., 2003); Stephen F. Hayward, *The Age of Reagan: The Fall of the Old Liberal Order, 1964–1980* (Roseville, CA: Prima Publishing, 2001); Mark Hamilton Lytle, *America's Uncivil Wars: The Sixties Era from Elvis to the Fall of Nixon* (New York: Oxford Univ. Press, 2006); John Anthony Maltese, "Speaking Out: The Role of Presidential Rhetoric in the Modern Supreme Court Confirmation Process," *Presidential Studies Quarterly* 25, no. 3 (1995): 447–55; Craig Shirley, *Reagan's Revolution: The Untold Story of the Campaign That Started It All* (Nashville: Nelson Current, 2005); and Melvin Small, *The Presidency of Richard Nixon* (Lawrence: Univ. Press of Kansas, 1999). The politics of the Ford administration are very ably recounted in Yanek Mieczkowski, *Gerald Ford and the Challenges of the 1970s* (Lexington: Univ. Press of Kentucky, 2005). Scholars of the Panama Canal Treaties fight should consult Howard B. Schaffer, *Ellsworth Bunker: Global Troubleshooter, Vietnam Hawk* (Chapel Hill: Univ. of North Carolina Press, 2003). Those of the future can look forward to Adam Clymer's forthcoming work on the politics of the debate over the Panama Canal treaties.

Useful material from or about Baker or his congressional colleagues can be gleaned from James A. Baker, III, with Steve Fiffer, *"Work Hard, Study . . . and Keep Out of Politics!": Adventures and Lessons from an Unexpected Public Life* (New York: G. P. Putnam's Sons, 2006); Barbara Bush, *Reflections: Life after the White House* (New York: Scribner, 2003); George H. W. Bush, *All The Best: George Bush: My Life in Letters and Other Writings* (New York: Scribner, 1999); Robert C. Byrd, *Robert C. Byrd: Child of the Appalachian Coalfields* (Morgantown: West Virginia Univ. Press, 2005); Adam Clymer, *Edward M. Kennedy: A Biography* (New York: William Morrow and Co., 1999); Karen DeYoung, *Soldier: The Life of Colin Powell* (New York: Alfred A. Knopf, 2006); William H. Frist and J. Lee Annis Jr., *Tennessee Senators, 1911–2001: Portrait of Leadership in a Century of Change* (Lanham, MD: Univ. Press of America, 1999); Lewis L. Gould, *The Most Exclusive Club: A History of the Modern U. S. Senate* (New York: Basic Books, 2005); Orrin Hatch, *Square Peg: Confessions of a Citizen–Senator* (New York: Basic Books, 2001); Mark O. Hatfield, *Against the Grain: Reflections of a Rebel Republican* (Ashland, OR: White Cloud Press, 2001); John Hayman with Clara Ruth Hayman, *A Judge in the Senate: Howell Heflin's Career of Politics and Principle* (Montgomery, AL: NewSouth Books, 2001); Jesse Helms, *Here's Where I Stand: A Memoir* (New York: Random House, 2005); Burton Hersh, *The Shadow President: Ted Kennedy in Opposition* (South Royalton, VT: Steerforth Press, 1997); Byron Hulsey, *Everett Dirksen and His Presidents: How a Senate Giant Shaped American Politics* (Lawrence: Univ. Press of Kansas, 2000); Robert G. Kaufman, *Henry M. Jackson: A Life in Politics* (Seattle: Univ. of Washington Press, 2000); Mark Kirchmeier, *Packwood: The Public and Private Life from Acclaim to Outrage* (New York: HarperCollins West, 1995); Paul Laxalt, *Nevada's Paul Laxalt: A Memoir* (Reno: Jack Bacon and Co., 2000); Kyle Longley, *Senator Albert Gore, Sr.: Tennessee Maverick* (Baton Rouge: Louisiana State Univ.

Press, 2004); Trent Lott, *Herding Cats: A Life in Politics* (New York: Regan Books, 2005); Eugene J. McCarthy, *No-Fault Politics: Modern Presidents, the Press, and Reformers* (New York: *Times* Books, 1998); Don Oberdorfer, *Senator Mansfield* (Washington: Smithsonian Press, 2003); John Rhodes with Dean Smith, *John Rhodes: "I Was There"* (Salt Lake City: Northwest Publishing, 1995); William G. Saxbe, *I've Seen the Elephant* (Kent: Kent State Univ. Press, 2000); Paul Simon, *PS: The Autobiography of Paul Simon* (Chicago: Bonus Books, 1999), and Lowell P. Weicker Jr., *Maverick: A Life in Politics* (Boston: Little, Brown and Co., 1995).

New information about the first six years of the Reagan administration can be found in Joan Biskupic, *Sandra Day O'Connor: How the First Woman on the Supreme Court Became Its Most Influential Justice* (New York: Ecco, 2005) and David Gergen, *Eyewitness to Power: The Essence of Leadership from Nixon to Carter* (New York: Simon & Schuster, 2000).

The best new treatise on the entire Reagan Presidency is Richard Reeves, *President Reagan: The Triumph of the Imagination* (New York: Simon & Schuster, 2005). An able synthesis of the Reagan-Bush era from the standpoint of a liberal academic is Michael Schaller, *Right Turn: American Life in the Reagan-Bush Era* (New York: Oxford Univ. Press, 2006). The best new material relative to Baker's tenure as Reagan's chief of staff is David Abshire, *Saving the Reagan Presidency: Trust Is the Coin of the Realm* (College Station: Texas A & M Univ. Press, 2005). Other valuable information can be found in David Cohen, "From the Fabulous Baker Boys to the Master of Disaster," *Presidential Studies Quarterly* 32, no. 3 (2002): 463–84; Anne Edwards, *The Reagans: Portrait of a Marriage* (New York: St. Martin's Griffin, 2003); John Ehrman, *The Eighties: America in the Age of Reagan* (New Haven: Yale Univ. Press, 2005); Jim Kuhn, *Ronald Reagan in Private* (New York: Sentinel, 2004); Peter Robinson, *How Ronald Reagan Changed My Life* (New York: Regan Books, 2003); and Richard Wirthlin and Winston C. Hall, *The Greatest Communication: What Ronald Reagan Taught Me about Politics, Leadership, and Life* (New York: Julian Wiley and Sons, 2004). Good recent work covering the Bork nomination can be found in Norman Vieira and Leonard Gross, *Supreme Court Appointments: Judge Bork and the Politicization of Senate Confirmations* (Carbondale: Southern Illinois Press, 1998), and David Alistair Yalof, *Pursuit of Justices: Presidential Politics and the Selection of Supreme Court Nominees* (Chicago: Univ. of Chicago Press, 1999).

Surprisingly, Nancy Kassebaum Baker has been the subject of very little academic inquiry. One brief work aimed at inspiring younger women is Eleanor Marshall White, *Women: Catalysts for Change: Interpretive Biographies of Shirley St. Hill Chisholm, Sandra Day O'Connor and Nancy Landon Kassebaum* (New York: Vantage Press, 1991). The best work covering the hallmark of her Senate career, the Kassebaum-Kennedy health-care reform is Adam Clymer's aforementioned biography *Edward M. Kennedy*. Surprisingly, nine of the next ten women who followed her into the Senate mention very little about her in their chronicle of their experiences in Barbara Mikulski, Kay Bailey Hutchison, Dianne Feinstein, Barbara Boxer, Patty Murray, Olympia Snowe, Susan Collins, Mary Landrieu, and Blanche L. Lincoln with Catherine Whitney, *Nine and Counting: The Women of the Senate* (New York: William Morrow, 2000).

At this point, information on Baker's service in Japan is best covered in English on the Web site of the U. S. embassy in Japan and in *Ambassador*, a video produced in 2002 for airing on public broadcasting stations by the National Geographic Society. But, all academic research since the hardback version has been greatly facilitated by the advent of the World Wide Web and I've employed it considerably. Those who created and operate Google and LexisNexis are to be commended. Still, I confess that I have not consulted any sources in Japanese, as my knowledge of it goes little beyond *sayonara*.

INDEX